EDUCATION FOR A MULTICULTURAL SOCIETY

EDUCATION FOR A MULTICULTURAL SOCIETY

Edited by

KOLAJO PAUL AFOLABI

CANDICE BOCALA

RAYGINE C. DiAQUOI

JULIA M. HAYDEN

IRENE A. LIEFSHITZ

SOOJIN SUSAN OH

HARVARD EDUCATIONAL REVIEW

REPRINT SERIES NO. 47

Library of Congress Control Number 2010942134
ISBN 978-0-916690-51-9

Published by Harvard Educational Review,
an imprint of the Harvard Education Publishing Group

Harvard Educational Review
8 Story Street
Cambridge, MA 02138

Cover Design: Josh Silverman

The typefaces used in this book are New Baskerville for text and
Franklin Gothic for display.

CONTENTS

ACKNOWLEDGMENTS

We give our sincerest gratitude to Ayana Kee for contributing to the vision for this volume, to the Harvard Education Publishing Group for helping us produce it, to the authors who have allowed us to reprint their work and who continue to enlighten us, and to our readers who will use this volume as inspiration to construct a better world for our children.

EDITORS' INTRODUCTION
THE KNOWLEDGE AND INSPIRATION
NEEDED FOR TRANSFORMATION

What is education for multiculturalism? Multicultural education has evolved from the simple recognition of racial, ethnic, and cultural differences to the realization that these experiences are inextricably linked to power, structures of oppression, and inequitable distribution of resources. Today, multicultural education is understood as both an idea and a process (Banks, 2009). Educators endorse the *idea* of multicultural education by examining language, race, culture, and power and fostering awareness of and respect for differences, which is necessary for the creation of a more just and equitable society (Au, 2009; Manning & Baruth, 1999). Moreover, they enact the *process* of multicultural education by teaching for social justice, honoring students' experiences, and committing to a stance of critical awareness and inquiry (Applebaum, 2002). In this volume, we present a body of knowledge that has influenced how educators think and teach. We hope these texts will now inspire innovation and a renewed commitment to what education ought to be in a multicultural world.

The original tenets of multicultural education recognized students' identities as salient features of learning and knowledge construction; educators were responsible for engaging these identities in increasingly complex and diverse cultural, racial, and linguistic environments (Banks, 2006; Manning & Baruth, 1999; Milner & Ross, 2006). This formulation, however, failed to analyze the importance of broader contexts within which students' lives are embedded or the lived realities of structural racism, lacked acknowledgement of experiences and systems of oppression beyond a Black/White racial dichotomy, and contained disconnects between theory and practice (May, 1999). The stance of *critical multicultural education* highlights multiple, shifting, and hybrid identities and their intersections in overlapping systems of oppression, and it attempts to bridge theory and practice by encouraging educators to recognize and resist the existing structures of domination and cultural oppression that are reflected in their practice in and outside of schooling spaces (Au, 2009; Ramsey, Williams, & Vold, 2003; Schramm-Pate & Jeffries, 2008).

Although in many ways an advance from earlier days when multiculturalism meant merely appreciating diversity, the stance of critical multicultural education is not enough—it is not enough merely to criticize injustice. We must actively *challenge* injustice; we must transform our collective and individual ways of being so that our critical consciousness does not stop with acknowledgement, understanding, and analysis but actually becomes radically caring practice. While we acknowledge that many other volumes trouble the notion of critical multiculturalism and call educators to action—what some would call transformative multiculturalism (Banks, 1996)—we often wonder why there is still so much work to be done to redress social inequalities. Surely, teachers are not lacking for resources and practical guides that lay out "how to" conduct multicultural education. Surely, school districts and state legislatures are not lacking initiatives and reform strategies. We aver that the field lacks inspiration: an inspiration that beckons us all to embrace differences, embody critical vigilance and bravery, and foster social imagination. In demonstrating how educators take stock of the inherent strengths of their students and school communities, talk back to dominant cultural narratives that oppress them, and offer transformative visions for what education in a multicultural society could be, this volume seeks to provoke inspiration for transformation.

This volume is not an exhaustive overview of multicultural education. It is not a textbook that will introduce readers to the basic tenets of a diversity curriculum or a manual containing decontextualized examples. The pieces in this volume do not trace the history of multicultural education or propose a multicultural canon. Instead, this volume provides material that can move readers toward the kind of critically caring practice that supports a truly competent and loving citizenry—a citizenry equipped for change. In selecting articles for this volume on multiculturalism, we asked: What are the narratives (and myths) that awaken us personally, staying with us long after we have read them? Who are the scholars that have appeared on our pages passionately decrying the status quo—changing the way we think about education and the shifting national discourse on quality education for all? Which voices and actions embody hope—opening our eyes to witness the beauty of restoring humanity and honoring the dignity of all people? We believe that it is the personal, the detailed, and the specific that move us as individuals and connect us to others, inspiring us to believe in our purpose and our possibility. It is in the particular that we come to understand the universal (Lawrence-Lightfoot & Davis, 1997); it is in concrete stories of different experiences of the world, in pointed arguments against domination, and in the uniquely imagined reenvisioning of society that the powerful whole of multiculturalism can be realized. In the acts of encountering the new, witnessing possibility, and seeing one's endeavor as part of something larger than oneself, one comes to be inspired to transform the self, community, and world.

Given the profoundly moving and indelible nature of the pieces we have selected for this reprint, it should be no surprise that they are among the most influential articles in the thought and practice of multicultural education. Lisa D. Delpit (1988) undeniably changed the course of mainstream dialogues in the field of literacy specifically and in education writ large with "The Silenced Dialogue: Power and Pedagogy in Educating Other People's Children"; her piece is among the most cited of all articles ever published in the *Harvard Educational Review*. It is also probably one of the most widely discussed articles among scholars and teachers alike—a less tangible but perhaps even more powerful measure of its impact on education. Similarly, one needs only to look to the near-universal citation of Dolores Delgado Bernal's (1998) "Using a Chicana Feminist Epistemology in Educational Research" in the *Harvard Educational Review*'s recent special issue on Latinos in higher education to witness the influence of her work on an entire generation of educational scholars. Moreover, we recognize the significant effect that the works of Steven Z. Athanases, Dorinda J. Carter Andrews, Paul Skilton-Sylvester, and Beverly Daniel Tatum have had on the ways in which educators put multicultural thought into actionable practice in their classrooms. The radical and seminal essence of these writers' words can be seen in everyday works of teachers who are committed to education that can transform classrooms and society alike into places of equity, justice, and harmony.

In reprinting these authors' revolutionary words, our primary purpose is to inspire readers to renew a broadly shared commitment to promoting education for a multicultural society. We believe that collectively, these articles have helped shape knowledge and practice in the field of multiculturalism, and thus we put them forth in hopes that they will continue to refine it. With these articles, we hope to remind educators and scholars of their dedication to this patient work—work that exhausts and invigorates them, work that promises great returns for their great labors—the work of identifying, critically examining, and challenging oppression in all its manifestations. This volume is for those who subscribe to the ideal that education is a means by which to transform society and who look to multiculturalism as a way to change and create how we, as a society, enact education. It is also for those who have been discouraged by the way multicultural education has been commodified, sanitized, and rendered impotent. We intend this volume to serve as living testimony to what is possible, the articles here bearing witness to this possibility.

The articles in this volume have been selected from the pages of the *Harvard Educational Review* for their capacity to inspire and for the weightiness of their words. True to form, the shaping of this book became in itself a process of inspiration for the editors, igniting connections to our own areas of scholarship and practice. We collaboratively savored and interweaved works that spoke to each other across time and space. In the pages of our journal, seminal works on diversity, identity, power, equality, and knowledge production have been born, sustained, and developed. Each of the articles in this volume is a gem in its own particular way; together, they reflect the rich palette of ideas that serve as touchstones, as particularly powerful works in the field that both cement and expand our understanding of multicultural education.

These works represent the empirical and theoretical, the practical and personal. In part I of this volume, readers will engage with compassionate asset-based pedagogies that honor the experiences of individuals and their communities. Acknowledging the varied capital inherent in students' funds of knowledge positions readers to become not only experts but learners, not only problem-solvers but listeners. In this listening stance, readers then encounter the articles in part II, which question the dominant narratives that have curtailed human capacity and consider the counter-stories offered against such limiting assumptions. Hearing these voices talk back to master scripts prompts readers to reexamine deeply held beliefs and their impact, to complicate and make visible what has become accepted as the status quo. These counter-narratives become the foundation of hope and possibility, activating the commitment to justice that already exists in our thinking and scholarship. Upon this foundation, in part III, readers are asked to reimagine their visions of education, to stand at the precipice of what *could* be. These bold—sometimes commonsense, sometimes radical, sometimes gentle, sometimes forceful—perspectives of possibility compel readers to believe in their own capacity for transformation. Having recognized the different experiences that inform our understanding of education and the need to talk back to limiting and limited conceptualizations of teaching and learning, readers can now engage with the work of transforming their inspiration into belief and action.

We need inspiration in the face of dehumanizing material conditions, impoverished imaginations, and limited spaces of opportunity. Teachers, who want to make their classrooms into spaces where children are their best selves and, therefore, do their best work, need inspiration. Principals and superintendents, who want to turn their schools into workshops where the tools for dismantling inequity are forged, need inspiration. Policy makers, who want to make reform initiatives with—not just for—the communities they serve, need inspiration. Researchers, who want to advance the dignity and liberation of *all* people through their scholarship, need inspiration. The work we do to make this difference, the work of transformation, needs the fuel of inspiration, energy, challenge, wonder, and beauty.

Inspiration comprises not only transformation in thought but also in action. In this volume, each of the contributors has shown us a possible vision for multicultural education—a vision we have often thought about yet postponed or deferred to others the task of carrying out. As editors, we acknowledge that inspiration, when shared, produces power—power to embrace differences, power to think critically, and even power to dream and create. We live in an era of constant reform, searching for the ultimate formula for a cure-all elixir.

In the midst of being bombarded with messages that demand action and results, we ask that you stand and pause to consider the words of the authors in this volume. We find that across these chapters, such moments of stillness and intentional reflection become the birthplace for transformation.

REFERENCES

Applebaum, P. (2002). *Multicultural and diversity education: A reference handbook.* Santa Barbara, CA: ABC-CLIO, Inc.

Au, W. (Ed.). (2009). *Rethinking multicultural education: Teaching for racial and cultural justice.* Milwaukee, WI: Rethinking Schools.

Banks, J. A. (Ed.). (1996). *Multicultural education, transformative knowledge, and action: Historical and contemporary perspectives.* New York: Teachers College Press.

Banks, J. A. (2006). *Race, culture, and education: The selected works of James A. Banks.* New York: Routledge.

Banks, J. A. (Ed.). (2009). *The Routledge international companion to multicultural education.* New York: Routledge.

Lawrence-Lightfoot, S., & Davis, J. H. (1997). *The art and science of portraiture.* San Francisco: Jossey-Bass.

Manning, M. L., & Baruth, L. G. (1999). *Multicultural education of children and adolescents* (3rd ed.). Boston: Allyn & Bacon.

May, S. (Ed.). (1999). *Cultural multiculturalism: Rethinking multicultural and antiracist education.* Philadelphia: Falmer Press.

Milner, H. R., & Ross, E. W. (Eds.). (2006). *Racial identity in education* (Vol. 3). Westport, CT: Greenwood Publishing Group, Inc.

Ramsey, P., Williams, L., & Vold, E. B. (2003). *Multicultural education: A source book* (2nd ed.). New York: RoutledgeFalmer.

Schramm-Pate, S., & Jeffries, R. B. (Eds.). (2008). *Grappling with diversity: Readings on civil rights pedagogy and critical multiculturalism.* Albany, NY: State University of New York Press.

PART I

TAKING STOCK

ACKNOWLEDGING AND HONORING
FUNDS OF KNOWLEDGE

PART I

TAKING STOCK
ACKNOWLEDGING AND HONORING
FUNDS OF KNOWLEDGE

In the first part of this volume, we draw together articles that honor the authentic experiences of people and communities. It has been said often that we need multiculturalism in education to combat the social troubles derived from living in an increasingly diverse society. However, rather than starting from this premise, these selected articles underscore that the United States has *always* been diverse and that our education system is most powerful when it recognizes the multiple cultures reflected in and shaped by the lives and experiences of students. We start here in order to recognize that education begins with appreciating difference. The authors of these pieces inspire us to consider how multiculturalism is enacted *with* children in educative spaces. They actively reframe multiculturalism to argue that schools and educational systems do not function to solve "problems" associated with diversity, but rather they function at their best through diversity and should honor the multiple ways of thinking and learning that are present, and always have been present, with our students. In recognizing diversity as a strength and describing the rich contributions of students' funds of knowledge to education, the moments described in these articles are at once individually profound and universally applicable.

In the first three articles of this section, readers are invited to consider the ways in which students—as individuals and as members of families and communities—bring funds of knowledge with them into classrooms (Moll, Amanti, Neff, & González, 1992). Multiculturalism is rooted in the premise that these local and cultural perspectives strengthen students' lives and provide both fodder and support for learning. In "Reading the World of School Literacy: Contextualizing the Experience of a Young African American Male," Arlette Ingram Willis (1995) speaks first as a mother whose children are continually placed in positions that require them to both accommodate and resist dominant notions of what is good and acceptable in their schooling contexts. Willis artfully layers the professional knowledge of a scholar and educator with the loving, empathic gaze of a parent. Her personal account of her son's experiences with literacy schooling affords an opportunity for practitioners to understand how unintentional disregard for students' home cultures and multiple sources of literacy can lead educators to commit "a sin of omission" by potentially ignoring or devaluing the rich cultural knowledge and experiences of students under their care (p. 16).

In the same way that Willis posits schools as cultural spaces that legitimize and privilege certain forms of knowledge and history, Patricia J. Saylor (1992) reminds us that d/Deaf children acquire literacy, communication, and socialization skills more readily in communities where Deaf Culture is honored and practiced. In "Teaching and Practice: A Hearing Teacher's Changing Role in Deaf Education," Saylor reflects on her experiences starting and working in BRIDGES—a bilingual/bicultural day care and family-service organization for both hearing and d/Deaf children. With poignant anecdotes, Saylor relates that parents have two choices—to try to "fix" their children or to "respect centuries of precedent and learn from the Deaf Community" (p. 47). She argues that d/Deaf children should not be encouraged to "overcome" deafness but should instead learn about the rich heritage of the Deaf Way and gain resilience, affirmation, and community. Saylor's article challenges us to expand our vision of culture beyond the typical constructs it suggests—that is, ethnicity, race, or gender—to encompass disability, a construct that continues to be described in deficit terms.

Django Paris (2009) further reinforces the importance of community and the need for protected, legitimate spaces for youth cultures in schools. In "'They're in My Culture, They Speak the Same Way': African American Language in Multiethnic High Schools," Paris explores how youth of various ethnic/racial backgrounds—Black, Latino, and Samoan—use African American Language (AAL) to transcend their divisions. Paris posits that high schools make possible a "pedagogy of pluralism." In these settings, where youth from multiple ethnic backgrounds come together, language serves as a bridging mechanism, creating a unique and protected youth space that is demarcated by fluency with AAL. Despite the widespread use of AAL among students, however, teachers in this study do not use the language as a resource. Thus, Paris reminds readers that schools must be "sites of critical language and literacy learning" for both students and teachers (p. 67).

In the final two articles, readers are reminded how educators might infuse a multicultural spirit throughout their thinking and practice. In "Indigenous Knowledges and the Story of the Bean," Bryan McKinley Jones Brayboy and Emma Maughan (2009) underscore how educators may be required to enter a new, unfamiliar world of knowing in order for multiculturalism to be enacted in classroom spaces. The authors describe a powerful vignette in which an Indigenous student teacher describes how she would teach about bean seeds—

typically within a unit on measurement, photosynthesis, and writing—from an entirely different perspective of connection, growth, and sustainability. Brayboy and Maughan argue for understanding an Indigenous Knowledge Systems perspective, in which knowledge—as action—is communal, contextual, and (re)produced within teaching and learning. Multicultural educators must bravely confront the limits of their knowledge and transform their lenses to see their students' worlds.

In a final act of transformation, we witness third-grade teacher Paul Skilton-Sylvester (1994) turn his classroom into a thriving cardboard neighborhood based on the authentic everyday experiences of his students. As his students participate in creating the economy and government of "Sweet Cakes Town," Skilton-Sylvester both validates students' current realities and dares them to imagine a different one. His students' responses to problems of homelessness, job dissatisfaction, and legal justice demonstrate the sincere commitment of a classroom community to tackle authentic challenges in society. By creating a "problem-posing" environment, Skilton-Sylvester provides educators with a vision and concrete ideas for thoughtful critical pedagogy (p. 117).

The articles in this section remind us of the strengths inherent in every community, encourage us to look for the good, and—having found the good—to build on it. In sharing stories of authentic struggles and powerful realizations that occur inside educative spaces, these authors underscore the importance of seeing students first as humans and considering their communities—whether conceptualized as places, cultures, or groups—as rich sources of knowledge. The following articles are vivid exemplars of the powerful synergy created when students' knowledge is honored and teachers become brave enough to be learners inside their own classrooms. In honoring and acknowledging differences, educators invite students to co-construct knowledge that bridges students' everyday lives to classroom life, thus creating spaces where students thrive and become their fullest selves.

REFERENCE
Moll, L., Amanti, C., Neff, D., & González, N. (1992). Funds of knowledge for teaching: Using a qualitative approach to connect homes and classrooms. *Theory into Practice*, *31*(2), 132–141.

READING THE WORLD
OF SCHOOL LITERACY

CONTEXTUALIZING THE EXPERIENCE OF
A YOUNG AFRICAN AMERICAN MALE

ARLETTE INGRAM WILLIS

Let me share a conversation that I had with my nine-year-old son, and the context in which it occurred:

It's a cold, frosty winter morning, and everyone has left for work or school except my youngest son Jake and me. I am busy applying last-minute touches to my makeup and encouraging Jake, in the next room, to "step it up." I wonder why he is dragging around; school starts in ten minutes and we haven't yet left the house. Jake knows the routine; I wonder if something is troubling him. So, I peek around the corner and find him looking forlorn—you know, a scowl on his face, a look of growing despair and sadness. I forget about the clock and attend to him.

"Jake, what's wrong? Why are you so unhappy?" I ask.

"We have the Young Authors [writing] Contest today, and I don't have anything to write about."

"Sure you do. There are lots of things you can write about," I encourage him. (I believe people write best about those subjects they know and care about.) *"Why don't you write about baseball or soccer?"*

"No," he replies. "A kid at our school wrote about cancer last year, and the story went all the way to the next state [regionals]."

"Well," I answer, "maybe you should write about something funny—like when you go to the barbershop. You and your brothers are always talking about your trips there."[1]

"Oh no, Mom, they wouldn't understand. When I just get my haircut, they always ask me, 'Why do you have that line in your hair?' 'It's not a line, it's a part,' *I try to tell them. I can't write about the barbershop. They won't understand."*

"Well," I say, trying to clarify what I really mean, "I don't mean write about getting a haircut. I mean writing about all the funny people that come in and the things that happen while you are at the barbershop. You and your brothers always come home tellin' a funny story and laugh about it for the rest of the week. That's what I mean by writing about the barbershop."

"No, Mom. They won't understand," he insists.

"What do you mean, 'they won't understand?' Who is this 'they'?" I ask.

"The people in my class," he replies, somewhat frustrated.

Jake continues, "You should read this story that M. wrote. It is a mystery story and it's really good. I can't beat that story. I'll bring you a copy of it if I can. I know it will win." (Sadder now that he has had time to consider his competition, Jake turns and walks toward his room.)

Wanting him to participate in the contest, I ask, "How do you know M.'s story is good?"

"She read it in class. Everybody said it's really good," he responds.

"Well, I still think you should try. You are a really good writer. Look at all the 'good stuff' you wrote in Mrs. S.'s room. You could rewrite some of it and turn it in."

Finally he answers, "I'll think about it," and we go off to school.

As I remember the conversation, Jake's tone of voice hinted at both frustration and defensiveness. I interpreted his use of phrases like "they always ask" and "I try to tell them" to mean that since he gets his hair cut every two weeks, it gets pretty tiresome answering the same questions from his classmates so frequently.[2] Furthermore, I interpreted his intonation to mean that he has had to stand his ground with other children who either do not agree with his definition of a "part," or who try to define its meaning for him.

I believe that Jake cannot bring this aspect of his life and culture into the classroom because he doesn't feel that it will be understood by his classmates and teacher. When Jake says "They won't understand," I interpret his words to mean that if his classmates cannot understand the simplest action in getting a haircut—the barber taking less than ten seconds to place a part in his hair—how can he expect them to understand the context and culture that surround the entire event. Also, I see Jake's reluctance to share something as commonplace in his home and community life as a haircut as a way of distancing this portion of his life from the life he leads at school. It seems that he has come to understand that as an African American he must constantly make a mediating effort to help others understand events that appear to be commonplace on the surface, but are in fact culturally defined.

Several interwoven incidents have helped me to understand the conversation with Jake. I will briefly describe them to provide the context for my understanding of the subtle, yet ever-present and unquestioned role of cultural accommodation that occurs in the school literacy experiences of children from diverse backgrounds. I have been teaching courses in multicultural literature at my university for several years. After my fall 1993 course, I reflected, using journal writing, on my growing experience teaching multicultural literature courses.[3] Teaching these courses has led me to a more informed understanding of how, in the practice of school literacy, there are many culturally defined moments of conflict that call daily for cultural understanding, knowledge, and sensitivity from teachers. These "moments" also challenge non-mainstream students to choose between cultural assimilation and accommodation, or resistance. My journal entries centered on my readings, research, and, most importantly, my daily conversations about school life with my three sons, who range in age from nine to seventeen. In my classes, I have often shared my sons' school experiences and my reactions to them in an effort to help my students understand how teachers' daily subtle and seemingly inconsequential decisions can affect the learning of the children they teach.

A striking example of a teacher's unintentional disregard for the cultural history, understanding, experiences, and voice of a student occurred when my oldest son struggled to meet the requirements of a national essay contest entitled, "What it means to be an American." One of the contest's restrictions was that students should not mention the concept of race. My son thought this was an unfair and impossible task to complete, since his African American identity is synonymous with his being American. Yet, his efforts to articulate the difficulty of the task to his English teacher were frustrated by her response that, although she was empathic, she did not have the authority to change the rules. I intervened and spoke with the teacher at length about my son's values, beliefs, and his unwillingness to compromise himself in order to compete in an essay contest in which he had little or no interest other than a grade.

My second son also had a similar experience involving unintentional cultural insensitivity. He is a member of the school band, which was having its fall concert. While attending, I noticed that all the music the band played was composed by Europeans or European Americans. I spoke with one of the band directors, and asked rhetorically if there were any songs that the band members could perform that were composed by people of color. She responded that she had never considered the choices she made as nonrepresentative of all the students who had to learn them, while I could see little else than the absence of cultural diversity. I was pleased when the winter concert included some Hanukkah tunes. It was a start.

REFLECTIONS

Though my conversation with Jake is now months old, it has continued to haunt me. I have been deeply concerned about a noticeable shift in my son's attitude toward writing. Jake's early writing experiences in kindergarten and first grade revealed that he found writing to be a natural outlet for self-expression. He often wrote for pleasure and has kept all of his drafts. Jake learned the process approach to writing in first grade and treasures his portfolio, which he had originally developed in that class. I have found him in his room revisiting a piece he had written earlier. However, this past year I have noticed a change in his level of production. Jake no longer writes detailed accounts. Instead, he spends a great deal of time thinking about what to write and how to say it. While I believe these are laudatory traits of a good writer, his teachers often accuse him of being under-productive.

Reflecting on our conversation, I sense that Jake believes (understands?) that his perceived audience will neither value nor understand the cultural images and nuances he wishes to share in his writing. Jake is a child wrestling with an internal conflict that is framed by the sociohistorical and sociocultural inequities of U.S. society. He is trying to come to grips with how he can express himself in a manner that is true to his "real self," and yet please his teacher and audience of readers who are, in effect, evaluating his culture, thinking, language, and reality.

Jake's perception of an unaccepting audience is not unique. Several researchers have expressed similar concerns about the narrowly defined culture of acceptable school literacy and the growing literateness of culturally and linguistically diverse children (Delpit, 1986, 1991, 1993; Gutierrez, 1992; Heath, 1983; Labov, 1972; Ovando & Collier, 1985; Reyes & Molner, 1991; Sawyer & Rodriguez, 1992).[4] Why is it clearer to children than to adults that there are systematic, institutional inequalities in the decisions teachers make about the "appropriate" methods and materials used to enhance their students' literacy development?

Like millions of culturally and linguistically diverse people, Jake understands the unstated reality of schooling in U.S. society: It is built upon a narrow understanding of school knowledge and literacy, which are defined and defended as what one needs to know and how one needs to know it in order to be successful in school and society. As Barrera (1992) explains:

> The school culture can be seen to reflect the dominant class and, so too, the cultures of literacy and literature embedded within the school culture. For this reason, the teaching of literacy and literature are considered to be neither acultural nor neutral, but cultural and political. (p. 236)

The real question is, why do we as educators continue this "sin of omission"— that is, allowing the cultural knowledge of culturally and linguistically diverse children to be ignored, devalued, and unnurtured as valid sources of literacy acquisition? Excerpts from the writings of five noted African Americans help to illustrate my point.

The Past Revisited

The problem of defining one's literary self is not a new one. As noted scholar W. E. B. Du Bois argued in 1903:

> After the Egyptian and Indian, the Greek and Roman, the Teuton and Mongolian, the Negro is a sort of seventh son, born with a veil, and gifted with second-sight

in this American world,—a world which yields him no true self-consciousness, but only lets him see himself through the revelation of the other world. It is a peculiar sensation this double-consciousness, this sense of always looking at one's self through the eyes of others. . . . One ever feels his twoness, an American, a Negro; two souls, two thoughts, two unreconciled strivings; two warring ideals in one dark body, whose dogged strength alone keeps it from being torn asunder. The history of the American Negro is the history of this strife,—this longing to attain self conscious manhood, to merge his double self into a better and truer self. (1903/1965, pp. 214–215)

Similarly, historian Carter G. Woodson (1933/1990) stated:

In this effort to imitate, however, those "educated people" are sincere. They hope to make the Negro conform quickly to the standard of the whites and thus remove the pretext for the barriers between the races. They do not realize, however, that if the Negroes do successfully imitate the whites, nothing new has thereby been accomplished. You simply have a larger number of persons doing what others have been doing. The unusual gifts of the race have not thereby been developed. (p. 4)

Poet Langston Hughes (1951) expressed a similar notion:

I guess being colored doesn't make me not like
the same things other folks like who are other races.
So will my page be colored that I write?
Being me, it will not be white.
But it will be
a part of you, instructor.
You are white —
yet a part of me, as I am a part of you.
That's American.
Sometimes perhaps you don't want to be a part of me.
Nor do I often want to be a part of you.
But we are, that's true!
As I learn from you,
I guess you learn from me —
although you're older—and white —
and somewhat more free. (pp. 39–40)

Novelist Ralph Ellison (1952) writes:

I am invisible, understand, simply because people refuse to see me. Like the bodiless heads you see sometimes in circus sideshows, it is as though I have been surrounded by mirrors of hard, distorting glass. When they approach me they see only my surroundings, themselves, or figments of their imagination—indeed, everything and anything except me. (p. 3)

And, finally, Toni Morrison (1992) refers to the phenomenon of double consciousness as "writing for a white audience" (p. xii). She asks:

What happens to the writerly imagination of a black author who is at some level always conscious of representing one's own race to, or in spite of, a race of readers that understands itself to be "universal" or race-free? In other words, how are "literary whiteness" and "literary blackness" made, and what is the consequence of these constructions? (p. xii)

Like other culturally and linguistically diverse people before him (including myself and every other person of color with whom I have shared this incident), Jake has encountered the struggle of literary personhood.

Questions and concerns flood my mind: Where, I wonder, has he gotten the idea of a "White" audience—that is, the sense that his classmates and others who read his writing will not appreciate what he has to share? When did his concept of a "White" audience arise? My questions persist: How long has Jake known, intuitively perhaps, that his school literacy experiences have been tempered through a mainstream lens? Will Jake continue to resist "writing for a white audience?" When do culturally and linguistically diverse children learn that they must choose between selfhood and accommodation?[5] When do they learn that "the best way, then, to succeed—that is, to receive rewards, recognition . . . is to learn and reproduce the ways of the dominant group?" (Scheurich, 1992, p. 7). Must there be only one acceptable culture reflected in current school literacy programs? What thoughts, words, and language is Jake replacing with those of the dominant culture in order to please his audience? Will he ever be able to recapture his true literate self after years of accommodation?

As a third grader, Jake is writing, but not for pleasure. Whereas once he wrote as a way of expressing himself or as a hobby, now he does not. He only writes to complete assignments. Much of the "joy" he experienced in writing for pleasure seems to have waned. I recently read some of his writings and noted that he concentrated on topics that do not reflect African American culture. For example, his most recent entries are about his spoon collection, running track, rocks, and football—pretty generic stuff.

My fears are like those of all parents who believe they have prepared their child, having done all that they have read and know a parent should do, yet see their child struggling with a history, a tradition, that is much larger than they can battle.[6] What can I do to help my son and children like him enjoy the freedom of writing and reading? How can I help them value the culturally relevant events in their lives? How can school literacy programs begin to acknowledge, respect, and encourage the diverse cultural knowledge and experiences that children bring to school?

In this article, I am speaking as a teacher educator and parent. This article is an attempt to begin conversations with my colleagues that will address cultural complexities so often ignored in literacy research and practice. For too long, the only perspective published was European Americans' understanding of literacy events. Over the past few years, other cultural perspectives have been published and, more recently, a few have questioned the connection between the theoretical notions of literacy and the historical, and daily, reality of institutionalized inequalities.

As a scholar, I can begin conversations with my colleagues about reexamining theories of literacy to include the role of culture and linguistic diversity. Moreover, teachers and teacher educators like myself can then extend these conversations to reinterpret literacy development, school literacy programs, and teacher education methods and materials to include the experiences of nonmainstream cultures. Finally, I can further extend these conversations into rethinking how we teach and practice school literacy.

BROADENING THE SCOPE

Several contemporary positions on literacy serve to enlighten our understanding of how literacy is defined in the field and how it is defined in practice. In this section, I will offer a brief look at several definitions. First, Cook-Gumperz (1986) describes two competing definitions of school literacy that are useful in framing this discussion. She states that "inherent in our contemporary attitude to literacy and schooling is a confusion between a prescriptive view of literacy, as a statement about the values and uses of knowledge, and a descriptive view of literacy, as cognitive abilities which are promoted and assessed through schooling" (p. 14). Second, a more expansive definition of how literacy is conceptualized is offered by Freire and Macedo (1987). They suggest that "literacy becomes a meaningful construct to the degree that it is viewed as a set of practices that functions to either empower or disempower people. In the larger sense, literacy is analyzed according to whether it serves a set of cultural practices that promotes democratic and emancipatory change" (p. 141). Further, they clarify their position on literacy by noting that "for the notion of literacy to become meaningful it has to be situated within a theory of cultural production and viewed as an integral part of the way in which people produce, transform, and reproduce meaning" (p. 142). Third, more general discussions of literacy define literacy as functional, cultural, or critical. Each of these concepts also refers to very different ways of thinking about literacy. Functional literacy refers to mastery of the skills needed to read and write as measured by standardized forms of assessment. This view of literacy is similar to Cook-Gumperz's (1986) notion of a descriptive view of literacy. The functional view promotes literacy as a cognitive set of skills that are universal, culturally neutral, and equally accessible through schooling, and is based on a positivistic ideology of learning. Further, this view is heavily dependent on the use of standardized testing measures as a proving ground for literacy acquisition. Most basal reading series and programmed reading approaches embrace the functional/descriptive view of literacy.

Cultural literacy is a term that is most often associated with E. D. Hirsch's 1987 book, *Cultural Literacy: What Every American Needs to Know*. Hirsch defines cultural literacy as "the network of information that all competent readers possess. It is the background information, stored in their minds, that enables them to take up a newspaper and read it with an adequate level of comprehension, getting the point, grasping the implications, relating what they read to the unstated context which alone gives meaning to what they read" (p. 2). Cook-Gumperz (1986) has labelled this form of literacy "prescriptive." In effect, this form of cultural literacy validates language forms, experiences, literature, and histories of some and marginalizes or ignores the language forms, experiences, literature, and histories of others. In the United States, the prescriptive view can be seen in the use of standard English, Eurocentric ways of knowing and learning, a Eurocentric literary canon, and a conventional unproblematic rendering of U.S. history. This form of the cultural/prescriptive view marginalizes the pluralistic composition of U.S. society by devaluing the language, contributions, and histories of some groups. Traditional or conventional approaches to school-based literacy take this form. McLaren (1988) argues that there is a second form of cultural literacy. He writes that this form of cultural literacy "advocates using the language standards and cultural information students bring into the classroom as legitimate and important constituents of learning" (p. 214). Cultural literacy, thus described, suggests that the language and experiences of each student who enters the classroom should be respected and nurtured. This form of cultural literacy recognizes that there are differences in language forms, experiences, literature, and histories of students that will affect literacy learning. Social constructivist theories fall into this prescriptive/cultural literacy category. These approaches to literacy emphasize the active engagement of learners in making meaning from print, the social context of literacy learning, and the importance of recognizing individual and cultural differences.

Critical literacy refers to the ideologies that underlie the relationship between power and knowledge in society. The work of Brazilian educator Paulo Freire has been influential to U.S. efforts to adopt a critical literacy position. Freire, among others, suggests that literacy is more than the construction of meaning from print: Literacy must also include the ability to understand oneself and one's relationship to the world. Giroux's (1987) discussion is worth quoting here at length:

> As Paulo Freire and others have pointed out, schools are not merely instructional sites designed to transmit knowledge; they are also cultural sites. As sites, they generate and embody support for particular forms of culture as is evident in the school's support for specific ways of speaking, the legitimating of distinct forms of knowledge, the privileging of certain histories and patterns of authority, and the confirmation of particular ways of experiencing and seeing the world. Schools often give the appearance of transmitting a common culture, but they, in fact, more often than not, legitimate what can be called a dominant culture. (p. 176)

Giroux goes on to state that:

At issue here is understanding that student experience has to be understood as part of an interlocking web of power relations in which some groups of students are often privileged over others. But if we are to view this insight in an important way, we must understand that it is imperative for teachers to critically examine the cultural backgrounds and social formations out of which their students produce the categories they use to give meaning to the world. For teachers are not merely dealing with students who have individual interests, they are dealing primarily with individuals whose stories, memories, narratives, and readings of the world are inextricably related to wider social and cultural formations and categories. This issue here is not merely one of relevance but one of power. (p. 177)

Similarly, Apple (1992) has argued for nearly a decade that "it is naive to think of the school curriculum as neutral knowledge. . . . Rather, what counts as legitimate knowledge is the result of complex power relations and struggles among identifiable class, race, gender, and religious groups" (p. 4). Critical literacy draws attention to the historical, political, cultural, and social dimensions of literacy. Most importantly, this form of literacy focuses on power relations in society and how knowledge and power are interrelated. Educationalists, practitioners in particular, have not yet fully grasped this position on literacy. The other forms of literacy, functional/descriptive and cultural/prescriptive, do not include, among other things, the notion of power relations in literacy instruction.

Philosophically, social constructivist notions (a form of prescriptive/cultural literacy) may be seen as comparable to those espoused by critical literacy. From the schema theorists of the early 1980s to the social constructivist theories of the 1990s, literacy development is understood to be a "meaning making process"—that is, socially mediated (Meek, 1982). Drawing primarily on the work of Halliday (1975), Vygotsky (1978), and Goodman (1989), a number of literacy researchers have stressed the universality of language learning. For example, Goodman's (1989) discussion of the philosophical stance of whole language is that:

At the same time that whole language sees common strengths and universals in human learning, it expects and recognizes differences among learners in culture, value systems, experience, needs, interests and language. Some of these differences are personal, reflecting the ethnic, cultural, and belief systems of the social groups pupils represent. Thus teachers in whole-language programs value differences among learners as they come to school and differences in objectives and outcomes as students progress through school. (p. 209)

However, I argue that the role of culture in the social constructivist theories is not as well defined as it needs to be in a pluralistic or multicultural society. While it is fair to say that unidimensional views of culture would not be supported by social constructivists, it is also fair to say that the multilayered complexity of culture, especially the cultures of historically oppressed groups, is not explicitly addressed by them either. By way of example, I will examine the prescriptive/cultural literacy foundation of whole language. Goodman (1986) argues that "language begins as means of communication between members of the group. Through it, however, each developing child acquires the life view, the cultural perspective, the ways of meaning particular to its own culture" (p. 11). But this definition fails to acknowledge that in addition to acquiring culturally "neutral" knowledge, some children must also acquire a Eurocentric cultural perspective to be successful in school. It is not sufficient to suggest that the language and culture of every student is welcomed, supported, and nurtured in school without explicitly addressing the power relations in institutions, social practice, and literature that advantage some and hinder others (Delpit, 1988; Reyes, 1992). School-based literacy, in its varying forms, fails to acknowledge explicitly the richness of the cultural ways of knowing, forms of language other than standard English, and the interwoven relationship among power, language, and literacy that silences kids like Jake.[7] To fail to attend to the plurality and diversity within the United States—and to fail to take seriously the historic past and the social and political contexts that have sustained it—is to dismiss the cultural ways of knowing, language, experiences, and voices of children from diverse linguistic and cultural backgrounds. This is not to imply that programs based on such theories need to be scrapped. It does mean that social constructivist theories need to be reworked to include the complexities of culture that are currently absent. It will also mean that teacher education will need to: 1) make explicit the relationship among culture, language, literacy and power; and 2) train teachers to use cultural information to support and nurture the literacy development of all the students who enter their classrooms.

When taken at face value, social constructivist theory would lead one to assume that new holistic approaches to literacy are culturally validating for all students. An examination of Jake's home and school contexts for his developing understanding of literacy illustrates that this is not always true. That is, we need to understand where he acquired language and his understanding of culture, as well as his history of literacy instruction, to understand how he is "reading the world" of school literacy and how his experiences with a variety of school literacy forms, including holistic approaches, have not addressed his cultural ways of knowing, experiences, language, and voice.

LITERACY CONTEXTS

Home Context

Literacy acquisition does not evolve in one context or through one type of event; rather, it is a complex endeavor that is mediated through culture. Jake's home literacy environment began with our preparations for him as a new baby. He was brought into a loving two-parent home in which two older brothers were awaiting his arrival. Jake also entered a print- and language-rich environment. He was read to when only a few months old, and continues to share reading (and now writing) with family members. Like the homes of many other middle-class children, Jake's is filled with language, and a range of standard and vernacular languages is used. Our talk centers around family issues, but also includes conversations about world events, neighborhood and school concerns, and personal interests. There are stories, prayers, niceties (manners), verbal games, family jokes, homework assignments, daily Bible reading and discussion, as well as family vacations and excursions to museums, zoos, concerts, and ball parks. Daily routines include reading and responding to mail, making schedules, appointments, grocery and chore lists, and taking telephone messages, all of which include opportunities for shared conversations. There is also a family library that consists of adult fiction, nonfiction, and reference materials. Conversations flow constantly and with ease as we enjoy sharing with each other.

Prior to Jake's entering school, we enjoyed music, games, songs, fingerplay, writing notes on unlined paper with lots of different writing tools, long nature walks, as well as trips to the store, library, barbershop, and church.[8] All these activities were accompanied by lots of talk to expand understanding and draw connections. In addition, Jake and his brothers all have their own bedroom library in which they keep their favorite books, collected since early childhood. Jake's written communications include telephone messages, calendar events, schedules, notes, recipes, invitations, thank-you notes, game brackets (Sega or Nintendo), and occasionally letters and poems.

Jake has a special interest in his collections of stickers, stamps, coins, puzzles, board games, maps, newspaper clippings, and baseball, football, and basketball cards. He also enjoys reading his bedtime story books, magazines (especially *Sports Illustrated for Kids*), and the newspaper (his favorite parts are the sports page, the comics, and the weather map).

What makes Jake's understanding of language and literacy so culturally different from his school's, although both are apparently based on middle-class standards, is that his home literacy events have been culturally defined and are mediated through his cultural understanding. Jake's world is African American; that is, his growing understanding of who and what he is has consciously and unconsciously been mediated through an African American perspective. We select our artwork, magazines, novels, television programs, music, videos, and movies to reflect interests in African American life and society.

School Context

Like most parents, I inquired about the kindergarten's literacy program before enrolling Jake in school.[9] I wanted to have some idea of how his teachers viewed literacy development and how they planned to conduct literacy instruction. My primary question was, "What approach to literacy will you use?" Jake's private, full-day kindergarten was founded by three Jewish women, two of whom taught the kindergarten class, while the third served as school administrator. The teachers informed me that they had taught for many years and were aware of the modern trends. They had therefore designed a program that included what they considered to be the strong points of several programs. Jake's classmates included twelve European Americans (eight were Jewish) and two African American children. His teachers tried to provide all the children with what they thought the children would need to know in order to be successful readers and writers in grade one. As a result, the classroom was colorful and full of print. Labels were placed on cubbyholes, activity centers, children's table chairs, and charts.[10] The reading material was an eclectic mix of basals, trade books, and a small library of children's classics.

In first grade, Jake attended a public elementary school. This classroom was a mixed-age group (grades one and two) of twenty-three children, including seventeen European Americans, four African Americans, and two Asian Americans. His teacher described her literacy program as literature-based, and she stressed reading and writing. This teacher read to the children, who also read individually or in small groups. The reading materials included recipients of the Caldecott award and other award-winning books, stories, and poems by children's favorite authors, classics of children's literature, and writing "published" by the students. The children especially liked to read folk tales. As they gained reading and writing skills, the children coauthored, published, and shared their own work. Students were also encouraged to read and write for pleasure. In all these works, I recall that very few were written about or authored by people of color, except for a few on the Caldecott list.

Jake attended a different elementary school for second grade. I eagerly met his new teacher and asked my standard question about literacy. She informed me that she used the basal approach, which she believed ensured that all the "skills" needed to be a successful reader would be covered. The particular basal series she used included "universal" themes and contained illustrations of various racial/ethnic groups but made little reference to the culture of the people. There were several "ethnic" stories, but I consider their authorship suspect, at best.[11] The series also included isolated skill development, vocabulary regulated text, several thematically organized stories, informational selections, and limited writing opportunities. This class of twenty-eight children included twenty European Americans, five African Americans, and three Asian Americans.

Not wishing Jake to repeat this basal approach in grade three, I spoke with other mothers in the neighborhood, soliciting information about the "good" third-grade teachers. After much prayer, I informed the principal of my choice. Now in third grade, Jake is experiencing what his teacher refers to as a whole language approach to literacy, which includes lots of reading and writing for meaning, working in cooperative groups, process writing, and having sustained time for reading and writing. Writing is a daily activity, and Thursday mornings are designated as Writing Workshop mornings with parent volunteers who assist students in a variety of ways, from brainstorming topics to editing their writing. The teacher allows time for individual and small group readings of trade books on a daily basis. Since my conversation with Jake, I have learned his teacher had selected the books she planned to use during the school year, ahead of time, and the children were allowed only to choose which of these books to read. All of the books were written by European American authors. Even the folk tales from other countries were rewritten by European Americans. Very few books by or about U.S. minorities have been read to students by the teacher, student teachers, or in the reading groups.

I cannot account for the moment-by-moment decisions Jake's teachers have had to make each day. However, I can review the philosophies behind the programs they use. Theoretically, each literacy program purports to be culturally neutral and not mediated by any dominant view of language, when, in fact, a Eurocentric, mainstream cultural view dominates. Darder (1991) argues that it is important to understand the historicity of knowledge:

> The dominant school culture functions not only to support the interests and values of the dominant society, but also to marginalize and invalidate knowledge forms and experiences that are significant to subordinate and oppressed groups. This function is best illustrated in the ways that curriculum often blatantly ignores the histories of women, people of color, and the working class. (p. 79)

Having held a conference with each of Jake's teachers and observed each class setting on several occasions, I can say without hesitation that each teacher believed that she was doing her best to meet the needs of each child in her classroom. That is, she was trying to foster a growing sense of literacy competence in each child. Yet, I don't believe that any of Jake's teachers were aware that they were also narrowly defining the cultural lens through which all children in the classroom were expected to understand literacy.

Thus, in four short years Jake has experienced a wide range of philosophies, approaches, and instruction in literacy, and, at the same time, a narrow ethnocentric view of school literacy. All of his teachers have meant to encourage his growth and development as a literate person. Why, then, have they failed to acknowledge an important part of who he is and what he *culturally* brings to the school literacy program? Reyes (1992) argues that teachers often fail to make adjustments in their approaches to literacy for culturally and linguistically diverse learners because

> the majority of [teachers] are members of the dominant culture, implementing programs designed primarily for mainstream students. Teachers implementing these programs tend to treat students of color as exceptions to the norm, as students who should be assimilated into the dominant group, rather than accommodated according to their own needs. (p. 437)

Some theorists, researchers, and teachers may suggest the counter argument; that is, that elements of the mainstream culture are apparent in all "parallel cultures" and that it is easiest to teach to the mainstream (Hamilton, 1989).[12] I would argue that to ignore, consciously or not, the culture and language that each child brings to the literacy table is to mis-educate him or her. As the research by Au (1993), Morrow (1992), and Reyes and Laliberty (1992), among others, has shown, when cultural and linguistic adjustments are made to school literacy programs, all children benefit.

You may wonder if I have tried to inform Jake's teachers of the narrowness of the literacy lens through which they seem to be defining literacy development and instruction. I admit that I have failed miserably to take a strong stand. Rather than confront them about the lack of culturally responsive literacy instruction, I have expressed my concerns for Jake's personal literacy growth. For example, I have shared multicultural book lists with Jake's teachers and offered to serve as a resource. I have honestly wanted to inform Jake's teachers of two things: one, the need to be more sensitive in their approach to the language and cultural experiences that children bring to the classroom; and two, the need to incorporate more books written by people of color to legitimize the contributions of all literate people. Yet I have also believed that expressing my thoughts might jeopardize Jake's educational future with some kind of backlash.

A STATUS REPORT

While literacy theorists, researchers, and practitioners continue to suggest that school literacy is culturally neutral, Jake's literacy experiences offer an intimate and compelling argument that, as currently practiced, school literacy has been and still is narrowly defined in terms of culture. Only the packaging is new.

Descriptions of my conversation with Jake have met with lots of head nodding and similar stories from many of my non-White students. Delpit (1988) has shared similar insights into what she correctly describes as the "silenced dialogue." The commonsense response among some people of color to school literacy (and schooling in general) has been to take a "way things are" attitude. Many people of color understand that there are inequalities in the educational system; however, we also understand that little can be done without massive school reform. So, to be educated in our current system requires accepting that "this is the way things are. If you want to advance you must learn to play the game." That is, institutionalized racism is something we all know, but see as an unavoidable part of education in U.S. society.

In sharing my analysis with my graduate students, several European Americans have questioned why I refer to Jake's school literacy experiences as being narrowly defined and inquired what is so "acultural" about his literacy education. They ask, "Aren't literature-based and whole language programs built upon notions of constructivist theory that embrace notions of culture?" Of course, my students' understanding is correct: Current holistic school literacy programs support constructivist theory. I guess that's what is so frightening.

While the rhetoric of school literacy programs suggests that culture is part of the theoretical framework, "culture" has been narrowly defined to mean middle-class European American culture. The tacit assumption is, then, that all children are being well served by the new literacy programs that are built on the "natural" language acquisition of middle-class European American children. However, natural language acquisition is mediated through the particular culture in which the child lives. The reality, then, as shared in this article, is that theoreticians, researchers, teacher educators, practitioners, and publishers of literacy approaches and programs are frequently unaware of their assumptions.

Some may truly believe that they are delivering on their promise to build on the culture and language of the child, but what they have been unable, or unwilling, to acknowledge is that school literacy, as it exists, is not universal or reflective of the language and culture of many children. They claim that current school literacy programs and practices are acultural. These programs, however, clearly put some children at a disadvantage, while giving an advantage to others. It is clear, even to a nine-year-old, that school literacy is narrowly defined.

DISCUSSION

In order to meet the needs of our U.S. society, which is rapidly becoming more culturally diverse, our literacy programs should offer more than sensitivity training, human relations, or attitudinal shifts to issues of culture and linguistic diversity. Programs are needed that will also help teachers transform their thinking about the role of language and culture in literacy development. It is simply not enough to inform teachers of what they do not know. Teachers need to question "cultural bumps," or mismatches in expectations of performance in literacy development (Garcia, 1994, personal communication). As Barnitz (1994) states, "Teachers must recognize difference as manifestations of cultural discourse which can be expanded rather than interrupted or suppressed" (p. 587).

What I see is an institutionalized racism that is grounded in the theories used to discuss literacy and to inform and educate teachers and teacher educators. I believe that we need to enhance pre-service teacher curricula and education. The current method of dispersing concepts of diversity, inclusivity, or multiculturalism across several courses, hoping students will synthesize these issues into a workable whole, has been ineffective. Pre-service teachers also need intensive education in understanding the dynamic role that culture plays in language and literacy development and in defining school literacy.

In a pre-service teacher education course I teach, I use literature authored by domestic minority men and women as a starting point for pre-service teachers to begin to reflect on their cultural assumptions about how they "read the word and the world" (Freire, 1985). The method has been effective in helping many students face their own, heretofore unvoiced, assumptions of their own culture and the cultures of other groups.

Most of my students are in their early twenties and have never really concerned themselves with issues of race. Even the students who are members of U.S. minority groups prefer not to discuss race, ethnicity, or culture openly. At the opening of class, for example, many of my students think that their cultural understanding will not affect the students they teach. They believe that their most important concern should be the subject matter and how to transmit effectively a love for their subject to their students. Some of my students also have difficulty understanding the notion of institutionalized racism in U.S. public education. It is at this point in the course that I begin to share the daily occurrences in the lives of my children. Further, some of my European American students see themselves only as "American" and do not wish to deal with their heritage. They want to minimize any tie to Europe and only concentrate on their "Americanness." Some students believe that most U.S. minority group members are poor people, and that most poor people (from all racial groups, but especially those seen most frequently in the media— African Americans and Latinos) really don't care about their children's education. Some also think that children from minority groups don't care about their own education. Most of my students have not even considered how to prepare to teach in multicultural or multilingual classrooms. They tend to live under the false assumption that they can get jobs in homogeneous, suburban school districts.

As in most pre-service teacher education courses nationwide, my students are predominantly European American women. However, in each of my classes, I have had at least one U.S. minority group member. The presence of members from these groups has helped give voice to the concerns of their various communities. My courses are elective, which I believe is important, because it means that the students in my class are interested in issues of diversity. In the best of all worlds, all students would be so inclined, but they are not.

One of the first things I do to help my students become aware of their own cultural understandings is to have them write an autobiographical essay. The essay requires them to trace their ancestry over four or five generations, and to explain their families' use of language, food traditions, and other interesting cultural habits. The essays are shared first in small groups and then with the whole class. In this way, students can readily understand that everyone is a product of their culture, knowingly or not. I too share my cultural and ethnic background. As a person of African, Native, and European American descent, yet who looks only African American, I use my background and life as a springboard for discussions of students' cultural diversity and the limited conception of "culture" in most schools. Since this is a semester-long course, we have the time to engage in many activities, such as community and faculty presentations, videos, and readings by U.S. minority members. However, I believe that some of the most productive work occurs in the small group discussions my students have with each other as they respond to literature written by U.S. minority group members. For example, recently we read a number of novels written by Asian Americans. Many of my students had not heard of the internment of Japanese Americans during World War II.

After my students and I have reflected upon the cultural assumptions from which we perceive our world (and those worlds that might differ from our own), we begin to address teachers' roles and how their cultural assumptions affect the decisions they make, their interactions with students, and their selection of teaching materials. I then give the students opportunities to use their growing understanding of cultural knowledge in lessons they design and teach. My students are all required to teach two literacy lessons during the semester. Many of them choose activities that require participants to work together in cooperative learning groups. Four examples come to mind. One student asked each of us to recall an event using the Native American concept of a "skin story"—drawing on animal pelts—to create pictograph symbols to relate that event. Another student separated class members by attributes they could not control (gender, hair color, size of feet). The "minority" group members (men in this case) were seated in the front of the classroom and were the only students the leader of the exercise asked to respond to her questions. In a third example, a student distributed a series of photographs to small groups and had each group classify the people in the photos, rating them on attributes such as who appeared most intelligent, most successful, and nicest. Finally, a student asked us to read current newspaper articles about war-torn countries and write a diary entry or letter to a government official from the perspective of someone in the country. Through such exercises and activities, my students have learned that culture is a complex issue, one that cannot be taken lightly. They learn to think and act reflectively and become predisposed to considering issues of race, class, gender, age, and sexual preference. Moreover, they understand that their decisions must be based on more than theory; they must also consider the interrelationship of power and knowledge.

I also design in-class lessons around students' responses to the authentic texts they have read. Throughout their field experiences, I have been impressed by the culturally responsive approach to literacy and literature that many of my students have taken with them into the field. For example, one of my students invited recent Asian immigrants to her eighth-grade class to be interviewed by her students. She believed that the face-to-face interactions her students had during the interviews allowed them to understand better the hardships endured by the new U.S. citizens. Another student taught *Huckleberry Finn*. She began the lesson by sharing the historical context in which the novel was written, a model I insist each student use in my class. When confronted by an African American student about the use of the word "nigger" in the novel, she was able to facilitate a group discussion on the use of derogatory terms. She believed that membership in my class enabled her to deal openly with the student and the offensive term. Her experience demonstrates that it is possible to create multicultural learning communities within classrooms that are based on critical literacy theory that validates and legitimizes all learners.

CONCLUSION

In this article, I have argued that for school literacy to begin to move beyond its "neutral" conception of culture, educators at all levels must acknowledge the role and importance of more than one culture in defining school literacy. Educators have not effectively built upon the culture and language of every child, and have set arbitrary standards of acceptance and defined them as normative. I have also argued for the reconceptualization and program development of school literacy, not to dismantle, but to strengthen, literacy frameworks. We can and must do a better job of inviting all students to the literacy table and including them in conversations on school literacy.

I had initial misgivings about sharing my conversation with Jake, as I feared that my thinking would be misinterpreted. My fears lay with the "predictable inability" (West, 1993) of some European Americans to consider honestly the shortcomings of programs they espouse as universal. In addition, I was concerned that my colleagues would view the conversation as one isolated event, ignoring the fact that there are countless instances of narrow cultural constructions of literacy in the daily lives of culturally and linguistically diverse children. I was also reluctant to give such an intimate look into my private world. Therefore, I hope that sharing the incident opens conversations about reconceptualizing and reforming school literacy. When I wonder if I've done the right thing, I recall Jake saying to his older brothers, "I want to share a picture of my real self."

NOTES

1. Going to the barbershop and getting a haircut is a bimonthly occurrence for many African American males. A number of Jake's classmates differed in their definition of what constituted a "part"; however, the other African American children in his class have a similar cultural understanding of the term.
2. As a Writing Workshop parent volunteer in his class, I know that Jake's class consists of ten European American boys, nine European American girls, four African American boys, two African American girls, and one Asian American girl. The class is taught by a European American woman with over twenty years of experience. Also, during this school year, there have been three student teachers (all European American women) and several other parent volunteers (also European American women).
3. In the fall of 1993 I taught a pilot course, which included multicultural education, reading methods for grades six–twelve, and literature for grades six–twelve with special emphasis on multicultural literature.
4. To me, "growing literateness" means an understanding of how language, reading, and writing fit into the communication patterns of home and school life. It can also mean the development of literate behaviors, the adoption of literate attitudes, and the confidence that allows one to define oneself as a reader and a writer.

5. Selfhood, as used in this article, means the awareness of oneself as a person, in particular as a person who belongs to a specific culturally and linguistically distinct group.
6. Cose's (1993) book, *The Rage of a Privileged Class,* gives examples of the frustration experienced by other middle-class African Americans who believed that by doing everything according to plan they would reap just rewards. For example, Cose quotes Darwin Davis, senior vice president of Equitable Life Assurance Society: "They [young Black managers] have an even worse problem [than I did] because they've got M.B.A.'s from Harvard. They did all the things that you're supposed to do . . . and things are supposed to happen" (p. 76).

   By "history," I mean how the inequalities that exist in schools reflect a much greater history of institutionalized inequalities. By "tradition," I mean teachers' tendency to teach how they were taught. Whether history or tradition is the overriding factor in this instance, I am not sure.
7. Silencing, as used by Michelle Fine (1987), "constitutes a process of institutionalized policies and practices which obscure the very social, economic and therefore experiential conditions of students' daily lives, and which expel from written, oral, and nonverbal expression substantive and critical 'talk' about these conditions. . . . Silencing constitutes the process by which contradictory evidence, ideologies, and experiences find themselves buried, camouflaged, and discredited" (p. 157).
8. "Fingerplay" is a term often used to describe actions made with the fingers as children sing a song. For example, the motions used with the song "The Itsy Bitsy Spider" are fingerplay.
9. During my years as a classroom teacher, many parents asked what type of reading program I planned to use. While most parents do not use the term "literacy programs" or inquire about writing programs per se, they do inquire about reading. I have also found that parents are interested in the methods used to teach spelling and vocabulary.
10. Activity centers are areas set aside for special activities. For example, the science center, math center, etc., all have activities specifically designed for children interested in learning more about a selected topic.
11. Many stories contained in basals, like the one Jake used in second grade, are written by teams of authors seeking to control vocabulary or teach specific skills. Basal stories are often abridged or edited versions of original works, and in some instances, such as folk tales, legends, and fairy tales, are translations or a retelling of the original.
12. Recently, Hamilton (1989) used the term "parallel cultures" to refer to the historical experiences of domestic minorities in the United States. "Parallel" conveys a sense of coexistence with the more dominant European American culture so loosely referred to as American culture. The term "domestic minorities" is used to refer to minority groups that have a long history in this country (African Americans, Asian Americans, etc.) but whose forefathers and foremothers lived elsewhere—except in the case of Native Americans.

REFERENCES

Apple, M. (1992). The text and cultural politics. *Educational Researcher, 21*(7), 4–11, 19.
Au, K. (1993). *Literacy instruction in multicultural settings.* Fort Worth, TX: Harcourt Brace Jovanovich.
Barnitz, J. (1994). Discourse diversity: Principles for authentic talk and literacy instruction. *Journal of Reading, 37,* 586–591.
Barrera, R. (1992). The cultural gap in literature-based literacy instruction. Education and *Urban Society, 24,* 227–243.
Cook-Gumperz, J. (Ed). (1986). *The social construction of literacy.* Cambridge, Eng.: Cambridge University Press.

Cose, E. (1993). *The rage of a privileged class*. New York: Harper Collins.

Darder, A. (1991). *Culture and power in the classroom: A critical foundation for bicultural education*. New York: Bergin & Garvey.

Delpit, L. (1986). Skills and other dilemmas of a progressive Black educator. *Harvard Educational Review, 56,* 379–385.

Delpit, L. (1988). The silenced dialogue: Power and pedagogy in educating other people's children. *Harvard Educational Review, 58,* 280–298.

Delpit, L. (1991). A conversation with Lisa Delpit. *Language Arts, 68,* 541–547.

Delpit, L. (1993). The politics of teaching literate discourse. In T. Perry & J. Fraser (Eds.), *Freedom's plow: Teaching in the multicultural classroom* (pp. 285–295). New York: Routledge.

DuBois, W. E. B. (1965). *The souls of Black folks*. New York: Bantam. (Original work published in 1903)

Ellison, R. (1952). *Invisible man*. New York: Random House.

Fine, M. (1987). Silencing in public schools. *Language Arts, 64,* 157–174.

Freire, P. (1985). Reading the world and the word: An interview with Paulo Freire. *Language Arts, 62,* 15–21.

Freire, P., & Macedo, D. (1987). *Literacy: Reading the world and the word*. South Hadley, MA: Bergin & Garvey.

Giroux, H. (1987). Critical literacy and student experience: Donald Graves' approach to literacy. *Language Arts, 64,* 175–181.

Goodman, K. (1986). *What's whole in whole language?* Portsmouth, NH: Heinemann.

Goodman, K. (1989). Whole-language research: Foundations and development. *Elementary School Journal, 90,* 207–221.

Gutierrez, K. (1992). A comparison of instructional contexts in writing process classrooms with Latino children. *Education and Urban Society, 24,* 244–262.

Halliday, M. (1975). *Learn how to mean*. London: Edward Arnold.

Hamilton, V. (1989). Acceptance speech, Boston Globe-Horn Book Award, 1988. *Horn Book, 65*(2), 183.

Heath, S. (1983). *Ways with words: Language, life and work in the communities and classrooms*. Cambridge, Eng.: Cambridge University Press.

Hirsch, E. (1987). *Cultural literacy: What every American needs to know*. Boston: Houghton Mifflin.

Hughes, L. (1951). *Theme for English B. In L. Hughes, Montage of a dream deferred* (pp. 39–40). New York: Henry Holt.

Labov, W. (1972). The logic of nonstandard English. In R. D. Abrahams & R. C. Troike (Eds.), *Language and cultural diversity in American education* (pp. 225–261). Englewood Cliffs, NJ: Prentice-Hall.

McLaren, P. (1988). Culture or canon? Critical pedagogy and the politics of literacy. *Harvard Educational Review, 58,* 213–234.

Meek, M. (1982). *Learning to read*. Portsmouth, NH: Heinemann.

Morrison, T. (1992). *Playing in the dark: Whiteness and the literary imagination*. Cambridge, MA: Harvard University Press.

Morrow, L. (1992). The impact of a literature-based program on literacy achievement, use of literature, and attitudes of children from minority backgrounds. *Reading Research Quarterly, 27,* 251–275.

Ovando, C., & Collier, V. (1985). *Bilingual and ESL classrooms: Teaching in multicultural contexts*. New York: McGraw-Hill.

Reyes, M. de la Luz. (1992). Challenging venerable assumptions: Literacy instruction for linguistically different students. *Harvard Educational Review, 62,* 427–446.

Reyes, M. de la Luz, & Laliberty, E. (1992). A teacher's "Pied Piper" effect on young authors. *Education and Urban Society, 24,* 263–278.

Reyes, M. de la Luz, & Molner, L. (1991). Instructional strategies for second-language learners in content areas. *Journal of Reading, 35,* 96–103.

Sawyer, D., & Rodriguez, C. (1992). How native Canadians view literacy: A summary of findings. *Journal of Reading, 36,* 284–293.

Scheurich, J. (1992). Toward a White discourse on White racism. *Educational Researcher, 22*(8), 5–10.

West, C. (1993). *Race matters.* Boston: Beacon Press.

Woodson, C. (1990). *The mis-education of the Negro.* Nashville, TN: Winston-Derek. (Original work published 1933)

Vygotsky, L. (1978). *Mind in society.* Cambridge, MA: Harvard University Press.

A HEARING TEACHER'S CHANGING ROLE IN DEAF EDUCATION

PATRICIA J. SAYLOR

A local television station has sent a camera crew to videotape the BRIDGES campers at a local skating rink. The camera is on; the light shines in my face so brightly that I cannot see my interviewer.[1] He asks, "How does it feel for the deaf to be living in a society of hearing people?"

I know I am on camera. My comments will be broadcast at 6 p.m. I smile broadly and say, "You know, I think it would be really inappropriate for me to answer that question since I am not Deaf myself."[2] He rephrases the question and asks me again. "I think it would be best to ask one of the Deaf staff members that question," I tell him, still smiling broadly, just in case he decides to use this clip.

After my third refusal, he turns off the camera and informs me that I need to answer because I am the "voice for these people." I inform him that I am not. I ask if it would be appropriate for me to answer the question, "How does it feel to grow up as a Black person in the South?" He is Black, and I am White. Finally, he seems to understand.

I offer to bring Connie or Donya over. I offer to interpret their answer to his question. Like so many hearing people, he is not willing to listen to what Deaf people have to say on behalf of their own experience. He decides not to interview them.

* * *

When Margaret Herring made her name tag at the end-of-summer picnic for BRIDGES 1990, it said, "Margaret Herring, Volunteer." Margaret had come to camp two mornings a week to supervise in the locker room and dress our

Harvard Educational Review   Vol. 62   No. 4   Winter 1992

preschoolers on swim days. She called them her "deaf grandchildren," and she had been so loving and concerned about them that I reminded her, "Margaret, you're not just a volunteer, you're the *grandmother* here." A few minutes later, Margaret had crossed out "Volunteer"; her tag now read, "Margaret Herring, Deaf Grandmother." Her husband's read "Russell Herring, Deaf Grandfather."

Margaret told a reporter, "I used to have just eight grandchildren, none of whom are deaf. Now I have about fifteen more, and they are all deaf." Margaret's acquisition of fifteen deaf grandchildren in five weeks relates directly to the changes I am experiencing as a hearing educator working in the field of deaf education. I realize that she, and other Deaf people like her, have something to offer these children that I never could.

Just over a year ago, I was teaching young deaf and hard-of-hearing children in a self-contained classroom in a public school. I was able to teach the fundamentals of reading, math, science, and social studies, but I soon realized that the thing I was not able to give these children was a strong sense of who they could be when they were grown.

This fact became most obvious to me when, toward the end of my first year of teaching, I invited Adam, one of my young deaf students, to accompany me to Washington, DC, to visit Gallaudet University, the only university for the deaf in the world. The thing he wanted to do most of all was to meet Dr. I. King Jordan, Gallaudet's first Deaf president. Dr. Jordan graciously invited us into his office and fielded questions from this six-year-old deaf child. Adam was most impressed. When we returned to school, he decided to write to this Deaf man. Weeks later, when he got his reply, he took it home and insisted that his parents frame it.

Adam seemed to be hungering for Deaf role models. While we were at Gallaudet, every time he met someone new he asked, "Are you Deaf?" More often than not the answer was yes, and the person would ask the same question of him. When Adam said he was, the person would make a sign that best translates, "You and I are the same." And Adam would grin. He told me that when he grows up he wants to go to Gallaudet University because "there are many, many Deaf people there and just a few hearing people."

A few days after we returned, Adam asked a Deaf teacher's aide in our classroom if she liked to be Deaf. She gave him the standard Deaf answer: Yes, she liked to be Deaf and sometimes wished the whole world were Deaf. Later, Adam asked me if I liked to be hearing. What could I say? I told him that I did, but that I thought being Deaf was fine too. I was just glad that he had this wonderful Deaf woman's input as well. Most deaf kids are not lucky enough to have any Deaf role models.

Shortly after my trip to Gallaudet with Adam, the mother of another child told me that every teacher her Black Deaf son ever had was a "hearing White woman." She wanted the opportunity for him to meet adults he could admire and in whom he could see his own future. Both my experience with Adam and that mother's comments convinced me that I wanted to change the role I played in the lives of deaf children.

I decided to use my administrative talents and skills to create an environment where deaf children could find the role models necessary to develop a strong sense of themselves, and where they and their families could see the potential for the linguistic and social competence they possessed. I knew that in order to create such an environment, I would have to work in cooperation with Deaf adults.

I had some reservations about moving into this new role. If I started the program, raised the funds, and became its director, I would be one more hearing person in charge of the information and services offered to families with deaf children. The more that hearing people are in charge, the fewer Deaf role models deaf children and their families have. Even if I hired Deaf people to work with the children, I would be the primary parent-contact person, and everyone involved in the program, whether hearing or deaf, adult or child, would have reinforced the idea that the hearing people are the ones in charge, and the Deaf people are the assistants.

The choices I saw for myself were to 1) leave the field altogether, 2) continue as a classroom teacher, or 3) redirect myself into a more administrative role. I did not want to leave the field; my heart and passion are in my work. Still, my reasons were clear for not continuing in the role I had. I had considerable experience directing quality children's programs for hearing children, and believed that deaf children deserved the same kind of opportunities. So, I decided that the administrative role was the most appropriate one to choose.

Thus BRIDGES was created. BRIDGES is a bilingual/bicultural day-care and family-service organization for deaf children and hearing children with Deaf family members. The idea behind BRIDGES is simple, but in the field of Deaf Education, our practices are rather revolutionary.

BRIDGES is based on the idea that the developmental delays typically experienced by deaf children are entirely preventable. What deaf children need for normal social and linguistic development is to mingle daily in a community of Deaf, fluent signers. Deaf children with Deaf parents have the opportunity to develop sign language naturally through this kind of interaction at home, but most deaf children of hearing parents do not.

Unfortunately, the typical deaf child of hearing parents is severely delayed in language and social development. These children are not able to acquire naturally the dominant language of their families because they cannot hear it. Therefore, it is not at all uncommon for a deaf child to arrive at school with a vocabulary of fifty or fewer words, little or no emergent literacy skills, and little or no conversational language skills. This delay is in sharp contrast with their hearing peers, who have usually acquired most of the morphological and syntactic rules of their language by the time they enter school.[3] Hence, the deaf child's language delay is usually accompanied by severe deficits in social skills and in the general knowledge required to function in the world.[4]

This early language deprivation adversely affects the deaf child's education, and may ultimately affect his or her ability to succeed and function independently as an adult. The average deaf high school graduate in the United States reads English at the third-grade level.[5] In the majority of deaf education programs, hearing teachers will speak English in the classroom while supporting their speech with a manually coded English Sign System. Some of the signs in these systems are borrowed and modified from American Sign Language (ASL) and others have been invented for educational purposes. However, given the lack of success in the current deaf education system in this country, it becomes obvious that spoken English, whether or not it is mixed with signs, is not sufficient for the education of children who cannot hear it.

With BRIDGES, I aim to create a unique environment where deaf children can develop language, cognitive, and social skills at the same rate as their hearing peers. In order to explain how this is possible, it is necessary to look briefly at the American Deaf Community.

Members of the Deaf Community in the United States do not usually consider themselves disabled, but rather part of a cultural and linguistic minority group. As a hearing person who signs, I am affiliated with, but not a member of, this culture.

Membership in the group is determined by the shared experience of being deaf (usually from birth or early childhood), by specific cultural values, and by the use of American Sign Language. There are active Deaf Communities in most major cities across the country.

The deaf child who is born into a family with culturally Deaf parents (fewer than 10 percent of deaf children fall into this category) does not experience any of the language or social delays of his or her peers living with non-signing, hearing families.[6] The Deaf child in a Deaf family is exposed to an accessible language from birth and is able to take advantage of critical periods for language acquisition that occur during the preschool years. These children, like their hearing counterparts, acquire cultural and social values and a sense of identity through language.

Later, these children typically become more fluent in English (usually through literacy) than their deaf peers from hearing families because they have a solid language base and knowledge about the world on which to build their education.[7]

Most of the deaf children born into hearing families are less fortunate. It has been my experience that fewer than 10 percent of hearing parents ever learn to sign well enough to converse fluently with their Deaf children—a statistic that is considered general knowledge within the field.

My vision for BRIDGES is to create a place where *all* deaf children (from Deaf or hearing families) can thrive. I want to see them develop their social skills, their language, and their knowledge about the world around them. With these skills, they will be able to move freely in both Deaf and hearing environments.

In the last two years, although BRIDGES has taken a lot of my time, it actually has not been difficult to establish. I approached the local YMCA's executive director in January 1990. He offered me space and administrative support if I could come up with the funding for a summer pilot program, which I received from a local foundation and service clubs. I put the word out in the local Deaf Community for staff, volunteers, and students. The first year there was a Deaf staff and lots of Deaf volunteers, who were joined by a hearing assistant the following year. The enrollment goal for that first year was ten children. We had twenty-three.

Some great things happened in the summer of 1990.

The BRIDGES pilot program was a five-week-long summer camp, which provided a place where being deaf presented few barriers. Because the hearing people at BRIDGES were in the minority, nearly all of the conversations were signed instead of spoken. When the children took field trips, fluently signing adults were available to explain where they were going and what to expect. When the children participated in activities with hearing teachers, interpreters were present to make sure two-way communication was possible. Deaf children aged three to thirteen came to camp every day and swam and played and learned in an environment that was almost completely accessible to them.

Preschoolers who arrived with almost no conversational language skills made incredible gains in the few short weeks they were involved in BRIDGES. Many deaf preschoolers arrived unable to ask or answer even simple questions, to comment on their environment, or to explain what they wanted or how they felt. Once at BRIDGES, most of them followed the same pattern: for three days they made no signs, the fourth day they began to copy the teacher's signs, and by the fifth day they were having short, meaningful exchanges.

On her fifth day at camp, four-year-old Isabelle emphasized that she wanted to ride the *rabbit*, not the giraffe, on the carousel at Pullen Park in Raleigh, North Carolina. By the end of the program, she was explaining abstract concepts she could not have discussed five weeks earlier. She told her teacher, "My brother and I have the same mother and father." Upon returning to the YMCA from a field trip, she wanted to know if it was time for the "boys and girls to go home now."

This was great progress for a child who would not even maintain eye contact when she arrived!

Hearing children who came to camp took home not only sign-language skills, but also an understanding of the experiences of their Deaf family members. Both of these gains benefitted the whole family. One ten-year-old girl with a deaf brother talked about feeling left out the first week of camp. She could not understand what was being said. I pointed out that her brother probably felt like that almost all the time. She said, "You know, I never understood that before."

A Deaf mother who brought her hearing son to BRIDGES said his sign-language fluency and attitudes about using sign language improved dramatically over the five-week period. He had been embarrassed to sign to her in public before, but after BRIDGES he began to take pride in the skills he possessed.

At the BRIDGES program, deaf children not only got to see signs being directed at them, but they had an opportunity to witness groups of Deaf people discussing and making decisions. They had the opportunity to "overhear" adult conversations daily. This experience is almost never available for deaf children unless their parents are members of the Deaf Community.

I remember a trip to the North Carolina Zoological Park I made with a group of mostly hearing teachers and deaf children. On that trip, we teachers had decided among ourselves which exhibits we would visit first, and then we had informed the children.

When the BRIDGES staff took the children to the zoo, they also decided among themselves the order of the day's activities. In this case, however, the children were able to witness the negotiation and decisionmaking process, and thus were able to take advantage of the incidental learning opportunities that come with being witness to adult conversations.

Parents had an opportunity to interact with people who did not view their children's Deaf experiences as negative. One woman approached the staff on a field trip to say that her nineteen-month-old daughter was deaf. She was answered with excitement and questions about her child. It was the first time that statement about her child had been received positively. Deaf adults from all over the Community volunteered their time to participate in the program and to be role models for these children and their families.

Margaret Herring, our "Deaf Grandmother," said that she had never spent any time with deaf children, and at camp, for the first time, she felt her contributions were valued. The Deaf cultural experience of children was also affirmed by the Deaf adults with whom they had contact. Adam had announced to a Deaf visitor at his school in the spring of 1990, "When I grow up, I am going to be hearing." That summer, a local Deaf man who had heard of this comment patiently explained to him that when he was young, he had been a deaf boy, too. He told Adam, "When you grow up, you will be a Deaf man, like me." Adam could see that he did not have to go to Gallaudet University to find Deaf people who made him feel good about his identity as a Deaf person.

In spite of the positive aspects and benefits of the program for both the deaf and hearing children, it was not possible to eliminate cross-cultural issues from this environment of Deaf-hearing contact. I was still the hearing person in charge, and the parents still came to me first to discuss their children's progress and program activities. Most of the parents do not have the sign-language skills even to converse fluently with their own children, and they therefore are not able to converse comfortably with the Deaf staff members. To help solve that problem and to encourage communication between parents and teachers, I plan to add a full-time interpreter to the staff when the program is established year-round.

When the BRIDGES Program requires interpreters, we use free-lance, certified local interpreters. I am careful to avoid the role of interpreter whenever possible. It would be an easy role to take on, but while I sign fairly well, I have had no training in the skill of interpreting. I feel this policy of using only certified interpreters is crucial if we are to maintain respect for the profession of interpreting and to encourage our children and their families to become well-informed consumers of these services. In the meantime, however, there is less communication between the staff and parents than I would like to see.

Most parents at BRIDGES are able to see the value of Deaf role models for their deaf children, but still have little or no understanding of Deaf Culture or its importance to their own families. Many will not use the term "deaf" in reference to their children, and most of them continue to talk to their children showing no apparent awareness that the children are understanding only a small fraction of what they are saying. Even the parents who know some signs use them primarily as a method to supplement their speech, rather than as the primary mode of communication.

Cultural differences between Deaf and hearing people can be a source of misunderstanding. For example, it is considered polite among Deaf people to share much more personal information than hearing people are accustomed to sharing among themselves. Sometimes this cultural difference leads Deaf people to perceive hearing people as distant, and hearing people to perceive Deaf people as nosy. The deaf children get mixed signals about what kinds of behaviors are appropriate. Cross-cultural awareness can ease tension between deaf and hearing adults, and also make it easier for them to explain to deaf children why some behaviors are appropriate in Deaf groups while others may be more appropriate among hearing people.

To address these issues, the year-round BRIDGES Program will include a parent-education component taught by Deaf instructors. Topics will include ASL, Deaf Culture, and cross-cultural concerns. Through this education, we hope to help hearing parents depend less on interpreters and other hearing people for information about their children. They will begin to be able to learn about Deaf Culture from Deaf people directly. They will develop the communication skills to participate in their deaf children's lives as fully as possible. Their children will then learn that their own experiences and culture as Deaf people are valuable. I do not, however, imagine that this respect for and value of Deaf Culture will happen in every family, nor that it will happen quickly. At least the BRIDGES environment has encouraged some communication between hearing parents and Deaf staff members. So far, it has been on the level of, "Where is my child's bathing suit?" or "Do I need to pack a lunch for her tomorrow?", but it is a start. Eventually, I hope discussions about educational decisions, parenting issues, communication, and Deaf Culture will occur between hearing and Deaf people.

Cross-cultural issues are also hard to overcome in the children's relationships. The school-age children at camp divided themselves into two groups, hearing and deaf, during independent play time. The preschool children were less segregated, but many of them did not yet have the language skills for cooperative, imaginative play.

One encouraging exception was Natalie, a preschool hearing child with Deaf parents. Natalie was by far the most fluent signer in the preschool group and moved freely between deaf and hearing play groups, signing or speaking as necessary. She is a true bilingual and could choose appropriately from her available communication strategies.

As a rule, very young deaf children are not able to be bilingual in ASL and English, as is Natalie.[8] Until they learn to read, they will not have access to spoken language. They can, however, become fluent users of ASL. Their second-language skills in English will then develop rapidly when they become literate through their elementary school education. Some of them may also develop varying degrees of spoken English proficiency with speech therapy. The use of speech therapy for deaf children has had widely varied success.[9] Some may develop speech that is intelligible only to their families and close friends. A few may learn to speak clearly enough to be understood by strangers, but many do not, and so choose not to use their speech by the time they are adults. Natalie and other children of Deaf parents show, however, that true bilingualism is a very realistic goal for young hearing children. If the siblings of deaf children could learn to sign fluently and to accept Deaf and hearing ways as equal, then there would be a positive impact on the families of deaf children.

When children who enter the BRIDGES Program are already in elementary school, their linguistic and cultural identities seem to be well established. Some experiences reach across cultural barriers, but most children, like their parents, are most comfortable communicating and socializing within their own cultural group.

These cross-cultural concerns make me even more aware of my role as a hearing administrator running a program for Deaf people. In an ideal situation, I would be working cooperatively with a Deaf person to codirect the program, which would be a model Deaf-hearing partnership for the staff and families involved. It is unrealistic, however, to expect a small, local program to support two directors. We are lucky to raise the funds to support one director, rent a van, buy program supplies, and pay the staff every summer. Perhaps in the future we will be able to incorporate more Deaf leadership into the program; for now, I do all the grant writing in my spare time, and speak to foundations and service clubs when I get a chance. It is not possible, at present, to change that administrative composition.

In spite of cross-cultural concerns, the summer program seems to be an excellent start for BRIDGES. The 1990 pilot summer program has successfully served as a catalyst to move us toward our goal of year-round operation.

The United Way gave us a Venture Grant of $12,000 to bring our facility up to day-care licensing standards; the state of North Carolina Division of Child Day Care Services awarded us the funds to purchase a van. We have applied for a federal grant from the Department of Education that would allow us to become a model demonstration preschool program. Although we were not awarded a grant the first year, a federal administrator tells me that every year we successfully raise local funds for the program, we will significantly increase our chances of receiving a five-year federal grant.

After the first summer of BRIDGES, I returned to teaching. This time the subjects were Spanish and American Sign Language at a local high school. Adam's older sister had circulated a petition requesting that a sign language class be offered at her high school, and the principal asked me to teach it. I needed year-round employment, and I saw this job as a way to continue my efforts to build bridges of understanding between Deaf and hearing cultures. My ASL classes included many hearing students with Deaf family members, neighbors, and friends.

While I had some reservations about teaching ASL (in some places it is considered "politically incorrect" for a hearing person who has not grown up in the culture to teach ASL), I made it clear to my students that I was not a native signer or a representative of the Deaf Culture, but that I would share with them the knowledge and skills that I had. I assigned readings and videotapes produced by Deaf people and provided opportunities for them to meet Deaf adults in our community. We exchanged letters and made a videotape to send to other high school students from the Eastern North Carolina School for the Deaf.

I invited one of the BRIDGES Deaf staff members and some local deaf children to accompany my ASL students and me on a field trip to the School for the Deaf. The tour was conducted by a hearing woman who unfortunately showed little awareness of Deaf Culture. She proudly showed off the school's audiological technology and bragged about the speech therapy students received.

During the rest of the afternoon, my students mingled in the dorms, watched a basketball game between two Deaf teams, and attended a party some of the Deaf students had prepared for them. As we were leaving, one of the Deaf students told me that my students had the best attitude about Deaf people of any hearing visitors they had ever had to the school. The Deaf student never fully explained what he meant when he said most hearing people had a very "bad attitude" about the Deaf. I was only glad that my students did not share it. The hearing students had approached the visit with the idea that they were guests of another culture, and I was pleased to know that it showed.

I had not planned to have a second summer program for deaf children in 1991. After the initial pilot program, I was focusing my attention on the goal of setting up year-round services. The parents, however, insisted that we have another day camp.

Groups who funded us the first year were approached, as well as a few other funding sources, and we were pleasantly surprised by the response. Some of the service clubs had already set aside funds for us. Local businesses came through with printing and t-shirts. Our major funding came from two local foundations, the Durham Merchants Association Charitable Foundation, and the Mary Duke Biddle Foundation.

The 1991 summer program had an expanded staff and served more children than the year before. Most of our children returned for a second year, and some new three-year-olds joined the program. The individuals' and the program's successes were as great as the first year.

I am confident that if the federal grant comes through to cover basic operating expenses, local funds can be raised to build a playground, set up a family resource library, and continue to provide summer opportunities for school-age children.

The BRIDGES Program has been so successful for the deaf children, it is hard to see why our methods are considered controversial. The revolutionary aspect of BRIDGES is the idea that Deaf adults are the most appropriate role models for deaf children. BRIDGES is different from most programs for deaf children because we don't consider being "more like hearing" to be necessarily better than being Deaf.

For years, the educational establishment has operated on the principle that in order to function in the "hearing world," deaf children need to assimilate and need to be as much like hearing people as possible. The more speech skills and auditory awareness they develop, the assumption is, the better off they will be, even if this focus on "speech and hearing" takes time away from academic studies and from more fluent and effective communication options. The reality of the Deaf Community shows us that this assumption is not true.

In March 1988, four Deaf students at Gallaudet University led a successful university-wide protest to install Dr. I. King Jordan as the first Deaf president in the institution's history. I was on campus during that eventful week. I saw student leaders take charge of the campus and work with the media. They set up press conferences, established a phone bank for fundraising, and achieved worldwide recognition for their cause. They changed the course of Deaf history in less than one week. No one will convince me that they did not know how to function in "the hearing world." It is significant that all of them sign ASL fluently; not once during that week did I hear them speak. All four come from Deaf families; from an early age, all four had the support and training of the Deaf Community to learn how to function as *Deaf* people in the hearing world.

As I was preparing for the BRIDGES 1991 summer program, I once again realized the importance of Deaf role models for deaf children. For example, when a new staff member, Richard, was preparing to come to his first BRIDGES staff meeting, I gave him directions over the phone (using a TTY—a telecommunications device). He had never been to the YMCA before and was coming from out of town. He assured me that if he got lost there would be no problem; he would stop and ask for directions.

Later I realized that I did not know how he would ask. I had no doubt that he could ask for directions without a problem, but I had no idea *how* he would. It struck me once again that there was a gap in my knowledge. If a deaf child asked me the best way to approach a hearing person and request information, I would have no idea what strategies to suggest. Richard, however, has years of experience interacting with hearing non-signers and would be an excellent resource for such questions.

Deaf people not only have a wealth of knowledge about how to cope in a sometimes hostile (or at least unaccommodating) environment, they also have a rich heritage of folklore, literature, customs, and values that can be a source of pride and self-esteem for young deaf children. Usually, hearing people (including teachers of deaf children) are completely ignorant of this heritage. Only through other Deaf people can deaf children have access to this rich source of pride and tradition in the Deaf Community.

At BRIDGES, we don't try to ignore or "overcome" Deafness in children. Instead, we nurture them through contact with Deaf adults who can share their stories and experiences. Most professionals working with deaf children and their families have a different perspective from that of the BRIDGES Community.

A school interpreter told me that a few years ago she brought two Deaf people to a group of parents of deaf preschoolers. The Deaf women talked about their experience and frustrations growing up with non-signing birth families. They told the parents how common it is for Deaf children to not want to go home from school to families with whom they cannot communicate. One parent cried. A couple of parents were so upset that they did not ever come back to the group. The interpreter suggested that maybe parents of young deaf children are not capable of handling the truth that Deaf adults share with them about what it means to grow up deaf.

My experience with parents of deaf children has been different. I think it is sometimes a relief for parents to have someone tell them that there is nothing wrong with their child. I have found that frequent exposure to a community of Deaf adults can be very positive for the families of deaf children. By seeing the Deaf teachers on a daily basis, the parents can begin to develop trusting relationships with them. Any one of the BRIDGES Deaf staff members would tell parents that they feel very positive about their Deaf identity. Some of their attitudes about themselves are bound to influence positively the parents' attitudes about their own deaf children.

Of course, these relationships take time to develop. I still find myself, uncomfortably at times, in the role of educating parents about the Deaf Community and the impact that being Deaf will probably have on their child and their family. Eventually, Deaf people will be doing this job instead of me, but for now, I persist.

I reassure the parents that a survey of existing literature demonstrates ample evidence that deaf children exposed to a natural sign language (as opposed to a "sign system" or one of the manual codes for English that are almost exclusively used in programs for deaf children) will go through a normal language acquisition process. This process almost exactly parallels the process hearing children go through when acquiring spoken languages.[10] I tell them that communication does not have to be any more of a struggle for their children than for hearing children.

For years, parents have been told that if they let their deaf children learn to sign, it will sap their motivation to learn to talk. More recently, they have been told that their children must learn a manual code representing English, rather than the language of the Deaf Community, ASL. In actuality, the skills and knowledge they learn through ASL and through interaction with a community that shares this language will make it easier for them to learn English. It is well known by educators that Deaf children from Deaf families who learn to sign early are almost always more successful students than those who do not acquire language until they are older.[11] The English skills of these children may or may not include speaking and auditory awareness or speech reading, but literacy is a realistic goal for almost all deaf children.

I tell parents that speech skills are a "convenience" for their deaf children, but not a prerequisite for success as an independent deaf adult. I tell them about the work of the Deaf student leaders during the "Deaf President Now!" protests at Gallaudet University.

Still, parents share their fears with me. They are given so much conflicting advice. They are afraid they will do the wrong thing. They are afraid that they will lose their children to a community of which they (the parents) cannot be a part. They are afraid life will be hard for their children. They are afraid their children will live a life of isolation. They are afraid that they will look foolish and incompetent if they try to sign with Deaf adults.

Conflicting advice is nothing new for parents of young deaf children. For decades, deaf children have been subjected to one "method" after another that attempts to minimize or annihilate what many Deaf people call the "Deaf Way." A local parent advocacy organization offers a videotape that informs parents of methods for communicating with their deaf children. The methods include: oral (lipreading and speaking); auditory/verbal (similar to oral, but in which the teachers cover their mouths when they talk to the children); cued speech (eight hand shapes made near the mouth while speaking); verbo-tonal (children and teachers move in rhythm with vocalizations); total communication (speech supported by some signs borrowed from ASL and others invented by educators); the modified Rochester Method (teachers finger-spell words as they speak); and vibro-tactile stimulation (the child wears a device on his or her body that vibrates with sound). Nowhere on the tape is ASL or the existence of a Deaf Community mentioned.

There are many "methods," but really only two choices. Parents may choose to follow one of the methods that denies the importance and contributions of the Deaf Culture and language and that tries to "fix" their children. Or, they may respect centuries of precedent and learn from the Deaf Community.

From Deaf adults, they can learn that having a Deaf child does have positive aspects. Parents have an opportunity to become familiar with a culture that they otherwise probably never would have encountered. They may become acquainted with a community of people who have a strong interest in the well-being of their child. And they can learn a new language, ASL.

Nevertheless, sometimes I find it hard to help parents see any positive aspects to their child's Deaf identity when there is so much negativity surrounding hearing loss. The parent advocacy organization mentioned above also presents a handbook to parents of recently identified deaf children. The first statement in the book tells them that finding out their child is "hearing impaired" (a label that many Deaf people find offensive) will probably make them feel as if someone has died!

While I agree that it is important to acknowledge the grief that parents experience when they find out that their child is not what they expected, it seems another message might be more helpful. I imagine what a different tone the book could have taken if it started with a quote from Dr. I. King Jordan: "Deaf people can do anything, except hear!"

I value children's relationships with their birth families. But I believe that continuing to foster an attitude that perceives hearing loss as a medical condition to be fixed, rather than an attitude that Deaf Culture is something to be nurtured and valued, will sabotage the relationship between deaf children and their hearing family members. As long as the deaf child is viewed as the defective member of the family, the parents will never be able to celebrate the Deaf child's language or culture, and a significant part of that child's identity will be lost. Even if the child is able to identify with other Deaf people later in life (and many of them do, in spite of their educational programs or their parent's efforts), the parents will be left out of one of the most significant parts of their child's life. I tell these mothers and fathers that they can have support in learning the language and culture of the Deaf Community, and that if they do that, they need not fear losing their children.

It takes one visit to a local Deaf Community event for parents to see that being Deaf will not condemn their children to a life of isolation. These community members are a tight-knit group who keep up with each other like an extended family. They are thrilled to see parents learning to sign for their deaf children, and almost all will support and encourage those efforts. Margaret Herring knows that deaf babies need a Deaf grandmother, but she also knows they need to be able to communicate with their own parents. She circulates, bounces babies, and makes a point of welcoming every family that brings a deaf child to the monthly Deaf Community dinners.

I also remind the parents that my parents and I are hearing. Yet as I grew up, I began to create a community for myself that was separate from my parents. It is the nature of all children to grow up and find their own communities. The fact that their children's community includes other Deaf people does not have to make them any less a part of their birth families than I am of mine.

So, my goal with BRIDGES is, in cooperation with Deaf people, to provide an environment where deaf children will have sufficient contact with fluent signers so that they can develop ASL as naturally as possible and at age-appropriate times. At the same time, the staff will provide support for their parents and siblings in learning the language and culture of the Deaf Community. Then, by the time these children are ready to enter school, they will have had several years of experience conversing and learning about their world. Their parents will have the skills necessary to allow the deaf child to be a contributing member of the family. The child will enter school with the base of language, knowledge, and family support necessary for a successful education.

We are not there yet, but after two summer programs, we are well on our way. Roadblocks are unavoidable, but with education and time, we make more and more progress. The roadblocks often come in the form of well-meaning, but misguided, professionals. The mother of a recently deafened toddler received informational materials from a friend she had known in the Peace Corps. The friend is now a doctor, and when he found out that her baby was deaf, he wanted to help. The emphasis of all his materials was on speech and hearing aids and surgical intervention. He warned her to stay away from sign language if she wanted her son to be able to function in the hearing world.

This parent tells me that her friend is very progressive about social issues. He supports and respects ethnic and cultural differences. I guess I should no longer be surprised, but I am consistently amazed that the same level of respect is almost never given to the language and culture of the American Deaf Community.

Perhaps this man's medical training prevents him from moving beyond a medical model of hearing loss to recognition of Deafness as a cultural identity. I only hope he does not encounter many parents with young deaf children.

* * *

Isabelle's mother tells me that she thinks Isabelle has a lot to say. She can't wait until her daughter has enough language to express herself. It is a comment I remember my sister making when her daughter was just under two years old.

It is July 1991. Isabelle lies on her blanket watching intently as Connie, one of the BRIDGES teachers, signs to own her daughter, Natalie. Natalie complains about having to lie down. Connie promises her a swim with her daddy that evening. For about five minutes they share the intimate, easy, fluid conversation of those who know and understand each other well. Isabelle's eyes never leave them.

A few minutes later, Connie turns her attention to Isabelle. They talk about Isabelle's family. Connie asks how many rooms there are in Isabelle's house and with which of her siblings she shares a bedroom. Isabelle obviously understands the topic and comments on her house, but she never makes it clear exactly who shares her room.

Connie asks if her mother works. Isabelle does not understand the question, and Connie rephrases it. Isabelle finally says something about sick babies. Connie looks to me and I inform her that Isabelle's mother is a neonatal intensive-care nurse. With that information, Connie is able to continue the conversation and elaborate, "Oh, your mother works in a hospital."

Sometimes Isabelle is frustrated and looks away, but each time, Connie gently brings her back to the conversation with a more accessible topic or an explanation she knows Isabelle will understand. I am amazed at Connie's patience and the success with which she engages this child. I have never been able to hold Isabelle's attention for more than one or two exchanges.

Connie pats Isabelle on the back and tells her it is time to go to sleep. She looks over at me and says, "Isabelle needs a Deaf person to converse with her every day. If she had that, she would be able to sign like Natalie." Natalie and Isabelle are both within weeks of their fifth birthdays.

* * *

Two years ago, a four-year-old girl I interviewed for a research project told me there were three kinds of people. They were either "Deaf, like my mom, a little bit Deaf, like my dad or *not* Deaf, like me!" To her, being Deaf was not negative, it was just a fact of life, like her brown hair. It would not occur to her to think she is any better than her parents because she is hearing and they are Deaf.

I used to teach in a program that the Harvard Graduate School of Education labeled as being for the "hearing impaired." Now I teach about Deaf Studies and ASL to hearing high school students. One night each week, a group of parents with deaf children come to my home to work on their sign language skills. In my spare time, I raise funds for a bilingual, bicultural program for the benefit of deaf children and their families. I wait for the break that will allow me to implement the program full-time.

People who know what I do frequently say I am involved in the field of "Speech and Hearing." It seems odd to me that they would focus on the things that most Deaf people do not do, speak and hear. I tell them that is not my field. My field is language and Deaf Studies, a very different thing.

NOTES

1. BRIDGES is not an acronym. The name describes a program created with the goal of building understanding between two cultures, the Deaf culture and the hearing culture.

2. In this text, as is becoming customary in the Deaf Community, there is a distinction between the words "deaf" and "Deaf." The word "deaf" refers to someone who does not hear or does not hear well, and "Deaf" refers to a cultural identification with members of the American Deaf Community.

3. Helen Trager-Flusberg, "Putting Words Together: Morphology and Syntax in the Pre-school Years," in *The Development of Language*, 2nd ed., ed. Jean Berko-Gleason (Columbus, OH: Merrill, 1989), p. 153.

4. Robert E. Johnson, Scott C. Liddell, and Carol J. Erting, *Unlocking the Curriculum: Principles for Achieving Access in Deaf Education* (Washington, DC: Gallaudet University Department of Linguistics and Interpreting and Gallaudet Research Institute, 1989).

5. Thomas E. Allen, "Patterns of Academic Achievement Among Hearing Impaired Students: 1983–1984," in *Deaf Children in America*, ed. Arthur N. Shildroth and Michael A. Karchmer (San Diego: College-Hill Press, 1986), pp. 161–206.

6. Raymond Trybus and Carl Jensema, *Communication Patterns and Education Achievement of Hearing Impaired Students*, Office of Demographic Studies Series T, No. 2 (Washington, DC: Gallaudet College, 1978).

7. Donald F. Moores, *Educating the Deaf: Psychology, Principles and Practices*, 3rd ed. (Boston: Houghton Mifflin, 1987).

8. For the purposes of this article, English is used as the example of a native spoken language.

9. I base this assertion on discussions with Deaf adults and personal observation.

10. Patricia J. Saylor, "Language Acquisition in Deaf Children: A Survey of Literature," Unpublished manuscript, 1988.

11. K. Brasel and Stephen P. Quigley, "The Influence of Certain Language and Communication Environments in Early Childhood on the Development of Language in Deaf Individuals," in *Journal of Speech and Hearing Research, 20* (1977), 95–107.

Author's Note: Clayton Valli, a noted Deaf Activist, informs me that the term "deafness" is something of a culturally sensitive term. Many Deaf people prefer the terms "Deaf Way" or "Deaf World." There were passages in this article where I could find no way to express adequately the meaning I was trying to convey without using the word "deafness," and I decided to leave it in. However, it is important to inform the reader that some Deaf people find the term distasteful.

"THEY'RE IN MY CULTURE, THEY SPEAK THE SAME WAY"

AFRICAN AMERICAN LANGUAGE IN MULTIETHNIC HIGH SCHOOLS

DJANGO PARIS

The title of this article comes from an interview I conducted with Miles,[1] an African American high school student I came to know during a year I spent doing an ethnographic study in his youth community. Miles was commenting on the linguistic reality of his multiethnic high school, describing the ways his Latino/a and Pacific Islander peers shared in his culture and his language. In this article, I explore the deep linguistic and cultural ways that Miles was right: that youth in his multiethnic urban high school employed linguistic features of African American Language (AAL) across ethnic lines. I begin by describing some of the characteristics of AAL and then show how language sharing in AAL happened and how youth across ethnic groups made sense of it. I also discuss the ways knowledge about AAL use in multiethnic contexts might be applied to language and literacy education and how such linguistic and cultural sharing can help us forge interethnic understanding in our changing urban schools.

To examine the ways youth shared in AAL across ethnicity and to facilitate a discussion of the educational and social implications of this sharing, I provide ethnographic and sociolinguistic data I collected over the 2006–2007 school year at South Vista High School. South Vista High is a public charter high school serving students from the city of South Vista, a working-class community of color in a major metropolitan area of the West Coast. South Vista was a predominantly African American city as late as 1990, but even then the city was beginning to experience dramatic demographic shifts. By the dawn of the twenty-first century, the Spanish-speaking Latino/a population had become a significant majority of the city's population.

The youth of South Vista were living through this change. Carlos, a Mexican American youth I worked with, put it this way: "It used to be all black people. It was a black city. . . . There was some Latinos, but over time they started moving away, and then more Latinos started moving in" (3/12/07).[2] During the year of my research, 17 percent of the students at South Vista High were African American, 10 percent were Pacific Islander, and 73 percent were Latino/a—mainly Mexican or Mexican American.[3]

The interviews and field notes I draw on here are the result of nine months of close fieldwork I conducted with a group of eight focus youth and the sixty young people in their peer networks. These focus youth included African American, Latino/a, and Pacific Islander young women and young men. I spent more than 400 hours participating with and observing these young people and conducted three semistructured, *ethnolinguistic* interviews with each focus youth over the school year.[4] I employed grounded theory to categorize major themes of youth language use and understanding and used sociolinguistic methods to look more closely at features of AAL in everyday talk.

My own interest in the nexus of ethnic and linguistic difference and school learning is fueled by my years teaching English in multiethnic schools as well as by my own identity as a black/biracial scholar with a black Jamaican immigrant father and a white American mother. My research relationships with these youth—as young people of color, as immigrants, and as speakers and hearers of many Englishes—were far from impersonal; in varying ways, these experiences were also part of my coming-of-age. Although here I focus on AAL in multiethnic high schools, the interviews and fieldnotes I present should be seen in light of my ethnographic work with these youth across community contexts, from home to church, classroom to basketball court, hip-hop show to soccer match. The AAL I observed, participated in, and recorded in these spaces, of course, was anchored in a historical context of oppression, resistance, and achievement. I attempt to attend to this context as I discuss AAL use across ethnicity at South Vista High.

THE NEED FOR INTERETHNIC LANGUAGE RESEARCH IN SCHOOLS

AAL is the most studied variety of English in the world, with over forty years of sociolinguistic scholarship investigating when, how, where, with whom, and why AAL has been and continues to be spoken by many African Americans (e.g., Baugh, 1983; Labov, 1972; Smitherman, 2006). These decades of scholarship have given us a rich understanding of the grammar, phonology, lexicon, and rhetorical traditions of AAL.[5]

Research into using AAL as a resource for classroom learning is also vast (Rickford, Sweetland, & Rickford, 2004). We know how to contrast AAL grammar with Dominant American English (DAE) grammar so that students come to see and attend to differences depending on social context and purpose (Godley, Sweetland, Wheeler, Minnici, & Carpenter, 2006).[6] We know much about the ways in which the features of spoken AAL carry into writing (Ball, 1995, 1999). We also know what it looks like to teach African American AAL-speaking students to maintain cultural competence while acquiring DAE (Alim, 2004; Ladson-Billings, 1995; Lee, 1995). We have a particularly robust and growing literature on the connections between hip-hop, AAL, and classroom learning (Alim, 2004, 2006; Kirkland, 2008; Mahiri, 2001; Morrell & Duncan-Andrade, 2002). And finally, we know quite a bit about how to train teachers to use AAL as a resource for classroom learning (Godley et al., 2006; Kirkland, 2008).

Yet research on AAL has remained focused solely on African Americans despite demographic change in our communities and schools. There is good reason for our focus on black speakers of AAL: AAL is a black-originated English that is intimately connected with a history of oppression, resistance, and rich linguistic and literary achievement in African America (Rickford & Rickford, 2000). And it is a language used by many African American young people in our schools and communities. However, demographic shifts coupled with the continued residential segregation of poor communities of color have increased the numbers of black and brown students who share the same communities and classrooms (Ball, 2006; Klein, 2004; Ladson-Billings, 2006; Massey, 2001). Understanding how AAL operates in such multiethnic schools will help us understand where our vast knowledge of AAL should be applied. It will also shed light on opportunities for a *pedagogy of pluralism*—a stance to teaching both within and across differences—in multiethnic schools.

This research is an attempt to push educational research further into the realm of interethnic youth communication. Building on seminal theoretical work focused on contact in multiethnic and multilingual contexts (Anzaldúa, 1987, 1999; Bakhtin, 1981; DuBois, 1903, 1965; Pratt, 1987, 1991), I have come to conceptualize *multiethnic youth space* as a social and cultural space centered on youth communication within and between ethnicities—a space of contact where youth challenge and reinforce notions of difference and division through language choices and attitudes. Very little research has brought social language knowledge and methodology to the multiethnic youth spaces so common in contemporary urban schools. Rampton's (1995) ethnographic and sociolinguistic study of language use in a multiethnic youth community in Britain provides a rare investigation into how language and ethnicity function among adolescents in such multiethnic space. Although not based in schools, Rampton's (1998) work moves beyond the study of in-groups and toward an understanding of what he later termed *plural ethnicities*. For Rampton, individuals can adopt plural ethnicities that challenge singular ethnicities in contexts where ethnic groups blur lines of linguistic and cultural ownership. In his analysis, he looked to understand the social rules of *language crossing*, moments when youth would cross into the languages of their peers during interactions.

Although Rampton referred to all instances of youth employing their out-group peers' languages as "crossing," my own analysis has pointed to some moments when AAL was crossed into and other times when it was shared. While language crossing may or may not be ratified by traditional in-group speakers, I refer to *language sharing* as those momentary and sustained uses of the language that are ratified—when use of the language traditionally "belonging" to another group is ratified as appropriate by its traditional speakers. Such sharing occurred at South Vista when African American students ratified the AAL use of their Pacific Islander and Latino/a peers. As I will show, this ratification can be expressed in several ways. Most often at South Vista, ratification occurred through African American AAL speakers continuing an interaction in AAL with their Latino/a or Pacific Islander peers and, by continuing an interaction, implicitly inviting their out-group peers to continue the language sharing. Another way AAL use was ratified as sharing was more simply when African American students did not protest, mock, or otherwise comment on the AAL use of their out-group peers, thereby implicitly deeming it as authentic.

While crossing and sharing have major implications for how we think about language, ethnicity, and schooling in multiethnic contexts, it is important that I avoid overstating what such practices can achieve in an unequal society. Although language is one primary marker of ethnicity and identity, other major markers of race, like skin color, play heavily into systems of discrimination, racism, and privilege. For this reason, I back away from Rampton's "plural ethnicities" and favor more specific terms of practice, such as *linguistic dexterity*—the ability to use a range of language practices in a multiethnic society—and terms of mind, such as *linguistic plurality*, consciousness about why and how to use such dexterity in social interactions. Such terms recognize the importance of interethnic practices without falsely implying that they surmount systemic barriers.

AAL GRAMMAR, LEXICON, AND RITUAL INSULT AMONG BLACK YOUTH AT SOUTH VISTA

All of the African American students I came to know at South Vista were bi-dialectal AAL speakers: their everyday speech both inside and outside the classroom showed major features of AAL, but they could also shift, to varying extents, into more dominant varieties of English. The research literature has long noted that many African Americans can and do systematically use features of AAL in their everyday speech (Baugh, 1983; Rickford & Rickford, 2000; Smitherman, 1977). Miles said this quite succinctly as we sat on a bench near the athletic field informally talking one afternoon. "*Every black person is bilingual*," he told me. "You gotta be because I was taught that it's harder for us, and you have to use their language to get by." (I use italics throughout the data examples to highlight youth perspectives on AAL as well as AAL features.)

Of course, not all African Americans can or do speak AAL. Like any language variety, it is socially and culturally learned and used. Only people who learn AAL and have reason to use it do so. Although this learning is often tied to race for reasons of solidarity and segregation, it is not always racially linked, as I will show at South Vista. Given Miles's statement, it was not surprising that my fieldnotes, formal interviews, and recordings of informal conversations with black youth were laden with lexical, grammatical, and phonological features of AAL as well as larger rhetorical traditions of AAL. I will provide a few brief examples here to give some voice to the prevalence of AAL use among South Vista's black youth. I will then follow this section by showing Latino/a and Pacific Islander youth engaging in the same structures, words, and rhetorical traditions as their African American peers.

I begin my analysis by recalling one afternoon when I was talking with African American youth Anthony as we headed over to basketball practice. I had been playing ball with the boys' and girls' teams for two months, and Anthony called me "Coach" as we walked. When I told him that he could just call me Django, Anthony replied, "But you ∅ like a second coach to me" (12/15/06). In our exchange, Anthony omitted the copula "to be," saying "you ∅ like" instead of the DAE "you *are* like." Basically, the option of omitting the copula "to be," a major feature of AAL grammar, is available to speakers when using the present tense of "is" and "are."[7]

Other major features of AAL grammar were commonplace among the African American youth I came to know. In a conversation I had with Terrell about a bootleg CD he was purchasing from a friend, he explained, "He *BIN* had it, he ∅ just waitin for me to have the money" (5/8/07). In addition to a copula omission, Terrell used the remote verbal marker *stressed been* in "He *BIN* had" to denote the fact that his friend had possessed the CD for some time and still had it. Part of a complex tense (when an action occurs) and aspect (how an action occurs) system, this feature is one of many that highlight how AAL semantics can differ significantly from DAE.

My ethnographic interviews with African American youth Miles and Rochelle also illustrated common AAL features. In one interview, Rochelle stated, "When *people call me out my name*, I don't really *be listening*" (12/4/06). Here Rochelle used a hallmark of AAL grammar known as the *habitual be*, in "I don't really *be* listening" for the DAE "I'm not usually/always listening." Rochelle's use of the habitual be is another example of the AAL tense and aspect system. In addition to the habitual be, Rochelle also used the AAL expression "people call me out my name," a phrase meaning when people insult or slander you (see Smitherman, 2006).

In addition to demonstrating AAL grammatical structures, verbal interactions between African American youth at South Vista were also laden with the AAL lexicon. One afternoon I was shooting hoops with African American youths Sharon and Miles. Miles was wearing his white socks up high, a retro look used by many NBA players.

Django: You got the old school look.

Sharon: No, he *do* that because he ø *hella ashy.*

Miles: No, it's like Baron Davis.

Sharon shakes her head: You ø ashy. *She walks off.*

In addition to the AAL optional *absence of third-person singular "s"* (or, here, "es") in "do" for the DAE "does," Sharon also omitted the copula. Yet grammar was not at the center of this interaction; the exchange hinged on the term *ashy.* Although there is much debate about what constitutes the entire AAL lexicon, *ashy* is considered a long-standing AAL lexical item. It is a generally negative term for dry skin that is uncared for. Sharon was calling Miles out for not taking care of his skin with moisture lotion. He protested that he looked like Baron Davis, a pro player, but Sharon was not having it. She even increased the stakes by calling Miles "hella ashy," using the regional adjective "hella" for "extremely."

Beyond AAL grammar and lexicon, the African American youth I worked with at South Vista participated in broader rhetorical traditions of black language. One common speech act was *the dozens,* also known in the literature as *capping.*[8] An extended form of *signifying,* or using "verbal hyperbole, irony, indirection, metaphor, and the semantically unexpected" (Smitherman, 2006, p. 70), the dozens are a form of ritual insult involving verbal wordplay centering on humorous insults to family members, friends, and the other participants. They are intended to be funny, often played to an audience. The following interaction that occurred in biology class shows Miles and Derek engaged in playing ritual insults on each other. The class was studying DNA duplication when Miles asked a question.

Miles: Why do people get mutations, deformities?

Teacher: Sometimes they don't copy right.

Miles: Then you end up short like Derek. *The class laughs.*

Derek retorts: Or dark like Miles. *More laughter.*

Miles: Or like Sharon. *More laughter. Sharon cuts her eyes at Miles, grinning. Miles shrinks back a bit, deciding he better not go further.* (2/28/07)

Miles asked an apparently straightforward question, yet he asked the question seemingly to set up his planned cap on Derek's diminutive stature (as Derek was the shortest boy in tenth grade). Miles's comment was certainly unexpected, a sort of verbal juke that brought some laughter. Yet Derek knew how to play as well and capped back, remarking on Miles's dark skin (which was dark in the broader spectrum of African American skin pigment), only for Miles to pass it off on Sharon, who had a skin color similar to Miles. Sharon, although verbally silent, participated in the exchange by *cutting* her eyes, a gesture of displeasure recognized in the African Diaspora that can be as loud as words. While the crack about skin color may seem particularly mean-spirited and is certainly laden with the pain of racist history, African American word-play and humor has often served the function of flipping the painfully real white and internalized oppression into the humorous (Carpio, 2008; Rickford & Rickford, 2000). The fact that the relative darkness of skin has historically had an impact on and continues to affect how African Americans view each other and are positioned by the dominant white culture is no laughing matter; yet to make it so simultaneously masks the internalized shame and gives momentary relief from it. It is also important that I point out that all of the people in the class, including the Latina teacher and myself, were people of color, which could have made such a joke more possible.

The use of AAL grammar and lexicon and participation in speech acts like signifying worked to sustain African American students' positions as members of the local and broader AAL speech community. Although social purposes and contexts vary in these examples, they were each acts of linguistic identity that placed youth within a tradition and a cultural community of "every black person" being "bilingual." Rochelle and Miles, for example, often spoke of "our" or "my" language in our discussions about AAL. And yet, as I will show, both Miles and Rochelle also understood that AAL was not theirs alone in South Vista. While these few moments taken from hundreds of examples in my fieldwork show that AAL was alive and well among the African American youth of South Vista, my goal here is to illuminate something far less studied but nevertheless central to understanding the role of oral language in division and unity in multiethnic schools: how do Pacific Islanders and Latinos/as also participate in AAL with black youth, and how do young people of all backgrounds make sense of this AAL sharing?

SHARING AAL AT SOUTH VISTA: GRAMMAR, LEXICON, AND RITUAL INSULT

It was an afternoon walk I had taken often during my months at South Vista. On any given day I would stroll over to the gym for basketball practice with any number of South Vista youth. On this afternoon I was walking with Samoan youth Soa and Latina youth Cynthia. There was an ease to our conversation that reflected many months of spending time together in the classroom and community. My ethnographic work, laden with rich interactions, had taken me from biology class to English class, from the basketball court to the home, and to many other school and community spaces. As we walked to the gym, we joked about a male ball player, Derek, who, despite his very small frame, was a favorite among many of the young women at South Vista.

Cynthia: Derek's a *gangsta.*

Django: A small *gangsta. We all chuckle.*

Cynthia: He *be teachin* everybody how to be *gangsta.*

Django: What he *be teachin?*

Soa: He taught me how to smoke weed. *They bust up laughing.*

Django: Ok, that is something. *I smile shaking my head.* (2/5/07)

Cynthia started the interaction with the hip-hop lexical item *gangsta* (an action or state of being that rejects dominant rules, or an action or state of being that shows prowess or wealth).[9] I could not resist a small cap myself. Cynthia, a bilingual Latina, continued by employing the habitual be, a major grammatical feature of AAL. I continued the participation, at which point Soa came with the unexpected and funny weed comment. While it is not my purpose here to debate the dangers or merits of Soa's comment (the teachers and administrators were aware of the prevalence of marijuana use), to be "gangsta" at South Vista meant resisting dominant rules of many kinds—cultural preferences both about how to speak and act and also about what to do. While I struggled at times with some of the choices made by the young people I worked with (e.g., truancy and substance use), I also worked to recognize these choices from youth perspectives. Linguistic resistance to DAE norms was certainly one major choice, a choice Cynthia made here by indexing youth identity through AAL grammar and lexicon.

AAL grammar and lexicon and the local hip-hop lexicon were also shared across ethnicity within the youth space of the classroom. Back in biology class, Latina youth Sierra and Samoan youth Ela got into the mix. The class was testing the effect of light on earthworms by blasting flashlights on the squirming organisms. The worms, which do not cherish bright light, thrashed about. "He ø *goin dumb,*" observed Sierra. After some chuckles, Ela agreed, "*Hyphy*" (1/10/07). In this interaction, Sierra omitted the copula and compared the worm's thrashing to a local dance known as "going dumb." In a typical version of this dance, the dancers let their limbs go loose and shake wildly, dipping up and down. Ela's agreement to Sierra's comment came through the more general term *hyphy*, a regional movement of bass-heavy club tracks, dance moves, and local lexicon led by rappers such as E-40 and the deceased father of hyphy, Mac Dre.

My ethnographic interviews with Mexican/Mexican American and Pacific Islander youth showed the use of many important AAL features (see table 1). Although there was considerable variation in the amount of AAL used by youth in interviews, they all did, in fact, use features of AAL.[10]

Carlos, Rahul, and Ela, for example, all used the habitual be. Coupled with instances from my observations, this use of the tense/aspect system of AAL shows the ways many nonblack youth had picked up an alternative sense of time and action in their everyday English—how they had come to embody Jordan's (1985) wonderful statement about the relationship between AAL grammar and mind: "The syntax of a sentence equals the structure of your consciousness" (p. 163). In addition to the habitual be, Carlos, Carla, Rahul, and Julio used the *existential it's* (Rickford & Rickford, 2000) in phrases like Carla's "*It's* some girls" for the DAE "There is/there are some girls." They also

TABLE 1   *AAL Features of Latino/a and Pacific Islander Youth*

Student	Feature	Examples
Carla	Zero copula	Next year my classes ø gonna be different
	Existential it is	*It's* some girls
Julio	Regularized agreement	People generally call you by the race *you is*
	Existential it is	*It's* really like nothing to do on my block
Carlos	Zero copula	You ø sorry
	Regularized agreement	Some dudes that *was* stealing cars
	Habitual be	Cause *they be tripping* about that
	Existential it is	*It was* a lot of black people
Ela	Regularized agreement	That's how the teachers in Samoa *is*
	Third-person singular "s"/ Zero copula	Every time he wake up, he ø always turning
	Habitual be	My big *mouth be saying*, "Uh uh, uh uh"
	Multiple negation [11]	*I don't got no* "F." *I don't got no* "B"
Rahul	Existential it is	*It's* times you have to use it
	Regularized agreement	When you *was* growing up
	Zero copula	They ø keeping me on check
	Habitual be	We *be talking* about cars
	Third-person singular "s"	He just *come* in my room
	Multiple negation	*I can't spit no rhymes*

employed the regularization of verb agreement patterns characteristic of AAL and other nondominant varieties of English as in Carlos's "Some dudes that *was* stealing cars."

Ela is a particularly interesting case of language sharing. Ela, who frequently used the habitual be, zero copula, multiple negation, regularization of verb agreement patterns, and absence of third-person singular "s," had arrived in South Vista from Samoa when she was twelve years old, only three years before our work together. Although these had been formative teenage years, for her to pick up and use grammatical features so often in her everyday English said a lot about the strong pull of AAL on Pacific Islander youth.

Beyond AAL grammar, participation by Pacific Islander and Latino/a youth in the AAL lexicon was pervasive in the multiethnic youth space of South Vista. Consider the following fieldnote excerpts documenting uses of "ashy" in multiethnic exchanges. The first example occurred in an exchange among Latina student Gloria, African American student Miles, and me.

I am sitting talking with Miles on the front benches. Gloria, who is wearing short pants, comes up to us and announces, "My legs are all *ashy*." Miles takes no notice of her comment, just glancing down at her legs. (3/20/07)

Another example of "ashy" was used in an extended exchange between Samoan youth Soa and African American youths Sharon and Ricky.

Soa and Sharon are sitting against a fence watching the boys play football. The girls are laughing and clowning the boys. I am standing with them and watching as well. Ricky runs out onto the field to play, tearing off his hoodie and throwing it down as he enters the field.

Soa: Ricky, you better not take that off, your arms *is hella ashy*! *She is too far away to see if they are, in fact, ashy.*

Sharon shakes her head: He ø ashy. *They laugh and I laugh with them.*

Soa launches into recounting what happened during geometry class. Ricky was near her, and she looked over at his arms and "they was hella ashy." She told him, "You better get some lotion." He went and asked African American student Rashida for lotion. Rashida told him he was hella ashy and gave it to him. We all laugh at the story. (4/5/07)

The word *ashy*—used in the first example by a Mexican American to refer to herself and in the second example by a Samoan and an African American to refer to an African American—was common in interethnic youth exchanges. These examples show sharing of one of the most secure items in the AAL lexicon, a word that has long been seen as an exclusively in-group term. While there is a long tradition of AAL-originated words (or meanings) making their way into mainstream popular use, the ratified sharing of "ashy" showed a particularly deep linguistic connection between the youth of color at South Vista.

Beyond the lexical item "ashy," Soa was also participating in ritual insult and verbal barbs characteristic of speech acts such as signifying and the dozens. I witnessed many occasions when Latino/a and Pacific Islander youth entered these speech acts at South Vista. Early in the basketball season, I sat next to Mexican American student Julio and Miles as we stretched on the gym floor before practice.

Miles: Mexican girls don't got no booty. It's all flat like. *He smiles and shakes his head.*

Julio feigns indignation: Yes they do, they got booty! *He is also smiling.*

Miles persists: They don't got enough food in Mexico to have booties. They got to do the J-Lo and get it pumped in.

Julio retorts: What about African girls, they don't got food neither.

Miles has the last word: It's in the bone structure, though, they just got booty. *And both bust up.* (11/8/07)

These "Mexican" versus "African" or "black" dozens sessions were common between Latino and African American males who shared social networks. In this session, the subject (or subjection) was women's bodies, although it was often wealth, employment status, and residency status. Here, Miles capped on what he deemed to be the unattractive bodies (specifically, rear ends) of an entire population of women. Julio protested. Miles, quick with the verbally unexpected, got two caps in. The first was that there wasn't enough food in Julio's homeland. The second was that the popular Latina star Jennifer Lopez, renowned in popular media for her attractive body (and, specifically, rear end), had to have surgery to be so good looking. Julio came back with a comment about the lack of food in Africa, but Miles had an answer for that, too, ending the exchange by taking up the racist/sexist mythology of black female body structure.[12]

It would be easy to continue in this vein, analyzing the racist/sexist content of this exchange, and objectification was paramount to this content. I see no analytic "out" for Miles and Julio on this count, save the point that both seemed to feel a racialized-sexualized allegiance to women from their own ethnic backgrounds. A possible additional saving grace was Miles's comment about "bone structure," which can be seen as another example of flipping pain and racist myth into an (objectified) appreciation. It seems he saw a sexualized beauty in the black female body and was attempting here to argue for the superiority of such beauty. But there were other themes about national origin and poverty that provide an important subtext to the turning of pain and shame into humor. While I found myself struggling to listen to this particular exchange (though I did have to laugh at the genius of the J-Lo comment), it also represents Julio's participation with Miles in AAL verbal wordplay that explicitly discussed difference.

One interpretation of such speech events could be that they were playing out community and national tensions between Latinos/as and African Americans, divisions that relate to the struggle for the scarce resources of the oppressed. I believe such an interpretation would be a dominant, divide-and-conquer read, though. Given an understanding of the role of ritual insult in building and sustaining relationships between people, and between people and their language, I am convinced that such loaded insult sessions provided the opposite function; that is, they helped make humor out of shame and pain by unifying Latino/a and African American youth in shared practice and marginalization. In doing so, these sessions resisted both popular conceptions of African American/Latino/a relations and, by invoking stereotypical rhetorics of body, skin, wealth, and gender, also resisted a racist legacy by showing such stereotypes as ridiculous or flipping them into compliments.[13] Both young men spoke of humor in separate interviews when I asked them about these kinds of interactions.

Julio: I be like, "You wanna work in my cotton field?" And he be like, "When you gonna cut my grass?" It's just jokes; it's like an inside joke or something like that. But, I mean, it's not to offend no one. It's just a way we get. (1/26/07)

Miles: We have—not like arguments—but you know, friendly—They be like, "Black people this" and I be, "Mexican that," and then, you know, they'll go back, and it's funny. We're having fun. (11/27/06)

I also observed young Pacific Islander and Latina women participating in AAL ritual insult with their black peers.[14] In one exchange, Ela capped on Miles as they worked in biology class to create Punnett squares (a diagram used to determine the probability of the genetic makeup for offspring). Miles was trying to create his diagram using a ruler; Ela sat at the table behind him, and I was behind Ela.

Miles: It's crooked. *He shakes his head looking down at his Punnett square.*

Ela: It would be. *She chuckles and keeps working on her diagram.*

Miles: I'ma get you! *Watch your back, Ela.*

Ela: I'ma get Django on you.

Miles: He ain't gonna do nothin', he ø scared. *He peers back at me with a smile.*

Django: Please. *I shake my head, staring in mock intensity at Miles.*

Ela: Looks like you ø scared. *She laughs at Miles who nods in defeat.*[15] (2/7/07)

Ela seized a moment of weakness by Miles to insult far more than his diagram. Her cap carried the broader meaning that Miles himself was crooked and unfit. Miles, within the play of the game, felt this insult and took a rather direct intimidation approach. Ela assessed all the verbal and physical tools available in her environment and chose to use me as a counterattack. Miles tried to call her bluff, but I was willing to play, too. My assist was just what Ela needed to finish Miles off. Not only was he "crooked," he was also now "scared."

* * *

While it is a significant research contribution to simply document the use of AAL grammar, lexicon, and speech acts in the everyday English of Latino/a and Pacific Islander youth, such use alone did not tell me much about the ways AAL worked within the ethnic geography of difference, division, and unity at South Vista. Nor was it evident whether such uses were instances of general crossing into AAL or whether they were ratified by the African American in-group as shared practices. In my interviews with youth across groups, I came to understand the processes involved in AAL use—that it was, by and large, seen by all parties as a shared linguistic repertoire across youth space. I also came to understand how youth explained what AAL was and why so many youth used it as something of a lingua franca in multiethnic youth space.

YOUTH UNDERSTANDINGS OF AAL SHARING

African American youth were keenly aware that their language was used by Latinos/as and Pacific Islanders. Though this participation was generally seen as unproblematic and caused far more social cohesion than social fissures in youth space, during a midyear interview Rochelle expressed reservations about some Latino/a AAL use.

> *Django:* Does it bother you when you hear the Mexican kids talking kinda black like that?
>
> *Rochelle:* Yeah.
>
> *Django:* It does? Like when all of them do it, or just some of them? Like some of them it's OK, some of them it's not?
>
> *Rochelle:* Some is okay because some be half-black, and some dudes be trying to talk like that just to get the attention. It's not funny. They ø gonna get beat up. (2/9/07)

Rochelle was aware that Latino/a youth participated in AAL, and her explanation of when such use was ratified by African American AAL speakers was complex. Rochelle sanctioned some AAL speech by "half-black" Latinos/as as authentic. She did not mean racially mixed youth (Rochelle did not have any Latino/a–black biracial youth in her peer network) but, rather, those Latinos/as she deemed "real" AAL speakers versus those who were feigning prowess for attention. Those who were faking, warned Rochelle, might be physically threatened. Although Rochelle's comment was atypical, and I never knew such violence to take place at South Vista (or even a comment or argument over inauthentic AAL use), these possible inauthentic uses show that some AAL participation by Latino/a and Pacific Islander youth might be perceived by African American youth as unratified language crossing rather than the more generally approved language sharing.

During an interview, Miles expressed a more general sentiment felt across ethnic groups at South Vista about AAL sharing. When I asked him what he thought about AAL use by nonblack youth at South Vista, Miles spoke of a community socializing process in multiethnic youth space.

> *Miles:* I'm not trippin. They're my homeboys, most of them. I'm cool with it. I don't think they're trying to steal anything. They're just being themselves because they were born here and raised here, but they were also born and raised in their house, so they can—they get the best of both worlds, I guess. (11/27/06)

Miles saw AAL use as a shared part of South Vista youth space. In fact, for Miles, such sharing promoted friendship across ethnicity, promoted Latino/a AAL speakers to be his "homeboys." Miles did not feel these ratified speakers were taking his language. Instead, he saw them as "being themselves," youth who grew up in an AAL-speaking environment with African American peers.

Though by saying "most of them" Miles left open the possibility that some participation could be inauthentic, the general thrust of his understanding was that AAL sharing was part of a community socializing process involving sustained linguistic and cultural contact between South Vista's ethnic communities. Even though Miles understood this, he also displayed some envy about the Spanish-speaking abilities of his peers. They got to speak his language, the shared language of multiethnic youth space, and also got to know the omnipresent Spanish, spoken by 70 percent of his school and community.[16] They got "the best of both worlds."

This was not the only time that Miles described this view of the community socializing process of AAL sharing. In a later interview, he furthered this notion:

> *Miles:* There's a lot of us in there that talk [AAL], well, not a lot, but you know, it's like for you who dress like they're black, you know, with the Girbauds, the long T's, you know. And there's some and they just speak slang like regular black people. It's like they were grown up here and it makes it cool at the same time. (3/26/07)

This statement falls in line with the socializing view of sharing. As he said, "They were grown up here." Yet Miles also provided two further understandings. One is the way he tied AAL use to other cultural ways of being, other identity markers of blackness in youth space. Here Miles used clothing as a prime marker. Girbaud, the hottest urban jean designer of the year, and long T-shirts were ways of indexing participation in black cultural discourse. This way of dressing coupled with "slang" made Latino/a and Pacific Islander AAL speakers "like regular black people." Pacific Islander and Latino/a youth I interviewed also attached AAL sharing to particular cultural activities. Julio, for instance, described his participation on the predominantly African American basketball team as a forum for speaking AAL. Fijian-Indian youth Rahul, who wrote and performed raps, talked of his role as an emcee as sharing in linguistic practices across race. These uses, attached to particular activities, were generally ratified as appropriate by the African American in-group. It seemed such ratification hinged on the speaker showing prowess in the given activity. Rahul's ability to rap, for example, was deemed considerable by the black peers he rhymed with, as was Julio's relative skill on the basketball court by the African American players on his team.

Miles, like Rochelle, expressed a feeling of ownership and solidarity about his culture; yet he also realized he shared that culture with the large and increasing number of Latinos/as and Pacific Islanders who "were grown up here." This was an awareness about AAL that Pacific Islander and Latino/a youth at South Vista also expressed. Ela, for instance, was clear that she and her Samoan peers used AAL as their everyday English, as she told me during an interview.

Django: When you're not talking Samoan—when you're talking with your friends in English—how would you describe the way you guys talk?

Ela: We talk ghetto a lot. Ghetto—like kids talk. They're like, "Man, he be cursing me—he's talking ghetto." (1/16/07)

Ela used the habitual be to give life to her description of what she called "ghetto." Other than "slang," "ghetto" was the most common term used by youth across groups to describe AAL. "Ghetto" at South Vista and in the broader urban youth and hip-hop culture was an adjective describing something as urban. Depending on context, "ghetto" could be positive, negative, or relatively neutral. Ela's use here was rather neutral to describe an everyday way of talk among peers.

Mexican American student Carlos also viewed AAL as the most common English used across youth space. When I asked him directly whether African Americans had a different way with words, he shared this view:

Django: Would you say that African American people in general have a way of talking? You said they only talk English. Do they talk English like everybody else or is their English different in any way?

Carlos: No, well they actually talk like everybody from South Vista, they talk slang, at least a little that you could tell, but they speak like that, too. So everybody here speaks the same in terms of the English. (1/22/07)

As Carlos considered my question, he came to the conclusion that "everybody here speaks the same in terms of English," since everybody speaks "slang." During a later interview, he provided maybe the most succinct statement of AAL linguistic socialization at South Vista. When Carlos came to South Vista from Michoacán, Mexico, in 1999, he spoke very little English. As he shared his personal story of learning English mainly from black youth in his first South Vista middle school, he expressed this general statement: "What happens is, like, when kids are coming—*like English learners*, since they're around black people sometimes, *they learn the slang instead of, like, the English-English*" (3/12/07).

Like Miles, Carlos realized that youth learning English in South Vista were likely to learn English within the long-standing African American community of South Vista. While Miles spoke of those Latino/a and Pacific Islander youth who were born in South Vista, Carlos added the perspective of immigrants, like himself and Ela, who learned to share in black speech as they learned to navigate a new city, a new country, a new language, and a new, hybrid identity.

AAL, EDUCATION, AND PLURALISM IN MULTIETHNIC SCHOOLS

At South Vista, many bilingual Latino/a and Pacific Islander youth worked to simultaneously forge identities as members of their particular ethnic communities *and* as members of broader youth culture. AAL was a major player in this work, and it offers important lessons for multiethnic schools and understandings of pluralist cultural spaces. While the use of Spanish, Samoan, or Fijian by the ethnic in-group often maintained ethnic solidarity and division (Paris, 2010), AAL served the opposite function: AAL was a shared practice that challenged notions of difference and division rather than reinforced them. Employing the words, the grammar, and the speech acts of black language provided a space of local youth prestige against the backdrop of shared marginalization in a white language- and white culture-dominated society. It was a shared counterlanguage that resisted the dominant norms of school and society.

In an interview one day, Miles proclaimed, "We all gotta stay together. We're the minorities" (1/19/07). Pluralism in multiethnic communities of color—what Miles called staying "together"—needs both within- and across-group practices to sustain it. AAL was the primary linguistic practice of cultural togetherness, though youth of all backgrounds also understood the need to maintain linguistic practices, like Spanish or Samoan, that were particular to their home and ethnic communities.[17] Yet, even as AAL was a tool of interethnic solidarity, it was somewhat troubling that black youth were the only group without an ethnic and linguistic safe haven within this multiethnic youth space. While most Latino/a and Pacific Islander youth could retreat into the important space of their own linguistic and cultural heritage, when African American youth used AAL, wore black-originated clothing styles, or listened to black-originated music, it was likely that youth of other ethnic groups understood their meanings and practices and would join in.

This tension certainly goes beyond language. Current demographic shifts in South Vista and other urban communities forecast a shrinking urban territory for the African American population (Zhou, 2001). With the shrinking numbers at South Vista came fewer exclusively owned practices. This tension was playing out in the lives of Rochelle and Miles and their Pacific Islander and Latino/a peers. They theorized about what it meant and, ultimately, saw the speaking on the wall: AAL would be shared just as their community had come to be shared. Remember that, just a generation before, South Vista had been a predominantly black community. In the face of demographic changes, AAL was echoing across social space from previous eras, and South Vista's African American youth were, in a sense, carriers of the linguistic and cultural torch for the black city their parents had known only decades before. These young people were passing their language into youth space and, through sharing it, ensuring its interethnic survival and importance in the community.

However, there is still a troubling tension between AAL as interethnic unifier and the lack of an ethnic safe haven for black youth. While African American youth did take a certain amount of pride in others being part of their language and their culture, they also struggled with the false linguistic shame of often seeing their shared practices as simply "slang."[18] Perhaps this tension would not seem so troubling if all the youth knew more about the structure and history of AAL. Adopting a *pedagogy of pluralism* would seek to use youth practices of AAL (as well as other heritage languages) in multiethnic schools to embrace, problematize, and extend understandings of interethnic language sharing *and* understandings of ethnic and linguistic solidarity. Such a pedagogical orientation puts schools in position to be sites of critical language learning that could bolster the pride of African American youth about their linguistic heritage, while simultaneously fostering more conscious respect from youth of other ethnic backgrounds. To be clear, I do not mean to imply that youth were not aware of the local and (through hip-hop) global prestige of AAL, but rather I am arguing that more consciousness could have increased respect for the language and its heritage speakers.

Still, AAL *was* a unifier in youth space. It worked to help youth, both consciously and unconsciously, move across divisions predicated on ethnic difference and seek common ground in an oppressive world. Unfortunately, South Vista High did not treat AAL as a unifier; in fact, the school did not seem to treat AAL much at all. Although I witnessed one attempt to use rap as a cultural entry point in an English class, the caring, dedicated, and well-qualified teachers of South Vista did not use the AAL lexicon or grammar as a resource for classroom learning during my year of observations. While I did not witness the old-school corrections of AAL speech that haunted previous eras ("No, it's not 'she in school!' It's 'she *is* in school!'"), and I found that South Vista's teachers were generally receptive to difference, there was no mention that a grammar was happening across ethnicity inside and outside the classroom. This omission saddened me. We dedicate entire classes to learning English, but teachers, their curriculum, and the broader structures of teacher preparation and linguistic ignorance are ill-equipped to use the Englishes of our students as critical resources in learning. Teacher education must contend with the demographic and linguistic realities of changing urban communities, and AAL will remain a central player in these changes.

Most simply, my work with the youth of South Vista suggests that we must reconsider where our vast linguistic and educational knowledge of AAL should be used. To date, this knowledge has mainly been applied to African American speakers of AAL. South Vista illuminates other urban youth who could benefit from using AAL as a resource for critical language and literacy learning. Although the teachers in South Vista taught in a predominantly Latino/a school, the student demographics belied the linguistic reality. If teachers had been encouraged to listen, they would have realized that AAL knowledge was required, just as knowledge of other heritage languages, like Spanish and Samoan, was required in order to understand and utilize their students' linguistic resources in the classroom. They would have also been treated to an amazing tapestry of practices that reached across groups to claim a linguistic and cultural plurality that often resisted traditional visions of racial strife in schools and communities. Such plurality sometimes seeped into classroom space but usually operated below the official script of classroom learning. Yet it begged to be given official space to foster and extend youth understandings of plural schools and plural communities. Such a classroom space would embody a pedagogy of pluralism, using youth language practices to explore the importance of ethnic difference and interethnic unity, helping youth and communities to build coalitions both within and across differences.

Our schools and communities are changing. Yet, as Miles knew, "We gotta stay together. We're the minorities." AAL use and understanding at South Vista was one aspect of the rich linguistic dexterity and plurality of our young people. Schools must take advantage of these resources to foster togetherness in the face of a difficult, unequal, and increasingly multiethnic society.

NOTES

1. All names are pseudonyms.
2. In this article, I follow *HER* policy using lowercase letters for the names of racial groups (e.g., "black," "white"). In other writing, I capitalize the names of racial groups to highlight the significance of the socially constructed categories of race in schools and society.
3. The majority of Latino/a and Pacific Islander students at South Vista were to some extent bilingual.
4. I use the term "ethnolinguistic" to describe interviews with both the ethnographic aims of gathering insider perspectives and the sociolinguistic aims of collecting everyday language use (Paris, 2008).
5. Although this is not a paper on the linguistics of AAL, I will give brief linguistic explanations of features to provide evidence of the ways the language was used across ethnicity.
6. I use "Dominant American English" instead of the commonly used "Standard English" to foreground unequal power relationships between the dominant variety of English and other varieties of English.
7. See Green (2002) and Rickford & Rickford (2000) for a complete discussion of all grammatical and phonological rules in this section, unless otherwise noted.
8. See Smitherman (2006) for the most current essay on *signifying* and *the dozens*.
9. I should note that the AAL lexicon and hip-hop lexicon have a close relationship, with many hip-hop terms finding a place in the vocabulary of AAL speakers, just as many AAL terms have always been a part of hip-hop culture. Alim (2006) calls the relationship between the AAL lexicon and the hip-hop nation lexicon a "familial one," denoting this strong dialogic relationship. See Smitherman (2006) for a thorough treatment of the term *gangsta* in black and hip-hop culture.
10. AAL features in these interviews also show the persistence of AAL use beyond everyday youth interactions, as I was the primary interlocutor.
11. All of the Mexican/Mexican American students I interviewed used multiple negation structures often. I do not represent them here since such constructions are also a feature of Chicano English (Fought, 2006).
12. Such racist, sexualized mythology about black female bodies in nineteenth-century European "anthropology," which sought to prove racial superiority through phenotype, is documented in prose and photography in Willis and Williams (2002).
13. See Carpio (2008) for an extended argument on the use of stereotypes in the humor of African American literature, stand-up comedy, and visual art as a resistance to the legacy of slavery.

14. This is an important point, as the study of the dozens and ritual insult has been dominated by analysis of male black exchanges (analyzed by male researchers) until recently
(Morgan, 2002; Smitherman, 2006).
15. *I'ma,* an AAL feature for first-person future action, represents a complicated morphological transformation from the DAE "I'm going to."
16. See Paris (in press) for a full discussion of Spanish at South Vista.
17. See Paris (in press) for a full discussion of the less extensive but important use of Spanish words and phrases by African American and Pacific Islander youth. For various reasons, including the small numbers of speakers, Samoan and Fijian languages were not
used by youth from other ethnic groups in my research (Paris, 2008).
18. This is an internalized shame that continues to haunt many in the African American
community (Baugh, 1999; Rickford & Rickford, 2000).

REFERENCES

Alim, H. S. (2004). *You know my steez: An ethnographic and sociolinguistic study of a black Ameri-
can speech community.* Durham, NC: Duke University Press.
Alim, H. S. (2006). *Roc the mic right: The language of hip hop culture.* New York: Routledge.
Anzaldúa, G. (1987, 1999). *Borderlands/La frontera: The new mestiza.* San Francisco: Aunt
Lute Books.
Bakhtin, M. M. (1981). Discourse in the novel. In M. Holquist (Ed.), *The dialogic imagina-
tion: Four essays* (pp. 257–422). Austin: University of Texas Press.
Ball, A. (1995). Text design patterns in the writing of urban African American students:
Teaching to the cultural strengths of students in multicultural settings. *Urban Educa-
tion, 30*(3), 253–289.
Ball, A. (1999). Evaluating the writing of culturally and linguistically diverse students: The
case of the African American vernacular English speaker. In C. Cooper & L. Odell
(Eds.), *Evaluating writing* (pp. 225–248). Urbana, IL: National Council of Teachers
of English.
Ball, A. (Ed.). (2006). *With more deliberate speed: Achieving equity and excellence in education—
realizing the full potential of Brown v. Board of Education.* National Society for the Study
of Education. Malden, MA: Blackwell.
Baugh, J. (1983). *Black street speech.* Austin: University of Texas Press.
Baugh, J. (1999). *Out of the mouths of slaves: African American Language and educational mal-
practice.* Austin: University of Texas Press.
Carpio, G. (2008). *Laughing fit to kill: Black humor in the fictions of slavery.* New York: Oxford
University Press.
DuBois, W. E. B. (1903, 1965). *The souls of blackfolk.* New York: Avon Books.
Fought, C. (2006). *Language and ethnicity.* Cambridge: Cambridge University Press.
Godley, A., Sweetland, J., Wheeler, R., Minnici, A., & Carpenter, B. (2006). Preparing teach-
ers for dialectally diverse classrooms. *Educational Researcher, 35*(8), 30–38.
Green, L. (2002). *African American English: A linguistic introduction.* Cambridge: Cambridge
University Press.
Jordan, J. (1985). Nobody mean more to me than you, and the future life of Willie Jordan.
In *On Call: Political Essays* (pp. 157–172). Boston: South End Press.
Kirkland, D. (2008). The rose that grew from concrete: Postmodern blackness and new
English education. *English Journal, 97*(5), 69–75.
Klein, H. (2004). *A population history of the United States.* Cambridge: Cambridge University
Press.
Labov, W. (1972). *Language in the inner city.* Philadelphia: University of Pennsylvania Press.
Ladson-Billings, G. (1995). Toward a theory of culturally relevant pedagogy. *American Edu-
cational Research Journal, 32*(3), 465–491.

Ladson-Billings, G. (2006). The meaning of Brown . . . for now. In A. F. Ball (Ed.), *With more deliberate speed* (pp. 298–313). Malden, MA: Blackwell.

Lee, C. D. (1995). A culturally based cognitive apprenticeship: Teaching African American high school students skills in literary interpretation. *Reading Research Quarterly, 30*(4), 608–630.

Mahiri, J. (2001). Pop culture pedagogy and the end(s) of school. *Journal of Adolescent and Adult Literacy, 44*(4), 382–385.

Massey, D. (2001). Residential segregation and neighborhood conditions in U.S. metropolitan areas. In N. Smelser, J. Wilson, & F. Mitchell (Eds.), *American becoming: Racial trends and their consequences* (pp. 391–434). Washington, DC: National Academies Press.

Morgan, M. (2002). *Language, discourse and power in African American culture.* Cambridge: Cambridge University Press.

Morrell, E., & Duncan-Andrade, J. (2002). Promoting academic literacy with urban youth through engaging in hip-hop culture. *English Journal, 91*(6), 88–92.

Paris, D. (2008). *"Our culture": Difference, division, and unity in multiethnic youth space.* Unpublished doctoral dissertation, Stanford University.

Paris, D. (2010). "The second language of the U.S.": Youth perspectives on Spanish in a changing multiethnic community. *Journal of Language, Identity, and Education.*

Pratt, M. L. (1987). Linguistic utopias. In N. Fabb, D. Attridge, A. Durant, & C. MacCabe (Eds.), *The linguistics of writing: Arguments between language and literature.* Manchester, England: Manchester University Press.

Pratt, M. L. (1991). Arts of the contact zone. *Profession, 91*, 33–40.

Rampton, B. (1995). *Crossing: Language and ethnicity among adolescents.* New York: Longman.

Rampton, B. (1998). Language crossing and the redefinition of reality. In P. Auer (Ed.), *Code switching in conversation: Language, interaction and identity* (pp. 290–317). London: Routledge.

Rickford, J., & Rickford, R. (2000). *Spoken soul: The story of black English.* New York: John Wiley and Sons.

Rickford, J., Sweetland, J., & Rickford, A. (2004). African American English and other vernaculars in education: A topic-coded bibliography. *Journal of English Linguistics, 32*(3), 230–320.

Smitherman, G. (1977). *Talkin and testifyin.* Detroit: Wayne State University Press.

Smitherman, G. (2006). *Word from the mother: Language and African Americans.* New York: Routledge.

Willis, D., & Williams, C. (2002). *The black female body: A photographic history.* Philadelphia: Temple University Press.

Zhou, M. (2001). Contemporary immigration and the dynamics of race and ethnicity. In N. Smelser, J. Wilson, & F. Mitchell (Eds.), *American becoming: Racial trends and their consequences* (pp. 200–242). Washington, DC: National Academies Press.

My deepest thanks to the young people I learned from in South Vista. Thanks as well to Arnetha Ball, Andrea Lunsford, John Rickford, and Guadalupe Valdés for their comments on earlier versions of this article. I alone am responsible for any faults herein.

INDIGENOUS KNOWLEDGES AND THE STORY OF THE BEAN

BRYAN MCKINLEY JONES BRAYBOY

EMMA MAUGHAN

You know, this is a funny place. I listen to the teachers as they teach, and it sounds like what happens when you push play and fast-forward on a tape recorder. The teachers, they talk so fast and they use these words that have four syllables when they could use [words] with two. So, there is a teacher that keeps saying "obfuscate" when she could say "hides behind" or something like that. Why the big words and the supersonic pace? We all need dictionaries to sit in on these classes. It's like you all [the faculty members] are trying to show us how smart you are.

We were in another meeting with the students in our Indigenous Teacher Preparation Program (ITPP) after an intense summer for our students, faculty, and staff. The ITPP students had earned eighteen credit hours in two summer sessions, and they were exhausted. The faculty had taught several courses, and the three support staff members had coordinated activity after activity and put out too many fires to remember, helping students find places to live, to bank, and to get health care for their children. As the meeting wound down, Henry Sampson,[1] a member of the program's leadership team, had asked the students how they were holding up.

Following the student teacher's comment on this "funny place" and the nods and chuckles in response, Henry asked if anyone else had something to say. This student, however, was not yet finished: "We're going to figure this out, because we have to be able to keep up with the fast talking. We'll get it. But when we do . . . [a long pause] the program is going to get us all our very own Mickey Mouse ears." Students laughed, hooted, squealed. The members of the program staff laughed and grinned. The student went on, "The reason I say this is because when these people [faculty] are talking so fast and being all impressive, they sound like Mickey and Minnie Mouse [another long pause]. I'm going to Disneyland, baby!" With this, the classroom erupted in pandemonium, and the staff could only watch as this group of "silent Indians" gave each other high fives, described how and where they would wear their mouse ears, and speculated on how much it would cost the program to send them to Disneyland.

In this defining moment for the ITPP, one student had clearly articulated what we, the staff and faculty, all knew but had not quite been able to say as clearly and directly as we should: The ways faculty approach issues of knowledge and knowledge production in our predominantly white institution are performative rather than relational and, therefore, very different from the ways of these bright Indigenous pre-service teachers.

This student's observation highlights stylistic issues, by pointing out that the faculty "talk so fast," as well as substantive issues, such as how we as faculty "are trying to show [them] how smart [we] are." She makes clear that teaching itself is a political act by pointing to the importance of word choice, pacing, and the implications of passing or failing a class for the Indigenous pre-service teachers who want to serve Indigenous elementary and secondary students. Teaching's political nature implicates the epistemic clashes inherent in how knowledge is used and how hierarchies of knowledge are produced and reproduced in educational institutions. These clashes raise critical connections between power and the (re)production and transmission of knowledge. In this essay, we make visible the ways in which knowledge clashes between Indigenous and non-Indigenous educators might be transformed from places of destruction to sites of hope and possibility.

As demonstrated in this short vignette, it is apparent that ITPP's challenge was to link knowledge and skill sets from a predominately white institution—in which specific kinds of identity performances and oral skills are valued—with Indigenous Knowledge and its (re)production, which demonstrate different, but equally worthy, values. This was not the only time we heard from students about observed differences in the ways that knowledge was created, produced, reproduced, and valued over the course of the program. We often heard comments that university teaching was "linear in a way that doesn't make any sense" or that the non-Indigenous students and faculty were "so focused on themselves, it is a wonder they can see or hear anyone else." The Indigenous students wanted to make connections that were more circular, or holistic,[2] in order to produce knowledge that served others.

In its long history, the schooling process for American Indians has been based on a hierarchy of knowledge wherein Indigenous Knowledges (IK) are framed as deficient (Adams, 1988; Lomawaima & McCarty, 2002, 2006). Here, we will examine what happens when Indigenous pre-service teachers are supported in recognizing the power of their own knowledge systems, when knowledge systems are not framed hierarchically, and when teachers are trained to recognize the connections between conventional Western schooling practices and Indigenous Knowledge Systems. We explore the possibility that Indigenous Knowledge Systems might offer distinct spaces in which educators and their students might be exposed to broader notions of what teaching and learning are and can be.

INDIGENOUS KNOWLEDGE SYSTEMS:
KNOWING, BEING, VALUING, DOING, TEACHING, AND LEARNING

The topic of Indigenous Knowledges has recently entered more mainstream conversation among education researchers (e.g., see Bang, Medin, & Atran, 2007; Battiste, 2008; Cajete, 2008; Pember, 2008; Villegas, Neugebauer, & Venegas, 2008). There have been calls to explore connections between "traditional" schooling and the ways that Indigenous peoples learn in the realm of science (Bang et al., 2007; Brayboy & Castagno, 2008; Cajete, 2000). Others have examined the ways that IK may inform, extend, and complicate how people learn, act, and think (Battiste, 2002, 2008; Villegas et al., 2008). Indigenous communities have long been aware of the ways that they know, come to know, and produce knowledges, because in many instances knowledge is essential for cultural survival and well-being. Indigenous Knowledges are processes and encapsulate a set of relationships rather than a bounded concept, so entire lives represent and embody versions of IK. Because of this, our attempt to offer a concise definition here creates some difficulty. Indigenous Knowledges are rooted in the lived experiences of peoples (Barnhardt & Kawagley, 2005; Battiste, 2002, 2008; Battiste & Henderson, 2000); these experiences highlight the philosophies, beliefs, values, and educational processes of entire communities. Indigenous peoples come to know things by living their lives and adding to a set of cumulative experiences that serve as guideposts for both individuals and communities over time. In other words, individuals live and enact their knowledge and, in the process, engage further in the process of coming to be—of forming a way of engaging others and the world.

As Indigenous student teachers begin the process of becoming licensed educators, they find themselves in an historic site of struggle for Indigenous peoples: teacher training (Smith, 1999; Vandergriff, 2006). In the context of this struggle, the lived implications of conflicting knowledge systems become more obvious. The teacher education program that we worked with, like many programs, could be rigid, narrow, and unforgiving to different ways of engaging the world. Additionally, teachers have historically been frontline actors in attempts to assimilate Indigenous peoples (e.g., see Lomawaima & McCarty, 2006; Adams, 1988).[3] Drawing on the experiences of Indigenous students, teachers, and peoples, we know that Indigenous Knowledge Systems are not vapid; rather, they are lively, fervent, and effectual, and in the search for holistic versions of teaching and learning amid struggle, they may be key sources of strength for Indigenous Peoples.

Within the larger concept of Indigenous Knowledge Systems, epistemologies, ontologies, axiologies, and pedagogies come to the fore. We have, to date, been working intensely with Indigenous epistemologies. We think, however, that we've been misguided in thinking that such work is simply about ways of knowing or coming to know. As lived knowledge, IK is intimately tied to ways of being, or ontologies. Though ontologists typically focus on exploring reality and whether or not beings are sentient, we think of ontologies a little differently than do philosophers interested in the idea of consciousness and whether or not human beings actually exist (e.g., see Heidegger, 1978; Husserl, 1969). We understand ontologies as capturing the process by which individuals—and communities—come to think of themselves, are framed by others, and are integrated into their local communities. Further, inherent in both knowledges and ways of being are value judgments—what does it mean to live a "good" life, to be a "good" person, and what are one's priorities in life? In considering axiologies, we aim to explore what is good, true, right, and beautiful, as we know these values to be deeply rooted in the ways Indigenous peoples view and engage the world.[4] Finally, we are interested in pedagogies because of the ways that Indigenous peoples come to think about, understand, and enact the processes of teaching and learning.

All of these ways of knowing, being, valuing, and doing make up Indigenous Knowledge Systems. As Mi'kmaq[5] scholar Marie Battiste (2002, 2008) notes, IK is systemic and systematic and has an internal consistency. Therefore, to seriously engage in conversations around connections between Indigenous Knowledges and their relationships to knowledge production and reproduction, we have to move beyond simple taxonomic distinctions of Indigenous epistemologies, ontologies, axiologies, and pedagogies to a more nuanced and holistic consideration of Indigenous Knowledges as entire systems.

These conversations of the role of IK in schooling are neither simplistic nor uniform. Importantly, even within a particular community, not everyone will operate from the same foundation of knowledges. As Battiste (2002) reminds us,

> Within any Indigenous nation or community, people vary greatly in what they know. There are not only differences between ordinary folks and experts, such as experienced knowledge keepers, healers, hunters, or ceremonialists, there are also major differences of experiences and professional opinion among the knowledge holders and workers, as we should expect of any living, dynamic knowledge system that is continually responding to new phenomena and fresh insights. (p. 12)

This diversity and plurality of knowledges is fundamental to the dynamism of knowledge systems and the survival of communities over time. The interconnectedness of knowledges, sources of knowledge, and experience are critical to understanding how Indigenous peoples have survived more than 500 years of genocide. These are peoples who have adapted and adjusted to their situations and confronted countless threats aimed at their extinction. This survival and commitment to perseverance is directly connected to Indigenous efforts to move outside of traditional categories of engaging the world intellectually and physically toward recognizing the interconnected nature of all things in the world.

We want to emphasize that our objective here is not to set up a dichotomy between Western[6] and Indigenous Knowledges, as this is not a particularly useful endeavor. Setting these knowledges in opposition to one another erases complexity and nuance, closing off spaces of potential and possibility. Battiste (2002) makes this point vividly:

> Indigenous scholars discovered that Indigenous Knowledge is far more than the binary opposite of western knowledge. As a concept, Indigenous Knowledge benchmarks the limitations of Eurocentric theory—its methodology, evidence, and conclusions—reconceptualizes the resilience and self-reliance of Indigenous peoples, and underscores the importance of their own philosophies, heritages, and educational processes. Indigenous Knowledge fills the ethical and knowledge gaps in Eurocentric education, research, and scholarship. By animating the voices and experiences of the cognitive "other" and integrating them into educational processes, it *creates a new, balanced centre and a fresh vantage point* from which to analyze Eurocentric education and its pedagogies. (p. 5, emphasis added)

Our goal is to focus on Indigenous Knowledge Systems in order to extend other knowledge systems and to locate "a new center" of teacher training. In this way, then, Western and Indigenous knowledges can be—in fact, must be—configured in a way that is complementary rather than contradictory. While we discuss here differences between knowledge systems, our purpose is not to reify a sense of binaries. We aim instead to examine how Indigenous Knowledges inform the work of Indigenous students and teachers and to consider how predominantly non-Indigenous educational spaces might come to value these knowledges as both worthy and useful.

CONTEXT AND PROGRAM BACKGROUND: THE INDIGENOUS TEACHER PREPARATION PROGRAM

This essay draws from the experiences of Indigenous pre-service teachers over the course of their teacher training. Western University's Indigenous Teacher Preparation Program was created in 2002 with a professional training grant from the U.S. Department of Education's Office of Indian Education. Just shy of $1 million, the grant provides funding to prepare 12 American Indian teachers to teach in schools serving American Indian populations through a three-year training program that includes one year of professional induction. In exchange for a stipend and other financial incentives designed to alleviate as many nonacademic stresses as possible, program participants commit to teaching in Indian-serving schools (as defined by the U.S. Department of

Education's Office of Indian Education) for the same number of years that the program offers them educational and financial support.[7] If participants are unable to earn licensure, they must reimburse the federal government for the services received from the university. After the grant award was announced, the grant leadership team was deluged by interested applicants: 132 applications for the 12 coveted spots.

Applicants reported a number of reasons for applying to ITPP. Among these was a commitment to providing Indigenous students with a more culturally responsive education. As one American Indian woman in ITPP described,

> I grew up on the reservation. When I was five, my parents decided that I should go to the boarding school for Indians because they thought I could get a good education there. It was like a military school where the teachers were strict and hit us if we spoke [our tribal language]. I hated it there, but I kept going because I thought education would make a difference. I didn't want the White people in town to call me a "dirty stinkin' Indian" or think they were better than me. . . . I guess I didn't realize that the teachers would also call me a dirty, dumb Indian . . . and the education I got was bad anyway and the White people still told me I was dirty and that I stunk. . . . That school [the Indian boarding school] could have helped me understand what I know today: My language is a good language and I should know it; I can be smart and Indian at the same time, and I'm not dirty, stinky, or dumb. I can do [many things well]. . . . I want to be a teacher so that my students can see that being smart and [Indian] can go hand-in-hand.

This powerful statement highlights the complicated relationships many ITPP students and staff had with formal schooling. This student points to the ways that schooling could be used to destroy the spirit of a young child and the hope and possibility of being "smart and Indian at the same time." ITPP was guided by the idea that Indigenous peoples could engage in self-determination through self-education, an idea that this quote speaks to powerfully.

Participants enter the program as college juniors or college graduates. They are admitted under the regular admissions policies and join the general student body cohort of pre-service educators in the teacher training departments. Although ITPP offers an introduction to American Indian studies and Indigenous Knowledges courses, the pre-service teachers are, for all intents and purposes, integrated into the general teacher preparation program.

It became clear to us in such a context that there were epistemological, ontological, axiological, and pedagogical differences between the ways that the American Indian participants and the non-Indigenous students, staff, and faculty were making sense of their experiences at the university. In an attempt to understand these discrepancies and find ways to articulate them to our partners at Western University, we set out to explore how ITPP participants were making sense of their daily experiences. In analyzing these differing and often contradictory knowledge systems as researchers, we found the work of comparing knowledge systems to be an intellectually challenging task, as each of us approached it from very different viewpoints, from divergent ways of knowing, being, valuing, and doing. One of the authors of this article is an Indigenous man who wrote the grant to fund this program, participated as a member of its leadership team, and understands Indigenous Knowledge Systems as a result of living them. The other author is an Anglo woman, a former graduate student, and a former writing instructor in the program. We both had almost daily interactions with the students, although one of us did so as an administrator and the other as a tutor and confidante. Most importantly, what we share is the belief that self-determination of Indigenous communities can be aided by self-education.

Our work in ITPP presented us with unique challenges. Among these was our struggle to support the university faculty members of our student teachers in their understanding of IK. We met with great difficulty in helping them recognize that the Indigenous pre-service teachers brought different epistemologies and ontologies with them to the experience of student teaching and that these needed to be recognized and valued. We also struggled to assist them in understanding that what makes a "good teacher" in a predominately American Indian school may look different than "good teaching" in the mostly white schools of the area surrounding Western University. As it turned out, it was one of our students who best supported the faculty in turning the corner regarding their understanding and valuing of Indigenous Knowledge Systems.

Soil and Sand: The Growth and Stagnation of Growing Minds

In an effort to assist the Indigenous pre-service teachers in recognizing the ways in which our university work translated to their home communities, we institutionalized weekly meetings. These meetings were born out of a number of conversations that a member of the leadership team, whom we call Henry, had with tribal leaders about their conceptions of what teachers working in their communities needed in order to be effective. Almost every elder and leader told him that the teachers needed to be able to connect with their children linguistically and culturally. These individuals also mentioned that teachers needed to show schoolchildren the ways in which their learning helps the entire community and how the curriculum relates to their everyday lives. In an effort to make the wishes of these tribal leaders a reality, we instituted the weekly meetings. At one of these meetings, the following scenario unfolded.[8]

It had been a difficult week for some of the student teachers. Their site teacher educators (STEs) questioned their readiness to take over the classes they would inherit in just a few weeks as student teachers. Implicit in this commentary was the way that the STEs might grade the student teachers. The university provides a rubric to STEs who evaluate their student teachers on a scale from one to five, with one being unacceptable and five being extraordinary. If student teachers receive anything below a three on any measure, they are not recommended for licensure, effectively denying them any opportunity to become licensed through "traditional" means. The student teachers were not aware of these conversations, but the faculty and program staff—heeding these informal evaluations by the STEs—were leaning toward removing the students from their placement sites.

We met at the school where the Indigenous pre-service teachers conducted their student teaching. The program had arranged to provide lunch, and we ordered pizza and drinks. We began the conversation by reviewing the week and discussing what was happening in classrooms. In the fourth-grade classroom, students were conducting experiments in which they attempted to grow bean plants in different kinds of soil (one in dirt, another in sand) with different amounts of water (one got more, another less). There were multiple and interdisciplinary objectives for the lesson: (1) a scientific experiment designed to find out what happens when certain seeds are planted in particular soils and watered with measured amounts of water; (2) an empirical component tied to mathematics, where students measured the growth of the plant as well as the daily amount of water provided to the plants; and (3) a written journal assignment where students recorded their measurements and described what they saw happening. The idea was to use this as a way to further examine the role of photosynthesis and to integrate reading and writing skills across subject areas. The assignment was prescribed to occur in a particular way; the conditions were intended to closely mimic work in a science lab with the idea that students would gather some additional knowledge of how scientists work.

After we had discussed the ways that students conducted the experiment and hypothesized about where the assignment might go, Henry asked one of the student teachers how she might teach this in her own community. She said,

> Well, first off, I wouldn't do it this way. I'd have to start at the beginning. . . . I would get a bunch of seeds that we plant over the course of a year and lay them out on a table and show them what the differences are . . . so, you know, a bean seed is different than a corn kernel and is different than a seed for pumpkins and other melons we might grow. They [the students] have to know what is what before they go planting these things. . . . Then I would talk about what each of the seeds did.

The conversation continued with her outlining what each of the seeds she described to us would "do." Henry asked why she would tell the students what the "seeds did." She responded,

> Well, they are going to plant them, right? So, you don't just plant any seed at any time. You need to know what you're planting, because you don't want to waste seeds, but you also don't want to plant something [if] you don't know what it will be. In my culture, we are very careful to make sure that every decision we make is thought about before we act. You don't plant some seed just because. It has a purpose and carries more stuff with it.

She informed us that in the process of planting, there were both metaphysical factors to consider as well as the spiritual nature of the planting process (which she described to one of the STEs as being "impossible to separate from everyday living"):

> Once I described the seeds and what they did, I would then ask [the students] to come in one night to school. We would probably do this a few times a year. Then we would look at the sky and the patterns of the stars. The constellations tell us when to plant certain things. So, I would tell them that when [a constellation] reaches the most eastern part of the sky, it is time to plant the corn, and that when [another constellation] reaches the apex of the sky, it is time to plant pumpkins. We can't do it earlier or nothing will grow, or it won't grow right. We have to do it that way . . . it's the way we do things. . . . These students have to know the right way to do it, and they can't plant these seeds at any time. . . . After the first frost, I'd tell them some stories to understand the importance of these things, so that they know.

After the student teacher discussed her own thoughts about this in more detail, Henry asked her about measuring the growth of plants and writing the measurements down and if she would do the assignment this way. In response, she said,

> Well, this is a little trickier. I'd not normally have them do it this way. You can look at it and know if it is growing; you don't need a ruler for that. And we wouldn't plant it in sand anyway; things don't grow well in sand, and everyone knows that. We'd plant the bean where we always do and have fieldtrips to make sure it's growing. I'd check in between to make sure it was okay, and if I had to do something to the plant, I'd take the class and show them, but they'd know how to do this by watching their parents or aunties and uncles, you know. . . . But with No Child Left Behind, and the other testing, I'd have to do this anyway, or at least I'd teach them how to read a ruler and to be ready for the test. They'd write other things down. I think our students have to be able to write and keep journals, and know why they do that.

She concluded by drawing our attention to the importance of bringing together forms of learning and knowing for the benefit of students and communities: "Our tribe is for education, and we know that we have to do better, but sometimes this does not make any sense. We have other ways of doing this, but I understand this much better now and think that I've learned a lot here . . . but me and [another student teacher] have something to teach you all, too."

During this conversation, the other student teacher nodded. At various points in the conversation, others would make comments such as, "Well, in [my reservation] we'd do it this way," in order to illustrate the related, but different, ways that other Indigenous peoples might think about the lesson. It was an important moment because it highlighted the nuanced ways in which these student teachers approached the tasks set before them. Henry was the only person asking questions of clarification, hoping to provide a fuller explanation for the university supervisor and STEs. He had asked the STEs to listen to what they heard and save their questions until after the student teachers had described what they would take away from the exercises.

As soon as the student teacher finished talking about the process, the conversation became excited. The STEs had many questions. One of the students, well versed in the cosmology of the tribal nation, explained the significance of a series of constellations and discussed the importance of understanding the metaphysical components of the planting process as it tied into her tribal culture. The student teachers were careful not to tell the STEs things that were inappropriate or that may otherwise violate the trust of their tribal nations. In the process, the pre-service teachers offered new possibilities for the STEs to consider, possibilities that include different ways of approaching assignments, contextualizing a topic area, and integrating student experiences directly into the lesson.

The Value of Student Teachers' Indigenous Knowledges

There are several critical points to be learned from the way that the Indigenous student teacher made sense of the lesson. Importantly, she began by making clear that she "wouldn't do it this way." From her perspective, the lesson itself was somewhat foreign and lacked a particular context. Importantly, Indigenous Knowledge Systems value contextualized knowledge that is local and particular to the setting. In her analysis of the exercise itself, this student teacher pointed to the fact that all knowledge cannot necessarily be universal in its application because of the importance of place, space, and context. Battiste (2002) is also clear on this point when she notes that "Indigenous Knowledge is also inherently tied to land, not to land in general but to particular landscapes, landforms, and biomes where ceremonies are properly held, stories properly recited, medicines properly gathered, and transfers of knowledge properly authenticated" (p. 13).

The student teacher made an axiological claim; that is, she appeared to be making a value judgment about the "best way" to conduct and engage in the lesson. Consider what Inupiat scholar Leona Okakok (1989) says about this when she writes, "To me, educating a child means equipping him or her with the capability to succeed in the world he or she will live in" (p. 253). She continues by making a powerful (and political) statement that "education is more than book learning, it is also value-learning" (p. 254). It was an interesting and logical move when the student teacher turned to her own ways of knowing and being as a source of guidance, much as Okakok encourages. The student teacher used her own ways of knowing to extend and complicate other ways of knowing and being, thereby locating a "new center."

The student teacher continued by arguing that she "would start at the beginning" and offered a way to contextualize the lesson itself. The process of contextualizing what is being learned and tying it to the actual lives of the children is an important part of Indigenous Knowledge Systems. It is not just a way of teaching but, rather, is tied into a particular pedagogy that more fully nuances the use of knowledge and ways of being. Indeed, she worked to contextualize knowledge for her students. Consider the important scholarship of Dakota and mixed-heritage scholar Mary Hermes (2005), who focuses on the importance of context in the language learning of Ojibwe students in schools. One of the elders/teachers in Hermes's (2005) study notes: "I asked them [the elders], 'Is a *ma'iingan* in a zoo a *ma'iingan?*' They said, 'No, it is a wolf.' Because *ma'iingan* requires a context. I can't take it out of context without changing the meaning. Everything in English is taken out of context. *Everything taught about Indians taken out of context is really in English—or in that way of thought*" (p. 50).

The student teacher, then, points to the fact that she is doing more than a science experiment. By "starting at the beginning," she contextualized the act of growing something, transforming it from a science experiment to a way of thinking about and engaging the world in which her students live everyday. It is neither sterile nor objective in the ways that many laboratories insist on treating the study of science. As Brayboy and Castagno (2008) assert, "Many Indigenous people [might] argue that their laboratory is the world and that their survival rested on puzzling over observations and phenomena and coming to make sense of them in ways that allowed them to survive" (p. 733). Indigenous science, then, is guided by a conscious move outside of laboratories into the world in which people live (e.g., Aikenhead, 2001; Kawagley, 2006). Thus, "starting at the beginning" signals a different "way of thought" and its concomitant behaviors. Evident here is a different knowledge system at work.

This emphasis on starting at the beginning is also connected to another fundamental difference between many Western and Indigenous Knowledge Systems. Within the Western tradition, the knowledge sought is propositional in nature (Burkhart, 2004). Individuals concerned with knowledge in this traditional Western sense focus on the search for eternal truths, laws, and principles that may be proven through the posing of hypotheses, test construction, and "scientific" experimentation. Indigenous Knowledges, however, are contextual and contextualized; they are lived and are an integral part of survival. Truth and knowledge cannot be ends in and of themselves. Battiste (2002) cogently addresses this when she writes, "Knowledge is not what some possess and others do not; it is a resourceful capacity of being that creates the context and texture of life. Thus, knowledge is not a commodity that can be possessed or controlled by educational institutions, but is a living process to be absorbed and understood" (p. 15). Again, we are struck by the fact that knowledge must be lived and is a verb. For many in Western knowledge systems, knowledge is a noun—rooted in things on the pages of a book or possessions. It is often stagnant, maybe something so abstract as to not even be tangible. Knowledge from an Indigenous perspective is active. For those who have knowledge, they must be vigorous in their acquisition and use of it. Okakok (1989) notes, "Though most of the education in our [Inupiat] traditional society was not formal, it was serious business. For us, education meant equipping the child with the wherewithal to survive in our world" (p. 256).

By utilizing the differences between seeds, the student teacher resisted a scripted approach to teaching just measurement and science; instead, she relied on the categorization inherent to knowing what seed grows into what plant: "They have to know what is what before they go planting things." Much of what she highlights here is rooted in notions of Indigenous Knowledges. It points to the practical nature of knowledge and moves away from the abstraction of planting something just to watch it grow and be able to measure it. The plant itself potentially represents more than just a learning tool and medium through which to engage in "scientific practices"; it is something that must itself first be known. There is sanctity in the knowledge and its use here that is an inherent part of Indigenous Knowledges. Doing things simply to do them—perhaps in the pursuit of knowledge for knowledge's sake—is not typically recognized as a part of Indigenous Knowledge Systems.

The student teacher highlighted the importance of contextualizing knowledge when she said, "Then I would talk about what each seed did." The active nature of this sentence points to the seed as alive and having purpose; it is not simply a "thing" to be viewed but an active and living object that "does" things. Framing the seed as something that "does" is a categorical shift in the ways that students in mainstream schools are asked to think about the subject matter and materials. Many Indigenous scholars and leaders indicate that Indigenous people are often concerned with the applicability and practical nature of the tools with which they are learning (Deloria & Wildcat, 2001; Marker, 2003). Respect for and responsibility over knowledge is also important because it demonstrates how knowledge is used and to what end. Indigenous Knowledges require responsible behavior, and this is often achieved by considering the ramifications of actions before they are taken.

The importance of purposeful action is central to this discussion because it is rooted in the beliefs of communities of people and points to the nature of responsible use of knowledge. Because all things are interrelated and connected, planting something that serves no purpose beyond learning is not logical when, from an Indigenous perspective, a plant can be grown both for the purpose of learning and for the purpose of feeding people.

In his book *The American Indian Mind in a Linear World,* Shawnee, Sac and Fox, Muscogee Creek, and Seminole scholar Donald Fixico (2003) writes:

> "Indian Thinking" is "seeing" things from a perspective emphasizing that circles and cycles are central to the world and that all things are related within the universe. For Indian people who are close to their tribal traditions and native values, they think within a native reality consisting of a physical and metaphysical world . . . people raised in the traditional ways of their peoples see things in this combined manner. (pp. 1–2)

A circular worldview that connects everything and everyone in the world to everything and everyone else, where there is no distinction between the physical and metaphysical and where ancestral knowledge guides contemporary practices and future possibilities, is the premise of many Indigenous Knowledge Systems. This fundamental holistic perspective shapes all other understandings of the world (Fixico, 2003; Marker, 2004; Stoffle, Zedeño, & Halmo, 2001). More specifically, holistic or circular understandings do not draw separations between the body and mind, between humans and other earthly inhabitants, and among generations. Instead, connections (like those between artificially separated disciplines) are central for knowledge production and the responsible uses of knowledge. These connections are also central to how many Indigenous people view their own places within the larger cosmos of all living things. When everything and everyone is connected, a person has a responsibility to act according to her surroundings. Thus, responsibility becomes a logical outgrowth of Indigenous philosophical understanding. A person understands that her actions affect everything else, and she is invested in maintaining necessary balance. According to Arapaho scholar Michael Marker (2003),

> This emphasis on relationships puts animals, plants, and landscapes in the active role of *teacher* and therefore results in a more holistic and integrated understanding of phenomena. This kind of holism resists constrictive and contrived taxonomies as well as disciplinary boundaries. It also produces a state of consciousness in the Aboriginal intellectual that makes no separation between scientific and moral understandings. (pp. 105–106)

When relationships are seen as pervasive and profound, they require attention. Proper attention to relationships requires efforts toward their maintenance, and it requires reciprocity.

In that session, the student teacher continued to emphasize the Indigenous Knowledge-based ways of recognizing the potential purpose and role of teaching the plant lesson. She immediately recognized the fact that students are going to do more than measure the plants; they must plant them first. Importantly, students must be aware of what they are planting before engaging in the process. For some Indigenous people, knowledge is the basis of power because it must be used toward a greater aim and goal. To plant something that is unknown potentially creates problems that could have been avoided: "In my culture, we are very careful to make sure that every decision we make is thought about before we act." In this statement she highlights the notion that knowledge and power must be handled with care and deliberation.

All decisions and actions carry ramifications, and the deliberateness of actions is intended to ensure that care is taken with all things. The deliberate nature may also be indicative of the seriousness with which learning occurs. Importantly, the student teacher elaborated by pointing to the fact that the planting of a seed "has a purpose and carries more stuff with it." She also implicitly chastised the teachers and the lesson by pointing out that, "We wouldn't plant it in sand anyway; things don't grow well in sand, and everyone knows that." The process of planting anything that is alive with the intention of nourishing it implies a responsibility to the plant and its care. In this particular tribal culture, the "more stuff" she referred to points to the spiritual and metaphysical acts that are tied to the nourishment of life. Also caught up in this is the critique of not planting the plants in sand: If it will not "grow well in sand," it makes little sense to do it; the plant suffers and the activity serves little purpose except to become "information." From an Indigenous perspective, planting a seed is more than just an experiment; it is a process of nurturing a living creature that bears fruit for life's sustenance.

In many ways, the student teacher appears to be asserting that students must learn more than what is found in books. This resonates with the late Lakota scholar Vine Deloria Jr. (1992), who argued that space must be made for students' moral development because the current educational system, as it stands, only produces professionals who know how to behave "properly" and does not develop whole persons who have a sense of their personal selves, because "professionalism overrules the concern for persons" (p. 46). In other words, according to Deloria, professionalism is the standard way to assess a person's goodness, and it is this oversimplified version of reality that creates blind spots in people's minds that lead to confusion and unrealistic interpretations of the world.

Importantly, the idea of the "more stuff" involved in planting these seeds also corresponds directly to the spiritual aspects of planting something for its nourishment and the nourishment of others. Some Indigenous notions of spirituality require that the metaphysical nature of things be considered in the daily lives of students and teachers. Curriculum and subject matter must be tied directly to the lives of students and their Indigenous teachers. Separating the two makes them arbitrary and fails to recognize the knowledge system that is rooted in the ways of the community. These materials become more than a simple individual exercise. Burkhart (2004) emphasizes the active nature of knowledge:

> Knowledge is what we put to use. Knowledge can never be divorced from human action and experience. . . . American Indian philosophers see the act of displacing oneself from the world in order to do philosophy not only as unnecessary but as highly problematic, since in doing so one is only guessing whether what one is striving after is really knowledge at all and whether the questions one has formulated are even really questions. (p. 21)

We can see what one knows by what one does; or, what one does, or puts to use, demonstrates the knowledge that individual has.

The student teacher continued with the connections between the curriculum and her own sense of native religion, suggesting that she would have the students "come in one night to school" where she would discuss the community's cosmology and make direct links to the seeds and when they get planted. In this way, few tasks at school are simple or unrelated to the everyday lives and spirituality of the students. When the student teacher said, "It is the way we do things," she points to the ontological and axiological basis that connects the everyday with the sacred—there is little disconnect, and she takes seriously her role to provide students with the larger reasons for engaging in school. School activities are mediated by the community norms and the way things are done. She elaborated on this when she argued that "these students have to know the right way to do it" and pointed to the fact that seeds and planting occur at particular times in particular places with the appropriate use of time and space. This description is culturally based teaching at its best and highlights the potential fluidity between the home and school.

Indeed, notions of the "right way to do it" go beyond notions of who does what better. From an IK framework, survival of a community is at the core of the matter. We simply cannot understand ways of knowing and being without a deep and abiding understanding of what community means and how, for many Indigenous peoples, community is at the core of our existence. Individuals, through self-discovery and selflessness, become whole, thereby insuring community survival. Interdependence of individual and community is essential. Lomawaima and McCarty (2006) write, "The ultimate test of each human educational system is a people's survival" (p. 30), a sentiment that is captured in Diné scholar Brian Yazzie Burkhart's (2004) insightful reworking of the Cartesian Principle. We know that Descartes based his own philosophies of knowledge and being on the principle "I think, therefore I am." Burkhart reconceptualizes an Indigenous version of this principle as "We are, therefore I am." At their core, then, the knowledge systems, ways of being, and teaching philosophies, for many Indigenous peoples, are focused on community and survival.

A healthy community is both the purpose and litmus test of knowledge. It is not dependent only on food and water for sustenance; creating and maintaining community health requires enrichment, aesthetics, emotional and spiritual expression, and the celebration of Indigenous/human creativity and intellectualism.[9] According to Deloria (1992), the freedom to think and act in ways governed by individual will promoted in some other knowledge systems can be detrimental, for it allows an individual to conceive of reality in whatever way she finds beneficial, which encourages her to disregard others and be blind to the repercussions of her thoughts and actions on those around her. Community-based knowledges require individuals to be concerned for the welfare of not just themselves but others as well.

Finally, the student teacher highlighted some of the conflicts between a way of teaching informed by IK and community practices and the standards and testing that currently drive curriculum and teaching. In her words, "This is a little trickier." She keenly noted that because of legislation like No Child Left Behind, she must assist her students in meeting the demands of myriad assessments. Ultimately, this student teacher makes what may be the most profound statement of all when she says that her "tribe is for education . . . but sometimes it doesn't make sense." In this statement, she is not arguing that education does not make sense; rather, she critiques a form of education that assumes that one size fits all and that achievement is rooted in individualism. This is a form of education that may not be valued in Indigenous communities, and her voice is a powerful critique of a system that claims to leave no one behind. Importantly, she pointed to the fact that as a future teacher, she has learned something from the university's program and will integrate it into her knowledge. She pushed the issue by letting us all know that while she is learning, the university and the teacher preparation program have something to learn from her. She is, of course, right. In a prescient moment, she foreshadows the effects of her comments on the educators with whom she works.

From Seed to Plant: Transformation, Transition, and Becoming Teachers

The student teacher's discussion of the lesson through an Indigenous lens changed the tenor of the meeting and quashed any concerns over the students' abilities to learn, teach, and think through problems in the classroom. The university faculty and staff had been having difficult conversations with the STEs and with Henry about whether or not these student teachers were going to be able to complete their student teaching assignments. Both of the STEs had privately questioned their student teachers' abilities to take over their classes, and one was adamant that the student teacher she was supervising was "not ready to do this work. She doesn't even have an understanding of the basics, let alone how to teach a child." The student teacher she discussed with such derision is the same student teacher who outlined the ways that she would teach the lesson of the bean.

The change in body language from this STE toward her student teacher was profound. She went from leaning away from the student teacher as she spoke to leaning in, engrossed by her version of the modifications she would make to the lesson. This STE was animated when she said, "Those are really good points. . . . I mean, of course we know that things grow in particular ways, and we can just tell our students this. . . . I also like the idea of us growing things in our classroom that the students can then take home and either eat or give away as gifts. . . . That's really good." Her analysis of what the student teacher described moved from "she doesn't even have an understanding of the basics" to "those are really good points." Buried in this transformation is the effect of actually watching the student teacher translate her knowledge into action. Demonstrating knowledge is an important key to the programmatic issues of the teacher-training program, and the student teacher demonstrated how she would rethink an entire lesson and actually put it to practical and informative use. In this example, there is evidence of the ways that differing knowledge systems can come together to create a unified vision of what makes sense. In this case, the sense making coalesces around the lessons of growing a bean plant.

This vignette and the connections it makes between knowledge and its production and transmission recall the comment by the Indigenous woman about her experiences in a boarding school and highlight the faulty logic that has been apparent in the education of Indigenous students for centuries. The school and its teachers framed her as a "dirty, dumb Indian." In response, she asserted the fact that she can be "smart and an Indian at the same time." She also noted that her teachers would have been more effective "if they only understood how good [her] ways are too." The bean lesson demonstrates precisely how "good [these] ways" are and shows how an Indigenous teacher can demonstrate that her "students can see that being smart and [Indian] can go hand-in-hand." Ultimately, we see, in this reframing of a lesson to be more in line with her students' cultural moorings, that "knowing what [her students'] lives are like and understanding what it means to be an Indian, [she] can be a better teacher" for her Indigenous students. Similarly, our hope in creating ITPP was to establish a way of reframing the educational experiences that many Indigenous peoples had with schooling. These pre-service teachers highlight one of the ways that Indigenous peoples might march toward self-determination through self-education.

CONCLUSIONS

The story of the bean highlights a number of issues for us. First, Indigenous knowledge systems are in danger of becoming something few Indigenous students are explicitly aware of in their daily lives. The need to understand this danger is imperative so that Indigenous students can make sense of their own experiences and their placement in institutions of higher education and K–12 schooling. Importantly, many individuals may be unaware of the rootedness of their own knowledge systems. For Indigenous students in higher education, being historically aware of the different ways that their own knowledge systems are marginalized or ignored allows them to better situate faculty feedback on their work and the ways that courses are run. This awareness allows for strategic accommodations in order to frame themselves as both "smart" in the context of the university and to maintain a sense of themselves as Indigenous people.

Second, these knowledge systems highlight the ingenuity of Indigenous peoples as members of functioning societies, as inventors, and as systematic, analytical thinkers. In the story we share here, student teachers began to transform the ways in which other teachers and their supervisors fundamentally understood teaching and learning. Recognizing this ingenuity is essential for Indigenous educators; they must have multiple sources of strength to draw on in their work with students in order to disrupt the ongoing damaging impacts of deficit thinking and colonization. Finally, it is imperative that all educators serving Indigenous peoples, whether they themselves are Indigenous or not, develop an awareness of the bases for Indigenous Knowledge Systems and production so they can support student learning in meaningful ways.

All knowledge systems are lived. Here we have examined one particular instantiation that has implications for the work we do. At the heart of much of what is called "cultural difference" is a set of deeper theoretical issues involving Indigenous Knowledges. The ways in which knowledge systems govern our lives—from how we value particular relationships to how we conceive of and deliver instruction on plant growth—may be difficult to see, especially if we are not familiar with knowledge systems other than our own. However, these misunderstandings are often at the crux of conflict and key sites of struggle, including Indigenous teacher education. Through the IK research of a large number of Indigenous scholars and the theorizing and action of students in the Indigenous Teacher Preparation Program, we have come to see more fully just how extensive the implications of Indigenous Knowledges are and how these knowledge systems are challenged and unrecognized by many of us in academia. We would be wise to follow the astute observations of Inupiat scholar Leona Okakok (1989), who noted, "We all know that we can go through life convinced that our view of the world is the only valid one. If we are interested in new perceptions, however, we need to catch a glimpse of the world through other eyes. We need to be aware of our own thoughts, as well as the way life is viewed by other people" (p. 248). In many ways, the Indigenous pre-service teachers' experiences and perspectives pushed the institution and the site teacher educators to consider "new perceptions," leading to a simple science lesson that opens up new possibilities.

In the bean lesson example, we are struck by the fact that Indigenous Knowledges are used to extend and create space to think more broadly about what teaching and learning is and what it might look like. In the process, the Indigenous pre-service teachers had an opportunity to demonstrate that they and their ancestors were, and are, brilliant in their ways of engaging the world. Rather than being closed down because of these clashes around different knowledge systems, the pre-service teachers opened up a wide range of possibilities for how to engage learning, contextualize assignments, and integrate differing knowledge systems during a classroom moment. This example highlights an axiological clash about what "good teaching" looks like; more importantly, it also demonstrates that openness to new ways of engaging teaching topics and areas can be sources of strength for both teachers and learners.

It is not enough for teacher education programs to simply claim commitment to the training of Indigenous educators. They must also be able to see that the construction of knowledge is socially mediated and that Indigenous students may bring other conceptions of what knowledge is and how it is produced with them to their teaching. As Battiste (2002) reminds us, "The immediate challenge is how to balance colonial legitimacy, authority, and disciplinary capacity with Indigenous Knowledge and pedagogies" (p. 7). Our hope is that by making explicit some fundamental aspects of Indigenous Knowledge Systems and how they are played out in the lives and teaching of our students, we contribute to a conversation that urges educators—specifically educators of American Indian teachers and students—to recognize these knowledge systems in their power, effectualness, and ontological manifestations.

Perhaps the best way to end this essay is by seeking the wisdom that comes from Indigenous Knowledge Systems. According to Chickasaw scholar and former president of Saskatchewan Indian Federated College Eber Hampton,

> The Europeans took our land, our lives, and our children like the winter snow takes the grass. The loss is painful but the seed lives in spite of the snow. In the fall of the year, the grass dies and drops its seed to lie hidden under the snow. Perhaps the snow thinks the seed has vanished, but it lives hidden, or blowing in the wind, or clinging to the plant's leg of progress. How does the acorn unfold into the oak? Deep inside itself it knows—and we are not different. We know deep inside ourselves the pattern of life. (cited in Battiste, 2002, pp. 28–29)

The pre-service teacher, in taking up Indigenous Knowledges to address a classroom lesson, demonstrated the power of the seed. Her reframing of the lesson highlighted "the pattern of life" and pointed us to a future full of hope and possibilities.

NOTES

1. Throughout this article, we use pseudonyms for individuals and institutions and we obscure some details as a way to maintain some sense of anonymity. In the essay, "we" refers to ourselves as authors and as members of the program staff.
2. We use the term "holistic" with the full understanding that it appears to have become a bit of a catchphrase in discussing issues related to Indigenous peoples. While we recognize the problems inherent in its use, we also know that this is the way that the students themselves talked about their own knowledge systems.
3. Lomawaima and McCarty's (2006) outstanding book, *"To Remain an Indian": Lessons in Democracy from a Century of Native American Education*, also points to the ways that front-line teachers rejected calls for assimilation and worked from a model of engaging Indigenous students in ways that led to choice and power.
4. There is a deeply moral and ethical component of Indigenous Knowledge Systems that scholars acknowledge (e.g., see Battiste, 2002; Deloria, 1969/1988; Okakok, 1989; Burkhart, 2004). In this way, IK encompasses a fourth dimension that includes the whole person and notions of the spiritual and metaphysical. There are deeply embedded components of values in these knowledge systems.
5. There are variations on this spelling for Indigenous peoples from both Canada and the U.S.
6. We understand that, like IK, Western knowledge systems are not monolithic. In many ways these Western ways of knowing are characterized by what many people think of as what occurs in formal schooling. We also believe, however, that many larger societal norms are connected to Western ways of knowing as well; these include an overemphasis on the individual, heavy competition, and the "right" way of doing everything from how to hold silverware, how to engage with teachers and in the intellectual process, and

how to "do school." None of these things is apolitical, and it is the "Western" ways that are often seen as those that have become normalized over time.

7. The opinions and analyses offered in this article are the authors' only and not necessarily those of the funding agency.

8. In order to protect the identities of the individuals involved in the following story, we use pseudonyms. Also, we have altered some nonessential details in order to make it more difficult to identify the individuals speaking. Our intention in this essay is not to paint any person or program in a negative light; rather, it is to use the vignette to point to places of possibility and transformation. Indeed, we eventually developed very good working relationships with faculty and program staff in these departments.

9. We acknowledge Terri McCarty's assistance in pointing out this nuance.

REFERENCES

Adams, D. W. (1988). Fundamental considerations: The deep meaning of Native American schooling, 1880–1900. *Harvard Educational Review, 58*(1): 1–28.

Aikenhead, G. (2001). Integrating Western and Aboriginal sciences: Cross-cultural science teaching. *Research in Science Teaching, 31*(3), 337–355.

Bang, M., Medin, D. L., & Atran, S. (2007). Cultural mosaics and mental models of nature. Proceedings of the National Academy of Sciences of the United States of America. Retrieved May 25, 2008, from www.pnas.org/cgi/doi.10.1073/pnas.0706627104

Barnhardt, A., & Kawagley, A. O. (2005). Indigenous knowledge systems and Alaska Native ways of knowing. *Anthropology and Education Quarterly, 36*(1), 8–23.

Battiste, M. (2002). Indigenous knowledge and pedagogy in first nations education: A literature review with recommendations. Ottawa: Indian and Northern Affairs Canada.

Battiste, M. (2008). The struggle and renaissance of Indigenous knowledge in Eurocentric education. In M. Villegas, S. R. Neugebauer, & K. R. Venegas (Eds.), *Indigenous knowledge and education: Sites of struggle, strength, and survivance* (pp. 85–92). *Harvard Educational Review* Reprint Series No. 44. Cambridge, MA: Harvard Education Press.

Battiste, M., & Henderson, J. Y. (2000). *Protecting Indigenous knowledge and heritage: A global challenge.* Saskatoon, Canada: Purich Publishing, Ltd.

Brayboy, B. McK. J., & Castagno, A. E. (2008). How might Native science inform "informal science learning"? *Cultural Studies of Science Education, 3*(1): 731–750.

Burkhart, B. Y. (2004). What coyote and thales can teach us: An outline of American Indian epistemology. In A. Waters (Ed.), *American Indian thought: Philosophical essays* (pp. 15–26). Oxford, England: Blackwell Publishing.

Cajete, G. A. (2008). Sites of strength in Indigenous research. In M. Villegas, S. R. Neugebauer, & K. R. Venegas (Eds.), *Indigenous knowledge and education: Sites of struggle, strength, and survivance* (pp. 204–207). *Harvard Educational Review* Reprint Series No. 44. Cambridge, MA: Harvard Education Press.

Cajete, G. (2000). *Native science: Natural laws of interdependence.* Santa Fe, NM: Clear Light Publishing.

Deloria, V., Jr. (1969/1988). *Custer died for your sins: An Indian manifesto (civilization of the American Indian).* New York: Macmillan.

Deloria, V., Jr. (Ed.). (1992). *American Indian policy in the twentieth century.* Norman: University of Oklahoma Press.

Deloria, V., Jr., & Wildcat, D. R. (2001). *Power and place: Indian education in America.* Golden, CO: Fulcrum Resources.

Fixico, D. (2003). *The American Indian mind in a linear world: American Indian studies and traditional knowledge.* New York: Routledge.

Heidegger, M. (1978). *Being and time.* Translated by J. Macquarrie & E. Robinson. Malden, MA: Blackwell Publishing.

Hermes, M. (2005). "Ma'iingan is just a misspelling of the word wolf": A case study for teaching culture through language. *Anthropology and Education Quarterly, 36*(1), 43–56.

Husserl, E. (1969). *Formal and transcendental logic.* Translated by D. Cairns. The Hague, Netherlands: Martinus Nijhoff.

Kawagley, A. O. (2006). *A Yupiaq worldview: A pathway to ecology and spirit* (2nd Ed.*)*. Long Grove, IL: Waveland Press.

Lomawaima, K. T., & McCarty, T. L. (2002). When tribal sovereignty challenges democracy. *American Educational Research Journal, 39*(2), 279–305.

Lomawaima, K. T., & McCarty, T. L. (2006). *"To remain an Indian": Lessons in democracy from a century of Native American education.* New York: Teachers College Press.

Marker, M. (2004). "Indigenous voice, community, and epistemic violence: The ethnographer's "interests" and what "interests" the ethnographer. *Qualitative Studies in Education, 16*(3), 361–375.

Okakok, L. (1989). Serving the purpose of education. *Harvard Educational Review, 59*(4): 405–422.

Pember, M. A. (2008, April 17). Diversifying pedagogies. *Diverse Issues in Higher Education.* Retrieved May 5, 2008, from http://www.diverseeducation.com/artman/publish/article_11004.shtml

Smith, L. T. (1999). *Decolonizing methodologies: Research and Indigenous peoples.* New York: Zed Books.

Stoffle, R. W., Zedeño, M. N., & Halmo, D. B. (2001). *American Indians and the Nevada test site.* Washington, D.C.: U.S. Government Printing Office.

Vandergriff, J. (2006, December). Native American teachers needed—and programs to prepare them needed even more. *Teachers College Record,* Retrieved December 28, 2006, from http://www.tcrecord.org.

Villegas, M., Neugebauer, S. R., & Venegas, K. R. (Eds.) (2008). *Indigenous knowledge and education: Sites of struggle, strength, and survivance. Harvard Educational Review* Reprint Series No. 44. Cambridge, MA: Harvard Education Press.

We are grateful for the many people who have engaged our work and assisted us in refining this essay. We'd like to thank Ray Barnhardt, Angelina Castagno, Karen Dace, Candace Galla, Perry Gilmore, Norma Gonzalez, Janet Hesch, J. P Leary, Teresa McCarty, Iva Moss, Brendan O'Connor, Michael Redman, Kristi Ryujin, Kristin Searle, Jessica Solyom, Adrienne Thunder, Sundy Watanabe, and Peterson Zah for providing thoughtful comments on earlier drafts of this paper and presentations. Although we cannot name them here, we are thankful for the participants and staff members in the teacher preparation program for their wisdom and guidance. We are especially indebted to Malia Villegas for her wisdom and her early encouragement and development of this manuscript and to Kristy Cooper and Mara Tieken for making this essay much better through their patient and gentle guidance and thoughtful ideas. Bryan is grateful for the financial and institutional support from the President's Professor of Education fund at the University of Alaska Fairbanks and Dean Eric Madsen's and President Mark Hamilton's Offices. Thank you all. All mistakes are our own.

ELEMENTARY SCHOOL CURRICULA AND URBAN TRANSFORMATION

PAUL SKILTON-SYLVESTER

"I want to get off welfare; I've been on food stamps all of my life!" Derek said to no one in particular. It was payday. Every Friday, each of my third graders received a paycheck or welfare payment. After cashing their checks at the classroom branch of the Fidelity Bank, they could spend their money, open their businesses, or report to work.

This was Sweet Cakes Town, a name chosen by students for the child-sized, red-brick neighborhood they created out of cardboard boxes in our classroom. (None of the students could explain to me why they seized upon one boy's odd suggestion for this name.) In this town, the businesses, government, and union were owned and run by the students. The economy of Sweet Cakes Town was not make-believe; Sweet Cakes dollars were legal tender for real goods and real services. Using money they earned from classroom jobs, students participated in the economy according to their individual interests. They could buy and manage businesses, rent a chess board at the toy store, rent paints at the Art Supply Store, borrow a book from the Free Library, plant seeds at the Wonderful World of Plants Store, sell one of their own paintings at the Art Gallery, rent an outfit at the Value Plus Clothing Store, get their hair corn-rowed at Shawntay's Beauty Salon, or feed the rabbit at the Sweet Cakes Zoo.

Derek's dilemma of finding a way off welfare was real both inside and outside the classroom.[1] The students' Philadelphia neighborhood had suffered the trauma of de-industrialization during the 1970s and 1980s, and 93 percent of our students were on public assistance (most recent figures available at time of writing) (School District of Philadelphia, 1991, p. 239). As in most eastern cities, factory closings compounded the historical effects of racial discrimination, leaving many African Americans and Latinos economically isolated.[2]

Harvard Educational Review   Vol. 64   No. 3   Fall 1994

As an elementary school teacher attempting to engage my students in real social and economic issues, I needed clear illustrations of what critical pedagogy could look like in the mainstream, K–12 public school systems of this country. In reviewing the current literature on education for social reform, I found a great deal of information on the theory of critical pedagogy, including work in the fields of adult literacy, higher education, feminist pedagogy, international development, and education for employment. Unfortunately, most of this was written in an abstract fashion, with little explanation of how one could make it work in an actual classroom.

Educational anthropologist John Ogbu (1978, 1988) has shown how students' views about their chances in the economy affect their school performance. Ogbu has found that as some African-American children grow older, they tend to engage in nonacademic activities and "become more aware of how some people in the community 'make it' without good school credentials or mainstream employment" (1988, p. 332). He has shown that such beliefs about success can lead to life strategies that undermine their school achievement. Similarly, in a study of twelve hundred Los Angeles high school students, Roslyn Arlin Mickelson found a significant relationship between the "economic returns" students anticipated from their education and how well they performed in school (1984, p. 112).

One could infer from Ogbu's findings that education cannot address the impoverishment in inner cities until changes have occurred in the economic opportunity structure. My own view, however, lies closer to that presented by Michael W. Apple and Lois Weis:

> If education can be no more than an epiphenomenon tied directly to the requirements of an economy, then little can be done within education itself. It is a totally determined institution. However, if schools (and people) are not passive mirrors of an economy, but instead are active agents in the processes of reproduction and contestation of dominant social relations, then understanding what they do and acting upon them becomes of no small moment. For if schools are part of a "contested terrain" . . . then the hard and continuous day-to-day struggle at the level of curriculum and teaching practice is part of these larger conflicts as well. The key is linking these day-to-day struggles within school to other action for a more progressive society in that wider arena. (Quoted in Erickson, 1987, p. 351)

In this article I describe one example of how education can address the inequality of a post-industrial society. I describe the evolution of a curriculum created with my students that involved the hands-on study of our neighborhood, as well as the creation of a child-sized model of the neighborhood in our classroom. I believe that the crucial element in the success of this curriculum was not in my personality as a teacher, but in the students' own creative power, which I tapped into by encouraging them to question, investigate, and interpret their experience of the world. As our classroom neighborhood evolved, it represented the opportunity for Derek and his classmates to imagine and actually live in, for a few hours a week, a future that defied the too-familiar statistics of their real-life chances.

In the second section of this article, I describe changes in the roles played by three students in the class. Finally, I discuss the implications of this curriculum for social transformation among the ghetto poor.[3] Overall, two questions guide this discussion: 1) How do we as teachers educate so that we do not replicate existing social inequalities? and 2) How do we avoid the twin pitfalls of a) stressing the obstacles to economic success, thereby encouraging defeatism, and b) stressing the possibilities for economic success and thereby encouraging the view that those who have not "made it" have only themselves to blame?

A CURRICULUM FOR URBAN TRANSFORMATION

Identifying the Problem and Becoming Part of the Solution

My interest in using education to address urban inequality began in the 1960s, as I was growing up in the suburbs of Detroit. I saw a city increasingly split between affluent suburbs where I saw only White people, and a run-down inner city where I saw mostly Black people. It was not until 1989, however, that I felt that I was making the least bit of progress in understanding what had been happening to Detroit. That year my parents gave me William Julius Wilson's *The Truly Disadvantaged* (1987) as a Christmas present, with the inscription " . . . that you may be part of the solution."

Wilson's *The Truly Disadvantaged* showed me our city through an economic lens in a time when much of the popular rhetoric blamed urban problems on the moral deficiencies of the poor (e.g., the need for "values"). Looking at the problem from Wilson's perspective, I wondered what role, if any, an urban elementary school teacher could play in helping to create the solution.

I had recently completed my teacher training at the Bank Street College of Education in New York City where, in the tradition of John Dewey and the Progressive education movement, curricula are developed around in-depth studies of various aspects of students' experiences. I began to think that if students were to overcome the obstacles presented by changes in the economy—or better yet, to play a role in breaking down these obstacles—they would first need practice imagining how they might do it. I began looking for a way to bring together students' experience of the economic conditions Wilson described with the integrated, experiential education I learned at Bank Street.

Around the same time, I was getting my feet wet as a teacher new to Philadelphia. In a curriculum guide issued by the school district, I found the suggestion to pay students classroom dollars for being "good classroom citizens" (School District of Philadelphia, 1989, pp. 34–39).[4] In this curriculum, students were to fill in a pay sheet, deciding whether they should receive pay for fulfilling the responsibilities of attendance, homework, getting along with others, and other classroom "jobs" (p. 36). The writers of the curriculum pointed out that this project could be extended in endless directions.

What I liked about this idea was that it seemed to provide the possibility of bringing economic experience into the classroom. The problem I had was that in the real world, one does not get paid for being a good citizen, but rather for doing one's job; those who are richest are not always the best citizens. With this in mind, I reframed the economic system so that children were paid for "the job of being a good student" rather than a good citizen; I structured the classroom economy to run parallel to an experiential economic study of the outside neighborhood; and I used students' questions and experience about both economies to chart the direction of our study.

The Evolution of the Classroom Economy

When the classroom economy first began, all student jobs were "government work" and I, the teacher, was the only boss. I began paying students for the job of being students, which included classroom jobs (e.g., distributing corrected work), academic performance, behavior, and a personal goal of their choosing (e.g., "I will get a job"). Students voiced no opposition to the power I reserved, which might be attributable to the reality that teachers are always the boss. A job chart at the front of the room listed government jobs, their rate of pay, and the name of the person currently holding each position. I later added a second chart listing "private sector" jobs. To apply for a job, students filled out an application. On the job application, students gave reasons why I should hire them and included their previous work experience and names of references. I returned these applications with written explanations for their acceptance or rejection. Students became familiar with the boss' criterion for a strong application. They learned, for example, that last year's teacher made a better reference than one of their friends, and that it was better to cite one's success at the last job than to state that one needs money. I once observed a boy start an application, then crumple it up to start over, saying, "I forgot, neatness counts!"

Students designed the money that we used. On the different denominations we had pictures of Rosa Parks, "Homey the Clown," Don King, and a student's mother. We printed the money on different colors of paper using our hand-cranked rexograph.

In our class, the students' schedule was highly structured, with the basic subjects being studied at the same time each day. In some progressive classrooms I have known, activities tend to be "decentralized," with two or three different groups engaged in different lessons at the same time. One group might be reading with the teacher, another working on dioramas, and still another testing each other on their spelling words. In contrast, my students seemed to do best when working as a class. Although students' ability levels varied greatly, there seemed to be a feeling of momentum when the entire class worked on an exercise, with the faster or more advanced students tutoring the others. Within this rather traditional routine, students had a great deal of input into the curriculum, great flexibility in the approaches they used to complete their work, and great responsibility when they earned it. Academic work and social behavior became the basis for the ebb and flow of the responsibilities and trust earned by students. When a child was responsible, I hired him or her for the most important work, such as collating homework packets. When the class as a whole earned my trust, we took more ambitious walking trips, such as to the local pond.

In the last ten minutes of every day, each child evaluated his or her "job of being a good student" by filling out a pay sheet. On the top half of the pay sheet was a grid for the student to fill in, with one column for each day of the week and a row for each aspect of the "job of being a student": their school work, behavior, and "government" job. Based on their self-evaluations, students wrote in how much they should be paid. I provided some parameters, such as that school work paid a maximum of twenty-five dollars per day. At the end of each column was a row for them to total each day's pay. On the bottom half of the sheet was a space for them to write their personal goal for the day. On Friday afternoons, I paid the students. They then had the chance to use their money to buy the use of activities. Yet, before they could spend their wages, they were required to pay rent for their desk and taxes needed for municipal salaries. Students who were unable to pay rent or taxes went on welfare.

Each month I asked the students, "How can we make the classroom more like the neighborhood?" Their responses directed our explorations. The first time I posed this question, students answered that we should start stores in the classroom. When William asked how much a store costs, I turned this question back to the class by asking them where we might go to find the answers. In the discussion that followed, we decided that we would take a walking trip to the soul-food restaurant named "Ziggie's Barbecue Pit," which was located on the same block as our school.[5]

The next day, with Ziggie forewarned of the invasion, we set out to learn about starting a business. Ziggie's was a dimly lit, homey establishment, with hundreds of snapshots decorating its walls. With students and parent chaperons sitting on the stools at the lunch counter and on the seats from Ziggie's long-deceased Chevy van, the press conference began. The regular customers listened with curious attention as Ziggie patiently answered the questions students posed to him. After a half-hour of talking with Ziggie, we returned to the classroom, and I asked the students what they had learned. From our conversation with Ziggie they recalled: *start small and save; buy wholesale for cheap and sell retail for less cheap;* and the motto of the patient entrepreneur, *little by little.* The students' over-sized thank you letter is still hanging on the inside of Ziggie's door.

After talking about the goods and services already available in our classroom, the students discussed what stores we should have in our classroom economy. For example, because we used educational games and puzzles in our classroom, the students decided that we needed a toy store. Once we knew what stores we needed, student builders painted red bricks on boxes large enough to be used as storefronts. Using a razor-blade knife, I cut "windows" out of the boxes so that the merchants could stand behind them and sell their wares through the opening. Positioned around the perimeter of the room, these storefronts framed our carpeted area. Store names painted by students hung from the ceiling over each establishment. Two potted trees, donated by a company that rents large indoor plants to corporations, added to the realism of the "neighborhood."

In January, in my role as "the government," I auctioned off the Arts Supply Stores, Fidelity Bank, the toy store, Value Plus Clothing Store, an Art Gallery, and the Sweet Cakes Zoo. This "privatization" provided material for a lesson on the law of supply and demand. The students subsequently decided to add more businesses to Sweet Cakes Town. With each new proposal, we were propelled out of the classroom and into the neighborhood, visiting businesses and a factory, inviting visitors to be interviewed, collecting specimens from the neighborhood pond, and doing research at the public library.

After each trip, students drew in a few more neighborhood landmarks on a 5-foot-by-4-foot "working map" of the neighborhood that hung on our wall. Earlier in the year, students had made maps of our classroom, the school, and the area directly surrounding the school. Once we had some shared understanding of what the map of the neighborhood would look like, I laid out the larger street grid on our working map. Following each trip, two or three students would make additions to this map in pencil, then compare them to an aerial photograph of the neighborhood (purchased from the local regional planning commission) before making their additions permanent.

In January, when we first added stores to our economy, I created a form that asked students to subtract their rent and taxes from their earnings on their pay sheets in order to find their gross and net pay. From this point on, their paychecks included only the net figure. By gradually increasing the complexity of these forms, the students had meaningful applications of math problems at a level that was both challenging and attainable. I once overheard a boy say to himself after correctly filling out his pay sheet, "Ya, I'm all that."

Retail buying time on Friday afternoons was as exhilarating as anything I have experienced as a teacher. I watched in anxious amazement as students followed their own purposes, whether they were working at their store or spending their money. Without anything else to do, I might rent a hat at Value Plus, or go to the Men's Styling Shop, where Derek would spray water on my head, style my hair, and then slap the chair with a towel as I got up, as barbers often do. During this time, the zoo keepers even let Frances the rabbit wander about the classroom. The amazing thing to me was that usually retail buying time worked; that is, students went about their business and didn't require me to play the role of disciplinarian.

On those occasions when retail buying time did start to get wild, I followed the advice of a wise teacher trainer, Barbara Moore Williams, who once told me, "Don't lecture—let the kids tell you what the problem is. The kids know it all!" When it got too noisy, I would call things to a halt using the traditional hand in the air and a finger over my lips. The students would do the same, and pretty soon it would be quiet. Then I would ask, "Why did we have to stop?" One of the kids would explain, "Because Tyree was running." Then I would ask, "What's the matter with running?" Somebody would say, "It's too wild for the classroom." I would say, "What's going to happen if I see running again?" They would say, "We'll have to stop retail buying time." This generally worked for us.

After a few months of learning from people in the neighborhood, students wrote nominations for neighborhood citizenship awards (e.g., "My neighbor, Mr. Davis, watches over the children on the block to make sure they are safe. He is like a guardian angel."). We invited those people, as well as all those whom we had interviewed in our study, to come to the classroom to receive awards for their contributions.

Along with studying their neighborhood, the mandated curriculum called for third graders to study the city of Philadelphia, the state of Pennsylvania, the United States, and the world. We began to study the city after about four months of studying our neighborhood, and later, we studied the state. Our point of departure for both of these projects were first-hand investigations of other neighborhoods. We visited the outdoor Italian market as an example of the diversity of Philadelphia, and the community of Landsdale as an introduction to rural Pennsylvania. In both of these studies, we established correspondence between our class and third-grade classrooms in the other neighborhoods. Throughout these units, the Sweet Cakes Town economy continued to develop within our classroom.

Economics and the Classroom Neighborhood

I structured the Sweet Cakes Town economy to mirror some of the changes that had occurred in the economy of the students' neighborhood in North Philadelphia.[6] For example:

- I listed high-paying jobs, such as gerbil cage-cleaning, but then explained to the kids that this job had moved to a classroom in the suburbs. We talked about how many of the jobs that used to be in the cities are now outside the cities and the strategies that adults use for overcoming this problem.
- I hired fourth-grade students who would work for nothing just so that they could get out of their class. These were our immigrant workers. My students responded to this by encouraging them not to work unless they were paid.
- I sent one student a letter via Sweet Cakes mail relating the bad news that a great aunt had died. Enclosed was the inheritance check, which gave us the

opportunity to discuss the fact that some people start off with more capital than others. Students reacted to this with quiet resignation.
• Students also dealt with recessions, layoffs, wage inequities, and alliances of capital.

Each of these obstacles was taken as a challenge to be overcome, rather than a defeat to be endured. After we read a biography of Cesar Chavez, student workers created their own union, which they named JBS Local 207 (standing for John Barnes School, room 207). It took a while for them to coordinate collective action. At first when I lowered their wages, one of them said, "I'm on strike," to which I replied, "OK, who wants her job?" At this point, many of the students raised their hands, and the striker backed down. Trying to make this as realistic as possible, I lowered their wages again and again. Eventually they realized that their individual good was dependent on each other, and except for two die-hard scabs, the workers waged a strike. The union leaders and I reached a bargain over lunch, and later the bargain was ratified by the rank and file.

Our classroom neighborhood study gave us an economic frame of reference for discussing a variety of real-life situations. For example, a work period was interrupted by two students yelling back and forth, "Your mother's homeless!" "No, your mother's homeless!" I intervened, and said that I was angry about their interruption and felt that we needed to discuss it as a class. We agreed that there were two issues at hand: one was that the two students were angrily arguing about something; the other was that homelessness was being used as an insult. I decided that the two students and I would discuss their dispute privately, but that the issue concerning homelessness would be addressed as a class.

I began this discussion by asking the students what kept people from being able to pay their rents. Jameel said, "They won't go out and get a job." We compared this explanation to what we experienced in our classroom economy, namely, the effects of intervening factors such as lay-offs, businesses relocating to the suburbs, jobs not paying enough, and people not having enough money to start a business. I emphasized that if a person is homeless, it is not something of which the person should be ashamed, but something of which our country should be ashamed. Individual students volunteered examples of honest and hardworking people they knew who were homeless. Only later did I learn that one of the students present for this conversation had recently moved to a homeless shelter with her family. I marveled at this, because even with such turmoil in her home life, she was excelling as a student, consistently making the honor roll.

It seems to me that impromptu discussions of economic issues complemented more structured discussions of inequality. For example, during the year, I used Margaret Davidson's (1986) biography of Martin Luther King, Jr., as one of our reading texts. In previous years, my students had always responded to King's fight against prejudice, but seemed to have trouble connecting their own lives with King's call for economic justice. This year, however, perhaps because of our classroom economy, students had an experiential vocabulary for talking about the economic factors behind inequality.

We also looked at language differences in an economic context. Knowing of the stigmatization of non-Standard English (NSE) in our society, I wanted to raise my students' awareness of the role that language differences play in social relations, but to do so in a way that did not demean the language style used in their homes. Assimilation was never the goal. Instead, I wanted them to see that one possible use of learning Standard English (SE) was *infiltration*: crossing over into a world where non-Standard English is not valued and using Standard English to achieve their own goals, while understanding that to do so need not mean giving up their identity as African-Americans or their loyalty to their home communities.

I therefore initiated discussions of the relative effectiveness of SE and NSE in different contexts. Students identified quotes from poetry we had studied and speeches by African-American leaders as "SE" or "NSE." Then we labeled quotes by students in the class in the same way. Finally, students identified a list of various situations with the type of English that would be most appropriately used there (e.g., speaking at home, writing a rap, asking for something from the principal, or applying for a job at a bank). I encouraged students to see language differences as options that could be invoked to suit their purposes in a given context, rather than as a once-and-for-all choice (Erickson 1987).

On a number of occasions, I saw informal evidence that these exercises might be raising students' awareness of their uses of language. For example, one afternoon as we were working on a science project, a boy with writing disabilities was dictating to me his observations about a snail that we had brought back from the neighborhood pond. The student said, "He ain't movin." As I started to write, he hurried to say, "He is not moving." I asked the boy if he was changing to Standard English and he looked at me perplexed. This suggested to me that while such labels as "Standard English" may have eluded him, this student had gained some practical awareness that he was able to switch codes and that he had knowledge of their appropriate contexts.

Democracy and the Classroom Neighborhood

As John Locke would have wanted it, the government of Sweet Cakes Town evolved naturally as problems arose between individuals. It seems that Lateef, the owner of the Value Plus Store, had been hiring new clerks each week rather than paying the old ones. Just when mob action seemed imminent, I separated the parties and suggested that we start a court. A judge was elected, jurors and lawyers picked, and for the time being, playground justice was held off. Before the trial, which was held a few days later, I invited an African-American lawyer to coach both the prosecution and the defense. Witnesses were sworn in on a coloring-book Bible found in a student's desk. In lieu of the black robe, the judge wore a black velvet evening gown on loan from Value Plus. At one point during the defendant's testimony, Judge Jameson blurted out, "Oh, he is *so* guilty!" giving us a chance to explore the notion of "innocent until proven guilty." In the end, Lateef was convicted and forced to pay all back wages.

Occasionally an offense was committed without the perpetrator ever being discovered. On a day when I was absent and the students had a substitute teacher, someone scrawled graffiti across the red-brick front of our toy store. At the beginning of the following day, I asked the students to answer the following questions: "What feelings are people showing when they hurt the classroom neighborhood? Who does it hurt? Does it solve the problem? What are other possible solutions?" In this way, I tried to get students to see that destructive behavior, like doing graffiti, is sometimes an expression of misplaced feelings like anger, which could be better used to solve the problem. The effective uses of anger came up again in our discussion of the L.A. riots that followed the Rodney King verdict. "Solve the problem!" became our class mantra.

Another day, we had problems with loitering students starting trouble during retail buying time. I overheard one girl explain, "I don't want to shop. I'm savin' my money for a business." Some students decided that we needed a "no loitering" law and called for the election of a government. I suggested to the students that they conduct a poll regarding which citizens should be allowed to vote. The boys said that girls should not vote, and the girls said that the boys should not vote. I used these experiences to provide a meaningful context for discussing the women's suffrage movement and the history of African Americans' struggle for voting rights in the United States.

As a result of these history lessons, the class decided on universal suffrage. With signs hanging from the ceiling, they designated each group of desks as a different city council district. They elected a city council representative from each table group and a mayor for the whole town. I asked each student to submit ten laws to their city council person. Student suggestions included "No more pay increases for city council" and "No air pollution."

Once when I asked how we could make the classroom more like the neighborhood, students suggested that we add roads and garbage collectors. "Who's going to pay for all this?" asked one realist. I turned this dilemma back to them and asked, "Who pays for these services in the outside neighborhood?" We discussed this, as well as the local controversy over the privatization of municipal services.

To learn more about how tax money was used, two student delegates and I telephoned Philadelphia's City Hall. Afterwards we received a pie chart of the city's expenditures in the mail, which I simplified for use with the children. This provided the basis for a discussion of students' views on spending priorities for city governments. Students created their own pie charts showing how they thought Sweet Cakes dollars should be used, and these suggestions were given to the mayor of Sweet Cakes Town. In our discussions about public and private services, students offered a variety of opinions about which services should be paid for with tax money and which should be handled privately. Eventually, the government paid for roads made out of black contact paper marked with yellow lane dividers, and instituted trash collection.

The mayor of Sweet Cakes Town was popular for nearly a month, until students realized he had hired only close friends to fill virtually all the government jobs, with some friends holding four jobs. We talked about how this happens in real life and discussed what options voters have when they feel their elected officials are not acting on their behalf. The mayor was roundly defeated in his bid for a second term.

By the time students decided that the town needed a mayor, they were already in the habit of going to the source for their information. Philadelphia's Mayor Rendell graciously accepted the children's invitation and came to Sweet Cakes Town to be interviewed about his job. During his visit, students gave him a large bar graph showing the results of the poll they had conducted to survey their parents' attitudes toward the mayor (at that point, the mayor was enjoying an 80 percent approval rating). As a final gesture of thanks, the mayor of Sweet Cakes Town gave Mayor Rendell the papier-mache "key" to our city.

The final project the citizens of Sweet Cakes Town undertook was a community works project: the students agreed to address the problem of small grocers in the neighborhood selling "crack." By writing a newspaper about Sweet Cakes Town and selling it on the street, they raised money for DARE, an anti-drug group. This project had to be squeezed into a single week, as the end of the school year was closing in on us. Our last day of school was a triumphant one. We returned to the streets of our neighborhood to sell the *Sweet Cakes News,* telling stories from students' study of the neighborhood. The response from the community was tremendous: in about two hours we sold 250 copies of *Sweet Cakes News* at 25 cents apiece. The students also gave copies to the merchants who had helped them during the year.

At the end of the year I asked students to carry the storefronts of Sweet Cakes Town to the trash. They asked to keep them, explaining to me that, if I didn't object, they would like to use them to start concession stands in the neighborhood. I didn't object.

Student Experience and the Standardized Curriculum

A series of questions guided the Sweet Cakes Town curriculum. Each day, when students filed into the classroom, an "opening exercise" sheet awaited them on their desks. The opening exercise typically included a few problems reviewing yesterday's math lesson and a single question concerning the neighborhood study, such as, "What are some things that money cannot buy?" which did not have a single "right" answer. These questions formed the basis of our morning discussions. Sometimes they served an instrumental purpose ("What special rules will we need for our trip to the pond?"); other times, they prepared us for the arrival of a visitor from the neighborhood ("Write one question that you have about the job of a dress designer."). By linking the questions from one day to the next, we developed themes while keeping students' experience and opinions at the heart of our study. For example,

Monday: In the Sweet Cakes Town system of jobs, what leaves you feeling bad, sad, or angry?

Tuesday: In the outside neighborhood system of jobs, what leaves people feeling bad, sad, or angry?

Wednesday: In the outside neighborhood, what are some *bad* things some people do if they are having a hard time making money?

Thursday: In the outside neighborhood, what are some *good* things some people do if they are having a hard time making money?

After ten minutes devoted to this opening exercise, students had an opportunity to volunteer their answers, which I recorded on chart paper, and a discussion usually ensued. With this format, I found that students would listen to each other more patiently and give thoughtful responses based on their considerable life experience. I tried to let students' questions and interests guide our study as much as possible, but this was negotiated in the context of the requirements that I faced and my own beliefs about what should be taught. My principal gave me great support and flexibility, but also insisted that the objectives of the curriculum be met, and that students be prepared for the standardized tests. Unfortunately, a new standardized test was implemented during the study of Sweet Cakes Town, making comparison of students' scores to previous years problematic.

To keep track of what mandated objectives we had met, I kept a list of them in my planbook and marked each one as we studied it (Donnan, 1988, p. 3).[7] Topics from social studies, such as "interdependence in the community," arose relatively naturally. But when other required topics did not come up, I looked for opportunities to raise them during the course of our investigation. For example, students were not clamoring to learn about commas, so with Raquel's permission, we began a writing class with the question, "Where are commas needed in Raquel's thank you letter to the people at the clothing store?"

Overall, I found that some of the most difficult issues of our study came from the students' own experiences in the community. The proper response to violence was an issue that confounded my easy answers. After discussing problems of urban violence, Black-on-Black violence, and the uses of political nonviolence, and after doing countless role plays of conflict resolution, I would be reminded again of how complicated my students' lives were. In a bit of writing that makes me laugh even while it saddens me, Macio wrote:

Being violent is bad to people. They steal from people. It is too bad that people are stealing from my mom. Me and my brother is going to kick some butts.

When I first began teaching in cities, I taught the gospel of nonviolence with less humility than I do today. Since then, I think that I have gained some understanding of my students' anger (and my own). I have a greater appreciation for how painfully difficult it can be to overcome anger and find solutions.

STUDENTS AND CITIZENS

Our class had, on average, twenty-four students, which was typical for third-grade classes in our school but down from thirty-four children the previous year. (This reduction was due to a vote by teachers in our school to use discretionary federal funds to reduce class size.) During the year, six students transferred in and eight transferred out. Of the entire class, one boy was Latino, and all others were African American. While Sweet Cakes Town evolved, not only was there turnover in student population, but students' roles within the town changed. Most students switched professions every month or two. Workers quit or were fired. Partnerships came and went as easily as third-grade friendships. Everyone held a job for some period, and no one held only one job. I will now describe three children who seemed to benefit socially and academically from their experiences in Sweet Cakes Town. While some students showed less personal and academic growth during the year, the experiences of these three students were not atypical among the group.

Derek

Derek, the boy quoted earlier who wanted to get off welfare, was handsome, funny, keenly observant of social interactions—a gifted mimic. At the beginning of the year, Derek requested to sit alone; he told me outright that he did not get along with other children. He was vehemently protective of his work being seen by the other students, but had a habit of yelling out humorous commentary to those very peers he held at a distance. A burly eleven-year-old, he could read at a kindergarten level. Despite this, or because of this, he refused to see a reading tutor. In the early stages of our classroom neighborhood, Derek created the character of "Kool Homie." Homie had a haircut known as a high-top fade, a big gold chain around his neck, sometimes a hat, and the local expressive walk. Week after week, Derek would pay for the clothes to dress up as Kool Homie, and act out stick-ups and muggings.

It was during this time that I heard Derek pronounce that he wanted to get off welfare, and that he had been on it all his life. Since Sweet Cakes Town did not have food stamps, I believe Derek was expressing the connection he saw between his life outside of school and his role in Sweet Cakes Town. In an effort to get off welfare, Derek applied for the job requiring the highest skill and receiving the highest wage: the filer of corrected work. The job paid forty Sweet Cakes dollars per day. Because he lacked experience, he did not get the job. Later that day another boy told Derek to apply for another job paying only $10.00 per day. Derek replied, "Who wants some $10.00 job! I don't want to get off welfare. . . . I applied to be a filer. That shows I want a job. Now I'm stayin' on welfare for the rest of my life. . . ."

I discussed with Derek the fact that he had not gotten the higher paying job for which he had applied because he lacked experience. We discussed strategies that people use to overcome this problem in the outside world, and Derek decided to volunteer as a work distributor for a week before applying to be a filer once again. Though he didn't get the filing job, he succeeded in being hired to water the plants (a job that paid a moderate wage).

With the money that Derek saved from his job, he was able to start the classroom branch of the Fidelity Bank. Making the most of our trip to a neighborhood bank, occasional lunch meetings with me, and hypothetical banking problems in math class, Derek proved greatly successful as a banker. He offered checking and savings accounts, as well as high-interest loans. As his business increased, he took on two partners. At the same time, he showed marked increases in social and academic confidence. However, though he regularly completed his math work, being older and bigger than the other children and barely able to read, he rarely attempted any language arts work in the classroom for fear of losing face.

One day in April, the kids told me that Derek had sold the bank. Because of the success he had had with the bank, I wondered why. When I talked with Derek, he would give me no explanation. A former teller, however, confided to me that Derek had sold the bank because people were bouncing checks: Derek thought this meant that he was in trouble. With the money from the sale of the bank, Derek bought the Value Plus Clothing Store and ran it successfully until the end of the school year.

Later in the year, I recommended that Derek be evaluated by our school's instructional support team (IST), a cross-disciplinary team charged with finding remedies when the school was failing to meet a child's needs. Derek was said to have a normal IQ, but also deficits in information processing, perceptual organization skills, and fine visual-motor perception and integration. As part of the IST effort to find support for students with learning problems within regular education classes, Derek was given intensive tutoring, which—this time—he accepted. When this tutoring failed to help him, the members of the IST, of which I was a part, recommended that Derek be switched to a special education class the following year.

Shawntay

Shawntay was a quiet, amiable girl. She did not cause trouble or draw attention to herself, but often did not finish her work. I found that as a teacher, I needed to keep deliberate track of her progress. Shawntay had good social skills, but remained peripheral to the social network. Moreover, I worried that her academic progress was hindered by low self-esteem. Like Derek, she too had been "held back" in first and second grades and now, in third grade, she was developing as an adolescent. In the early part of the year, the school psychologist found that Shawntay was dyslexic, but it was decided that she should remain in our classroom, where she seemed to be making progress.

Shawntay was the student who bought the bank from Derek. After the purchase, she found herself having great responsibility, but lacking a good understanding of how to run a bank. When people came to her asking for "their money," she neglected to keep track of how much she was giving out. When we realized the problem, she arranged to pay Derek to take time out from his new business to train her in banking (our first highly paid consultant). Although Shawntay learned to run the bank, she never really seemed to take a liking to it. She sold the business after a few months.

With the money she made from selling the bank, Shawntay opened a beauty parlor in May. Here she thrived. Shawntay's Beauty Parlor offered hair braiding, manicures, and make-up consultation. She did a brisk business, and soon her idea for a beauty parlor was copied by Tyree, who began a styling salon for "men." Shawntay's business career proved to be a springboard for political life; now, as an esteemed leader among the girls, she was elected to a seat on the city council. In the process, she showed marked improvement in her math skills, going from B's to A's.

William

William was a thoughtful, quiet boy who was well-liked by his classmates. In reading and math he performed on grade level. He had gotten an A in reading for the previous year, even while getting an F in behavior. My journal notes from the beginning of the year describe William as "sullen" and "sulky." Sometimes, William would become emotionally removed and perform a "go-slow" for an afternoon. William occasionally gave me a glimpse of the experiences he was having outside of school that might be draining his vigor. In response to a homework assignment asking students to write a true story about their neighborhood, William wrote the shortest of stories, but one that told volumes:

> One day on a weekend my best friend's dad got shot. I didn't know that he would get killed because he was good to people.

Despite such troubles, William came alive when we started the classroom economy. He was the first to apply for a job and the first to hold more than one government job at a time (at one point he held four). During this time William saved his money, keeping it in a big "knot" in his front pocket. It was he who inquired how much a business cost and, not suprisingly, he was the first to buy a store of his own.

Over the course of the year, William demonstrated a great entrepreneurial spirit. William's first store was the toy store, for which he hired his long-time friend Tyree as manager. With their profits, the two bought the Art Supply Store and hired Ray as a manager. William was the town's first mayor (it was his fall from power that I mentioned earlier). William's first appointment was again his friend Tyree. On Fridays, William and Tyree stayed in the classroom during recess to calculate revenues and expenditures for that fiscal week. Eventually, William and Tyree completed them on their own. One day when they requested to use silent reading time to finish their calculations, I heard William say to his buddies, "Don't bug me—I'm busy!" As he left that day I told him that he had done a good job on the budget. He grinned from ear to ear as he walked out through the gate of the schoolyard.

After William was defeated in his bid for re-election, he returned to running his businesses with Tyree. In the springtime, they started a plant store where students could plant seeds and then pick up their plants a week or so later.

LEARNING FROM SWEET CAKES TOWN

In this section, I return to the first of the questions with which I began this article: How can we teach children so that we do not simply replicate the existing social inequalities? Following are the seven primary insights I gained from my experiences with my students in our development of Sweet Cakes Town.

Creating opportunities for repeated, meaningful applications of academic skills

As has long been recognized by educational advocates among the poor, "self-efficacy" is a hollow term when one lacks the skills necessary to accomplish one's goals (Freire, 1993, p. 59; Lukas, 1986, p. 36). But, too often, "skills" and "knowledge" have been dichotomized, as if the two needed to be taught separately, as if the meaningfulness of a task could not increase the process of skill acquisition. Besides running counter to empirical research (Sticht, 1987), this dichotomization contradicts the common experience many of us have of learning deeply and quickly something that we care about.

Sweet Cakes Town involved students in what I call "meaningful drill." For example, at the end of each day, students computed their daily pay using multiplication and addition with carrying. At the end of each week, they also calculated their weekly pay, using addition with carrying and subtraction with borrowing. This was not math taught as practice for some task that the students might face in future years, but real math applied to make things happen in their present lives. Traditionally, most of what are called "applications" of math skills, such as story problems, ask students to pretend that they are using skills in a real situation. Unfortunately, it is all too possible for a student to go from kindergarten through twelfth grade and never use math for a real purpose. In Sweet Cakes Town, the calculations were as real as the privileges that the students could buy with their money. Similarly, I believe students' involvement in issues that mattered to them dramatically enhanced their acquisition of hard skills in reading, writing, science, and geography. It seemed that students learned skills faster in Sweet Cakes Town because they needed them, and they routinized their new skills by using them every day.

Providing opportunities for students to imagine themselves in new roles

For years, sociologists have told us that schools prepare lower socioeconomic status (SES) students to become lower SES adults, and upper SES students to become upper SES adults. Though this problem is partly a sin of omission, there are other dimensions to it that I will address later. Schools have failed to broaden their students' range of possibilities, leaving students to choose from the limited options that they see around them.

Options that Derek saw were playing "Kool Homie," standing on the street corner, or being a thief. Though Derek was not satisfied being on welfare, other options did not seem accessible to him. There were obstacles in his way, such as his lack of experience, the lack of role models to teach him how one gets experience, and, not least of which, a school system that had failed to find successful ways to teach him. I believe he needed to develop a strategy and to know that others (such as the lawyer who visited our classroom) have succeeded in overcoming the obstacles that face African Americans from the inner city.

By allowing students to imagine themselves in new roles, Sweet Cakes Town was, I like to think, a dream that we as a class dreamed together. The power of dreams to transform a life is explained by Ernst Bloch:

> Dreams come in the day as well as at night. And both kinds of dreaming are motivated by wishes they seek to fulfill. But daydreams differ from night dreams; for the day dreaming "I" persists throughout, consciously, privately, envisaging the circumstances and images of the desired, better life. The content of the daydream is not, like that of the night dream, a journey back into repressed experiences and their associations. It is concerned with an, as far as possible, unrestricted journey forward, so that instead of reconstituting that which is no longer conscious, the images of that which is not yet can be phantasied into life and into the world. (quoted in Simon & Dippo, 1987, p. 102)

Derek, Shawntay, William, and most other children in the class proved eminently successful at daydreaming new futures—as a banker, the owner of a hair styling salon, or an entrepreneur.

Helping students to divorce academic success from "acting White"

As has been observed by Fordham and Ogbu (1986), success in school is often perceived by African-American children as "acting White," which makes having a positive racial identity and succeeding in school seem mutually exclusive. Erickson (1987) has pointed out that this perception can be exacerbated or ameliorated depending on the behaviors of teachers and school personnel. He cites a comparative study of two classrooms: in one, the teacher frequently corrected the students for using "Black English"; in the other, the teacher did not correct students' language (Erickson, 1987, p. 346, citing Piestrup). At the end of the year, students who had frequently been corrected were speaking a *more* pronounced dialect in the classroom. Students who were *not* corrected were using language that was closer to "Standard English."

Erickson explains this data using contrasting metaphors of a "boundary" and a "border" (used first by Barth, 1969). In the classroom where Black English was stigmatized, a boundary was created between the world of the student and the world of the teacher. With each correction, the students' *defense* of their own cultural style grew, raising the wall a bit higher. The ultimate impact of this boundary was a sacrifice of the mutual trust that is needed for a student to risk attempting new academic tasks. In contrast, in the classroom where Black English was not stigmatized, this boundary became a border that the students could cross in both directions without threat of giving up an aspect of their cultural identity (Erickson, 1987, p. 350).

Whereas Fordham and Ogbu (1986) have shown the effects of a closed labor market on African Americans' attitudes about education, Erickson's (1987) analysis shows how the actions of people in schools can affect these attitudes. In our classroom, one way we incorporated the observations of Fordham and Ogbu and Erickson into the neighborhood study was in the treatment of language difference. I presented both Black English and Standard English as options that were appropriate and useful in certain contexts (Ladson-Billings, 1992). More generally, I attempted to show that academic skills are tools in the ongoing struggle for equality (Freire, 1993; Ladson-Billings, 1990). As educators, we need to find new ways to show students that achieving academic success can be "acting Black."

Allowing students to take pro-active stances in relation to those in power

In Sweet Cakes Town, the students not only had the chance to imagine themselves as grown-ups in roles of power, they also had power right then and there to influence the classroom study, each other, and me as their teacher. In the drama of the classroom economy, they experimented with strategies for using power: as workers who sue a corrupt boss, as exploited union members who strike for a fair wage, or as constituents who rally for a new mayor. In other words, as modern-day Davids, they found that the Goliaths of their day were within their range.

But beyond these chosen roles, Sweet Cakes Town also gave students a chance to experience new relationships between themselves and the authority figure with whose power they are most familiar: their teacher. Writers discussing such diverse topics as social reproduction, critical pedagogy, the hidden curriculum, process consultation, and education for empowerment have observed that having a passive role in educational institutions prepares students for taking a passive role vis-à-vis authority figures later in life: that is, a role as object rather than subject (Bowles & Gintis, 1976, p. 56; Freire, 1982, p. 59; Giroux, 1977, 1978, pp. 148–151; Schein, 1988, p. 9; Sleeter, 1991, p. 15). In contrast, problem-posing education replaces this vertical relationship between teachers and students with a horizontal one, a dialogue (Freire,

1982). In the case of Sweet Cakes Town, students were part of the process of guiding the course of study.

In our classroom, as students created a model of the neighborhood, they were *encoding* aspects of their culture (Freire, 1986). Derek's character Kool Homie was a code packed with elements of the situation faced by some African-American men. Derek had an understanding of how one might portray himself as an African-American male in a closed economy. I shared with Derek my belief that he could make it in the mainstream economy. In our daily discussion of Kool Homie, jobs, and strategies for getting jobs, the two of us came to a new understanding of his relationship to street corner life, as well as to how he could envision a different relationship.

Problem-posing education provides an opportunity to prepare the next generation for relationships qualitatively different than those we know between authorities and subordinates, such as bosses and workers or government leaders and constituents. Such changes are well-suited to current innovations in management practices, as U.S. corporations begin to realize the loss inherent in treating human beings like machines and move to less hierarchical, more team-oriented approaches to management (Byrne, 1993; Stewart, 1992, 1993).

For my students to play a role in changing their relationships to authority figures, they had to learn how to get, keep, and use power to participate in defining these relationships. The need for such practice will be developed below in my next-to-last recommendation.

Creating curricula that treats reality as something to be questioned and analyzed (Giroux, 1979)

When teachers change their students' role in acquiring knowledge, I believe they also change the nature of the students' relationship to that knowledge. In more traditional forms of education, knowledge is deposited into the minds of uncritical students (Freire, 1982). Henry Giroux has pointed out that in such "banking" pedagogy, knowledge is treated as a set of objective "facts" (Giroux, 1979). He says that

> knowledge is divorced from human meaning and inter subjective exchange. It no longer is seen as something to be questioned, analyzed and negotiated. Instead, it becomes something to be managed and mastered. In this case, knowledge is removed from the self-formative process of generating one's own set of meanings, a process that involves an interpretive relationship between knower and known. (Giroux, 1979, p. 250)

Such "banking" instruction has been contrasted with a "mining" pedagogy, where teachers view their task as drawing knowledge *out* of the student, rather than depositing it within (Ladson-Billings, 1990, p. 340). Ira Shor (1980) says that when students are allowed to bring their experience into the classroom, teachers are able to help students see the familiar and accept it in a new light: "By identifying, abstracting and problematizing the most important themes of student experience, the teacher detaches students from their reality and then re-presents the material for systematic scrutiny" (1980, p. 100).

For example, when two students taunted each other, saying, "Your mother's homeless," I believed that the students had internalized the popular ideology of blaming the victim. Consequently, I related that example to their experience in Sweet Cakes Town, showing that factors outside of an individual's control sometimes interfere with a person's ability to pay the rent.

Similarly, as students in Sweet Cakes Town studied their environment, they created their own understanding of how their community works and where its hope lies. The structures of knowledge that they created were not isolated, abstract, and theoretical, but interrelated, concrete, and practical. To borrow terms from Lev Vygotsky (1978), the informal knowledge of their experience was organically connected to the formal knowledge of school learning. Or, from Pierre Bourdieu's (1977) perspective, the students used the "cultural capital" *from* their community to create "dividends" to *take back* to their community.

Creating opportunities for students to develop strategies and hope for overcoming barriers to economic success in the mainstream

So far in this discussion, I have talked about aspects of my curriculum aimed at changing conditions internal to the students: their perceptions about their role in the world, their perceived relations both to those in power and to knowledge itself. But urban, African-American children of lower socioeconomic status also face obstacles to success that are external to them, obstacles that they will need to understand if they are to stand a chance (Sleeter & Grant, 1986). First, there are those obstacles Black people have always faced in the United States: prejudice, residential ghettoization, poor education, lack of capital, and lack of networks to obtain capital, to name a few. Secondly, postindustrial changes in the economy have constructed new obstacles to economic success for those isolated in the inner cities: lack of jobs, jobs moving further out of the city where there is no public transportation, lack of access to job information networks, jobs that require higher skills, or, I would add here, that require them to speak differently than they do at home.[8] In the face of these obstacles to economic success, there are new self-destructive alternatives, such as crack cocaine, which also threaten to pull them down. As teachers, we want to say to our students, "If you try, you will make it," but we know that it's not that simple, and to say it is that simple is to imply falsely that those who did not make it did not try.

This brings me to the second of the two questions with which I began: *How do we avoid the twin pitfalls of a) stressing the obstacles to economic success, thereby encouraging defeatism, and b) stressing the possibilities for economic success, thereby encouraging the view that those who did not make it have only themselves to blame?* Some might argue that it is better to teach the bootstraps "myth," believing that a false hope is better than none. This, of course, would ultimately leave students unprepared for the obstacles ahead. Our students face the stark realities of the inner cities every day. As teachers we must face our responsibility to abandon the innocuous social studies curricula that do not take into account the abandoned buildings and crack vials that students pass on any walking trip to the fire station. We must help our students cope with their present problems, and prepare them to overcome future obstacles. I believe that children who are economically isolated in U.S. inner cities need to be educated about the structural obstacles to their success, while also being taught that with strategic planning and collective effort these obstacles are surmountable.

Offering opportunities for students to experience social structures as impermanent and changeable for the sake of those people who live within them (Freire, 1993)

In the students' creation of Sweet Cakes Town, they had the opportunity to question why certain conditions exist, and to try out new approaches in such areas as legislation, taxation, social services, and labor/management relations. Here the importance of the imagination in social change becomes clear. I would like to explain this connection with a passage written by Northrop Frye (1964) about the literary imagination. What Frye says about the literary imagination I find equally applicable to the social imagination exhibited by my students in the creation of Sweet Cakes Town. While he wrote this in 1964, referring to the imagination of Canadians, I have taken the liberty of inserting the United States of our time:

> Just as [the material world] looks real, so this ideal world that our imaginations develop inside us looks like a dream that came out of nowhere, and has no reality except that we put into it. But it isn't. It's the real world, the real form of human society hidden behind the one we see. It's the world of what humanity has done, and therefore can do, the world revealed to us in the arts and sciences. This is the world that won't go away, the world out of which we built the [United States of 1964], are now building the [United States of 1994], and will be building the quite different [United States of 2004]. (Frye, 1964, p. 152)

My students found that they could change their roles in Sweet Cakes Town, as well as alter its social structures. Thus we see that the template for the society of the future need not be what the students have seen, but what they can imagine.

NOTES

1. Students' names have been changed for confidentiality.
2. Many of my assumptions about the causes of our urban situation come from the work of William Julius Wilson. Recently, he provided a concise summary of his landmark work: "I argue in *The Truly Disadvantaged* [Wilson, 1987] that historic discrimination and a migration flow to large metropolitan areas that kept the minority population relatively young created a problem of weak labor-force attachment within this population, making it particularly vulnerable to the ongoing industrial and geographic changes in the economy since 1970. The shift from goods-producing to service-producing industries,

increasing polarization of the labor market into low-wage and high-wage sectors, innovations in technology, relocation of manufacturing industries out of the central city, periodic recessions, and wage stagnation exacerbated the chronic problems of weak labor-force attachment among the urban minority poor" (Wilson, 1990, p. 6).

3. In response to Gans's (1990) suggestion that the term "underclass" is no longer useful due to the pejorative connations it has taken on through misapplication, Wilson (1990) has suggested the substitution of the term "ghetto poor."

4. For other classroom uses of "micro-societies," see McCarthy and Braffman (1985), and Richmond (1989).

5. In many schools, the spontaneity of going on field trips is curtailed by the time it takes to issue and receive signed permission slips. The Philadelphia school system helps teachers to avoid this problem by issuing permission slips that allow children to go on neighborhood walking trips throughout the year.

6. Philadelphia, like most Eastern, industrial cities, had been decimated by the loss of manufacturing jobs in the last two-and-a-half decades. In the period between 1975 and 1979 alone, the city lost 128,000 jobs, or one out of six (Katz, 1986, p. 276).

7. See Elliot Wigginton (1989) for another framework for bringing together students' interests and mandated curricula.

8. The split between low-wage (goods producing) and high-wage (service producing) sectors of the economy was not addressed in the curriculum, but would be wisely included in future neighborhood studies.

REFERENCES

Barth, F. (1969). *Ethnic groups and boundaries: The social organizational of culture difference.* Boston: Little, Brown.

Bowles, S., & Gintis, H. (1976) *Schooling in capitalist America.* New York: Basic Books.

Bourdieu, P. (1977). *Reproduction in education, society, and culture.* London: Sage.

Byrne, J. (1993, December). The horizontal corporation. *Business Week,* pp. 76–81.

Davidson, M. (1986). *I have a dream.* New York: Scholastic.

Donnan, C. (1988). Following our forebears footsteps: From expedition to understanding. In V. Rogers, A. D. Roberts, & T. P. Weinland (Eds.), *Teaching social studies: Portraits from the classroom* (pp. 3–11). Washington, DC: National Council for the Social Studies.

Erickson, F. (1987). Transformation and school success: The politics and culture of educational achievement. *Anthropology and Education Quarterly, 18,* 335–356.

Freire, P. (1982). *Pedagogy of the oppressed.* New York: Continuum.

Freire, P. (1986). *Education for critical consciousness.* New York: Continuum.

Freire, P. (1993). *Pedagogy of the city.* New York: Continuum.

Frye, N. (1964). *The educated imagination.* Bloomington: Indiana University Press.

Fordham, S., & Ogbu, J. (1986). Black students' school success: Coping with the "Burden of 'acting White.'" *Urban Review, 18,* 176–206.

Gans, H. J. (1990). Deconstructing the underclass: The term's danger as a planning concept. *Journal of the American Planning Association, 56,* 271–277.

Giroux, H. A. (1977). The politics of the hidden curriculum. *Independent School, 37,* 42–43.

Giroux, H. A. (1978, December). Developing educational programs: Overcoming the hidden curriculum. *Clearing House,* pp. 148–151.

Giroux, H. A. (1979, December) Toward a new sociology of curriculum. *Educational Leadership,* pp. 248–253.

Katz, M. B. (1986). *In the shadow of the poorhouse: A social history of welfare in America.* New York: Basic Books.

Ladson-Billings, G. (1990). Like lightning in a bottle: Attempting to capture the pedagogical excellence of successful teachers of black students. *Qualitative Studies in Education, 3,* 335–344.

Ladson-Billings, G. (1992). Reading between the lines and beyond the pages: A culturally appropriate approach to literacy teaching. *Theory Into Practice, 31,* 312–320.

Lukas, J. A. (1986). *Common ground: A turbulent decade in the lives of three American families.* New York: Vintage Books.

McCarthy, L. P., & Braffman, E. J. (1985). Creating Victorian Philadelphia: Children reading and writing their world. *Curriculum Inquiry, 15,* 121–151.

Mickelson, R. A. (1984). *Race, class, and gender differences in adolescent academic achievement attitudes and behaviors.* Unpublished doctoral dissertation, University of California, Los Angeles.

Ogbu, J. (1978). *Minority education and caste.* New York: Academic Press.

Ogbu, J. (1988). Variability in minority school performance: A problem in search of an explanation. *Anthropology and Education Quarterly, 18,* 312–335.

Richmond, G. (1989). The future school: Is Lowell pointing us toward a revolution in education? *Phi Delta Kappan, 71,* 232–236.

Schein, E. H. (1988) *Process consultation: Vol. 1. Its role in organizational development.* Reading, MA: Addison Wesley.

School District of Philadelphia. (1989). *Social studies grade three.* Philadelphia: Office of Curriculum.

School District of Philadelphia. (1991). *Superintendent's management information center, 1990-1991.* Philadelphia: School District of Philadelphia, Office of Assessment.

Shor, I. (1980). *Critical teaching and everyday life.* Boston: South End Press.

Sleeter, C. E. (1991). Multicultural education and empowerment. In C. E. Sleeter (Ed.), *Empowerment through multicultural education* (p. 15). Albany: State University of New York Press.

Sleeter, C. E., & Grant, C. A. (1986). Success for all students. *Phi Delta Kappan, 68,* 297–299.

Simon, R., & Dippo, D. (1987). What schools can do: Designing programs for work education that challenge the wisdom of experience. *Boston University Journal of Education, 169*(3), 101–117.

Sticht, T. (1987). *Cast off youth: Policy and training methods from the military experience.* New York: Praeger.

Stewart, T. (1992, May). The search for the organization of tomorrow. *Fortune,* pp. 92–99.

Stewart, T. (1993, December). Welcome to the revolution. *Fortune,* pp. 66–77.

Vygotsky, L. S. (1978). *Mind in society.* Cambridge, MA: Harvard University Press.

Wigginton, E. (1989) Foxfire grows up. *Harvard Educational Review, 59,* 24–49.

Wilson, W. J. (1987). *The truly disadvantaged.* Chicago: University of Chicago Press.

Wilson, W. J. (1990, February) Studying inner city dislocations: The challenge of public agenda research. 1990 Presidential address. *American Sociological Review,* pp. 1–14.

Those who know my teaching know that it has been a wildly uneven road to any success. As any teacher, I am indebted to the wisdom and generosity of others. Credit and thanks must first go to my students, and the many members of the community who supported us. For reasons of confidentiality, all of the above must go unnamed. I am also indebted to the wisdom of my mentors: Scott Tiley, my fifth-grade teacher; Virginia Miller of Bank Street College; Fran Motola of PS 87; Joan Billen, formerly of the Bank Street School for Children; Ewa Pytowska, of the Intercultural Training Resource Center; Barbara Moore Williams of the School District of Philadelphia; the principal of my school. Lastly, I am indebted to the many people who patiently helped me with the preparation of this manuscript: Nancy Brooks, Frederick Erickson, David Kinney, Michael B. Katz, Karl Otto, Ellen Skilton-Sylvester, and my family.

PART II

TALKING BACK

THE POWER OF COUNTER-NARRATIVES
TO CHALLENGE DOMINANT DISCOURSES
IN EDUCATION

TALKING BACK

THE POWER OF COUNTER-NARRATIVES TO CHALLENGE
DOMINANT DISCOURSES IN EDUCATION

For the second part of this volume, we selected articles that complicate and contest existing narratives that limit, marginalize, or render invisible the humanity and potential of certain groups of people. A multicultural perspective requires educators to recognize and cultivate the capital that students bring with them from home. Nevertheless, schools are often subtractive spaces, requiring students to deny and diminish the complexities of their lived experiences, forcing them to position themselves within dominant conceptions of achievement. These articles dispose of commonly accepted deficit-based models, which fail to see the cultural wealth and educational capital within oppressed communities and challenge readers to talk back to the institutions that reify and enact narratives of oppression. These authors invite readers to reenvision what it means to be literate, successful, and intelligent, and thus they ask us to redefine what schooling could be in a society of many cultures.

In her seminal article, "The Silenced Dialogue: Power and Pedagogy in Educating Other People's Children," Lisa D. Delpit (1988) speaks to the skills/process debate in literacy instruction, boldly calling this debate fallacious and the dichotomy false. She uses this debate, however, to position her exploration of the real question—that of "communicating across cultures and addressing the more fundamental issue of power, of whose voice gets to be heard in determining what is best for poor children and children of color" (p. 141). Delpit broadens our understanding of the sociology of education by using the skills/process debate to illustrate two major points: first, that one can acquire power by knowing the rules of the culture of power; and second, that those in power are the least willing to acknowledge its existence. She argues that students should be taught to understand the value of the codes they already possess as well as the dominant codes, as facility with these dominant codes grants power in this country. Teachers, then, are not simply the conveyors of the culture of power but potentially the initiators and mediators of a true dialogue, "seeking out those whose perspectives may differ most" (p. 142) and understanding the power of hearing what they say.

Implicitly taking up questions of power, Signithia Fordham (2010) challenges the notion that we live in a postracial era in "Passin' for Black: Race, Identity, and Bone Memory in Postracial America." She implicates America's hurried march toward racial amnesia in the dismal academic performance "of the descendants of the enslaved and of those who enslaved them" (pp. 165–166). In telling the stories of two high school girls—one Black and one White—Fordham demonstrates the impact of an educational system that simultaneously denies America's entire racial history and still clings to essentialized notions of race. Fordham posits that as the nation's "one remaining obligatory institution," schools are a unique space to deconstruct and critically analyze dominant discourses that keep both educators and students locked in a peculiar performance of racial identities (p. 166). She challenges schools to begin the work of interrogating race as a social category in the United States if we are really to be a postracial society.

Like Fordham, Dorinda J. Carter Andrews (2008) asks us to rethink commonly accepted notions of the relationship between race and education. Andrews'[1] "Achievement as Resistance: The Development of a Critical Race Achievement Ideology Among Black Achievers," examines the achievement ideology of high-performing Black students at a predominantly White high school. In this work, she directly takes on ideas about Black achievement and the often-cited acting White thesis. Andrews finds that these students enact an intentional ideology of resilience, which simultaneously enables them to understand the material and symbolic dimensions of race and to see their race as an integral factor in their achievement. Although Andrews is able to find evidence of this ideology among only a small group of students, she is hopeful that schools can be involved in helping students develop achievement ideologies that affirm their racial identities and incorporate academic achievement as a natural part of those identities.

Unfortunately, the strengths of students' identities are often invalidated by the very institutions that purport to educate them. In Sonia Nieto's (1998) "Fact and Fiction: Stories of Puerto Ricans in U.S. Schools,"[2] we find a beautiful melding of fiction and empirical research that both documents and celebrates the history of an identity that is largely unknown to educators. Her sharp critique of educational research on Puerto Ricans reminds us that we have focused too long on "what Puerto Rican youngsters *did not have, did not know,* and *could not do,* and, as a result, neglected to consider what students *already had, knew,* and *could do*" (p. 221). Nieto transcends the deficit lens that has often been applied to Puerto Rican students and their communities and provides powerful counter-narratives to these portrayals through fiction. Nieto asks us to consider that for every story we have heard of Puerto Rican subjugation and marginalization, there is an equally valid one of Puerto Rican resistance and acceptance.

While Nieto boldly shows us the power of fiction to change the minds of educators, Steven Z. Athanases (1996) reminds us of the power of literature to change the minds of students. In "A Gay-Themed Lesson in an Ethnic Literature Curriculum: Tenth Graders' Responses to 'Dear Anita,'" Athanases portrays a teacher's efforts to open a dialogue on the oppressive conditions that homosexuals face in American society. Noticing that many students are steeped in the homophobic narratives used to deny people their basic human rights, the teacher, Reiko Liu, uses author Brian McNaught's heartfelt letter to Anita Bryant as a counter-narrative in her classroom. Many of the students claim to be against homosexuality on religious grounds; however, McNaught's perspective as an Irish Catholic allows them entrée into a discussion of differences and students start to connect homophobia with other equally virulent forms of oppression. Athanases's research demonstrates the power of changing not just the lenses that we use as researchers but the lenses with which we empower students to see the world.

The articles in this section embody the collective voices of people who have been inspired to talk back to what they see as their misrepresentation in research, literature, discourse, and the world. Although this section is a celebration of strength and resilience within marginalized communities, we ask readers not to deny the material conditions or injustices that many of the people referenced in these articles have suffered. The unilateral denigration of people's cultures, communities, and lives will not lead to a rich multicultural society based on principles of justice, fairness, and equality. We present these counter-narratives as messages of hope and possibility for a pluralistic and open-minded future.

NOTES

1. This article was originally published under the name Dorinda J. Carter.
2. This article by Sonia Nieto was originally published in both English and Spanish as part of the Summer 1998 symposium "Colonialism and Working Class Resistance: Puerto Rican Education in the United States" in the *Harvard Educational Review* (Vol. 68, No. 2, Summer 1998, pp. 133–163). The title of the Spanish-language version of the article is "Realidad y Ficción: Historias de Puertorriqueños en Escuelas Estadounidenses."

THE SILENCED DIALOGUE

POWER AND PEDAGOGY IN EDUCATING
OTHER PEOPLE'S CHILDREN

LISA D. DELPIT

A Black male graduate student who is also a special education teacher in a predominantly Black community is talking about his experiences in predominantly White university classes:

> There comes a moment in every class where we have to discuss "The Black Issue" and what's appropriate education for Black children. I tell you, I'm tired of arguing with those White people, because they won't listen. Well, I don't know if they really don't listen or if they just don't believe you. It seems like if you can't quote Vygotsky or something, then you don't have any validity to speak about your *own* kids. Anyway, I'm not bothering with it anymore, now I'm just in it for a grade.

A Black woman teacher in a multicultural urban elementary school is talking about her experiences in discussions with her predominantly White fellow teachers about how they should organize reading instructions to best serve students of color:

> When you're talking to White people they still want it to be their way. You can try to talk to them and give them examples, but they're so headstrong, they think they know what's best for *everybody*, for *everybody's* children. They won't listen: White folks are going to do what they want to do *anyway*.
>
> It's really hard. They just don't listen well. No, they listen, but they don't *hear*—you know how your mama used to say you listen to the radio, but you *hear* your mother? Well they don't *hear* me.
>
> So I just try to shut them out so I can hold my temper. You can only beat your head against a brick wall for so long before you draw blood. If I try to stop arguing with them I can't help myself from getting angry. Then I end up walking around praying all day "Please Lord, remove the bile I feel for these people so I can sleep tonight." It's funny, but it can become a cancer, a sore.

So, I shut them out. I go back to my own little cubby, my classroom, and I try to teach the way I know will work, no matter what those folk say. And when I get Black kids, I just try to undo the damage they did.

I'm not going to let any man, woman, or child drive me crazy—White folks will try to do that to you if you let them. You just have to stop talking to them, that's what I do. I just keep smiling, but I won't talk to them.

A soft-spoken Native Alaskan woman in her forties is a student in the Education Department of the University of Alaska. One day she storms into a Black professor's office and very uncharacteristically slams the door. She plops down in a chair and, still fuming, says, "Please tell people, just don't help us anymore! I give up. I won't talk to them again!"

And finally, a Black woman principal who is also a doctoral student at a well-known university on the West Coast is talking about her university experiences, particularly about when a professor lectures on issues concerning educating Black children:

If you try to suggest that that's not quite the way it is, they get defensive, then you get defensive, then they'll start reciting research.

I try to give them my experiences, to explain. They just look and nod. The more I try to explain, they just look and nod, just keep looking and nodding. They don't really hear me.

Then, when it's time for class to be over, the professor tells me to come to his office to talk more. So I go. He asks for more examples of what I'm talking about, and he looks and nods while I give them. Then he says that that's just my experiences. It doesn't really apply to most Black people.

It becomes futile because they think they know everything about everybody. What you have to say about your life, your children, doesn't mean anything. They don't really want to hear what you have to say. They wear blinders and earplugs. They only want to go on research they've read that other White people have written.

It just doesn't make any sense to keep talking to them.

Thus was the first half of the title of this text born—"The Silenced Dialogue." One of the tragedies in the field of education is that scenarios such as these are enacted daily around the country. The saddest element is that the individuals that the Black and Native American educators speak of in these statements are seldom aware that the dialogue has been silenced. Most likely, the White educators believe that their colleagues of color did, in the end, agree with their logic. After all, they stopped disagreeing, didn't they?

I have collected these statements since completing a recently published article (Delpit, 1986). In this somewhat autobiographical account, entitled "Skills and Other Dilemmas of a Progressive Black Educator," I discussed my perspective as a product of a skills-oriented approach to writing and as a teacher of process-oriented approaches. I described the estrangement that I and many teachers of color feel from the progressive movement when writing-process advocates dismiss us as too "skills oriented." I ended the article suggesting that it was incumbent upon writing-process advocates—or indeed, advocates of any progressive movement—to enter into dialogue with teachers of color who may not share their enthusiasm about so-called new, liberal, or progressive ideas.

In response to this article, which presented no research data and did not even cite a reference, I received numerous calls and letters from teachers, professors, and even state school personnel from around the country, both Black and White. All of the White respondents, except one, have wished to talk more about the question of skills versus process approaches—to support or reject what they perceive to be my position. On the other hand, *all* of the non-White respondents have spoken passionately on being left out of the dialogue about how best to educate children of color.

How can such complete communication blocks exist when both parties truly believe they have the same aims? How can the bitterness and resentment expressed by the educators of color be drained so that the sores can heal? What can be done?

I believe the answer to these questions lies in ethnographic analysis, that is, in identifying and giving voice to alternative world views. Thus, I will attempt to address the concerns raised by White and Black respondents to my article "Skills and Other Dilemmas" (Delpit, 1986). My charge here is not to determine the best instructional methodology; I believe that the actual practice of good teachers of all colors typically incorporates a range of pedagogical orientations. Rather, I suggest that the differing perspectives on the debate over "skills" versus "process" approaches can lead to an understanding of the alienation and miscommunication, and thereby to an understanding of the "silenced dialogue."

In thinking through these issues, I have found what I believe to be a connecting and complex theme: what I have come to call "the culture of power." There are five aspects of power I would like to propose as given for this presentation:

1. Issues of power are enacted in classrooms.
2. There are codes or rules for participating in power; that is, there is a "culture of power."
3. The rules of the culture of power are a reflection of the rules of the culture of those who have power.
4. If you are not already a participant in the culture of power, being told explicitly the rules of that culture makes acquiring power easier.
5. Those with power are frequently least aware of—or least willing to acknowledge—its existence. Those with less power are often most aware of its existence.

The first three are by now basic tenets in the literature of the sociology of education, but the last two have seldom been addressed. The following discussion will explicate these aspects of power and their relevance to the schism between liberal educational movements and that of non-White, non-middle-class teachers and communities.[1]

1. Issues of power are enacted in classrooms.

These issues include: the power of the teacher over the students; the power of the publishers of textbooks and of the developers of the curriculum to determine the view of the world presented; the power of the state in enforcing compulsory schooling; and the power of an individual or group to determine another's intelligence or "normalcy." Finally, if schooling prepares people for jobs, and the kind of job a person has determines her or his economic status and, therefore, power, then schooling is intimately related to that power.

2. There are codes or rules for participating in power; that is, there is a "culture of power."

The codes or rules I'm speaking of relate to linguistic forms, communicative strategies, and presentation of self; that is, ways of talking, ways of writing, ways of dressing, and ways of interacting.

3. The rules of the culture of power are a reflection of the rules of the culture of those who have power.

This means that success in institutions—schools, workplaces, and so on—is predicated upon acquisition of the culture of those who are in power. Children from middle-class homes tend to do better in school than those from non-middle-class homes because the culture of the school is based on the culture of the upper and middle classes—of those in power. The upper and middle classes send their children to school with all the accoutrements of the culture of power; children from other kinds of families operate within perfectly wonderful and viable cultures but not cultures that carry the codes or rules of power.

4. If you are not already a participant in the culture of power, being told explicitly the rules of that culture makes acquiring power easier.

In my work within and between diverse cultures, I have come to conclude that members of any culture transmit information implicitly to co-members. However, when implicit codes are attempted across cultures, communication frequently breaks down. Each cultural group is left saying, "Why don't those people say what they mean?" as well as, "What's wrong with them, why don't they understand?"

Anyone who has had to enter new cultures, especially to accomplish a specific task, will know of what I speak. When I lived in several Papua New Guinea villages for extended periods to collect data, and when I go to Alaskan villages for work with Alaskan Native communities, I have found it unquestionably easier—psychologically and pragmatically—when some kind soul has directly informed me about such matters as appropriate dress, interactional styles, embedded meanings, and taboo words or actions. I contend that it is much the same for anyone seeking to learn the rules of the culture of power. Unless one has the leisure of a lifetime of "immersion" to learn them, explicit presentation makes learning immeasurably easier.

And now, to the fifth and last premise:

5. Those with power are frequently least aware of—or least willing to acknowledge—its existence. Those with less power are often most aware of its existence.

For many who consider themselves members of liberal or radical camps, acknowledging personal power and admitting participation in the culture of power is distinctly uncomfortable. On the other hand, those who are less powerful in any situation are most likely to recognize the power variable most acutely. My guess is that the White colleagues and instructors of those previously quoted did not perceive themselves to have power over the non-White speakers. However, either by virtue of their position, their numbers, or their access to that particular code of power of calling upon research to validate one's position, the White educators had the authority to establish what was to be considered "truth" regardless of the opinions of the people of color, and the latter were well aware of that fact.

A related phenomenon is that liberals (and here I am using the term "liberal" to refer to those whose beliefs include striving for a society based upon maximum individual freedom and autonomy) seem to act under the assumption that to make any rules or expectations explicit is to act against liberal principles, to limit the freedom and autonomy of those subjected to the explicitness.

I thank Fred Erickson for a comment that led me to look again at a tape by John Gumperz[2] on cultural dissonance in cross-cultural interactions. One of the episodes showed an East Indian interviewing for a job with an all-White committee. The interview was a complete failure, even though several of the interviewers appeared to really want to help the applicant. As the interview rolled steadily downhill, these "helpers" became more and more indirect in their questioning, which exacerbated the problems the applicant had in performing appropriately. Operating from a different cultural perspective, he got fewer and fewer clear clues as to what was expected of him, which ultimately resulted in his failure to secure the position.

I contend that as the applicant showed less and less aptitude for handling the interview, the power differential became ever more evident to the interviewers. The "helpful" interviewers, unwilling to acknowledge themselves as having power over the applicant, became more and more uncomfortable. Their indirectness was an attempt to lessen the power differential and their discomfort by lessening the power-revealing explicitness of their questions and comments.

When acknowledging and expressing power, one tends toward explicitness (as in yelling to your ten-year-old, "Turn that radio down!"). When de-emphasizing power, there is a move toward indirect communication. Therefore, in the interview setting, those who sought to help, to express their egalitarianism with the East Indian applicant, became more and more indirect—and less and less helpful—in their questions and comments.

In literacy instruction, explicitness might be equated with direct instruction. Perhaps the ultimate expression of explicitness and direct instruction in the primary classroom is Distar. This reading program is based on a behaviorist model in which reading is taught through the direct instruction of phonics generalizations and blending. The teacher's role is to maintain the full attention of the group by continuous questioning, eye contact, finger snaps, hand claps, and other gestures, and by eliciting choral responses and initiating some sort of award system.

When the program was introduced, it arrived with a flurry of research data that "proved" that all children—even those who were "culturally deprived"—could learn to read using this method. Soon there was a strong response, first from academics and later from many classroom teachers, stating that the program was terrible. What I find particularly interesting, however, is that the primary issue of the conflict over Distar has not been over its instructional efficacy—usually the students did learn to read—but the expression of explicit power in the classroom. The liberal educators opposed the methods—the direct instruction, the explicit control exhibited by the teacher. As a matter of fact, it was not unusual (even now) to hear of the program spoken of as "fascist."

I am not an advocate of Distar, but I will return to some of the issues that the program—and direct instruction in general—raises in understanding the differences between progressive White educators and educators of color.

To explore those differences, I would like to present several statements typical of those made with the best of intentions by middle-class liberal educators. To the surprise of the speakers, it is not unusual for such content to be met by vocal opposition or stony silence from people of color. My attempt here is to examine the underlying assumptions of both camps.

"I want the same thing for everyone else's children as I want for mine."

To provide schooling for everyone's children that reflects liberal, middle-class values and aspirations is to ensure the maintenance of the status quo, to ensure that power, the culture of power, remains in the hands of those who already have it. Some children come to school with more accoutrements of the culture of power already in place—"cultural capital," as some critical theorists refer to it (for example, Apple, 1979)—some with less. Many liberal educators hold that the primary goal for education is for children to become autonomous, to develop fully who they are in the classroom setting without having arbitrary, outside standards forced upon them. This is a very reasonable goal for people whose children are already participants in the culture of power and who have already internalized its codes.

But parents who don't function within that culture often want something else. It's not that they disagree with the former aim, it's just that they want something more. They want to ensure that the school provides their children with discourse patterns, interactional styles, and spoken and written language codes that will allow them success in the larger society.

It was the lack of attention to this concern that created such a negative outcry in the Black community when well-intentioned White liberal educators introduced "dialect readers." These were seen as a plot to prevent the schools from teaching the linguistic aspects of the culture of power, thus dooming Black children to a permanent outsider caste. As one parent demanded, "My kids know how to be Black—you all teach them how to be successful in the White man's world."

Several Black teachers have said to me recently that as much as they'd like to believe otherwise, they cannot help but conclude that many of the "progressive" educational strategies imposed by liberals upon Black and poor children could only be based on a desire to ensure that the liberals' children get sole access to the dwindling pool of American jobs. Some have added that the liberal educators believe themselves to be operating with good intentions, but that these good intentions are only conscious delusions about their unconscious true motives. One of Black anthropologist John Gwaltney's (1980) informants reflects this perspective with her tongue-in-cheek observation that the biggest difference between Black folks and White folks is that Black folks *know* when they're lying!

Let me try to clarify how this might work in literacy instruction. A few years ago I worked on an analysis of two popular reading programs, Distar and a progressive program that focused on higher-level critical thinking skills. In one of the first lessons of the progressive program, the children are introduced to the names of the letter *m* and *e*. In the same lesson they are then taught the sound made by each of the letters, how to write each of the letters, and that when the two are blended together they produce the word *me*.

As an experienced first-grade teacher, I am convinced that a child needs to be familiar with a significant number of these concepts to be able to assimilate so much new knowledge in one sitting. By contrast, Distar presents the same information in about forty lessons.

I would not argue for the pace of the Distar lessons; such a slow pace would only bore most kids—but what happened in the other lesson is that it merely provided an opportunity for those who already knew the content to exhibit that they knew it, or at most perhaps to build one new concept onto what was already known. This meant that the child who did not come to school already primed with what was to be presented would be labeled as needing "remedial" instruction from day one; indeed, this determination would be made before he or she was ever taught. In fact, Distar was "successful" because it actually *taught* new information to children who had not already acquired it at home.

Although the more progressive system was ideal for some children, for others it was a disaster.

I do not advocate a simplistic "basic skills" approach for children outside of the culture of power. It would be (and has been) tragic to operate as if these children were incapable of critical and higher-order thinking and reasoning. Rather, I suggest that schools must provide these children the content that other families from a different cultural orientation provide at home. This does not mean separating children according to family background, but instead, ensuring that each classroom incorporates strategies appropriate for all the children in its confines.

And I do not advocate that it is the school's job to attempt to change the homes of poor and non-White children to match the homes of those in the culture of power. That may indeed be a form of cultural genocide. I have frequently heard schools call poor parents "uncaring" when parents respond to the school's urging that they change their home life in order to facilitate their children's learning by saying, "But that's the school's job." What the school personnel fail to understand is that if the parents were members of the culture of power and lived by its rules and codes, then they would transmit those codes to their children. In fact, they transmit another culture that children must learn at home in order to survive in their communities.

"Child-centered, whole language, and process approaches are needed in order to allow a democratic state of free, autonomous, empowered adults, and because research has shown that children learn best through these methods."

People of color are, in general, skeptical of research as a determiner of our fates. Academic research has, after all, found us genetically inferior, culturally deprived, and verbally deficient. But beyond that general caveat, and despite my or others' personal preferences, there is little research data supporting the major tenets of process approaches over other forms of literacy instruction, and virtually no evidence that such approaches are more efficacious for children of color (Siddle, 1986).

Although the problem is not necessarily inherent in the method, in some instances adherents of process approaches to writing create situations in which students ultimately find themselves held accountable for knowing a set of rules about which no one has ever directly informed them. Teachers do students no service to suggest, even implicitly, that "product" is not important. In this country, students will be judged on their product regardless of the process they utilized to achieve it. And that product, based as it is on the specific codes of a particular culture, is more readily produced when the directives of how to produce it are made explicit.

If such explicitness is not provided to students, what it feels like to people who are old enough to judge is that there are secrets being kept, that time is being wasted, that the teacher is abdicating his or her duty to teach. A doctoral student in my acquaintance was assigned to a writing class to hone his writing skills. The student was placed in the section led by a White professor who utilized a process approach, consisting primarily of having the students write essays and then assemble into groups to edit each others' papers. That procedure infuriated this particular student. He had many angry encounters with the teacher about what she was doing. In his words:

> I didn't feel she was teaching us anything. She wanted us to correct each others' papers and we were there to learn from her. She didn't teach anything, absolutely nothing.
>
> Maybe they're trying to learn what Black folks knew all the time. We understand how to improvise, how to express ourselves creatively. When I'm in a classroom, I'm not looking for that, I'm looking for structure, the more formal language.
>
> Now my buddy was in [a] Black teacher's class. And that lady was very good. She went through and explained and defined each part of the structure. This [White] teacher didn't get along with that Black teacher. She said that she didn't agree with her methods. But *I* don't think that White teacher *had* any methods.

When I told this gentleman that what the teacher was doing was called a process method of teaching writing, his response was, "Well, at least now I know that she *thought* she was doing *something*. I thought she was just a fool who couldn't teach and didn't want to try."

This sense of being cheated can be so strong that the student may be completely turned off to the educational system. Amanda Branscombe, an accomplished White teacher, recently wrote a letter discussing her work with working-class Black and White students at a community college in Alabama. She had given these students my "Skills and Other Dilemmas" article (Delpit, 1986) to read and discuss, and wrote that her students really understood and identified with what I was saying. To quote her letter:

> One young man said that he had dropped out of high school because he failed the exit exam. He noted that he had then passed the GED without a problem after three weeks of prep. He said that his high school English teacher claimed to use a process approach, but what she really did was hide behind fancy words to give herself permission to do nothing in the classroom.

The students I have spoken of seem to be saying that the teacher has denied them access to herself as the source of knowledge necessary to learn the forms they need to succeed. Again, I tentatively attribute the problem to teachers' resistance to exhibiting power in the classroom. Somehow, to exhibit one's personal power as expert source is viewed as disempowering one's students.

Two qualifiers are necessary, however. The teacher cannot be the only expert in the classroom. To deny students their own expert knowledge is to disempower them. Amanda Branscombe, when she was working with Black high school students classified as "slow learners," had the students analyze rap songs to discover their underlying patterns. The students became the experts in explaining to the teacher the rules for creating a new rap song. The teacher then used the patterns the students identified as a base to begin an explanation of the structure of grammar, and then of Shakespeare's plays. Both student and teacher are experts at what they know best.

The second qualifier is that merely adopting direct instruction is not the answer. Actual writing for real audiences and real purposes is a vital element in helping students to understand that they have an important voice in their own learning processes. Siddle (1988) examines the results of various kinds of interventions in a primarily process-oriented writing class for Black students. Based on readers' blind assessments, she found that the intervention that produced the most positive changes in the students' writing was a "mini-lesson" consisting of direct instruction about some standard writing convention. But what produced the *second* highest number of positive changes was a subsequent student-centered conference with the teacher. (Peer conferencing in this group of Black students who were not members of the culture of power produced the least number of changes in students' writing. However, the classroom teacher maintained—and I concur—that such activities are necessary to introduce the elements of "real audience" into the task, along with more teacher-directed strategies.)

"It's really a shame but she (that Black teacher upstairs) seems to be so authoritarian, so focused on skills and so teacher directed. Those poor kids never seem to be allowed to really express their creativity. (And she even yells at them.)"

This statement directly concerns the display of power and authority in the classroom. One way to understand the difference in perspective between Black teachers and their progressive colleagues on this issue is to explore culturally influenced oral interactions.

In *Ways With Words,* Shirley Brice Heath (1983) quotes the verbal directives given by the middle-class "townspeople" teachers (p. 280):

"Is this where the scissors belong?"

"You want to do your best work today."

By contrast, many Black teachers are more likely to say:

"Put those scissors on that shelf."

"Put your name on the papers and make sure to get the right answer for each question."

Is one oral style more authoritarian than another?

Other researchers have identified differences in middle-class and working-class speech to children. Snow et al. (1976), for example, report that working-class mothers use more directives to their children than do middle- and upper-class parents. Middle-class parents are likely to give the directive to a child to take his bath as, "Isn't it time for your bath?" Even though the utterance is couched as a question, both child and adult understand it as a directive. The child may respond with "Aw Mom, can't I wait until . . . ," but whether or not negotiation is attempted, both conversants understand the intent of the utterance.

By contrast, a Black mother, in whose house I was recently a guest, said to her eight-year-old son, "Boy, get your rusty behind in that bathtub." Now I happen to know that this woman loves her son as much as any mother, but she would never have posed the directive to her son to take a bath in the form of a question. Were she to ask, "Would you like to take your bath now?" she would not have been issuing a directive but offering a true alternative. Consequently, as Heath suggests, upon entering school the child from such a family may not understand the indirect statement of the teacher as a direct command. Both White and Black working-class children in the communities Heath studied "had difficulty interpreting these indirect requests for adherence to an unstated set of rules" (p. 280).

But those veiled commands are commands nonetheless, representing true power, and with true consequences for disobedience. If veiled commands are ignored, the child will be labeled a behavior problem and possibly officially classified as behavior disordered. In other words, the attempt by the teacher to reduce an exhibition of power by expressing herself in indirect terms may remove the very explicitness that the child needs to understand the rules of the new classroom culture.

A Black elementary school principal in Fairbanks, Alaska, reported to me that she has a lot of difficulty with Black children who are placed in some White teachers' classrooms. The teachers often send the children to the office for disobeying teacher directives. Their parents are frequently called in for conferences. The parents' response to the teacher is usually the same: "They do what I say; if you just *tell* them what to do, they'll do it. I tell them at home that they have to listen to what you say." And so, does not the power still exist? Its veiled nature only makes it more difficult for some children to respond appropriately, but that in no way mitigates its existence.

I don't mean to imply, however, that the only time the Black child disobeys the teacher is when he or she misunderstands the request for certain behavior. There are other factors that may produce such behavior. Black children expect an authority figure to act with authority. When the teacher instead acts as a "chum," the message sent is that this adult has no authority, and the children react accordingly. One reason this is so is that Black people often view issues of power and authority differently than people from mainstream middle-class backgrounds.[3] Many people of color expect authority to be earned by personal efforts and exhibited by personal characteristics. In other words, "the authoritative person gets to be a teacher because she is authoritative." Some members of middle-class cultures, by contrast, expect one to achieve authority by the acquisition of an authoritative role. That is, "the teacher is the authority because she is the teacher."

In the first instance, because authority is earned, the teacher must consistently prove the characteristics that give her authority. These characteristics may vary across cultures, but in the Black community they tend to cluster around several abilities. The authoritative teacher can control the class through exhibition of personal power; establishes meaningful interpersonal relationships that garner student respect; exhibits a strong belief that all students can learn; establishes a standard of achievement and "pushes" the students to achieve that standard; and holds the attention of the students by incorporating interactional features of Black communicative style in his or her teaching.

By contrast, the teacher whose authority is vested in the role has many more options of behavior at her disposal. For instance, she does not need to express any sense of personal power because her authority does not come from anything she herself does or says. Hence, the power she actually holds may be veiled in such questions/commands as "Would you like to sit down now?" If the children in her class understand authority as she does, it is mutually agreed upon that they are to obey her no matter how indirect, soft-spoken, or unassuming she may be. Her indirectness and soft-spokenness may indeed be, as I suggested earlier, an attempt to reduce the implication of overt power in order to establish a more egalitarian and non-authoritarian classroom atmosphere.

If the children operate under another notion of authority, however, then there is trouble. The Black child may perceive the middle-class teacher as weak, ineffectual, and incapable of taking on the role of being the teacher; therefore, there is no need to follow her directives. In her dissertation, Michelle Foster (1987) quotes one young Black man describing such a teacher:

> She is boring, bo::ring.* She could do something creative. Instead she just stands there. She can't control the class, doesn't know how to control the class. She asked me what she was doing wrong. I told her she just stands there like she's meditating. I told her she could be meditating for all I know. She says that we're supposed to know what to do. I told her I don't know nothin' unless she tells me. She just can't control the class. I hope we don't have her next semester. (pp. 67–68)

But of course the teacher may not view the problem as residing in herself but in the student, and the child may once again become the behavior-disordered Black boy in special education.

What characteristics do Black students attribute to the good teacher? Again, Foster's dissertation provides a quotation that supports my experience with Black students. A young Black man is discussing a former teacher with a group of friends:

> We had fu::n in her class, but she was mean. I can remember she used to say, "Tell me what's in the story, Wayne." She pushed, she used to get on me and push me to know. She made us learn. We had to get in the books. There was this

* *Editor's note:* The colons [::] refer to elongated speech

tall guy and he tried to take her on, but she was in charge of that class and she didn't let anyone run her. I still have this book we used in her class. It's a bunch of stories in it. I just read one on Coca-Cola again the other day (p. 68).

To clarify, this student was proud of the teacher's "meanness," an attribute he seemed to describe as the ability to run the class and pushing and expecting students to learn. Now, does the liberal perspective of the negatively authoritarian Black teacher really hold up? I suggest that although all "explicit" Black teachers are not also good teachers, there are different attitudes in different cultural groups about which characteristics make for a good teacher. Thus, it is impossible to create a model for the good teacher without taking issues of culture and community context into account.

And now to the final comment I present for examination:

"Children have the right to their own language, their own culture. We must fight cultural hegemony and fight the system by insisting that children be allowed to express themselves in their own language style. It is not they, the children, who must change, but the schools. To push children to do anything else is repressive and reactionary."

A statement such as this originally inspired me to write the "Skills and Other Dilemmas" article. It was first written as a letter to a colleague in response to a situation that had developed in our department. I was teaching a senior-level teacher education course. Students were asked to prepare a written autobiographical document for the class that would also be shared with their placement school prior to their student teaching.

One student, a talented young Native American woman, submitted a paper in which the ideas were lost because of technical problems—from spelling to sentence structure to paragraph structure. Removing her name, I duplicated the paper for a discussion with some faculty members. I had hoped to initiate a discussion about what we could do to ensure that our students did not reach the senior level without getting assistance in technical writing skills when they needed them.

I was amazed at the response. Some faculty implied that the student should never have been allowed into the teacher education program. Others, some of the more progressive minded, suggested that I was attempting to function as gatekeeper by raising the issue and had internalized repressive and disempowering forces of the power elite to suggest that something was wrong with a Native American student just because she had another style of writing. With few exceptions, I found myself alone in arguing against both camps.

No, this student should not have been denied entry to the program. To deny her entry under the notion of upholding standards is to blame the victim for the crime. We cannot justifiably enlist exclusionary standards when the reason this student lacked the skills demanded was poor teaching at best and institutionalized racism at worst.

However, to bring this student into the program and pass her through without attending to obvious deficits in the codes needed for her to function effectively as a teacher is equally criminal—for though we may assuage our own consciences for not participating in victim blaming, she will surely be accused and convicted as soon as she leaves the university. As Native Alaskans were quick to tell me, and as I understood through my own experience in the Black community, not only would she not be hired as a teacher, but those who did not hire her would make the (false) assumption that the university was putting out only incompetent Natives and that they should stop looking seriously at any Native applicants. A White applicant who exhibits problems is an individual with problems. A person of color who exhibits problems immediately becomes a representative of her cultural group.

No, either stance is criminal. The answer is to *accept* students but also to take responsibility to *teach* them. I decided to talk to the student and found out she had recognized that she needed some assistance in the technical aspects of writing soon after she entered the university as a freshman. She had gone to various members of the education faculty and received the same two kinds of responses I met with four years later: faculty members told her either that she should not even attempt to be a teacher, or that it didn't matter and that she shouldn't worry about such trivial issues. In her desperation, she had found a helpful professor in the English Department, but he left the university when she was in her sophomore year.

We sat down together, worked out a plan for attending to specific areas of writing competence, and set up regular meetings. I stressed to her the need to use her own learning process as insight into how best to teach her future students those "skills" that her own schooling had failed to teach her. I gave her some explicit rules to follow in some areas; for others, we devised various kinds of journals that, along with readings about the structure of the language, allowed her to find her own insights into how the language worked. All that happened two years ago, and the young woman is now successfully teaching. What the experience led me to understand is that pretending that gatekeeping points don't exist is to ensure that many students will not pass through them.

Now you may have inferred that I believe that because there is a culture of power, everyone should learn the codes to participate in it, and that is how the world should be. Actually, nothing could be further from the truth. I believe in a diversity of style, and I believe the world will be diminished if cultural diversity is ever obliterated. Further, I believe strongly, as do my liberal colleagues, that each cultural group should have the right to maintain its own language style. When I speak, therefore, of the culture of power, I don't speak of how I wish things to be but of how they are.

I further believe that to act as if power does not exist is to ensure that the power status quo remains the same. To imply to children or adults (but of course the adults won't believe you anyway) that it doesn't matter how you talk or how you write is to ensure their ultimate failure. I prefer to be honest with my students. Tell them that their language and cultural style is unique and wonderful but that there is a political power game that is also being played, and if they want to be in on that game there are certain games that they too must play.

But don't think that I let the onus of change rest entirely with the students. I am also involved in political work both inside and outside of the educational system, and that political work demands that I place myself to influence as many gatekeeping points as possible. And it is there that I agitate for change— pushing gatekeepers to open their doors to a variety of styles and codes. What I'm saying, however, is that I do not believe that political change toward diversity can be effected from the bottom up, as do some of my colleagues. They seem to believe that if we accept and encourage diversity within classrooms of children, then diversity will automatically be accepted at gatekeeping points.

I believe that will never happen. What will happen is that the students who reach the gatekeeping points—like Amanda Branscombe's student who dropped out of high school because he failed his exit exam—will understand that they have been lied to and will react accordingly. No, I am certain that if we are truly to effect societal change, we cannot do so from the bottom up, but we must push and agitate from the top down. And in the meantime, we must take the responsibility to *teach*, to provide for students who do not already possess them, the additional codes of power.[4]

But I also do not believe that we should teach students to passively adopt an alternate code. They must be encouraged to understand the value of the code they already possess as well as to understand the power realities in this country. Otherwise they will be unable to work to change these realities. And how does one do that?

Martha Demientieff, a masterly Native Alaskan teacher of Athabaskan Indian students, tells me that her students, who live in a small, isolated, rural village of less than two hundred people, are not aware that there are different codes of English. She takes their writing and analyzes it for features of what has been referred to by Alaskan linguists as "Village English," and then covers half a bulletin board with words or phrases from the students' writing, which she labels "Our Heritage Language." On the other half of the bulletin board she puts the equivalent statements in "standard English," which she labels "Formal English."

She and the students spend a long time on the "Heritage English" section, savoring the words, discussing the nuances. She tells the students, "That's the way we say things. Doesn't it feel good? Isn't it the absolute best way of getting that idea across?" Then she turns to the other side of the board. She tells the students that there are people, not like those in their village, who judge others by the way they talk or write.

> We listen to the way people talk, not to judge them, but to tell what part of the river they come from. These other people are not like that. They think every-

body needs to talk like them. Unlike us, they have a hard time hearing what people say if they don't talk exactly like them. Their way of talking and writing is called "Formal English."

We have to feel a little sorry for them because they have only one way to talk. We're going to learn two ways to say things. Isn't that better? One way will be our Heritage way. The other will be Formal English. Then, when we go to get jobs, we'll be able to talk like those people who only know and can only really listen to one way. Maybe after we get the jobs we can help them to learn how it feels to have another language, like ours, that feels so good. We'll talk like them when we have to, but we'll always know our way is best.

Martha then does all sorts of activities with the notions of Formal and Heritage or informal English. She tells the students,

In the village, everyone speaks informally most of the time unless there's a pot-latch or something. You don't think about it, you don't worry about following any rules—it's sort of like how you eat food at a picnic—nobody pays attention to whether you use your fingers or a fork, and it feels so good. Now, Formal English is more like a formal dinner. There are rules to follow about where the knife and fork belong, about where people sit, about how you eat. That can be really nice, too, because it's nice to dress up sometimes.

The students then prepare a formal dinner in the class, for which they dress up and set a big table with fancy tablecloths, china, and silverware. They speak only Formal English at this meal. Then they prepare a picnic where only informal English is allowed.

She also contrasts the "wordy" academic way of saying things with the metaphoric style of Athabaskan. The students discuss how book language always uses more words, but in Heritage language, the shorter way of saying something is always better. Students then write papers in the academic way, discussing with Martha and with each other whether they believe they've said enough to sound like a book. Next, they take those papers and try to reduce the meaning to a few sentences. Finally, students further reduce the message to a "saying" brief enough to go on the front of a T-shirt, and the sayings are put on little paper T-shirts that the students cut out and hang throughout the room. Sometimes the students reduce other authors' wordy texts to their essential meanings as well.

The following transcript provides another example. It is from a conversation between a Black teacher and a Southern Black high school student named Joey, who is a speaker of Black English. The teacher believes it very important to discuss openly and honestly the issues of language diversity and power. She has begun the discussion by giving the student a children's book written in Black English to read.

Teacher: What do you think about that book?

Joey: I think it's nice.

Teacher: Why?

Joey: I don't know. It just told about a Black family, that's all.

Teacher: Was it difficult to read?

Joey: No.

Teacher: Was the text different from what you have seen in other books?

Joey: Yeah. The writing was.

Teacher: How?

Joey: It use more of a southern-like accent in this book.

Teacher: Uhm-hmm. Do you think that's good or bad?

Joey: Well, uh, I don't think it's good for people down this a way, cause that's the way they grow up talking anyway. They ought to get the right way to talk.

Teacher: Oh. So you think it's wrong to talk like that?

Joey: Well . . . *[Laughs.]*

Teacher: Hard question, huh?

Joey: Uhm-hmm, that's a hard question. But I think they shouldn't make books like that.

Teacher: Why?

Joey: Because they not using the right way to talk and in school they take off for that and li'l chirren grow up talking like that and reading like that so they might think that's right and all the time they getting bad grades in school, talking like that and writing like that.

Teacher: Do you think they should be getting bad grades for talking like that?

Joey: *[Pauses, answers very slowly.]* No . . . No.

Teacher: So you don't think that it matters whether you talk one way or another?

Joey: No, not long as you understood.

Teacher: Uhm-hmm. Well, that's a hard question for me to answer, too. It's ah, that's a question that's come up in a lot of schools now as to whether they should correct children who speak the way we speak all the time. Cause when we're talking to each other we talk like that even though we might not talk like that when we get into other situations, and who's to say whether it's—

Joey: *[Interrupting.]* Right or wrong.

Teacher: Yeah.

Joey: Maybe they ought to come up with another kind of . . . maybe Black English or something. A course in Black English. Maybe Black folks would be good in that cause people talk, I mean Black people talk like that, so . . . but I guess there's a right way and wrong way to talk, you know, not regarding what race. I don't know.

139

Teacher: But who decided what's right or wrong?

Joey: Well that's true . . . I guess White people did.

[Laughter. End of tape.]

Notice how throughout the conversation Joey's consciousness has been raised by thinking about codes of language. This teacher further advocates having students interview various personnel officers in actual workplaces about their attitudes toward divergent styles in oral and written language. Students begin to understand how arbitrary language standards are, but also how politically charged they are. They compare various pieces written in different styles, discuss the impact of different styles on the message by making translations and back translations across styles, and discuss the history, apparent purpose, and contextual appropriateness of each of the technical writing rules presented by their teacher. *And* they practice writing different forms to different audiences based on rules appropriate for each audience. Such a program not only "teaches" standard linguistic forms, but also explores aspects of power as exhibited through linguistic forms.

Tony Burgess, in a study of secondary writing in England by Britton, Burgess, Martin, McLeod, and Rosen (1975/1977), suggests that we should not teach "iron conventions . . . imposed without rationale or grounding in communicative intent, . . . [but] critical and ultimately cultural awareness" (p. 54). Courtney Cazden (1987) calls for a two-pronged approach:

1. Continuous opportunities for writers to participate in some authentic bit of the unending conversation . . . thereby becoming part of a vital community of talkers and writers in a particular domain, and
2. Periodic, temporary focus on conventions of form, taught as cultural conventions expected in a particular community. (p. 20)

Just so that there is no confusion about what Cazden means by a focus on conventions of form, or about what I mean by "skills," let me stress that neither of us is speaking of page after page of "skill sheets" creating compound words or identifying nouns and adverbs, but rather about helping students gain a useful knowledge of the conventions of print while engaging in real and useful communicative activities. Kay Rowe Grubis, a junior high school teacher in a multicultural school, makes lists of certain technical rules for her eighth graders' review and then gives them papers from a third grader to "correct." The students not only have to correct other students' work, but also tell them why they have changed or questioned aspects of the writing.

A village teacher, Howard Cloud, teaches his high school students the conventions of formal letter writing and the formulation of careful questions in the context of issues surrounding the amendment of the Alaska Land Claims Settlement Act. Native Alaskan leaders hold differing views on this issue, critical to the future of local sovereignty and land rights. The students compose letters to leaders who reside in different areas of the state seeking their perspectives, set up audioconference calls for interview/debate sessions, and, finally, develop a videotape to present the differing views.

To summarize, I suggest that students must be *taught* the codes needed to participate fully in the mainstream of American life, not by being forced to attend to hollow, inane, decontextualized subskills, but rather within the context of meaningful communicative endeavors; that they must be allowed the resource of the teacher's expert knowledge, while being helped to acknowledge their own "expertness" as well; and that even while students are assisted in learning the culture of power, they must also be helped to learn about the arbitrariness of those codes and about the power relationships they represent.

I am also suggesting that appropriate education for poor children and children of color can only be devised in consultation with adults who share their culture. Black parents, teachers of color, and members of poor communities must be allowed to participate fully in the discussion of what kind of instruction is in their children's best interest. Good liberal intentions are not enough. In an insightful study entitled "Racism without Racists: Institutional Racism in Urban Schools," Massey, Scott, and Dornbusch (1975) found that under the pressures of teaching, and with all intentions of "being nice," teachers had essentially stopped attempting to teach Black children. In their words: "We have shown that oppression can arise out of warmth, friendliness, and concern. Paternalism and a lack of challenging standards are creating a distorted system of evaluation in the schools" (p. 10). Educators must open themselves to, and allow themselves to be affected by, these alternative voices.

In conclusion, I am proposing a resolution for the skills/process debate. In short, the debate is fallacious; the dichotomy is false. The issue is really an illusion created initially not by teachers but by academics whose world view demands the creation of categorical divisions—not for the purpose of better teaching, but for the goal of easier analysis. As I have been reminded by many teachers since the publication of my article, those who are most skillful at educating Black and poor children do not allow themselves to be placed in "skills" or "process" boxes. They understand the need for both approaches, the need to help students to establish their own voices, but to coach those voices to produce notes that will be heard clearly in the larger society.

The dilemma is not really in the debate over instructional methodology, but rather in communicating across cultures and in addressing the more fundamental issue of power, of whose voice gets to be heard in determining what is best for poor children and children of color. Will Black teachers and parents continue to be silenced by the very forces that claim to "give voice" to our children? Such an outcome would be tragic, for both groups truly have something to say to one another. As a result of careful listening to alternative points of view, I have myself come to a viable synthesis of perspectives. But both sides do need to be able to listen, and I contend that it is those with the most power, those in the majority, who must take the greater responsibility for initiating the process.

To do so takes a very special kind of listening, listening that requires not only open eyes and ears, but open hearts and minds. We do not really see through our eyes or hear through our ears, but through our beliefs. To put our beliefs on hold is to cease to exist as ourselves for a moment—and that is not easy. It is painful as well, because it means turning yourself inside out, giving up your own sense of who you are, and being willing to see yourself in the unflattering light of another's angry gaze. It is not easy, but it is the only way to learn what it might feel like to be someone else and the only way to start the dialogue.

There are several guidelines. We must keep the perspective that people are experts on their own lives. There are certainly aspects of the outside world of which they may not be aware, but they can be the only authentic chroniclers of their own experience. We must not be too quick to deny their interpretations, or accuse them of "false consciousness." We must believe that people are rational beings, and therefore always act rationally. We may not understand their rationales, but that in no way militates against the existence of these rationales or reduces our responsibility to attempt to apprehend them. And finally, we must learn to be vulnerable enough to allow our world to turn upside down in order to allow the realities of others to edge themselves into our consciousness. In other words, we must become ethnographers in the true sense.

Teachers are in an ideal position to play this role, to attempt to get all of the issues on the table in order to initiate true dialogue. This can only be done, however, by seeking out those whose perspectives may differ most, by learning to give their words complete attention, by understanding one's own power, even if that power stems merely from being in the majority, by being unafraid to raise questions about discrimination and voicelessness with people of color, and to listen, no, to hear what they say. I suggest that the results of such interactions may be the most powerful and empowering coalescence yet seen in the educational realm—for *all* teachers and for *all* the students they teach.

NOTES

1. Such a discussion, limited as it is by space constraints, must treat the intersection of class and race somewhat simplistically. For the sake of clarity, however, let me define a few terms: "Black" is used herein to refer to those who share some or all aspects of "core black culture" (Gwaltney, 1980, p. xxiii), that is, the mainstream of Black America—neither those who have entered the ranks of the bourgeoisie nor those who are participants in the disenfranchised underworld. "Middle-class" is used broadly to refer to the predominantly White American "mainstream." There are, of course, non-White people who also fit into this category; at issue is their cultural identification, not necessarily the color of their skin. (I must add that there are other non-White people, as well as poor White people, who have indicated to me that their perspectives are similar to those attributed herein to Black people.)

2. *Multicultural Britain: "Crosstalk,"* National Centre of Industrial Language Training, Commission for Racial Equality, London, England, John Twitchin, Producer.

3. I would like to thank Michelle Foster, who is presently planning a more in-depth treatment of the subject, for her astute clarification of the idea.

4. Bernstein (1975) makes a similar point when he proposes that different educational frames cannot be successfully institutionalized in the lower levels of education until there are fundamental changes at the postsecondary levels.

REFERENCES

Apple, M. W. (1979). *Ideology and curriculum.* Boston: Routledge & Kegan Paul.

Bernstein, B. (1975). Class and pedagogies: Visible and invisible. In B. Bernstein, *Class, codes, and control* (Vol. 3). Boston: Routledge & Kegan Paul.

Britton, J., Burgess, T., Martin, N., McLeod, A., & Rosen, H. (1975/1977). *The development of writing abilities.* London: Macmillan Education for the Schools Council, and Urbana, IL: National Council of Teachers of English.

Cazden, C. (1987, January). *The myth of autonomous text.* Paper presented at the Third International Conference on Thinking, Hawaii.

Delpit, L. D. (1986). Skills and other dilemmas of a progressive Black educator. *Harvard Educational Review, 56,* (4), 379–385.

Foster, M. (1987). *It's cookin' now: An ethnographic study of the teaching style of a successful Black teacher in an urban community college.* Unpublished doctoral dissertation, Harvard University.

Gwaltney, J. (1980). *Drylongso.* New York: Vintage Books.

Heath, S. B. (1983). *Ways with words.* Cambridge: Cambridge University Press.

Massey, G. C., Scott, M. V., & Dornbusch, S. M. (1975). Racism without racists: Institutional racism in urban schools. *Black Scholar, 7*(3), 2–11.

Siddle, E. V. (1986). *A critical assessment of the natural process approach to teaching writing.* Unpublished qualifying paper, Harvard University.

Siddle, E. V. (1988). *The effect of intervention strategies on the revisions ninth graders make in a narrative essay.* Unpublished doctoral dissertation, Harvard University.

Snow, C. E., Arlman-Rup, A., Hassing, Y., Josbe, J., Joosten, J., & Vorster, J. (1976). Mother's speech in three social classes. *Journal of Psycholinguistic Research, 5,* 1–20.

I take full responsibility for all that appears herein; however, aside from those mentioned by name in this text, I would like to thank all of the educators and students around the country who have been so willing to contribute their perspectives to the formulation of these ideas, especially Susan Jones, Catherine Blunt, Dee Stickman, Sandra Gamble, Willard Taylor, Mickey Monteiro, Denise Burden, Evelyn Higbee, Joseph Delpit Jr., Valerie Montoya, Richard Cohen, and Mary Denise Thompson.

PASSIN' FOR BLACK

RACE, IDENTITY, AND BONE MEMORY
IN POSTRACIAL AMERICA

SIGNITHIA FORDHAM

Barack and Michelle Obama, guilty. Barbara Jordan, guilty. Cornel West, guilty. Michael Jordan, guilty. Dorothy Gilliam, guilty. Lani Guinier, guilty. Walter White, guilty. Patricia and Vanessa Williams, both guilty. Halle Berry, guilty. Fannie Lou Hamer, guilty. Faye Harrison, guilty. Oprah Winfrey, guilty. Anatole and Bliss Broyard, both guilty. Eartha Kitt, guilty. Michael Eric Dyson, guilty. Claude Steele, guilty. Shelby Steele, not guilty. Clarence Thomas, not guilty. Armstrong Williams, not guilty. Roy Innis, not guilty. Ward Connelly, not guilty. John McWhorter, not guilty.

What makes all of these persons eligible for a common status? Their skin color, which varies along a spectrum from midnight to daylight, is certainly not an adequate explanation. So what is?

All of the individuals listed as guilty are *passin' for Black*—embracing a socially constructed identity as if it were inherent in the body or based on genetic inheritance—despite the lightness or darkness of their skin. The few who are innocent of this masquerade are not culturally Black, even though they do not differ in apparent ancestry from those who identify themselves as culturally Black.[1] Many of those who are socially defined as Black, as well as those who acknowledge their biracial or multiracial identity, have a parent or grandparent who was socially defined as White, and some of them could have passed for White themselves. Indeed, Anatole Broyard did, until his daughter uncovered his origins. Passin' for White is an open secret. Passin' for Black is strange, yet so familiar as to be taken for granted.

Slavery was a profoundly sexual institution (Hine, 1993). In a striking departure from the patrilineal rules of the dominant Anglo-American kinship system, every enslaved mother's child was enslaved, regardless of who the father might have been. And, by a perverse logic, all slaves carried the stigma of Blackness—as do their descendents today.

In "postracial" America, passin' for Black means that I, like most other Americans of African ancestry, am a pallbearer of my enslaved female ancestors' pain and shame, the living embodiment of the cruel sexual violation they endured. Their pain and anguish awaken me from my dreams of an authentic postracial America. Anxious and uncertain, I am incapacitated by memories, terrified and immobilized. I want to know what it is about this historical era that makes America eligible for the designation "postracial."

MEMORY

I sit at America's diversity table trying desperately to channel this country's romanticized notion of immigration: peoples from all over the world choosing to come to this land of liberty and unlimited opportunities.

I close my eyes and try to envision my great-grandfather, twelve generations removed, disembarking eagerly, luggage and letters of credit in hand, at Charles Town or some other colonial American port, a free person not even subject to the scrutiny later immigrants endured at Ellis Island.[2] The image does not work. Instead, I see him held captive in the bowels of a ship, with men standing over him holding whips. I see his son running desperately from a mob in the dead of night, dogs barking furiously in pursuit of his scent, men on horseback with lighted torches trying to catch him before he reaches the Canadian border. His self-deportation efforts end in his recapture. He is branded or has a limb amputated; he is forced to live in a country where he is not a citizen. Property, even in human form, is not free to decide where it will live, how it will labor, or when it is worn out and discarded.

I imagine his grandson as depicted in the movie *Rosewood* (Singleton & Poirier, 1997), sitting down to Thanksgiving dinner in a middle-class home with his family and friends.[3] I see an angry White mob gathering outside the house preparing to destroy everyone inside and the entire Black community known as Rosewood. Why? One self-appointed vigilante justifies the planned atrocity by observing that the owner of the home has a piano and he does not. I try not to hear the lashes of the whip as he is hauled away and hung; I try to disremember the stench of his burnt flesh hanging from a tree.[4]

I switch lineages, channeling my great-grandmother to the twelfth power. The sharp-edged image that emerges dispels the cloudy tint of pride in ancestry that surrounds European Americans' colonial genealogies and the sentimental nostalgia that shades sepia photographs of arrivals at Ellis Island. What I see is my female ancestors' pain: their naked bodies at auctions violently inspected by prospective buyers, their bloated breasts leaking the milk intended for the children they birthed or recently nursed. I hear their unanswered screams for protection as their uteri are violently, routinely possessed, like Pauli Murray's (1978) grandmother, Harriet, in *Proud Shoes*. I sense their love for children, whose paternity they may or may not have known, but whom they bore and nurtured for as long as they were allowed, seared in their hearts and hovering in their dark brown eyes. I watch in horror as they are forced to leave their families in order to populate the Cotton Kingdom and breed another enslaved population, making the pigment in their skin—"high yella to jet Black"—the boundaryless marker of all our kin.

Given this sordid history and racialized pain, why am I and many other descendants of America's only enslaved population committed to passin' for Black? We are compelled to disremember our traumatic past in order to authenticate a postracial America. Why is it that we cannot acknowledge the complex, multiracial history of so many Black Americans and the complicity of White Americans in our lineage? Why are we acceptable only if we are willing to erase our social and cultural history? For many Black Americans, this act of disremembering is often impossible, since today race is constructed concurrently as a biological reality and as a cultural performance.

Because I am an anthropologist of African descent, my sensibilities have been shaped both by my disciplinary training and by the bone memory of my ancestors' enslavement. I embody their pain; even before conscious memory, I know their suffering. Their involuntary migration to America was followed by their involuntary detention. Citizens of nowhere, they sought to escape "the peculiar institution" and the country that upheld its legality, joining what Frederick Douglass called "a dark train going out from the land, as if fleeing from death" (Blassingame, 1982, p. 245). The Underground Railroad began on the margins of Southern plantations and waterways, passed from house to wagon to barn to ship, conducted by Black as well as White, women as well as men. It paused briefly in the supposedly free states, and continued on toward a destination beyond these borders, often past death itself. Yet today, we—their descendents—are here.

Are my enslaved ancestors my kin? What about their owners, who are also among my progenitors? If we define kinship not in biological terms, not as a matter of DNA lineages reconstructed retrospectively by scientists, but in social terms, as a matter of recognition, relatedness, and reciprocity, they are not. According to Hortense Spillers (1987), African-descended people whose ancestors were enslaved are "unrelated both to their begetters and to their owners . . . [and] find themselves in the situation of being orphans" (p. 74). Spillers cites the work of Claude Meillassoux: "The offspring of the [enslaved] female does not 'belong' to the Mother, nor is s/he 'related' to the 'owner,' though the latter possesses it, and in the American context, often fathered it, and, as often, without whatever benefit of patrimony" (p. 74). Within the dominant society's legal definition of kinship, the enslaved offspring of White patriarchs were simultaneously owned and disowned. African Americans' sense of connection to their African foremothers was disallowed. Those ties were often sundered by White masters and mistresses who sold "uppity" adults and "offensive"—that is, biracial—children to slave traders, just as kinship ties had previously been sundered by captivity and the Middle Passage.

My historically determined inability to identify my biological kin has placed me in the position of being compelled to disremember. My ancestors, faced with a similar dilemma under much more wrenching immediate circumstances, opted for a fictive kinship system (Fordham, 1996). What anthropologists call fictive kinship is an attempt to knit together what has been lost and broken, a survival strategy and a mode of resistance. Their grounded philosophy was simply this: if African ancestry courses through an American's veins, she is kin; since she is kin, reciprocal expectations and obligations apply.

This confusing complexity is implicated in my role as my ancestors' pallbearer. I am ambivalent about bearing this burden at an endless funeral: I want and do not want to be the living embodiment of my ancestors. I am honored that I have been given the opportunity to try to redeem their desecrated memory, but I am afraid that I am not up to the task, that I am not as strong as they were, even though what I have to endure is less devastating.

In this ostensibly postracial era, I try to locate spaces, or even one place, where I can shed the pall and find public recognition of my ancestors' violated but ever-renewed humanity. As a descendant of those who could not escape enslavement, I am a lost and orphaned daughter, meandering in a blindingly impenetrable fog. Like them, I have no viable way of belonging where I am. Will I find my humanity in the arbitrary, unpredictable severance of my kith and kin's connections to each other, embodied most powerfully in my great-great-great-grandmother's tears and fears, in her sense of connection with Africa and Africans, ancestry and community that has been handed down to her descendants only as longing? How is my humanity to be affirmed when I cannot look into the human faces on two huge continents, Africa and North America, and find my cousins? My White cousins several times removed do not even know of my existence, as our shared lineage was officially denied. How can we meet and acknowledge each other? I am a guest in everybody's house. No place belongs to me; no one recognizes me. I am indelibly homeless and kinless.

I search the ebony eyes and the chocolate-to-vanilla skin of strangers on two continents. As I scan the faces of people gathered in culturally specific institutions, I want to know: Are you my cousin? If you are, what American state or African country are you from? I look into the blue eyes and the paper-white skin of people I have been told are my enemies, seeking a reflection of me. Are you my cousin? I silently ask. If you are, I think to myself, what American state or European country are you from? Why have you not acknowledged me?

These unsettled images undermine both the hegemonic system of racial classification and the emergent ideology of a post-raceless America.[5] We would be well served to reexamine the meanings of race and to consider how I, and others who share my ancestral history, are passin' for Black.

As I reflect on the second emancipation, when, like most of my generation, I was compelled to participate in the transformation of American apartheid, it is the violence that remains most indelibly seared in my mind. As I try to verify the accuracy of the refrain that "we shall overcome," I confront the socially imposed limitations that still exist today: de facto segregation in the public schools, social segregation in transportation and housing, bankers' rapacious red-lining and overlending, and occupational segregation and wage discrimination based on race and gender. I recognize the enormous inequality that is generated and reproduced because the working poor are forced to sell their labor for so much less than the living wage needed to survive in a country where conspicuous consumption is the norm. All this knowledge ravages my self-esteem and my confidence in the future that awaits the next generation.

In order to shore up my own and my people's damaged sense of self, I make a futile effort to find any space in my country where America's hallowed ideals are put into practice. I migrate endlessly, trying to avoid the gaze of those who watch with camera-ready eyes, searching for a place where my racialized identity does not mutate my gendered self. I look for a space that will make me feel safe, where I will experience a sense of belonging. Indeed, because I am racially constructed, migration is my middle name, my indelible link to an undesired past. I have come to realize that running from the past is not possible because this history haunts the present. My dilemma surpasses Faulkner's (1951) claim that "[t]he past is never dead. It's not even past" (p. 92).

For me, not only is the past neither dead nor past, but it is embedded in the deepest marrow of my bones. Memories lodged so deep within cannot be evaded. Wherever I go, whatever I do, this racialized history envelops me. Inevitably, it pulls me back, compelling me to disturb the peace of my ancestors by trying to fulfill their dreams and aspirations.

In order to have even a remote chance of reclaiming their humanity, it is my words, not my body, that must migrate well beyond the pages on which they are printed or the walls within which they are spoken. In academia, it is widely accepted, even expected, that words travel. Words that reproduce themselves across space are longed for and clearly identified as commodities, objects created to be consumed. Migrating bodies, by contrast, are generally perceived as out of place, watched, and policed, their behaviors and practices under constant surveillance, their lack of stasis a challenge to the sense of belonging so central to human survival.

How, or even why, should I shed my memories of dehumanization through enslavement and rape, the unmitigated violence of lynching committed against Black bodies in the wake of the first emancipation? Is it possible, I wonder, for the millions of people like me to be American without a racial history? Is it even remotely possible to be both raceless and passin' for Black?[6]

What haunts me most about the lives of my ancestors is localized in their knees, backs, and eyes: knees that will not or cannot bend because they refuse to bow and scrape; backs that served as bridges and, despite the scars they bore from the lash, unwittingly reinforced their own and their descendants' enslavement; jet-black eyes that cannot mask their pain and so must be averted or lowered so as not to offend dominant Whites.

I seek, unsuccessfully, to establish boundaries between *us* and them, to find my way to a home I have never known. Most of those of African ancestry who sought to find a refuge within or outside the United States failed; they were captured and returned, forced to live in a country where they were viewed as commodities purchased by their owners and as raw labor whose productive and reproductive powers were to be extracted against their will. White men too poor to own slaves became overseers and patrollers for the slave owners, as did officials in the so-called free states and territories. When my ancestors fled to areas within the United States where slavery was not allowed, they always remained fearful of capture and return. The desperate measures they took in their exodus affect my life hundreds of years later. The bone memory of how their bodies' sweat equity was denied, and even erased, is the fuel that propels my commitments and visions.

[S]KINSHIP AND RACIAL IDENTITY

My academic interest in the notion of postracial America was evoked not only by my own personal history but also by the unique social history of my enslaved ancestors in this country. Today, most people—not each and every person, but most people—who are identified as having African ancestry self-consciously seek to pass for Black.

For the first time in my life, I have been forced to admit that I, like most of my Black kinspeople, am an American hybrid. My hybridity is not just a matter of the name I call myself, African American. My ancestors include White as well as Black people, which makes me quintessentially American. Acknowledging skinship forced me out of my own, ostensibly unadulterated, racialized closet. With this admission regarding my fragmented pedigree, I reluctantly acknowledge that I, too, am guilty of passin' for Black.

But why should anyone take my argument seriously—a visibly Black body claiming to be merely passin' for Black? In this context, as Aretha Franklin (1985) put it, "Who's zoomin' who?" The dark hue of my skin, my Black discourse style, the arrogance of my hair, and the African cast of my physical features all make a mockery of my assertion that I am guilty of merely passin' for Black. Or do they?

My goal is not to revisit the ongoing debate about whether we should add a new racial category to the U.S. Census; I accept the recommendation made by the American Anthropological Association (1997). Rather, I aim to challenge essentialized notions of racial categories. What does it mean to say a person is Black? Or White, Asian, Latina/o? If I self-identify as African American, does that mean that I must appear Black in order to be perceived as a "real" Black person—that I cannot be wealthy, can only sing the blues, cannot have very light skin or straight hair, and must assume a specific discourse style? Alternatively, am I Black if my father is Black and his father was White, or if my father and grandfather are White but my mother and grandmother are Black? The meanings of "biracial" are contested. Today, the claims of racial belonging made by young adults born from interracial unions vary markedly (Kilson, 2001). So, a definition is in order.

As I use the term, "passing" is a collective rather than an individual act. It is more than the physical and mental flight that is possible when a socially defined Black person successfully disregards fixed racial boundaries. Passin' for Black is neither a benign social practice nor an individual deviation; it is, instead, a subversive group process, the ultimate act of transgression. The term is intended to convey the chutzpah involved in African Americans' contemporary practice of trespassing backward to Black.

Virtually every socially defined Black person in America is passin' for Black—regardless of their skin color, hair texture, and facial features. So compulsory is the performance of racialized identity that the meaning of Black has been assumed rather than interrogated. Indeed, the lives of Black people are still so polluted with the violence that accompanies racism that our racialized identity has become a master status, superceding everything else about us. In recent academic debates, Blackness has been problematized as an artifact of the distant past or an artifice of performance (Young, 2007). But this conceptual flexibility has yet to reshape the American system of racial classification. Today, passing not only involves the willful violation of recognized racial boundaries (Kroeger, 2003), it also suggests that the constructed identity itself—Blackness—is stolen. Passin' for Black is symptomatic of the fragile and fleeting nature of social categorization in contemporary America.

American slavery depended on the reproductive freedom and social dominance of White males and the enslaved labor and reproductive capacity of African American females (Hine, 1993; Roberts, 1997). Consequently, I argue, race is a synonym for kinship within the Black community.[7] The connections between race and kinship differ among Black and White Americans. Kinship is embedded in the practice of choosing to be Black and denied by attempts to police the boundaries of White. Bounded social groups—not individuals within particular social groups—are either kith or kin or a hybridized version of both. African Americans, who form one bounded group, have reinvented themselves, transforming a stigmatized racial identity into an ethnic marker and encompassing every Black mother's child despite their non-Black paternity. Defending the putative purity of Whiteness, by contrast, requires White males to disown their progeny.

White males' reproductive power—strengthened by their ability to coerce others—and Black females' *freedom from choice* had immense consequences for the construction of American racial categories. Traditional anthropological kinship schema, like dominant White American constructions of race, conflate biology and social ideology. Biologically, White and Black Americans are kin. They share not only a social history but a common ancestor: the White American male. The White American male's ability to reproduce an enslaved population propelled him to the unprecedented patriarchal status of master and father, owner and procreator. His power meant he could forcibly impregnate enslaved Black women (Giddings, 1984; Gordon-Reed, 2008; Gwaltney, 1980; Harris, 1993; Spillers, 1987) and, at the same time, enjoy the privilege of reproducing with White women. The "one drop rule," based on the core principle that White is pure, established a hierarchy of fallacious classifications.

In addition to the endemic torture of coerced intercourse and involuntary reproduction suffered by Black women, and witnessed by their fathers, husbands, and sons, were the rare occasions when White females chose to reproduce with males who were socially identified as Black. This nightmare of race-mixing haunted White men who, paradoxically, both disowned and owned their enslaved children. These White women were—and are still—compelled to "bear . . . Blackness" (Hodes, 1997; Robinson, 2003; Rothman, 2003; Sollors, 2000). Bearing Blackness erased White women's racial connection to their own children.[8] In contrast, women socially defined as Black, who either involuntarily or with some degree of choice conceived children with men defined as White were—and still are—not free to define their sons and daughters as White.

Against this historical backdrop, scholars have failed to acknowledge the full social import of the "one drop rule" for what anthropologists identify as kinship (for exceptions, see Davis, 1991; Johnson, 1989; Ladner, 1977; Piper, 1996). The common knowledge that Black women conceived children with White men who coerced them in the fields, the household, the workplace, or on the street is denied rather than acknowledged. As Ralph Ellison (1995) noted, "the Negro looks at the White man and finds it difficult to believe that the 'grays'—a Negro term for White people—can be so absurdly self-deluded over the true inter-relatedness of Blackness and Whiteness" (p. 109).

Virtually nothing in the literature helps us to understand how the imagined Black community emerged from a hybridized, creole population. Even more critically, the significance of White males' reproductive power is lost in the practice of viewing Black Americans' efforts to reclaim this component of their racialized heritage. Instead, even novels by African Americans present passing for White as the quintessential marker of a pathological identity: Nella Larsen's *Passing* (1929); James Weldon Johnson's *The Autobiography of an Ex-Colored Man* (1912); the movie *Imitation of Life* (Sirk, 1959), based on Fannie Hurst's 1933 novel; Henry Louis Gates's "White Like Me" (1996).

Blackness is an American cultural invention. People of African ancestry have had to learn two contradictory things concurrently: how not to be White and how to become Black. Codification of bifurcated racial categories forced everybody within the imagined African American community, regardless of skin color and their alleged, immediate, or remote paternity, to steal a fictive, pristine Black identity. This obligatory appropriation was resisted for more than a century. The civil rights revolution ushered in an inversion of the long-established denigration of Blackness and the abandonment of this dominant historical response. Today, an individual's assertion that she is Black is unlikely to be challenged, either within or outside this cultural group. Consequently, to argue that passin' for Black is problematic both within and outside the African American community appears illogical. The salience of this issue, however, appears in the popular inquiry, "Am I Black enough for you?"

Ironically, passin' for Black is the mantra of the children of the first emancipation. The overwhelming majority of the children of the second emancipation who describe themselves as "biracial" mean that their mothers are White and their fathers are of African ancestry. Passin' for Black is not a synonym for biracial. Instead, this concept shows how the Black community turned Blackness into a badge of honor rather than shame. As initially constructed, the one drop rule meant that every child who could not claim a White mother was socially defined as Black. A chosen Blackness transforms the biracial or hybridized body with African ancestry into the socially constructed, racialized Black person. The critical question that begs an answer is: What does it mean to pass for Black?

TWO NARRATIVES

Throughout this analysis, I have described how "passin' for Black" is my generation's hellish connection to a past that is, strangely, both indelibly remembered and unknown. This connection and the resultant skinship has propelled me into a space where "cousins" who are officially defined as my enemy are more likely my kin, but deny my kinship status; and, in striking contrast, "cousins" who are socially constructed as undeniably my biological kith and kin see me as their enemy, as is reflected in the aggression statistics against Black women, including what is widely labeled "Black-on-Black crime."

When I began this project, I naively assumed that the children of the second emancipation whose parental heritage is officially acknowledged, unlike the children of the first emancipation, would not be burdened by the memories and denials that have scrambled previous generations, including my own. To my surprise and my chagrin, I have had to acknowledge that the race and gender borders and boundaries affecting the children of the second emancipation remain messy, nonlinear, and embodied, hemorrhaging on their race and gender identities in ways that are parallel to, and in some instances, surpass what happened in earlier generations.

Here, I share two composite cases from my recent research study on female competition in a predominantly White high school that I pseudonymously call Underground Railroad High (UGRH), located in upstate New York.[9] The contrasting experiences of these young women illuminate how this phenomenon is manifested among high school students. In each of these composite cases, the young woman sought to escape the racialized identities to which she felt inappropriately assigned, though each did so in different directions.

Ethnographers routinely protect the privacy of their informants by giving them pseudonyms and changing identifying details about their lives. They often create composite characters, sometimes theorizing them as Weberian ideal types that have heuristic value. I pledged to school officials, the participants in the study, and their parents that the young women's identities would be concealed. In this study, I have approached the task of conveying the truths of my subjects' lives as they know them while shielding them from the embarrassment and pain that being identified would entail in a particular way—and, of course, with their consent. In keeping with the sense that Americans like me who are passin' for Black are displaced bodies, I have constructed composite portraits that retain the integrity of my informants' voices while displacing their bodies. The words of my informants are quoted directly as taken from their diaries, our interviews, and my field notes. But their bodies have migrated. They have been mixed and merged into categories that reflect the racial categories recognized and normalized at the school and within the society at large. Each voice is that of a single informant, confined in the privacy of her diaries, conversations with me in formal and informal interviews, and the pages of my field notes. Like me and most Americans of African ancestry, Chloe's and Brittany's bodies are composites; but each young woman's words are hers alone.

Chloe

I met Chloe for the first time as she sat with her White girlfriends in a remote corner of the school cafeteria.[10] Chloe's name was one of three on a list of "biracial" girls that I was given by teachers, counselors, and administrators who were helping me identify subjects for my study of female aggression and bullying.

Initially, I had trouble finding her in the cafeteria, because, unlike most of the other "Black" students who ate lunch in the cafeteria, she was not sitting at the Black table. During the entire period of my interactions with her at UGRH, I never saw her sitting at the Black community table. She told me she had never sat at that table, not even once. She always sat with her BFF (best friend), who was White, and her other White girlfriends. A couple of Black female students also noted her consistent absence from the Black table and her exclusive association with Whites. Several of the adults told me that she suffered from depression. Her Black school peers were far less charitable.

Chloe is seen as a Black girl by everyone but herself. Her primarily White friends see her as Black; the Black peers she seeks to avoid at school see her as Black and wonder why she is always trying to "act White"; her family members, including her mother, see her as Black; and the people in her suburban church community think of her as a Black girl. Black is Chloe's least favorite identity but the one that she cannot dislodge. She is as close to White as any

American of African descent can get: her mother is socially defined as White and her father is Black. In "post-racial" America, being the child of a White mother is the most prestigious lineage a Black person can have, and the status of this segment of the population is rapidly advancing in the current socio-political climate.

Chloe constantly reminds people that although she looks Black, she is not Black and does not want to be defined as Black. Still, she knows that neither her White nor her Black peers at school assent to her self-proclaimed White-ness, and her frustration over this issue has plunged her into depression. I wrote in my field notes:

> After several conversations with her counselor at school, Chloe and the coun-selor agreed that she desperately needed help. Chloe decided to admit herself voluntarily to a hospital and spend three weeks in the adolescent psychiatric ward (known as "the partial") at St. Teresa [fictitious name of a local hospital], which offers day treatment for people who are having mental health problems, includ-ing depression. To cope with the stresses Chloe associated with her racialized existence and the sense of not belonging anywhere, she strategically decided to spend the three weeks just before spring break committed to the cause of trying to heal. She didn't return to school until after spring break and didn't see any of her friends for four weeks.[11]
>
> The hospital stay did reduce Chloe's stress, but she still has days when she feels as though she can't cope. She struggles to make do with the once-a-week therapy session that her counselor has arranged for her in the wake of the long hospital stay. Some weeks the stress is so great, she skips her Wednesday classes and can barely wait until therapy on Thursday. Chloe told her counselor about the anxiety attacks and hoped that she would be able to get her schedule changed from one to two days per week. No such luck. The counselor claims that, by law, the school system can only offer students one therapy session a week. (May 17, 2005)

Chloe blames her hair, whose unruliness stigmatizes her as Black. As long as she can remember, she has hated her hair—or, more accurately, she has hated the way others regard her hair, and their view has distorted her sense of herself. Chloe's internalization of others' rejection of her hair resembles the crippling form of double consciousness W. E. B. Du Bois (1903) describes in *The Souls of Black Folk.* Her mother kept trying to groom it like her own, waging a constant battle that was impossible to win. When Chloe was in elementary school, she cried when her classmates—all of whom were White—teased her about her hair. When her father was home, he consoled her, telling her that "sticks and stones might hurt my bones but words don't bother me" and reas-suring her that she was the prettiest girl in the world. Sometimes she prayed that a merciful God would change her hair, enabling her to claim the White identity she believes is her birthright.

Chloe is caught in a constant tug-of-war with her mother over her self-assertion and her sexuality. Her mother wants her to embrace a White-identi-fied notion of femininity, giving up her own power and learning how to act, or at least appear to be, helpless. This image of frailty is the opposite of the dominant gender norms practiced in the Black community. Chloe feels that her mom is trying to infantilize her in order to make her appear less capable of taking care of herself. She is exhausted by the sporadic efforts she makes to comply and suspects that this strategy is unrewarding.

Curiously, like many other non-White girls in America, Chloe desires to be valued and respected in the impressive ways that the White females she knows in real life and observes on television and other media appear to be. These women include her mother, especially when she was Chloe's age. Chloe's rookie adult status, coupled with her limited firsthand experiences, have forced her to conclude that White girls (and White women) are the most sexually desired females on the planet, regardless of race or ethnicity. However, unlike her contemporary White female peers—who appear to disidentify with or, at the very least, devalue their Whiteness while celebrating their one acknowledged identity (femaleness)—Chloe covets the pristine property of Whiteness (see Harris, 1993) not the femaleness merged to it. She wants to jettison her Black identity for a White identity because she views it as the critical currency in the mating and dating game. She recognizes that Whiteness—not femaleness—is the carat in her non-Black friends' lives; their femaleness is drenched in the privilege of Whiteness. If she were socially defined as White, she reasons, her hair would not be defined as kinky, regardless of the density of its curl pattern. This conundrum—desiring both to be and not be a White girl, to both be and avoid being a Black girl—is the bane of her young life.

I observed Chloe's racial and gender ambivalence in multiple contexts: at school, at home, and in other settings. The intersectionality of these social constructs made it difficult for me to determine which of these issues complicated her life more. Over time, however, I became convinced that gender was the primary complicating construct. Two of her diary entries, one describing her school life and the other her family life, are illustrative:

> I went to school today which was a ton of fun because we had a substitute. Everyone was being loud and crazy and the substitute loved it. Two of the girls that sit next to me (both White) had fun talking to me. They kind of tease me because a boy in the class has a crush on me but I don't mind that they tease me, we are friends. There is a very annoying (Black) girl that sits on the other side of me. She never shuts up and always thinks she is right. We were reading a poem and the substitute asked a question and the girl got it wrong. For once. Well everyone started laughing at her and eventually she told them to shut up. (May 17, 2005)

> Happy Mother's Day! What a day it was. We went out to lunch with about 16 of my family members. Nothing really interesting happened but my great aunt did get an attitude. My aunt (Black) pulled me aside and told me not to worry about her life any more and that it was none of my business, this after the previous day she came to me, as an adult, and told me that she was going to divorce my millionaire uncle. The family knew from the beginning that she was a liar and only wanted the money. She told me that she never loved him. This just about sent me

through the roof. How could you have two great kids (my cousins) with a man you don't love?! Well of course I made the mistake of telling my non-trustworthy mother and look where it got me, in the corner of the restaurant being lectured by a witch who I am embarrassed to say is my aunt. (May 8, 2005)

Chloe's parents met in the public school in the city that fueled the growth of the suburban community where their daughter was born and now lives. During their adolescence, the schools were less segregated than they are today. Her Black father was the star of the football team; her mother was the captain of the all-White cheerleading squad. Their friendship evolved into courtship, love, and marriage, despite their racial differences. Some twenty-five years ago that was really risky. Neither went to college; he joined the military, and she became a full-time mother after Chloe, their first child, was born. For this unconventional couple, the conventional model of marriage did not work well. Because so many of their White friends did not approve of their inter-racial marriage, isolation became the centerpiece of their lives. Her mother coped with her depression by drinking; her father survived by being away or working nonstop.

The only Black people Chloe loves unconditionally are her father and her little brother. She loves her father's chocolate-brown skin; thick, arrogant, Black hair; super-dark brown eyes; and wide, crooked smile. He works hard to support and protect his family. Anything she tells him she wants or needs, he makes heroic efforts to get for her. He recently retired from the military after serving for more than twenty years on a submarine. Now he works as a police officer in a suburban town. His constant absence from home has fueled her parents' estrangement. Her father tries to avoid interacting with her and her little brother when their mother is present.

Although Chloe says that she loves her little brother, she feels burdened by her responsibility for him. When her mother sinks into an alcoholic depression, she struggles to take care of him, even though she is only four years older. Her maternal grandmother, who lives down the street, helps during the worst times. Still, she feels that the "adultification" of her childhood has been forced; it was not a chosen role or one into which she grew.[12] Chloe reports that no one takes care of her, or shows any concern, except her father, who is rarely home. Her pain and confusion are virtually invisible to everyone but her. She suffers, but her suffering goes unnoticed.

Chloe shares that her love for her father and brother does not extend to other people defined as Black, including her father's family. She knows that people are supposed to be concerned about their relatives, but obligation is different from affection. Her connection to her father's mother and her Black lineage is the real barrier between her and the unadulterated White identity she so deeply desires. She does not know why, but when she is in her Black grandmother's presence, she feels like a partitioned or divided person: one part above the ground, the other below. When Chloe talked with her father's sister about this, her aunt responded by saying that Chloe's grandmother struggles at every moment to contain the violence and loss that permeates her life. According to Chloe's aunt, her grandmother endures only to demonstrate her power in the face of unbearable suffering, masking the excruciating pain of being alive and dead at the same time. A chill ran down Chloe's spine as she heard her father endorse this explanation.

The intimately intertwined issues of gender and race are at the core of Chloe's discomfort. In adolescence, she is trying to separate from a troubled family. She wants desperately to share her mother's and maternal grandmother's White identity. She shops, visits, and interacts constantly with her White BFF. As she observes how seamlessly her BFF travels through the world, she aches to live like that, to be the beneficiary of doubt.[13] When she is with her White friends, though, doubt rebounds against her.

Chloe remembers being invited to join the Black-identified step team during her first year in high school. The Black girl who is now the team's captain asked her more than once. Chloe was horrified. Not only would she "never be caught dead" engaging in such a spectacle, but she was outraged that, just because her hair texture and skin tone are not conventionally associated with Whiteness, a Black girl would assume that she wanted to belong to this group. More than any other activity that Black females engage in at UGRH, participation in the step team compels a girl to perform what is seen as Blackness. Chloe smiled politely and made up a flimsy excuse about having to take care of her little brother after school. She engages only in activities that are marked White, not Black. But when she tried out for the cheerleading squad, she was rejected because, as one of the coaches told her, she does not have "bouncy hair."

Being identified as Black is what annoys her most: nobody will allow her to be who she wants to be. She loves science and, although she did not get an A in biology, she is convinced that she understands enough about genetics to know that her genetic makeup disqualifies her for the label Black. How can she be Black when her mother is White? She realizes that her father is Black and is willing to concede that she is at least partially Black. But, she reasons, since she is only partially Black, she should be able to choose between the two identities rather than being compelled to be Black. Because no one will allow her to choose her identity, she takes revenge on Black females, as expressed in her diary.

Today I went to the mall with my brother and we saw two girls from school. The two girls were black and they were arguing with each other about who was going to do the rest of the driving. It's funny because both of these girls are out of school so I wouldn't trust either of them to drive me. When we walked by my brother and I just laughed at how stupid they sounded. The one girl who looked younger wanted to drive and was yelling at the other girl to let her drive. When my brother and I had passed them we turned back to look and they were grabbing at each other for the keys. It may have been playful, but it didn't seem like it. (May 5, 2005)

Chloe dates Black guys. At this high school, lots of White girls date Black guys. But she works hard not to become friends with African American girls. She does not want their image to rub off on her. She would never, ever sit at the "Black table" in the cafeteria because Black girls are sitting there. She does not play basketball or sing in the glee club or the gospel choir. Instead, she plays squash. She is a member of the swim team, even though she must constantly struggle with her hair after practice. She sits with her White-only gal pals on the other side of the cafeteria and becomes anxious when other Black girls are in her classes, because she fears that they will call attention to her Blackness.

Only one of the teachers at the school is Black, so Chloe does not feel that she has to be concerned about how they perceive her. Since most of the teachers know her mother is White and because she has no friendships with Black girls, they often give her the benefit of the doubt, which they do not often do for Black girls in their classes. She has noticed that teachers and other school staff reward her for her distance from other Black students. Chloe works hard to make sure her teachers praise her for being "a very nice girl."

Brittany

"That White boy hit me. That White boy hit me. I hate that White boy. Make that White boy stop hitting me." As I stood in the school hallway trying to make sense of this strange linguistic construction, a White teacher who also heard this young woman's complaint offered a racial characterization: "She talks like a Black girl." Several other adult White women smiled knowingly, confirming the teacher's assessment.

Focusing on the adult's statement rather than on what this student said, I asked no one in particular, "*Is* she a Black girl?" Silence. The teachers looked at me blankly and walked away. One of the White women standing nearby told me that the student is White. But I wondered about the conundrum of her racial identity. I was seeing this student for the first time and, given the wide range of skin colors and hair textures in what is known as the "Black" community, it is dangerous to make assumptions about who is and is not Black. Admittedly, she has light-colored skin, which is frequently associated with the essentialized racial category White. But for me the important questions are: How does the student self-identify? What does it mean to her to "talk like a Black girl" at this school? What does it mean to be a Black girl, and who makes that determination? As an adult female who self-identifies and is perceived by others as Black, I felt like Alice in Wonderland in a world turned upside down.

Brittany, the speaker and the subject of this conversation, did not share my puzzlement and distress. As I observed and got to know her, I realized that she is secretly pleased when someone, especially an adult, accuses her of "acting Black."[14] The women who view her as White like themselves are aghast at her "inappropriate" racial performance and attempt to restrain her by telling me—a stranger whom they see first as Black, second as female, and third as an anthropologist who is studying their school—that Brittany is guilty of deliberately appropriating a Black female discourse style, maybe even a Black identity.

In Brittany's social world, the "White boy" is as strange to her as he would be to most Black girls. She grew up in the urban core that spawned the suburb to which she was recently forced to move. Until last year, she lived in the city with her mother and grandmother. After her parents' divorce, her mother took Brittany back to the urban neighborhood where she had grown up. The neighborhood had "changed," however; as the second generation of Italian Americans moved away, African Americans and other families of color moved in. So Brittany grew up surrounded by Black children. Her best friend was the Black girl her age who lived nearby. Through junior high, her friendship circle extended to include other Black girls. Brittany fit right in: she braided her hair, listened to rap music, and wore the kind of clothes her friends wore—when she could get away with it. She joined the step team as well as the cheerleading squad, the gospel choir, and the glee club. Brittany's Black BFFs embraced her unconditionally. Brittany desires to convince everyone that she is Black like them.

Like the vast majority of the Black girls at UGRH, Brittany is passing for Black, but not in the traditional sense. Socially defined as White, Brittany is drawn to the Black community because in her previous schools she was an assimilated minority among a Black peer majority. Her decision to pass for Black—an identity inversion—compels school officials to interpret her identity construction as pathological, going beyond what is widely attributed to Black Americans who opt to pass for White (see, e.g., Larsen, 1929; Piper, 1996; White, 1998). School officials and her White peers identify her as White, an "identity confer[ring] tangible and economically valuable benefits [that are] jealously guarded as a valued possession, allowed only to those who me[e]t a strict standard of proof" (Harris, 1993, p. 1726). Moreover, because Brittany self-identifies as a Black female and does not engage in physical violence— merely talking (and behaving) like a Black girl—she unwittingly captures the essence of female competition: relational aggression.[15]

An entry from Brittany's diary clearly exemplifies the complicity of language in describing female aggression and competition, not only at UGRH but among women more generally. Primarily because of their language practices at this school (and elsewhere), African Americans, especially African American girls, are viewed as "aggressive" even when they do not engage in physical violence. This is why it was extremely difficult for me to get beyond the idea of physical violence as the central criterion of Blackness when school officials offered possible study participants. Being misidentified as a Black girl made Brittany guilty of what most adults and students at the school recognized as "aggression," or the desire to harm another. Her direct discourse style, as reflected in the entry from her diary, does not embody what Delpit (1988) identifies as the "veiled use of power" or what I describe as the language of uncertainty. Instead it embodies the central criterion in hegemonic female "ways with words" (Heath, 1983).

> I was at school all day. I was going to skip last block cuz Asha, my [Black] friend, is having her birthday party [in the City]. It will be a lot of fun. Asha is just like me. She likes guys better than most girls just like me . . . Sometimes they annoy me cus their [they are] girls, but I can't chill with guys all the time . . . Rick came to pick me up . . . This kid really likes me . . . [a girl in one of my classes] told me he talks about me all the time. Then I and Rick went to Asha's house. There were so many girls there . . . Some I had seen at school or when I went to school [in the City]. Yea, I already didn't like some of 'em. Then they were complaining . . . Then I smoked and just let them do their "little" thing while I did mine . . . Then that was over and it was time for the birthday cake (at 10:30 at night?). Then I went to go do that and I was smoking a bong and I went to go to move to go upstairs and I remembered I had my bong, so I accidentally exhaled towards some girl. Some girl bitch walked [up] and was like "Bitch." It was an accident. My bad. You don't gotta call me a bitch. So I heard her say that, and I was, "Did you just call me a bitch?" She . . . hasn't even tasted life. And she got the nerve. You don't walk up to a girl and <u>ever</u> disrespect her. (March 4, 2005)

Brittany has always been aware that her mother and grandmother are proud to be Italian. Like her father, they identify as White. In order to please her family, she pretends to do so too—but only in their presence. As long as she can remember, Brittany has thought of herself as a Black girl with very light skin and dark, wavy, rather limp hair. Admittedly, these physical features are not commonly associated with Black girls. But she talks, acts, and behaves as she imagines a Black girl would. She tries out this racial performance on her Black female peers. In the city, she succeeded. Now, in this predominantly White suburban school, she feels that she does not belong anywhere. Part of the problem is that she has been sent to live with her father and his new wife. But Brittany believes that happened because her parents agreed that she was bound to go astray if she stayed in the city at an "inferior" school whose student body is predominantly Black and Brown.

Brittany knows that White girls at her new school do not accept her, even though they identify her as White like them. She avoids these girls because, to her, Whiteness seems like baggage, an identity to be negotiated, if not entirely shed. During her first week at school, she sat at a different table every day. The White girls never even introduced themselves, much less asked her who she was. At each table, Brittany was a silent audience of one, expected to listen to the gossip but invisible and unimportant in her own right.

The teachers in the suburban school, like those in the inner city, are almost all White women. They encourage Brittany to excel academically but constantly curtail her attempts to perform what she imagines as Blackness instead of what they imagine as Whiteness. Their ambivalence toward Brittany emerged in the wake of her extraordinary performance on an IQ test in elementary school and her achievements on state-mandated exams in junior high. Her grades vary widely and unpredictably. In the city, her teachers deplored Brittany's inclusion in the Black peer group. Again and again, they told her how smart she was but explained that her friendships were a threat to her academic future. They told her mother that she was "running with the wrong crowd," coded language for those "loud Black girls" who, her mother agreed, were a bad influence (see Fordham, 1993). One teacher even told her mother that she was playing dumb in order not to outshine her Black peers. Brittany remembers her teachers rewarding her disproportionately for any academic effort, in striking contrast to their low expectations of her Black friends.

In the city, Brittany found the diversity of her classmates' experiences stimulating. She loved their freedom of movement, of talking and interacting. She especially liked the Black girls' direct way of speaking. In the Black community, she observed, women are expected to speak for themselves, to say what they think about what is happening in their lives. Her family could not stand the idea of her acting on her own behalf and talking in a way that they regarded as inappropriate for a young lady. Brittany shared that she was made keenly aware of this every day after school when her mother and grandmother would tell her, in no uncertain terms, "Brittany, use your inside voice . . . Brittany, don't act like those Black girls at your school."

Brittany's mother keeps telling her to "be nice." Her mother's major preoccupation in life seems to be making sure that no one has any reason to form a negative opinion of her—or her daughter. Growing up in a middle-class Italian American family, she was taught to be a "people pleaser," even if she had to fake it. Brittany resents her mother's advice and does not see why women should hide both their competence and their competitiveness beneath a veneer of civility and politeness. The White girls at school act like the White women at her mother's job: supportive of one another, ever so nice in face-to-face interactions, sharing intimate details of their lives, but, as soon as one woman or girl does something that makes her stand out from the others, out come the claws.

As Brittany sees it, behaving like a White girl is too constraining. When she tries to embody White femininity, her sense of suffocating compression is so intense that she flees from it, despite the chagrin of her mother and grandmother and the disapproval of her teachers. The Black girl's costume does not appear to constrict her; she feels like she is able to breathe. She walks upright, without a hollow in her waistline, without having to speak in a squeaky voice from her throat rather than more powerfully from her abdomen. Brittany wonders whether the anorexia that is rampant among the White girls at her school but not among their Black counterparts is an indication of the expectation that White females should not take up space.

White women like her mother and grandmother are supposed to depend on men to protect and take care of them, but Brittany realizes that their lives belie their advice: both are on their own. Like the Black girls at her old school, she did not see anyone running to protect or take care of her. At her new school, she noticed right away that whenever a fight broke out, whether it was between the Black girls or between a Black girl and a White girl, or even among the boys, the "good" girls—the "nice" White girls—were always on the sidelines watching rather than drawn into the fray, even when they were the source of the gossip or rumors that fueled the altercation. Brittany's mother and grandmother repeatedly remind her that she is an individual and advise her to do her work and forget the other kids. "Good girls" do not fight for themselves; they get others to defend them. If someone does something that is unacceptable to you, they insist, go tell the teacher or principal; these adults will take care of it for you.

Brittany feels that her mother and grandmother are distressed when she becomes involved in the conflicts that arise at school; even when she is the target, they are not sympathetic. Instead, they insist that acting like and being identified with Black girls jeopardizes her future. Brittany wants to believe that they have her best interests at heart. But when she tries to stand alone and be just a bystander at school, she feels vulnerable.

Perhaps as a result, Brittany's mother and grandmother have not succeeded in getting her to disengage from her Black and Brown peers. Instead, they responded to Brittany's stubborn insistence on acting like her imagined and chosen self by sending her to live with her father in a predominantly White suburb—a decision that shocked Brittany. Here, they fervently hoped, Brittany would be forced to behave appropriately. In the city, she had been caught sneaking out of the house to see the Black guy she was surreptitiously dating. (She was not supposed to be dating at all; they kept telling her that she was too young, although she was sixteen.) Brittany's mother and grandmother were so distraught at her covert defiance that they summoned her father and his new wife to a family meeting just before the end of her ninth-grade school year. Each of her parents blamed the other for her out-of-control behavior. In an informal conversation, Brittany shared a memory of her mother arguing that her father had abdicated his responsibilities and was never as engaged in her life as he should have been; he put his career ahead of his daughter's well-being. As her father turned beet red with indignant anger, her mother argued that she was not strong enough to keep their daughter out of the clutches of the ghetto in which she was forced to live.

Brittany's mother explained that a White girl coming of age in a predominantly Black community is vulnerable because, as is shown every day on television, she is so much more desirable than any of the other females that she is a marked target for sexual violence, including rape. Brittany listened in shocked silence as her mother told her father that she and the other White girls at her inner-city school are especially vulnerable because the Black guys find them more beautiful than the Black girls, which makes the Black girls as well as the Black guys more aggressive toward the White girls. Then came the coup de grace. Her mother's voice rising in distress, she shrieked at Brittany's father,

"Your daughter is acting like a whore . . . your daughter is running around with Black boys."

The decision was swift, though Brittany remained in denial as long as possible because the prospect of leaving her family and friends and going to live with her father and his new wife in a lily-White suburb was too painful to contemplate. Brittany recalls how scared she was of leaving the only family and community she had ever known and of being alone in a way that she had never been before. Now, members of the school staff repeatedly say in her presence that she "talks like a Black girl." They identify Brittany as White and assume that she is inappropriately passin' for Black.

CONCLUSION

In both cases presented here, passin' for Black is the problem each girl must overcome in order not to be seen as "strange fruit," misrecognized as an individual because of her racial "abnormality." Chloe's presumed Black skinship compels virtually everyone to identify her as biologically "Black" even though she disavows any cultural connection to Blackness. In striking contrast, Brittany, who is biologically defined as "White" but socially defines herself as Black, is also racially misrecognized. Her efforts to embrace a Black identity are parodied in the widely used refrain "she talks like a Black girl" and manifested in her social isolation, academic failure, and frayed female reputation.

Why does Chloe insist on being White, or at the very least, not Black? Why does Brittany attempt to disavow being White and seek, instead, to become Black? Chloe's consignment to a Black identity has made her physically sick, making Blackness a "disease" she has to overcome. Similarly, Brittany is not allowed to forgo her unearned privilege, Whiteness, and is instead assigned to White America's social purgatory: lower-class status. Each girl is denied the opportunity to embrace the identity she desires primarily because of the color of her skin, although it must be acknowledged that Chloe thinks, with some justification, that it is not her skin but her hair that is the primary reason she cannot be known as a White girl. Why are racialized categories both so influential and so resistant to disremembering? These phenomena subvert the claim of a postracial America.

So what does all this mean for the schooling of children and adolescents who are either voluntarily or involuntarily passin' for Black in what is supposedly a postracial America? How do we both honor their bone memories and minimize the impact of these cultural and structural issues on their academic performance, which continue so powerfully even when young people assert that they have no knowledge of enslavement and that they are not victimized by racism?

I return to two of the claims made earlier in this essay—Darlene Clark Hine's (1993) claim that "slavery was a [profoundly] sexual institution" and Faulkner's (1951) observation that "the past is never dead. It's not even past"—

because they are powerfully instructive as I struggle to transform my role as a pallbearer in the endless funeral of my female ancestors. In passin' for Black, I see myself as paying homage to my foreparents, especially my grandmother—at least twelve generations removed—for her pain and suffering and for her will to survive, which made it possible for me to be here, her body out-of-place granddaughter. If these claims and observations are even partially accurate, will I ever be able to discard the unbleached shroud of my racially infused skinship? Will I always be homeless, unable fully to claim either America or Africa as my homeland? Obviously, I do not desire to be kinless, but I am. I do not desire to be an orphan, but I am. I want my enslaved ancestors and their owners to acknowledge and embrace me, their long-lost daughter, but they have not. Am I then forever a body out of place—too Black to be White and too White to be Black, too female to be masculine yet too masculine to embody America's quintessential image of femininity? Clearly, I long for my cousins and the attendant recognition, relatedness, and reciprocity. Since disremembering is not an option, is passin' for Black—that is, embracing a socially constructed identity as if it were inherent in the body or based on genetic inheritance—my only option? Will my bone memory permanently confine me to this racial and gender "gray zone" (Levi, 2004, p. 90), a geographical place and personal space that indicate that I do not belong? Should I become a fugitive and seek self-deportation, à la Harriet Tubman's Underground Railroad? Where could I go, except into yet another exile? I want to be accepted as entitled to what is considered integral to being an American citizen: living in any neighborhood you desire; matriculating at the school of your choice; being able to obtain the job that is rewarding and that meshes with your academic and social skills; marrying the person of your choice without regard for his or her racial identity; voting without any qualifications beyond residence and citizenship. I want to be able to claim as rights what have previously been reserved as privileges for Whites-only. All this, it seems clear to me, is not only doable in a postracial America but is the central criterion that would make it so.

Parallel social and cultural issues are affecting the lives of the students I studied at UGRH. They, too, despite their birth during the second emancipation, are tethered to a racial and gender "gray zone"—a "zone of ambiguity which radiates out . . . [creating] terror and obsequiousness" (Levi, 2004, p. 90), a social space that tells them that they do not belong. But what does disremembering mean for the schooling of children and adolescents who are either voluntarily or involuntarily passin' for Black in what is supposedly a postracial America? How do we prepare practitioners to engage a profession in which denial is so prominently displayed?

First, acknowledge, acknowledge, acknowledge and challenge, challenge, challenge. As I remain bolted to the diversity table, I realize that only by embracing America's entire racial history do we have even a remote chance of transforming the academic performance of the descendants of the enslaved and of those who enslaved them. The invisible and unacknowledged umbilical cord that connects us to America's rapacious social, political, and economic histories is so deeply embedded in cultural policies and practices that avoidance of the pain affiliated with that history is not an option. We all share this history. The children of the enslaved are impaled on a crucifix of low expectations, not because we cannot perform academically but because the people who should challenge and support us appear not to believe we are worth the effort that entails.

This problem is most visibly evident in the denial of both the angst and the powerful social forces arrayed around race matters on the part of predominantly White, mainly female, teachers—many of whom are liberals and were drawn to this profession by a desire to help others. Denial makes students' confusion all the more severe and leaves them with few resources to counter or even critically analyze the influences of the dominant culture around them—except for commercial youth culture, which is not much better even in its inversions.

Our nation's leaders must create, nurture, and even compel a nonnegotiable sense of belonging that encompasses all Americans. My observations in various schools—the nation's one remaining obligatory institution, both north and south of the Mason-Dixon Line—reveal that the most consistently dysfunctional curricular practices in America's public schools are those that deliberately and willfully avoid the most painful chapters in our nation's history, especially those chapters centered around enslavement, segregation, and racial discrimination. Healing or transformation cannot begin until what has been done in America's name—historically—is offically acknowledged, accounted for, and seared in the school curriulum. Children and adolescents whose family and collective histories include enslaved ancestors suffer because everyone avoids what is most critical to their sense of belonging: affirmation of the uniqueness of their lives in America's social history.

The very structure of public schooling is intended to reinforce the ideal of rugged individualism enshrined in the nation's dominant narrative, a practice that is diametrically opposed to the ethos of connectedness generally embraced among the descendants of the enslaved. This *equality means sameness* approach compels each student to become a competitive, self-sufficient entity capable of performing all required social and academic functions in ways that do not differ in level of proficiency from any of her peers.

Finally, as the case studies included here suggest, "postracial" is oxymoronic when applied to America. What is "post" about these issues is their slow decline, not their erasure. Race remains a major social category in America, although its social and cultural constructedness is becoming increasingly obvious. Racial and national identities are not innocuous, state-mandated historic relics that have no impact in our lived experiences. Instead, these identities continue to profoundly shape human practices and interactions even when we use language that suggests otherwise. Passin' for Black is the quintessential embodiment of both the bone memory of enslavement and the chameleon-like nature of race in contemporary America.

NOTES

1. In the United States, racial categories were defined under slavery and remained unchanged through the first emancipation during the Civil War and the second emancipation brought on by the civil rights movement.

2. Charles Town was the name of the port in South Carolina to which, during the colonial period, more newly enslaved Africans were brought than to any other port on the British mainland or in North America. After the Revolution, the name of the port was changed to Charlestown to deemphasize the name of the English king after whom the port was named.

3. *Rosewood* is based on a 1923 race riot in a small Florida town in which between 70 and 250 African Americans were killed and the rest driven out as the all-Black town was burned to the ground. The precipitating event was a White woman's accusation that a Black man had raped her; in fact, she had been beaten by her White lover and wanted to prevent her husband from finding out. Rather than a lynching, this event was an organized attack on an entire Black community. The events were investigated in 1982 by newspaper reporter Gary Moore and became the subject of a CBS News report and documentary on the Discovery Channel in 1984. In 1994, the Florida state legislature officially recognized the massacre and paid $2 million in reparations to the survivors and their families.

4. The word "disremember" signifies the deliberate, always incomplete effort to expunge my cultural DNA (e.g., my Black ancestors' American enslavement and racial segregation), including the social knowledge I acquired early in life that I do not exist outside of it. I seek to achieve this goal not necessarily because it is part of my personal memory, but because it's part of the "bone memory" I have inherited.

5. "Post-raceless," in this article, is intended as a synonym for "postracial."

6. Passin' for Black is the internal, group symbol of a uniquely Black American kinship system—or, kinship sans blood. It is a collective rather than an individual process and is the metaphor I use to describe the emergence of a "new [African-descended] people" (Williamson, 1995) in North America, Black Americans. I also use it convey Black Americans' efforts to create family and community out of the chaos of their status as property.

7. In the (imagined) Black community, "race" functions as a synonym for "kinship" because it all comes down to [s]kinship, to the assumption that all Black folks are kindred (and perhaps an implicit denial that Blacks are also kin of Whites). Moreover, despite the draconian measures of the enslavers to mask their familial connection to us (see Ball, 1998), this breach of social conventions metastasized, compelling our bones to disremember, refusing to embrace all efforts at dissimulation, unwittingly revealing, in the process, our skinship. This is most clearly manifested in our "hair, skin and bones"—the wide range of skin colors, hair textures, facial features, and body shapes within what is known as the Black community.

8. During the colonial period, when there were still Whites who were bound to long years of labor, White bound-servant women who bore visibly Black babies were sentenced to an extension of their years of servitude and/or, if they had willingly consorted with an enslaved Black man, to becoming slaves for life themselves. That ended (at various times in different places, but everywhere after the Revolution) when White men decided to make the lines between freedom and slavery much clearer and made sure that most Whites were formally free. Still, in the early nineteenth century, there were many servants among those who bore mixed-race children. These servants were pros-

ecuted for bastard-bearing, since they were not allowed to marry during their term of servitude.

9. These are condensed versions of two of the five case studies in my next book, *Downed by Friendly Fire: Black Girls, White Girls and Female Competition at Underground Railroad High.* These characters have been created from specific subsets of the twenty informants in my two-and-a-half year study of female aggression.

10. Chloe represents a composite of three young women in the study who define themselves as biracial. As such, this is my take on these young women's stories as I observed and studied them during my time at UGRH. My observations and interaction with Chloe were invariably painful, not because she was rude, unkind, or thoughtless but because of our generational-specific connection to an undesired past. I embodied the race and gender contradictions she so clearly despised and that she attributed to our generational difference. Indeed, she was a model citizen in her interactions not only with me, but with everyone who she thought would add value to her life. Since her experiences resonated with me—not personally, but because she was so aware of the pain implicit in the long history of Black racial identity—I looked forward to any opportunity to interact with her. One of my favorite informants, she was a mirror reflection for my racial experience before and during the second emancipation. As the diary entries suggest, there was no love lost between her and the females she identifies as Black at the school. She recognized the Black girls at UGRH as her presumed biological skinship group, but that was neither desired nor comforting. Consequently, in her presence and in reading her diary entries, I religiously sought to be the meandering, postracial, disembodied anthropologist, a historical Black female.

11. Throughout, the specific diary entries are excerpted from the journals of different participants and are reproduced in their own words.

12. Adultification is the process by which the behaviors of Black children, male and female, are "refracted," or "stripped of any element of childish naïveté," and seen as "adultified," making "their transgressions, sinister, intentional and fully conscious" (Ferguson, 2000, p. 83).

13. Being given "the benefit of the doubt" is an endemic feature of privilege. Chloe's White friends are snared in a web of privilege that enables them to escape so many of the damaging and disfiguring aspects of the stigma affiliated with Black and Blackness. For example, law officials often allow her White friends, males and females, to avoid getting traffic tickets by giving them a warning; teachers at UGRH do not give their White students zeros for not turning in their work because they believe them when they say that their parents took them to the opera and they forgot to retrieve it from the car.

14. The concept of "acting Black" has been written about widely in the literature. See, for example, Willie (2003).

15. Intriguingly, language in its broadest sense, which includes images and logic as well as speech, is the most widely used form of nonphysical violence in human interactions, although it is rarely recognized as such. According to Bourdieu and Wacquant (2004), "Symbolic violence is the kind of violence exercised upon a social agent with his or her complicity" (p. 272).

REFERENCES

American Anthropological Association. (1997). Draft of official statement on "race." *Anthropology Newsletter, 38*(6), 26–27.

Ball, E. (1998). *Slaves in the family.* New York: Farrar, Straus and Giroux.

Blassingame, J. W. (Ed.). (1982). *The Frederick Douglass papers: Speeches, debates and interviews* (pp. 243–248). New Haven, CT: Yale University Press.

Bourdieu, P., & Wacquant, L. (2004). Symbolic violence. In N. Scheper-Hughes & P. Bourgois, *Violence in war and peace* (pp. 272–275). Malden, MA.: Blackwell Publishing.

Davis, F. J. (1991). *Who is Black? One nation's definition.* University Park: Pennsylvania State University Press.

Delpit, Lisa (1988). The silenced dialogue: Power and pedagogy in educating other people's children. *Harvard Educational Review, 58*(3), 280–298.

Du Bois, W. E. B. (2007). *The souls of Black folk.* Oxford: Oxford University Press. (Original work published 1903).

Ellison, R. (1995). Shadow and act. In J. F. Callahan (Ed.), *The collected essays of Ralph Ellison* (pp. 47–341). New York: Modern Library.

Faulkner, W. (1951). *Requiem for a nun.* New York: Random House.

Fordham, S. (1993). "Those loud Black girls": (Black) women, silence and gender "passing" in the academy. *Anthropology and Education Quarterly, 24*(1), 3–32.

Fordham, S. (1996). *Blacked out: Dilemmas of race, identity and success at Capital High.* Chicago: University of Chicago Press.

Ferguson, A. (2000). *Bad boys, public schools and the making of Black masculinity.* Ann Arbor: University of Michigan Press.

Franklin, A. (1985). Who's zoomin' who? On *Who's zoomin' who?* [Album] Arista Records.

Gates, H. L., Jr. (1996). White like me: African American author Anatole Broyard. *New Yorker, 72*(16), 66–81.

Giddings, P. J. (1984). *When and where I enter: The impact of Black women on race and sex in America.* New York: HarperCollins.

Gordon-Reed, A. (2008). *The Hemmingses of Monticello: An American family.* New York: W. W. Norton.

Gwaltney, J. (1980). *Drylongso: A self-portrait of Black America.* New York: Random House.

Harris, C. (1993). Whiteness as property. *Harvard Law Review, 106*(8), 1709–1791.

Heath, S. B. (1983). Ways with words: Language, life and work in communities and classrooms. New York: Cambridge University Press.

Hine, D. C. (1993). "In the kingdom of culture": Black women and the intersection of race, gender, and class. In G. Early (Ed.), *Lure and loathing: Essays on race, identity, and the ambivalence of assimilation* (pp. 337–351). New York: Allen Lane, Penguin Press.

Hodes, M. (1997). *White women, Black men: Illicit sex in the nineteenth century.* New Haven, CT: Yale University Press.

Hurst, F. (1933). *Imitation of life.* New York: P. F. Collier.

Johnson, J. W. (1989). *The Autobiography of an ex-colored man.* New York: Viking. (Original work published 1912).

Kilson, M. (2001). *Claiming place: Biracial young adults of the post-civil rights era.* Westwood, CT: Greenwood.

Kroeger, B. (2003). *Passing: When people can't be who they are.* New York: PublicAffairs, Perseus Books Group.

Ladner, J. (1977). *Tomorrow's tomorrow: The Black woman.* Garden City, NY: Anchor Books.

Larsen, N. (1929). *Passing.* New York: Knopf.

Levi, P. (2004). The gray zone. In N. Scheper-Hughes & P. Bourgois (Eds.), *Violence in war and peace* (pp. 83–90). Malden, MA: Blackwell.

Murray, P. (1978). *Proud shoes: The story of an American family.* Boston: Beacon Press. (Original work published 1956).

Piper, A. (1996). Passing for White, passing for Black. In E. K. Ginsberg (Ed.), *Passing and the fictions of identity* (pp. 234–271). Durham, NC: Duke University Press.

Roberts, D. (1997). *Killing the Black body: Race, reproduction, and the meaning of liberty.* New York: Pantheon.

Robinson, C. F. (2003). *Dangerous liaisons: Sex and love in the segregated South.* Fayetteville: University of Arkansas Press.

Rothman, J. D. (2003). *Notorious in the neighborhood: Sex and families across the color line in Virginia, 1781–1861*. Chapel Hill: University of North Carolina Press.

Singleton, J. (Director), & Poirier, G. (Writer). (1997). *Rosewood* [Motion picture]. United States: Warner Brothers.

Sirk, D. (Director). (1959). *Imitation of life* [Motion picture]. United Kingdom: Universal International Pictures.

Sollors, W. (Ed.). (2000). *Interracialism: Black-White intermarriage in American history, literature, and law*. Oxford: Oxford University Press.

Spillers, H. (1987). "Mamma's baby, papa's maybe": An American grammar book. *Diacritics, 17*(2), 65–81.

White, W. (1998). *A man called White: The autobiography of Walter White*. Athens: University of Georgia Press. (Original work published 1945).

Williamson, J. (1995). *New people: Miscegenation and mulattoes in the United States*. Baton Rouge: Louisiana State University Press.

Willie, S. S. (2003). *Acting Black: College, identity and the performance of race*. New York: Routledge.

Young, V. (2007). *Your average nigga: Performing race, literacy and black masculinity*. Detroit, MI: Wayne State University.

Earlier versions of this paper were presented at the 1997 annual meeting of the American Anthropological Association and in 1996 at the Institute for African American Studies at the University of Connecticut.

ACHIEVEMENT AS RESISTANCE

THE DEVELOPMENT OF A CRITICAL RACE ACHIEVEMENT
IDEOLOGY AMONG BLACK ACHIEVERS

DORINDA J. CARTER ANDREWS*

INTRODUCTION

Many individuals hold deeply to the idea that the United States is "the land of opportunity," where people can go as far as their own merit takes them. In other words, one's social and economic mobility are achieved primarily through individual effort and hard work; regardless of race, gender, socio-economic status, or other social identity, individuals can claim a piece of the American Dream by "pulling themselves up by their bootstraps." This idea that individual agency is the primary determinant of social and economic mobility and success is commonly known as the myth of meritocracy.[1] Not only do many individuals think that the system of obtaining upward mobility *should* operate based on individual merit, they also believe that this is how the system actually *does* operate in the United States (MacLeod, 1987). In this ideology, structural conditions (e.g., joblessness, poverty, racism, classism, sexism, etc.) do not prohibit or even constrain individuals from achieving their personal goals.

This myth of meritocracy can also apply to schooling, suggesting that people who demonstrate high performance through hard work and individual effort in formal education can achieve positive future outcomes. Students who espouse this mainstream achievement ideology (MacLeod, 1987) about schooling typically believe that "if I work really hard and always put forth maximal effort in school, I can achieve my current and future goals." Like the larger myth within U.S. society, this ideology is typically associated with the beliefs and attitudes that white and/or middle-class students hold about the value of schooling (O'Connor, 1997). The mainstream achievement ideology

* This article was originally published under the name Dorinda J. Carter.

Harvard Educational Review   Vol. 78   No. 3   Fall 2008

requires individuals to take ownership of their successes and failures, and it fails to account for structural conditions that might constrain or even impede students' abilities to achieve their maximum potentials in school and life. To extend the bootstraps metaphor, the fact that some individuals come to school with no laces for their boots—or no boots at all—is seldom considered. Similarly, that many students are afforded or denied access to opportunities based on the perceived value of their boots is also often an afterthought or simply never considered.

In this article, I investigate a conceptual gap in the current literature on race and achievement ideology by applying the lens of critical race theory to consider the achievement ideologies of nine high-achieving African American students attending a predominantly white public high school. I first provide an overview of the current discourse regarding the relationship between race, achievement ideology, and school behaviors of African American students. I then discuss critical race theory (Delgado & Stefancic, 2001) as an analytical framework to challenge the boundaries of mainstream achievement ideology and provide a lens for understanding how race and racism can inform one's attitudes and beliefs about schooling. I then propose six tenets of a critical race achievement ideology (CRAI), which emerges both from my research participants' descriptions of their experiences and from other empirical work. Ultimately, CRAI provides a new concept of successful African American students' approaches to school achievement.

AFRICAN AMERICANS, ACHIEVEMENT IDEOLOGY, AND SCHOOL BEHAVIORS

Do African American students believe schooling is a vehicle for their upward social and economic mobility? If so, do their school behaviors promote school success? What roles do race and racism play in shaping black students' schooling dispositions and academic performance? Decades of research related to these questions have yielded varied answers, indicating that African Americans cannot be examined as a monolithic group, especially regarding their beliefs about the utility of schooling and their subsequent school behaviors. What we have learned from this research is that black students' perceptions of schooling as a racialized and classed process inform the way they adjust to the learning environment, and their behaviors can play out as either adaptive or maladaptive for school success. What is missing from the literature is an explicit examination of how racial and achievement self-perceptions interact to shape students' achievement ideologies and school behaviors, particularly adaptive behaviors. This study attempts to address this gap in the literature.

The ethnographic research of John Ogbu (1978, 1987, 1991, 2003) is widely cited in characterizing the achievement ideology of black students and their resultant school behavior. His work, both alone (1991, 2003) and in partnership with Herbert Simons (1998), uses a cultural-ecological framework to suggest that many black students hold negative beliefs about the link between schooling and opportunity. Specifically, they do not view schooling as an avenue for achieving positive life outcomes because they perceive race-based labor market discrimination as a relatively permanent barrier that cannot be overcome through the educational system. Both a shared history of discrimination and the perception that schools are primarily controlled by whites lead black students to actively resist activities and behaviors associated with academic success, since these activities are equated with assimilation into the white middle class and thus viewed as compromising a black social identity and group solidarity. Ogbu asserts that the collective and oppositional ideology of many black students leads to maladaptive behavioral strategies for school and subsequent relatively poor academic success. Where the cultural-ecological analysis falls short is in considering how individuals' self-perceptions inform their ideological constructions and resulting school behaviors. This process is inherently cultural and, in part, shaped by individual perceptions of societal structures.

Other research linking the achievement ideology and school behaviors of black students describes these students as embodying incongruent attitudes and behaviors. Described as an attitude-achievement paradox, research posits that some black students believe in the mainstream achievement ideology but do not exhibit school behaviors that support high academic performance (Ford, 1991; Mickelson, 1990). These adolescents value education in the abstract, believing that hard work and individual effort result in a high return on investment. However, their concrete attitudes are informed by their perceptions of the American opportunity structure, perceptions that differ based on the ways in which race, ethnicity, and social class shape individuals' and groups' experiences within this opportunity structure (Mickelson, 1990). Similar to Ogbu's work, this argument recognizes how the interaction between structural conditions and individual agency can affect academic achievement. However, it does not closely consider the connections between how black students' thoughts about the significance of race to their lives and the significance of achievement to their self-definition inform the embodiment of maladaptive school behaviors and subsequent academic underperformance.

A growing body of psychological and sociological literature highlights the significance of understanding racial identity and its relationship to achievement ideologies and school behaviors. Sellers, Smith, Shelton, Rowley, and Chavous (1998) posit that an individual's beliefs about the significance of race will influence his or her behavior during specific events in a specific context. For example, in the school context, heightened racial salience (or the extent to which one's race is a relevant part of one's self-concept at a particular moment or in a particular situation) might moderate the extent to which one's racial beliefs influence his or her interpretation of a specific event in school and subsequent behavior in response to this event. A black student who has strong racial pride and heightened sensitivity to negative intellectual stereotypes about his or her racial group may take on a prove-them-wrong attitude in the classroom where those stereotypes exist (D. Carter, 2005). This type of higher racial salience is related to higher academic achievement (Sellers, Chavous, & Cooke, 1998). The psychological work of Robert Sellers and his colleagues is a move in the right direction toward examining the significance that some black students attribute to "blackness" as being part of their self-definition and how this informs their achievement ideology, school behaviors, and academic performance. However, Sellers et al. do not focus on the interrelatedness of racial and *achievement* self-conceptions and the resulting achievement ideologies.

In addition to the work of Robert Sellers and his colleagues (Sellers, Chavous, & Cooke, 1998; Sellers, Smith, Shelton, Rowley, & Chavous, 1998), other educational scholars who use sociological frameworks suggest that some students of color can successfully negotiate primary and dominant cultural codes in school in order to acquire academic success while also affirming and maintaining strong pride in their racial and ethnic heritages within the school context. Gibson (1988) calls this "accommodation without assimilation." Some students of color, who believe education can be a vehicle for upward mobility, strive to do well in school by acquiring the cultural codes required for school success while also recognizing the value of their own cultures, navigating effectively between their primary cultures and the dominant culture. Prudence Carter (2005) calls these types of students "cultural straddlers" and describes them as "hav[ing] bicultural perspectives; they are strategic movers across the cultural spheres" (p. 30). She characterizes these students as those who "play the game" of schooling (i.e., "do school"), embrace the cultural codes of both school and home community, or verbally critique the mainstream culture of schooling while simultaneously performing well academically.

Other sociological research has described these cultural straddlers in similar but unique ways, emphasizing that these students' knowledge of a limited opportunity structure does not constrain their academic and life pursuits. These scholars note that structural barriers such as racism and other forms of discrimination do not discourage these students from achieving their goals (Bergin & Cooks, 2002; Flores-González, 2002; Floyd, 1996; Hemmings, 1996; Mehan, Hubbard, & Villanueva, 1994; O'Connor, 1997; Sanders, 1997). What differentiates these black achievers from other black students who develop strategies for maintaining academic success is that they do not view school success as white property; therefore, they do not contend with the burden of "acting White" (Fordham & Ogbu, 1986) or feel the need to demonstrate "racelessness" (Fordham, 1988) in order to achieve in school. These students resist and defy these ideas by embracing the notion that school achievement is a raceless human trait that can be pursued by individuals of any racial or ethnic group. These and other researchers find that some black students maintain academic success by developing an acute understanding that, although racism might block their success, they will develop adaptive strategies for navigating this barrier in school; thus, maintaining a positive racial self-conception facilitates this process. This type of achievement ideology includes more nuanced constructions of how race might operate as a structural barrier to constrain one's success.

While the work of these scholars contributes to our understanding of how black achievers navigate the process of schooling in culturally affirming ways, absent from the literature is a focus on understanding the implications of embodying such an ideology in a predominantly white public school setting. Additionally, the complicated nature of how some black students situationally racialize and/or deracialize the task of achieving academic success also has not been explicitly studied. This study attempts to address gaps in the existing discourse on African Americans, achievement ideology, and school behaviors by focusing on the interrelatedness of students' racial and achievement conceptions, their achievement ideology, and their resultant adaptive school behaviors in a predominantly white learning environment. This work combines the psychological and sociological discourses to arrive at a new understanding of how race and achievement ideologies inform black students' school success.

CRITICAL RACE THEORY AND ACHIEVEMENT IDEOLOGY: A NEW LENS

One way to examine and better understand black students' racial constructions as they relate to their thoughts about schooling is through a critical race theory (CRT) framework. CRT began as a legal movement by activists and scholars interested in studying and transforming the relationship among race, racism, and power (Delgado & Stefancic, 2001). Today, many educational scholars use CRT to analyze racial injustice in schools as it is enacted through educational issues, policies, and ideology (Ladson-Billings, 1999; Ladson-Billings & Tate, 1995; Solórzano, Ceja, & Yosso, 2000; Solórzano & Yosso, 2001; Tate, 1997). This approach challenges the mainstream achievement ideology, which dismisses any presence of social inequality in the United States and any structural conditions that might interact with people's exertion of individual agency to achieve upward mobility. CRT acknowledges the significant role of various forms of discrimination that impede the achievement of black students and other members of subordinate racial and ethnic groups. The basic tenets of CRT focus on:

1. racism as normal in American society and strategies for exposing it in its various forms;
2. the significance of experiential knowledge and the use of storytelling to "analyze the myths, presuppositions, and received wisdoms that make up the common culture about race and that invariably render blacks and other minorities one-down" (Delgado, 1995, p. xiv);
3. challenges to traditional and dominant discourse and paradigms on race, gender, and class by showing how these social constructs intersect to affect people of color;

4. a commitment to social justice; and
5. an examination of race and racism across disciplinary fields (e.g., psychology and education).

According to Roithmayr (1999), "Critical race theory can be used to 'deconstruct' the meaning of 'educational achievement'" (p. 5). As an analytical framework, it furthers our understanding of how race and racism inform black students' achievement ideology and school behaviors, and it counters the hegemonic myth of meritocracy that leads individuals to believe that racism, as a structural barrier, is nonexistent. Therefore, the intersection of critical race theory and the mainstream achievement ideology calls for a different kind of achievement ideology that considers how the structural condition of racism interacts with black students' individual agency in their pursuit of academic success and upward social and economic mobility.

An examination of the data presented in this article reveals an achievement ideology held by these high-achieving black students that counters Ogbu's and Mickelson's theories. These students have an achievement ideology that is collective and resistant in nature rather than collective and oppositional. Instead of embodying romantic tenets of the mainstream achievement ideology (Mehan et al., 1994), these students view achievement as a means to an end, considering what it means to achieve as a *black* person. By conceptualizing success in the context of being a proud member of the black community, some participants develop an achievement ethos that reflects an understanding of success despite systemic forces that oppress black people in society. Even though studies show that some black students with a high awareness of racial discrimination respond in resilient ways using strategies that are conducive to academic success, seeing race as an important aspect of one's self-definition and being aware of the effects of racism on one's life is not enough to sustain academic achievement and school success (Oyserman, Gant, & Ager, 1995). According to Oyserman, Gant, and Ager (1995), a third dimension of an African American identity is needed to maintain school persistence and high levels of performance. These and other scholars posit that black youth must conceptualize achievement as occurring within, rather than separate from, the context of being African American in order to sustain high levels of school success (Azibo, 1991; Oyserman et al., 1995; Perry, 2003). In other words, being academically successful and being black cannot be perceived as dichotomous, nor can academic success be viewed as a white character trait.

By conceptualizing achievement as embedded within one's sense of self as an African American, youths will not experience contradiction and tension between achievement and their African American identity (Oyserman et al., 1995). Thus, school success is dependent on (1) seeing oneself as a member of the racial group (i.e., connectedness); (2) being aware of stereotypes and limitations to one's present and future social and economic outcomes (i.e., awareness of racism); *and* (3) developing a perspective of self as succeeding as a racial group member (i.e., achievement as an African American) (Oyserman et al., 1995). Oyserman's work is theoretical in nature and does not include empirical data that highlights the voices of black students. The present study extends these theoretical constructs by illuminating explicit instances where black students' ideas and behaviors confirm Oyserman's conceptualization.

RESEARCH QUESTIONS

This study investigates an important gap in the current literature on race and achievement by asking if the lens of critical race theory can illuminate ways that successful African American students in a highly racialized context may use resistant or adaptive approaches to support their school success. This article explores how successful African American students shift from the mainstream achievement ideology through an examination of the schooling attitudes and beliefs of nine high-achieving black students attending a predominantly white, suburban public high school.[2] Research questions guiding this investigation include:

1. How do high-achieving African American students describe and understand the behaviors they employ in classroom, social, and extracurricular domains in a predominantly white high school?
2. How do these students' perceptions of values, behavioral norms, and expectations in these domains inform the behaviors they employ in these different domains within the school context?
3. How, if at all, do these students view these domains as fundamentally different along racial lines?

By using CRT to examine students' responses related to these questions, race and racism become central to deconstructing black students' schooling experiences in a predominantly white learning environment. Their lived experiences become counternarratives about the role of race in shaping some black students' achievement ideologies and school behaviors.

My study adds to the literature by exploring the unique achievement ideology of my participants: They are able to undertake the complicated work of viewing achievement as a human, raceless trait while simultaneously viewing the task of achieving as racialized. As a theoretical concept, my study attempts to shift the paradigm of current thinking about how one's attitudes and beliefs about the utility of schooling couple with adaptive behavioral strategies for school success by highlighting the continued presence of racism as a structural barrier to this success. While there are other forms of discrimination that might also impede students' achievement (e.g., sexism, classism, heterosexism, etc.), in this study race emerges as a salient factor as these high-achieving black students navigate their predominantly white high school context and develop adaptive behavioral strategies to maintain school success and a positive racial self-conception.

Here I want to clarify how the key terminology of achievement and success are being used in this article. I use the term *school success* to characterize both academic and social success. I believe that school success should not simply be measured by an individual's academic performance but also by achievement in the extracurricular activities in which he or she participates and by an individual's ability to maintain acceptance by the social groups of which he or she desires to be a part; thus, school success is a holistic outcome of positive child development. More broadly defined, *success* is the achievement of a desired outcome related to an individual's quality of life, such as completing high school, entering college, or owning a business. In this study, the students' measures of school success included getting good grades, feeling good about themselves, having a strong social support network, and being goal oriented (D. Carter, 2005). They considered success beyond high school to be going to college, obtaining financial stability, and achieving specific career aspirations, among other things (D. Carter, 2005). In this article, my use of the term *achievement* indicates a student's accomplishment of specific tasks or goals. I refer to both *academic success* and *academic achievement* as a student's ability to maintain high performance in academic courses at the school.

METHODOLOGY

Research Site

I collected this interview and observational data between September 2003 and May 2004 at Independence High School,[3] a predominantly white, upper-class, suburban, four-year comprehensive public high school in eastern Massachusetts. Of the 2,181 students enrolled during the 2003–2004 school year, approximately 80.7 percent were white, 9.5 percent Asian, 5.6 percent black, 4 percent Hispanic, and 0.18 percent American Indian (D. Carter, 2005, p. 64). Of the 121 students identified as black, only eighteen were enrolled in an honors or AP course at the time of this study. Only fifteen African American students in the school had a B (3.0) or higher cumulative grade point average, approximately 12 percent of the black student population at Independence High—a very bleak statistic. These numbers represented concrete evidence for the principal's concern over black student underperformance that had existed for several years at Independence High. I believed that examining how race was operating in this learning environment might reveal some information regarding black students' achievement patterns at Independence. That is, among those black students who were performing at high levels in this type of learning environment, a degree of resiliency to the structural barriers perpetuated by racism might be a factor in their success.

Study Participants

I recruited African American students in tenth through twelfth grade who were identified as high achievers based on enrollment in at least one college prep or honors/AP course, participation in at least one extracurricular activity, and also one or more of the following criteria: a GPA of 2.8 or higher,[4] consistent honor roll status, and/or teacher recommendation. After conducting a screening interview with all students who volunteered to participate, I purposively selected (Maxwell, 1996) nine students (four females and five males) to participate in the study. I was interested in studying students who self-identified as black/African American and were considered high achievers.[5] Some students participated in the local busing program, which allowed African American students from the inner city to attend school in the suburbs. Participants ranged in age from fifteen to eighteen and came from single-parent families, two-parent families, and families with an extended family member (e.g., aunt, uncle, grandmother) as the primary guardian. Table 1 summarizes demographic data for the study sample.

Although each participant self-identified as black or African American, they varied in ethnic identity: Some were born to two African American parents, others had two parents of different racial/ethnic backgrounds, or some had two parents of Caribbean descent. This variation provided an interesting examination of how race and ethnicity impacted these students' schooling experiences and achievement ideologies. For example, those students born to West Indian parents were considered second-generation immigrants and most closely resembled Mary Waters's (1999) classification of West Indian students identified as "American" and "Ethnic" in the way that they described their affiliation with African American culture and its significance to their self-definition. For this group, their ethnic heritage was the most salient part of their "racial" identity. For participants with mixed heritages, they described "blackness" as the most salient cultural aspect of their racial identity.

Data Collection Procedures and Analysis

Using the Three-Interview Series method (Seidman, 1998), I conducted three in-depth, semi-structured interviews with each participant. Although each interview followed a protocol, I also explored topics that the participants introduced. I asked students to provide examples of and rationales for their behavioral choices in school. I also asked them to provide examples of how they perceived race as impacting their schooling experiences, if at all. This deeper probing served as an entry into these students' lives and allowed me to help them make sense of their experiences as well as help me understand how they related these lived experiences from their particular racial/ethnic background to their school experiences and behaviors. All interviews were conducted at the school site, audiotaped, and later transcribed verbatim by an external transcriber. Primary interview questions focused on students' definitions of success, the construction of their academic and racial self-concepts, and their motivation(s) to succeed. I also asked students whether or not they perceived race to be a factor in their schooling and who and/or what sources of support contributed to their success.

TABLE 1   *Demographic Data for Study Sample (N = 9)*

Name	Gender	Age	Self-Reported Racial Identification	GPA
Rodney	Male	17	African American	3.20
Derek	Male	18	African American and Puerto Rican	3.01
Rachel	Female	17	Mainly African American and also recognizes Cape Verdean and Haitian roots	3.11
Leslie	Female	15	Biracial (Black/White)	3.00
Kelis	Female	17	Black or West Indian	3.00
Kimmy	Female	15	Black/African American and also recognizes West Indian roots	3.11
Mark	Male	17	Black/African American	2.89
Samantha	Female	16	African American and also recognizes Jamaican roots	3.09
Aaron	Male	17	African American and also recognizes Haitian roots	3.22

In addition, I shadowed each participant for two consecutive school days and observed his or her behaviors in classroom and nonclassroom settings in the school. After writing several analytic memos about each participant, I observed some participants for an extra school day in order to clarify some of my initial assumptions. After completing the third interview with each participant, I conducted a sixty-minute focus group interview with five of the participants (although all participants were invited, not all could be present). The focus group provided participants with an opportunity to interact with and debate one another as they responded and reacted to each other's comments regarding questions I used in the individual interviews.

To understand both my participants' attitudes and beliefs about the utility of schooling in achieving life outcomes and how their perceptions of race and racism factored into behavioral strategies for school success, I used a grounded theory approach (Strauss & Corbin, 1998). Through this approach, I inductively developed an analytic framework through constant interaction across the study's data; essentially, the theoretical findings are grounded in the actual data collected (Maxwell, 1996). Therefore, while concepts from the existing literature were considered in my initial analysis of the data (e.g., racism, achievement ideology, racial identity), I used both open and focused coding to analyze my data and allowed codes and larger themes to emerge from the data regarding the interrelatedness of race, racial identity, achievement ideology, and school behaviors (such as critical race consciousness, struggle, burden to succeed, and achievement as a human characteristic). I also employed thematic analysis and narrative analysis and created participant profiles to further examine my data. The narrative summaries and participant profiles were helpful in building cross-case matrices to compare participants' experiences based on emerging themes. This analytic strategy helped me develop the concept of a critical race achievement ideology by pulling together salient themes related to race, achievement ideology, and racism.

Role of the Researcher: Insider Status—Asset and Liability

I believe that my role as a young (twenty-something) African American researcher with both experience as a high school teacher and a schooling background similar to those of the participants proved advantageous for establishing trusting relationships with the students. In an initial informational meeting, I told participants that I had been a high-achieving student who attended predominantly white schools in the South. I described why this study was important to me personally and professionally. Thus, before engaging in any interviews with me, participants learned about me as a researcher and individual and understood what it was that I hoped to learn from them—that is, how they were experiencing their school and what behaviors they employed in the school context. I tried to be as transparent as possible with participants with the hope of establishing a foundational trust. As a result, the students seemed very willing to share stories about their experiences at Independence High with me.

I also believe that my race contributed to the building of these trusting relationships. Many of the participants indicated that they felt more at ease discussing sensitive topics such as race and racism with a person who shared their racial group affiliation. My age was also an asset. Many of the participants stated that I reminded them of an older sister with whom they could share some of the intimacies of their experiences in this predominantly white learning environment. Participants' awareness that I was a former high school math teacher led them to believe that I had firsthand knowledge of the challenges of classroom activity, both from a student perspective and a teacher perspective. Thus, I was able to develop a rapport of trust with participants because I allowed them to see who I was beyond the role of researcher.

While my identity as a black woman was advantageous to the study, I also believe it posed some challenges. The biggest challenge involved the interview process. Participants had a difficult time describing their identities and analyzing their school experiences through a racial lens. I faced challenges managing my expectations for students' abilities to answer race questions with their expectations that I would understand what they meant by their limited responses to my interview questions related to race and racism. I assumed that participants would talk openly about race with me because I was black; however, their responses to race questions were shallow in some instances, because they assumed that I could extrapolate meaning from their short answers. Participants would continuously say, "You know what I mean?" because they perceived that our shared racial group heritage meant that I understood their limited responses to race-related questions. I learned that I had to probe further to extrapolate deeper meaning from participants' limited race talk. In many cases, I had to ask participants to provide concrete examples or stories to clarify their point.

FINDINGS

Overall, my analysis of the data from this study suggests that the achievement ideology of these students incorporates a critical consciousness about the role race plays as a potential structural barrier constraining their school and life success. Rather than espousing beliefs about schooling that lead to maladaptive behaviors and subsequent underachievement, these students have schooling dispositions that facilitate their enactment of resilient adaptive behaviors to navigate what they perceive to be a racially hostile school context (see D. Carter, 2005). My use of the descriptor "resilient" is very intentional, indicating that these students' stories illuminate their commitment to surmount the negative racialization of the task of achieving in their predominantly white school. In the process of "doing school" in an environment in which academic success is defined in mainstream, hegemonic ways, these students are able to maintain high academic performance *and* a positive racial self-conception. These students embody a critical race achievement ideology that allows them to both view themselves as achieving within the context of being black and also overcome perceived racism in their school environment.

CRAI emerged from careful analysis of participants' voices and behaviors in a yearlong qualitative investigation. It is a construct that arises from black achievers' attitudes and beliefs about the utility of schooling for obtaining positive life outcomes and their understanding of their resilient and adaptive school behaviors for success in a predominantly white learning environment. This achievement ideology has, at its core, a critical understanding of the role race plays in one's educational experiences and life outcomes and facilitates a psychological resistance to racism as a potential barrier to success. Their achievement ideology operates as a strategy to achieve traditional definitions of mainstream success while simultaneously aiding them in redefining success. Although these students attempt to deracialize achievement (i.e., view achievement as a general human trait) in describing their school experiences, they still perceive the task of achievement as racialized based on their experiences with racism in their predominantly white high school.

The remainder of this article focuses on describing the components of CRAI, revealing how this type of ideological disposition represents an acute awareness of and resistance to the mythical bootstraps theory. Throughout this article, I will not detail the ways in which these students' school behaviors represent resilient adaptation to schooling; however, I will provide a few examples so the reader can gain some insight into how a critical race achievement ideology facilitates school success for these nine students and allows them to maintain a strong racial self-concept.

THE DEVELOPMENT OF A CRITICAL RACE ACHIEVEMENT IDEOLOGY

In my study, the interrelatedness of race and achievement as primary components of these students' identities facilitates the development of the critical race achievement ideology (see Figure 1). These students view themselves as achieving in the context of being black, and, for them, the task of achieving is racialized, given their experiences in a racially biased school context. Although achievement is a part of their self-definition, they construe it as a human characteristic rather than a black or white characteristic (see D. Carter, 2005). Nonetheless, their attitudes and beliefs about achievement are not constructed in a vacuum. I argue that their understandings of how race operates in their daily lives inform their constructions of achievement beliefs, attitudes, and self-definitions and influence their racialization and deracialization of the task of achieving at various times in the school context. Thus, their achievement ideology integrates a sense of individual agency with an awareness and understanding of racism as a structural condition designed to impede upward mobility.

In brief, a critical race achievement ideology is both a psychological and a behavioral framework that considers the act of performing at high levels in school an act of resistance against the mainstream achievement ideology and

FIGURE 1   *The Interrelatedness of Race and Achievement Self-Constructions*

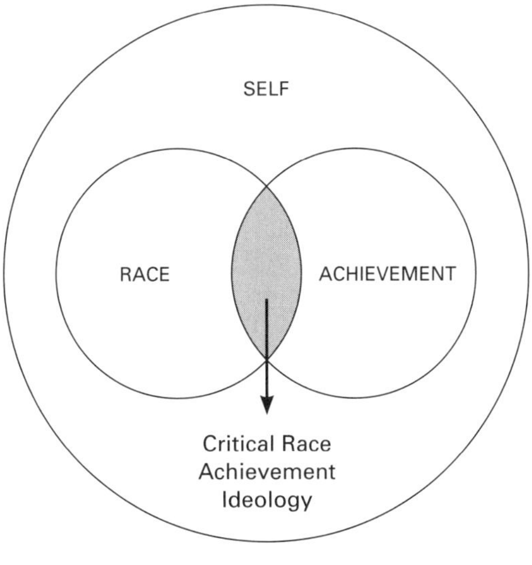

SELF

RACE   ACHIEVEMENT

Critical Race
Achievement
Ideology

(D. Carter, 2005)

183

notions of school success as a white character trait and act. It reflects aspects of Ward's (2000) concept of resistance in that it forms when African American students internalize messages from family members and other adults in their lives that build a strong racial self-concept—resistance born from "love and purpose, racial pride, and connection" (p. 55). It is a resistance for survival in that these black students' psyches are constantly under attack in a learning environment in which their racial group membership is often associated with anti-intellectualism and/or intellectual inferiority.

CRAI primarily originates in students' views of themselves as successful members of their racial group and their school successes as individual and collective racial group accomplishments. These two self-views emanate from strong racial and achievement self-definitions; participants in this study espouse an achievement ideology that draws on their self-conceptions as racially and academically competent individuals.[6] The positive meaning of race in their everyday lives, as well as the significance of achieving as a member of a subdominant racial group in the United States, informs how these students think about the importance of education and schooling to their future. It also informs the adaptive behaviors and strategies that they enact in order to achieve within a racist environment. In the Independence environment, these black achievers are surmounting what they perceive to be a culturally oppressive learning environment and redefining achievement through the embodiment of a critical race achievement ideology. Using participants' words, I describe the six dimensions of the ideology below.

Students believe in themselves and feel that individual effort and self-accountability lead to school success.

Possessing a sense of self as an achiever and internalizing the concept of hard work and individual effort are two character traits necessary to sustain school success. Participants in this study possess a belief in self that facilitates their achievement motivation and subsequent enactment of achievement-oriented behaviors in school. For example, Kimmy and Aaron talk about themselves as good students and describe the roles that hard work and ownership of learning and academic performance play in school success:

> A good student is a student that puts forth 100 percent effort at all times . . . does as much as they can to improve themselves in any particular subject. . . . Just gives 100 percent effort and don't slack off. [DC: Do you see yourself as a good student?] I would say so. I would say I'm a good student. . . . I know what I wanna get out of life, so you know, I'm just trying to work toward the goals I've set for myself. In order to reach those goals, I know I have to work hard, try the best I can. (Aaron, senior)

> [DC: What does it mean to be a good student?] To pretty much work hard. Try your best at whatever you do. Try to achieve. [DC: Do you see yourself as a good student?] Yes. I work hard in school, try to get good grades. . . . Like if I'm strug-

gling or not understanding something in class, I always go to my teacher and ask can they explain it, or I ask right after class, or I'll come after school and they'll show me and give me examples of how to do different things. Like I went to my math teacher a lot this year, just cuz I was struggling more than usual. (Kimmy, sophomore)

Kimmy and Aaron both value effort as part of their self-conceptions as being good, successful students. In turn, in large part they hold themselves accountable for their academic successes and failures. Kimmy, for example, explains that she seeks additional help from teachers when she does not clearly understand a concept discussed in class. In their comments, Kimmy and Aaron do affirm the dominant narrative of how one "makes it" in the United States. They believe in the importance of hard work and individual effort for upward social and economic mobility, and they value a strong work ethic because they perceive that the return on investment is quite beneficial. Kimmy and Aaron believe that high school is preparing them "for the outside world of adulthood and independence" and to "go to college." Steele (1997) posits that this kind of identification with school—such that it is part of one's self-definition—is necessary to sustain school success. For such an identification to form and persist, one must perceive that one has the skills and resources to prosper in the domain: These students identify with schooling as a domain in which they are accountable to themselves for their outcomes.

Participants in this study tend to attribute their successes to academic competence and hard work and their less-than-satisfactory performance to lack of effort, misguided priorities, and inconsistent focus. They sometimes attribute limitations in their overall ability to succeed to racism experienced in the school context. These students claim ownership for their performance and strive to use their personal strengths to improve their weaknesses. Samantha (a junior) underscores this when articulating that she tries to work on her weak points in school in order to improve her overall self. "If I see that I have a weak point in something, I'm gonna try to work on it, and if I have a strong point in something, then I'm gonna continue to do that." Kimmy talks about seeking the help and guidance of teachers after school when she is struggling with concepts from class. These students believe that their locus of control is internal rather than external (Weiner, 1986); their academic behaviors and outcomes are guided by their personal decisions and efforts rather than fate, luck, or other external factors. (They do, however, also perceive that limitations to their overall success can sometimes be attributed to structural barriers such as racism, which is characteristic of an external locus of control.)

Students also demonstrate their confidence in self and individual effort in the goals they set. They believe that their goals are realizable, and their performance in school is consistent with their expectations. For example, Aaron wants to become a medical doctor or lawyer. He achieved a perfect score on the SAT, has maintained a high GPA, involves himself in extracurricular activities, and maintains enrollment in honors and AP courses. He believes he is taking the necessary steps to acquire the skills that will aid him in meeting his career goals. His motivation, optimism about his future, and academic achievement are enhanced by his belief in his abilities and the value of hard work and his self-accountability for his school success. When asked how important he thought his performance in high school is to his future success, Aaron stated, "I think it's been very important, cuz if I didn't do as well as I did, I don't think I could have gotten into some of those places [referring to college acceptances]." Similarly, Rodney (junior) aspires to open his own autobody shop after college, and he is taking the necessary business electives in his senior year to gain the skills that he perceives will be beneficial to operating a business. It is clear that these students expect to realize their middle- and upper-class ambitions by maintaining high academic performance in school. They believe in their personal competence and have strong achievement self-concepts.

Other research corroborates the link between these beliefs and high academic performance. O'Connor (1997) found these personal character traits (i.e., belief in personal competence and strong achievement self-concepts) in the resilient black students in her study. Similarly, in a study of twenty low-income African American high school seniors, Floyd (1996) found that students expressed a belief in persistence and optimism as critical resources for being successful in school. What differentiates my study is the ability of my participants to articulate their racial salience and centrality and to embody and enact achievement-oriented behaviors that derive from these articulations.

Belief in one's abilities and an ethic of hard work, combined with a commitment to hold oneself responsible for achievement outcomes, are necessary ingredients for school success, and study participants utilize this self-confidence to resist experiences with racism in the school context. However, this character trait alone is not enough to sustain high academic achievement, a positive racial identity, or a positive future outlook. In fact, O'Connor (1997) found this to be true with some of her study participants. They did not possess strategies for overcoming constraints to their social and economic mobility; they also did not have examples of black role models who overcame barriers to success in their own lives. O'Connor suggests that these students need models and people who can convey to them how to personally negotiate these structural constraints. This finding suggests that other dimensions of a critical race achievement ideology are necessary in order to maintain school success and a strong racial self-concept.

Students view achievement as a human, raceless character trait embedded in their sense of self as a racial being.

In order to maintain school success without rejecting one's racial identity, the student must develop a perspective of self as a succeeding racial group member. This is a very important component of CRAI. School and life success should not come at the expense of one's racial identity. By conceptualiz-ing achievement as embedded within one's sense of self as a black person, it is unlikely that adolescents will experience contradiction and tension between being an achiever and being black. Rachel (a senior) believes that she is black *and* smart and emphasizes how her father has instilled this belief in her.

> When I was little he used to, like, tell me all the time that I'm black and I'm dif-ferent from people and for me, I dunno, just I have to work hard because you know white people don't think highly of black people, you know? Stuff like that. . . . It's kinda good cuz in a way I'm really, like, aware of the fact that I'm black. . . . My dad has taught me a lot about my background. So I still know about my history and what it is—what it actually means to be black. And I'm secure in my sense of self. I'm secure in my race and how smart I am.

In feeling secure about her intellect, Rachel views achievement as a human characteristic that can be obtained by anyone, regardless of race; however, the task of achieving is racialized for her because she feels that she has to work harder than other students given her racial identification. Her father has racially socialized her to the world around her, and being an achiever is a char-acter trait embedded in Rachel's self-definition as a black person.

Kimmy also expresses her belief in herself as a succeeding black person: "Well, it's known for black people to struggle and stuff, like, [in] school and everything. And to me, I just feel as though I'm gonna be one of those black people that's gonna make it and prove a lotta people wrong that black people can achieve and do good in school." Kimmy is motivated to prove wrong a neg-ative racial stereotype that she perceives others hold: that African Americans are anti-intellectual and underperform in school. Instead of responding in maladaptive ways, she demonstrates achievement-oriented behaviors in school that allow her to convey to her peers that black students are as intelligent as any other students. Both Rachel and Kimmy do not operate from a deficit mentality about black intellectual capacity; instead, they see achievement as intrinsic to who they are as racial beings. Several scholars and empirical stud-ies suggest that conceptualizing achievement as occurring within the context of being black sustains high levels of school success (Azibo, 1991; Oyserman et al., 1995; Perry, Steele, & Hilliard, 2003). Thus, my participants do not possess an attitude achievement paradox (Mickelson, 1990; Ogbu & Simons, 1998); their achievement attitudes, beliefs, and behaviors are aligned so as to facili-tate high academic performance in the school context. This component of CRAI serves to challenge dominant discourses regarding black anti-intellectu-alism by illustrating how some black students deconstruct normalized concep-tions of achievement in order to maintain their own school success.

The alignment of achievement beliefs, attitudes, and behaviors is nurtured in several ways. Many of these students possess strong racial and ethnic self-concepts, which, through positive racial socialization (as seen through the words of Rachel's father), help them view themselves as successful. As Rodney states, "I like being what I am. I think that my race is very strong, and I like associating myself with that." This high racial centrality and positive racial regard is nurtured by a counternarrative conveyed by parents who emphasize pride and self-respect as members of the racial group (Perry, 2003; Ward, 2000). This racial socialization also includes messages about expectations for academic achievement. These students' race-conscious parents are explicit in expressing the importance of high levels of achievement as a member of a subdominant racial group in America. Rachel's father, for example, encourages her to work twice as hard for her achievement because she is black and "white people don't think highly of black people."

School success, then, becomes both an individual goal and a collective goal as a result of receiving these racialized achievement messages. Like Rachel's father, black parents and other adults in this study are teaching the concepts of collectivism, black familialism, and the value of kin networks. These students develop a collective identity that includes achievement (Bowman & Howard, 1985); it is not oppositional, as Ogbu suggests. As expressed in Kimmy's earlier remark, students show an awareness of a historic collective struggle within the black community for educational equity and access as a means to upward mobility. Thus, the notion of collective struggle, the salience of group identity, and theories of "making it" produce adaptive instead of maladaptive educational outcomes. O'Connor (1997) also found this to be the case in her research, as students' knowledge of black struggle did not discourage them from achieving; rather, this knowledge fueled the belief that achievement was possible, since members of the race had already overcome perceived insurmountable barriers such as racism, propelling some students to work harder. Similarly, students in my study were compelled to achieve based on their knowledge of "black struggle." Rodney expresses his support for the collective struggle when describing his success as an obligation to members of his racial group: "I'm not sayin' that I'm trying to move all black people out of the ghettos, but, definitely, I wanna make a difference . . . I wanna succeed." This view of success as an individual and collective group accomplishment helps students internalize success as a member of a racial group and maintain success and a strong racial self-definition. This awareness of the black struggle is also indicative of these students' critical race consciousness, another component of the critical race achievement ideology.

Students possess a critical consciousness about racism and the challenges it poses to their present and future opportunities as well as those of other members of their racial group.

In addition to believing in individual effort and seeing oneself as a succeeding member of the racial group, an individual must possess a critical consciousness about how race informs present and future opportunities in order to resist racism in ways that are adaptive for school success and the maintenance of a strong racial self. Several students demonstrate a critical awareness of the asymmetrical power relationships that exist between blacks and whites in America, and they express high ambitions while simultaneously registering high degrees of critical consciousness. For example, Derek (a senior) describes his perception of the effects of white privilege in his schooling and the larger society: "I think going to school out here, you see it's the white kids who can get bad grades and not do well on SATs and go to Penn State and go to the University of Virginia and go to UMass, but once they meet their quota for us—maybe one or two you gotta accept—and that's it. So that's part of the power." Derek sees racism as operating in both real and potentially imagined ways in his own life. His perception that colleges use quotas to racially diversify their student body is real to him but inaccurate in the larger society; however, he alludes to a critical awareness that white students are advantaged by the color of their skin when college admissions decisions are being made. He acknowledges what he perceives to be a racial hierarchy in U.S. society and describes how it might systemically disadvantage blacks. His awareness of the role race plays in potentially determining his future informs his behavioral responses in order to overcome the obstacle of racism (see D. Carter, 2005). For Derek, the existence of societal racism as a potential barrier to his success motivates him to persist in a school that he perceives as racially hostile. His attitude at Independence is "I'm here to do what I have to do so that when I have a family they won't want for nothing."

Rodney describes his critical awareness of racial differences in educational equity and access when expressing thoughts on civil rights.

> There was this white kid who said he didn't believe in civil action. Like if a white kid and a black kid get the same score on a test, and they're trying to get into college, it usually goes to the black kid, right? That's civil rights. Civil action is like the action of civil rights. He said he didn't believe that. He said he shouldn't have to pay for what happened if he wasn't directly connected to that problem [particularly referencing slavery]. . . . I know all the white kids here have tutors. If I get the same grades as a white kid who had, like, two tutors—of course I should get more respect! I did that by myself, you know? I got parents who didn't even finish high school and they're trying to help me with my math homework. I do it myself. I stay after till five or six o'clock and get help from teachers!

Rodney perceives that he has to work harder than his white counterparts for the same educational benefits (i.e., admissions to college) simply because of the color of his skin. He acknowledges that several of his white peers have private tutors, something that his family cannot afford for him; thus, these students are advantaged in terms of their academic preparation. For Rodney, achieving is racially loaded. He also alludes to his views on white privilege and black disadvantage when comparing educational opportunity. Both Derek and Rodney possess a critical awareness of racial (and economic) inequities that exist in society and in their school. However, they do not allow these inequities to impede their school success and future ambitions; rather, they persist in school by developing behavioral strategies for overcoming the institutional and structural racism that they see as barriers to their success. The racism is a motivator to prove wrong negative societal stereotypes that might exist about them as African Americans and African American males. A critical consciousness about the effects of racism on one's current and future opportunities can serve to academically motivate black students. A student in the O'Connor (1997) study who possessed a high degree of racial consciousness and affirmed her affiliation with the black community believed that, in the absence of struggle, blacks had no hope of "breaking the hold that Whites had on them" (p. 595). Students in my study express similar sentiments. They embrace the struggle and express a sense of power through the belief that blacks can improve their social and economic opportunities via consistently high educational achievement. Thus, a critical race consciousness fosters academic motivation and facilitates the development of a critical race achievement ideology in many of the participants.

Similarly, in her study of twenty-eight urban African American eighth graders, Sanders (1997) found that the high achievers in the sample had a heightened awareness of racial barriers to their success and were therefore compelled to demonstrate increased academic effort in the face of this obstacle. Some of the high achievers viewed racism as a challenge and saw their school success as an opportunity to counter societal stereotypes that depict black students as anti-intellectual and academically disengaged. My study builds on this work by connecting black achievers' views on racism to their achievement ideology. Several participants in my study embody similar beliefs. For example, Samantha strives to prove herself and "change that stereotype about black people when [she does] well in [her] classes." In one of her interviews, Rachel suggests that black students new to Independence High should counter racial stereotypes by "work[ing] extra hard to be better than them [white students], and, like, don't accept their mentality." Realizing that the process of attaining school success requires different strategies than those used by their white counterparts, these students demonstrate their critical awareness of the racial inequities that exist in school but they don't allow those inequities to deter them from achieving their school and life goals. Although their strategies for school success construct the task of achieving as racially loaded, their ideas about who can be successful (i.e., themselves) are race neutral; thus, achievement is again viewed as a human characteristic.

Students possess a pragmatic attitude about the value of schooling for their future.

Students view education as a vehicle for social and economic mobility. Understanding the value of an education for future success is necessary for developing positive achievement beliefs and maintaining school success. Students in this study view schooling as instrumental to future life outcomes and conceptualize education as highly significant. This is explicitly illustrated in their descriptions of the purpose of school. Participants believe school helps you "get a good education so you can go to college" (Kimmy), "provides a mental and educational background for the future" (Derek), and prepares you for adulthood and life (Rodney). Kelis (a senior) clearly understands the utility of an education:

> Like, if you don't have a high school diploma, the job that you have is not gonna pay great, which is not gonna put you on a good economic status in society and then you're not gonna live in a good neighborhood or you're not gonna be able to provide for your family—if you have one—the best way you can, so it all stems from, like, at least graduating from high school.

For these students, high school success sets them on the path for a positive future that includes college completion and a stable professional career. For example, Leslie (a sophomore) wants a financial position better than that of her mother: "I know that [doing well is] definitely gonna help me. I really want to go to college, and be successful. I just wanna be . . . well-off, I guess. So I guess that's my motivation. I don't wanna struggle to afford things, cuz my mom has gone through a lot, and I just feel like that's what I strive for." Having self-identified her family as lower-middle-class, Leslie desires to use her education as a medium for becoming financially stable as an adult.

Aaron also understands schooling as a means of opening doors to enhanced future opportunities: "The better you do in school, the more opportunities you give yourself later on." Rachel describes similar sentiments in wanting to achieve more than members of her family have: "Well, for me it's important, but I dunno if I think that for everyone it's important to do well in school. I wanna be better than most of my family, and I actually, like, wanna graduate and, like, make something of myself. . . . For me, I just have a lot of ambitions, and I just wanna make sure that I have the background to achieve those." She has goals that she is determined to achieve. Wanting to make something of herself is a primary ambition and one that she knows requires additional schooling. She speaks of wanting to explore a number of careers, including law, physical therapy, and foreign language interpreting. Although she is entertaining a range of career ideas, she does not think that any of these are beyond her reach. Her high academic marks at Independence High support her belief that she is on the right path to future success and highlight her strong self-definition as an achiever. Where research has reserved this kind of thinking for immigrant students and voluntary minorities (Ogbu & Simons, 1998), the students in this study defy the myth that black students do not believe economic mobility is achievable through school persistence.

Performing well in school is very important for the students in this study. They internalize the belief that "the better you do in school, the more opportunities you give yourself later on" (Aaron). These students have specific career aspirations that they believe are contingent on high academic performance and postsecondary education. They aspire to become middle- and upper-class individuals in society. Thus, their academic motivation stems from believing in schooling as a means to a specific end: upward social and economic mobility. This pragmatic attitude about the value of schooling both buffers these students from negative environmental influences that might impede their school success and facilitates their academic motivation and persistence in school.

Students value multicultural competence as a skill for success.

Black students must be committed to acquiring the cultural capital that is often viewed as oppositional to African American cultural formations (Perry, 2003). For example, the individual must value the acquisition of mainstream speech, behaviors, and interaction patterns because they are required for full participation in mainstream society. Thus, students must understand the utility of acquiring various social and cultural codes for navigating the school context and then know when to situationally apply specific sets of codes. Many of the students in this study develop behavioral strategies akin to those of "border crossers" (Delgado-Gaitan & Trueba, 1991) or cultural straddlers (P. Carter, 2005), allowing them to move within and between various subcultures in the school and to understand the utility of acquiring the cultural capital of various cultural formations (including those for success).[7] By attending school in a racially integrated environment, the students in this study learn how to exist in a predominantly white context where white cultural styles and interaction patterns are dominant. They learn to navigate black cultural styles, white cultural styles, cultural styles required for school success, and other cultural styles in their daily school lives. Similar to the cultural straddlers in Prudence Carter's (2005) work, my participants are socially successful among their African American peers and also possess multiple cultural tool kits that allow them to interact with peers from other racial and ethnic backgrounds.

Several participants in this study express the value of exposure to diverse experiences that comes from interactions with students from various racial and ethnic groups at Independence High School. Specifically, students talk about belonging to both racially homogenous and diverse peer groups. In describing the value in having a diverse group of friends, Rachel says, "I also have white friends too, because it's important to have a variety [of friends]. In the real world outside of school, you have to interact with people of different races regardless of what you do. You have to come in contact with Chinese people, Philippine people, and if you start younger having relations with people like that, it makes it easier to continue doing it. Like, I think it's good to get a perspective from everyone, so I try as best as I can to have a variety of friends." Kimmy also believes that having racially diverse peer groups is essential for long-term success, remarking, "I think it's important to just be able to communicate with other people that are not like you, cuz eventually you're gonna have to when you go out for jobs and things like that."

Even though participants might sometimes find it hard to interact with racially and ethnically diverse peers, they value the social and cultural capital that can be acquired through relationships with students from diverse backgrounds, both racially and economically. In one of his interviews, Derek speaks explicitly about his conscious decision to interact with more white students as he approaches his senior year. He believes that he can learn the skills of economic mobility from students that he perceives already hold such knowledge. Rachel, Kimmy, and Derek express their desire to acquire the skills they think are necessary for school and future success by proactively learning the norms, habits, and interaction patterns of diverse students. In this manner, they value the ability to negotiate various cultural styles and tastes; thus, they become multicultural by code switching. Like high-achieving Chicano/a students in Gandara's (1995) research, the students in this study find ways to affirm their cultural identities in school while simultaneously working hard to enhance future opportunities. These students can "keep it real" (P. Carter, 2005) with their same-race peers while simultaneously negotiating cultural codes of school and their nonblack peers.[8] They do more than succeed in a nonblack context; they also incorporate key cultural tools for achievement from their same-race peers and mainstream learning environment to enact their achievement ideology. They are cultural negotiators, able to integrate multiple sets of cultural codes into their schooling schema.

Cross, Strauss, and Fhagen-Smith (1999) suggest that some black students utilize a bridging function to move between black and white cultures. For these students, race is highly central to their self-definition, and they are comfortable with what makes them black and what makes them American. They might also value what can be learned from interacting with people who share a range of cultural backgrounds and experiences. The bridging function refers to those competencies, attitudes, and behaviors that make it possible for a black person to immerse himself or herself in another group's experience, absent any need to suppress one's sense of blackness. The individual is able to move back and forth between his or her conception of black culture and the ways of knowing, acting, thinking, and feeling that constitute a nonblack worldview (in this case, a white worldview). Some of my participants demonstrate bridging behavior as a form of code switching in the school context. For example, through participant observations I learned that Rachel was savvy in using the classroom domain as a space to learn achievement-oriented behaviors of her white peers without suppressing her sense of racial identity. In her upper-level courses, Rachel initiated conversations with white peers regarding strategies for completing classroom assignments and homework material. She was attentive to her peers' scheduling of study times and offered to join them when possible. However, she was adamant in stating, "I don't change who I am in the classroom just because I'm the only black student. I know who I am, and I'm secure in my race and how smart I am."

Other individuals engage in code-switching behaviors by temporarily accommodating to the norms and regulations of a group or a specific domain within the school context. According to Cross et al. (1999), code switching differs from bridging in that code-switching interactions avoid sharing racial and cultural interests and differences. Code switching allows black students to act, think, dress, and express themselves in ways that maximize the comfort level of the person, group, or organization with whom they are communicating. Participants also code-switched when situationally accommodating domain norms, particularly in the classroom. When describing her shift in language between the classroom and social domain, Kimmy revealed, "Outside of class, I speak a lot of slang." She describes the difference in her behavior between these two domains: "In class I'm focused. I don't let anybody distract me. Outside of class I'm usually wild and whatever." Kimmy shifts her behavior between these domains to accommodate the behavioral norms of each social context. She perceives that it is not an appropriate academic behavior for her to act "wild" in the classroom; thus, she reserves this behavior for when she is with friends in a nonacademic setting.

Whether their behavior is termed bridging or code switching, what is important is that high-achieving black students who value achievement and their constructed sense of blackness learn to shift cultural and social codes in their school context without culturally assimilating (Gibson, 1988). These students are able to speak, act, think, and interact in ways that are situationally appropriate for domains within the school. In this manner, they acquire the necessary skills and behaviors for academic achievement and school success *and* maintain the construction of blackness central to their self-definition. Thus, the ability to enact various cultural styles for various cultural contexts—multicultural competence—enables these students to maintain success within the context of also being black.

Students develop adaptive strategies for overcoming racism in the school context that allow them to maintain high academic achievement and strong racial/ethnic self-definitions.

Black students must develop adaptive strategies for school adjustment and success that reflect positive achievement attitudes and beliefs and a desire to overcome racism as a potential barrier to success. It is not enough to believe in one's self and be aware of racism and other structural inequities as barriers to success; the individual must also decide how she or he will deal with such challenges. These strategies can encompass resistance to racism, and they must aid students in maintaining high academic achievement and a strong racial/ethnic self-concept. According to Ward (2000), healthy resistance strategies teach black teenagers

1. to be aware of the sociopolitical context of race in America and the role that racism plays in shaping the attitudes, beliefs, values, and behaviors of Americans of all racial and ethnic backgrounds;
2. to develop the ability to accurately assess the threat of racism to themselves and other members of the black community and then determine the most appropriate course of action;

3. to take a stand for beliefs, practices, and ideologies that promote positive self-validation and racial group affirmation;
4. to seek solutions that empower them through a positive sense of self and the strengthening of kin networks in the larger black community;
5. to develop effective and self-affirming offensive and defensive strategies that have positive long-term implications for their lives; and
6. to identify and reject unhealthy resistance when they see it in themselves or others.

In this study, students develop strategies for dealing with racism in classroom and nonclassroom domains that reflect varying degrees of resistance (see D. Carter, 2005). Sometimes the strategies are survival tactics designed to maintain both cultural integrity and emotional and psychological stability. These strategies are positive forms of resistance in that they do not hinder students' academic progress. These behaviors do not represent opposition to schooling; rather, they represent strategies to counter racism as normative in these students' lives. Although the confines of this article prevent me from detailing all of the strategies that students employ, a few examples illustrate the resistant and adaptive behaviors that can result from a critical race achievement ideology. For instance, when feeling that she is being positioned as a racial spokesperson in the classroom, Kimmy responds by remaining silent.

> For most of my classes, I'm the only black person in the room, and it feels like there's a lotta pressure or attention on me and . . . if there were more black people in my classes, I guess it would just take a lotta pressure off me. Like when we talk about, uh . . . racial issues, and like, talk about blacks and whites, like I'm expected to know, like, everything. . . . I guess they assume just cuz we're black that we know everything about Africa, what went on in Africa.

The perceived pressure to be a black history expert causes her to be less vocal in race-related classroom discussions. Silencing oneself might seem like an avoidance strategy, but it could also be a survival strategy that allows Kimmy simultaneously to resist this perceived racism and protect her emotional and mental health in the classroom environment. In other cases, students challenge their white peers and teachers to own and reconceptualize their racist assumptions and behaviors. For example, when Rodney perceives that a teacher does not value his ideas in a history classroom because of his race, he does not sit quietly: "I'll be like, 'What up? How come you don't want my stuff written on the board?' I'll be like, 'Write mine on the board.' [DC: You'll say that to the teacher?] Yeah. They'll be like 'Okay, fine.' It does make a difference, you know? Even that little thing proves something to me, you know?" Whether the teacher's behavior is intentional or not, Rodney feels that that the teacher deems him unworthy of adding anything valuable to the class discussion because he is black. Given this perception, the teacher's inaction results in Rodney being positioned as invisible in the classroom. Rodney responds by self-initiating visibility as he verbally confronts the teacher in front of other class members. These and other adaptive resistance strategies allow these students to reject external conceptions of who they should be as racial and academic beings and rely on their own conceptions of self as proud black achievers. Additionally, with these adaptive resistant behaviors, these students counter the racism in schools as a normal condition and racial inequality in education as a given.

Although some studies find that black students develop maladaptive strategies such as oppositional school attitudes or academic disengagement because they cannot see the usefulness in fighting forces that are designed to oppress them (Mickelson, 1990; Ogbu, 2003), other studies indicate that many black students develop resistant adaptive strategies that allow them to achieve and maintain a strong racial self-definition (O'Connor, 1997; Sanders, 1997). The participants in my study have also developed such resistant adaptive behavioral responses to schooling. Thus, a necessary component and result of a critical race achievement ideology is the development of adaptive strategies that resist racism and promote positive adjustment, allowing students to effectively navigate within and across multiple school domains (i.e., classroom, social, and extracurricular). As stated earlier, this work differs from that of O'Connor and Sanders in that black achievers' behaviors are examined in relation to their racial and achievement self-conceptions and achievement ideologies.

DISCUSSION

Based on these findings, I posit six components of a critical race achievement ideology that reflect an ideology of resistance, resilience, and a redefinition of achievement.

1. Students believe in themselves and feel that individual effort and self-accountability lead to school success.
2. Students view achievement as a human character trait that can define membership in their racial group.
3. Students possess a critical consciousness about racism and the challenges it presents to their present and future opportunities as well as those of other members of their racial group.
4. Students possess a pragmatic attitude about the utility of schooling for their future as members of a subdominant racial group.
5. Students value multicultural competence as a skill for success.
6. Students develop adaptive strategies for overcoming racism in the school context that allow them to maintain high academic achievement and a strong racial/ethnic self-concept.

Embodying any one, or only a small subset, of the components of the critical race achievement ideology is not sufficient for maintaining school success and a strong affiliation with one's racial group. I believe that the individual must possess beliefs and attitudes about schooling that are aligned with *all* of these components, because they build on one another and address different dimensions of this conceptualization of success. By internalizing these dimensions, black students can be black in whatever ways they construct blackness and can also maintain academic success.

So how is a critical race achievement ideology manifested in the everyday life of a high-achieving black student attending a predominantly white high school? The following profile of Rachel, compiled from her interviews, illustrates her conception of this achievement ideology and shows how it facilitates her enactment of resilient adaptive strategies in school.

> The purpose of school is to get educated so you can make something of yourself and be an important part of the world. I want to explore careers like being a lawyer, physical therapist, or foreign language interpreter. For me it's important [to do well] in school. I wanna be better than most of my family, and I actually, like, wanna graduate and, like, make something of myself. . . . For me, I just have a lot of ambitions, and I just wanna make sure that I have the background to achieve those. It's good to know where you come from, and especially when— cuz society treats black people different, or minorities in general different. So it's important to know where you come from. It's important to know those things, because it affects your everyday life depending on your skin color. It really does. It's important to me to identify with my race and have that knowledge. When I was little [my dad] used to, like, tell me all the time that I'm black and I'm different from people and for me, I dunno, just, I have to work hard because you know white people don't think highly of black people, you know? My dad has taught me a lot about my background. So I still know about my history and what it is—what it actually means to be black—and I'm secure in my sense of self. I'm secure in my race and how smart I am. So if it happens that I'm stuck in an all-white school and all my friends are white, I'm still secure enough in my sense of self and in my background that I can still have all my friends and not lose myself. I've seen probably more racism in one setting [at Independence] than I've seen in my entire life. So that in itself has taught me a lot cuz I've learned how to deal with it more and not accept it, but how to handle that situation. It's difficult, but I mean, sometimes it is—I just speak my mind, you know. If someone's views I don't like, I'll tell them and I'll be like, "Hey you know what? Your view sucks!" I have white friends too, because it's important to have a variety. Because in the real world outside of school, you have to interact with people of different races regardless of what you do. If you start younger having relations with people like that, it makes it easier to continue doing it.

Rachel's profile highlights all six components of the critical race achievement ideology. She believes in her academic abilities, possesses a critical race consciousness, and has developed strategies for overcoming racism in her school context. She also understands the pragmatic value of an education and has acquired the multicultural skills that will aid in current and future successful relationships and networks. She views herself as a succeeding member of her racial group and is proud of her racial heritage; she does not feel pressure to reject her racial identity in order to succeed. Possessing this type of achievement ideology equips Rachel and the other participants with the necessary armor for overcoming racism and enacting resistant adaptive strategies that lead to school success and maintenance of a positive racial identity.

CONCLUSIONS

This research expands our understanding of how some black students' racial and achievement self-conceptions inform their achievement ideologies and resulting adaptive behaviors for school success. This work has the potential to help educators better understand the nuanced relationships among race, achievement ideology, and school behaviors and see what can be done to help students develop healthy strategies for maintaining school success and a positive racial identity, particularly in learning environments that are perceived as racially hostile. I am not suggesting that simply embodying a critical race achievement ideology will lead to students' sustained school success; however, I do believe that the development and maintenance of this type of ideology in black students—particularly those who are being educated in predominantly white school contexts—can foster positive attitudes and beliefs about schooling and adaptive behaviors for success. I do not believe that this is the only achievement ethos for black student success. In fact, research shows that some black students perform at high levels in school by rejecting their racial heritage, essentially becoming raceless (Fordham, 1988) and conforming completely to mainstream cultural patterns (i.e., cultural assimilation) (Gibson, 1988). A critical race achievement ideology, however, assumes that a student believes in achievement as a characteristic of his or her racial group and values both achievement and racial group affiliation as a part of his or her self-definition. It also enables a student to enact resilient behaviors within and across domains in the school environment, given a high level of racial critical consciousness about structural inequities that she or he might face. The resulting adaptive behaviors for schooling do not come at the expense of rejecting or downplaying one's racial and ethnic identity. Thus, achievement is internalized by the student and represents an individual and collective accomplishment.

Findings from this research cannot be generalized across black achiever populations in predominantly white high schools. These nine achievers only represent a subgroup of black students at Independence High School. Because I did not study average- or underperforming black students, it is not clear whether they espouse any components of a critical race achievement ideology and, if so, what other factors may contribute to their level of academic performance and school success. This sample of nine students has a variety of cultural backgrounds, including diverse parental upbringing, socioeconomic status, and ethnic group traits, each of which may also inform students' beliefs about the utility of schooling for future success. Also, given the specific learning context of this research, one cannot draw conclusions about the presence or absence of this type of achievement ideology in other high school contexts with very different racial demographics. A larger study comparing the achievement attitudes of black students across high schools with a variety of racial compositions can shed more insight on whether black students' racial and achievement self-concepts illuminate a critical race achievement ideology or some other kind of ideology. If CRAI is present, it may look different across settings.

Despite the fact that this achievement ideology was found in a small sample of nine students in one predominantly white high school, it has implications for classroom practice. Facilitating the development of a critical race achievement ideology in black students is a tall order for educators and institutions of learning, but it is a necessary one. These nine achievers convey that schools and educators need to be counterhegemonic in their practices, challenging traditional dominant discourses and paradigms about what it means to be successful and who is successful. Instead of constructing achievement as a quality of particular subgroups, schools must create a culture of achievement that can include any individual, regardless of racial or ethnic identification (Perry, 2003). Additionally, educators must become more aware of the lived experiences of African American students in predominantly white schools, particularly in those learning environments where susceptibility to racism and negative racial stereotyping is high. Understanding how African American students in predominantly white schools perceive their learning context and then respond to these perceptions can allow educators to access the students' brilliance, a trait that is often suppressed in the face of racist barriers to success. By helping these students to understand the educational persistence of their ancestors despite racism as a potential obstacle to their success and to view achievement as a human, raceless trait, we can begin to eliminate underachievement among black students.

NOTES

1. Throughout this article, my use of "success" refers to the mainstream definition characterized by high social status and material wealth achieved through upward social and economic mobility. This is not how the students define success, as is discussed later in the article.
2. I use the terms "black" and "African American" interchangeably to refer to people of African descent through U.S. slavery and those of Caribbean descent who live in the United States.
3. The school and students' names have been changed to maintain anonymity.
4. At the time of this study, there were only nine students who had a cumulative GPA of 3.0 or higher. I found out that some of these students were biracial (black/white), and although the school identified them as black, their parents did not want them to participate in the study. Thus, I had to expand my GPA criterion to include black students with a C+ or higher GPA in order to have enough students for a screening sample.
5. I define "high achieving" as maintaining academic and social success in the school context.

6. The constraints of this article do not allow me to present how the students discuss their racial and achievement self-conceptions. For more detailed information on this, see D. Carter (2005).

7. The confines of this paper do not allow me to go into detail regarding the behavioral strategies that participants in this study employed for school success. For a detailed explanation of this, see D. Carter (2005).

8. Prudence Carter (2005) uses the term "cultural straddlers," indicating that these type of students "juggle" multiple cultural tool kits. I prefer to think of their behaviors as cultural negotiation. For me, *straddling* implies indecisiveness regarding the embodiment of certain cultural codes. *Negotiation* implies an integration of multiple sets of cultural codes. I believe that my study participants are cultural negotiators. While Carter's students share some similarities in their racial and achievement ideologies with my participants, our terminology differs.

REFERENCES

Azibo, D. A. Y. (1991). An empirical test of the fundamental postulates of an African personality metatheory. *The Western Journal of Black Studies, 15*, 183–195.

Bergin, D. A., & Cooks, H. C. (2002). High school students of color talk about accusations of "Acting White." *The Urban Review, 34*(2), 113–134.

Bowman, P., & Howard, C. (1985). Race-related socialization, motivation, and academic achievement: A study of black youths in three-generation families. *Journal of the American Academy of Child Psychiatry, 24*(2), 134–141.

Carter, D. J. (2005). *"In a sea of White people": An analysis of the experiences and behaviors of high-achieving Black students in a predominantly White high school.* Unpublished doctoral dissertation, Harvard University, Cambridge, MA.

Carter, P. L. (2005). *Keepin' it real: School success beyond Black and White.* New York: Oxford University Press.

Cross, W. E., Strauss, L., & Fhagen-Smith, P. (1999). African American identity development across the life span: Educational implications. In R. Hernández Sheets & E. R. Hollins (Eds), *Racial and ethnic identity in school practices: Aspects of human development* (pp. 29–47). Mahwah, NJ: Lawrence Erlbaum.

Delgado, R. (Ed.). (1995). *Critical race theory: The cutting edge.* Philadelphia: Temple University Press.

Delgado, R., & Stefancic, J. (2001). *Critical race theory: An introduction.* New York: New York University Press.

Delgado-Gaitan, C., & Trueba, H. (1991). *Crossing cultural borders: Education for immigrant families in America.* New York: Falmer.

Flores-González, N. (2002). *School kids/Street kids: The identity development of Latino students.* New York: Teachers College Press.

Floyd, C. (1996). Achieving despite the odds: A study of resilience among a group of African American high school seniors. *Journal of Negro Education, 65*(2), 181–189.

Ford, D. Y. (1991). *Self-perceptions of social, psychological, and cultural determinants of achievement among gifted Black students: A paradox of underachievement.* Unpublished doctoral dissertation, Cleveland State University, Cleveland, OH.

Fordham, S. (1988). Racelessness as a factor in Black students' success: Pragmatic strategy or pyrrhic victory? *Harvard Educational Review, 58*(1), 54–84.

Fordham, S., & Ogbu, J. U. (1986). Black students' school success: Coping with the burden of "acting White." *Urban Review, 18*(3), 176–206.

Gandara, P. (1995). *Over the ivy walls: The educational mobility of low-income Chicanos.* Albany, NY: SUNY Press.

Gibson, M. A. (1988). *Accommodation without assimilation: Sikh immigrants in an American high school.* Ithaca, NY: Cornell University Press.

Hemmings, A. (1996). Conflicting images? Being Black and a model high school student. *Anthropology & Education Quarterly, 27*(1), 20–50.

Ladson-Billings, G. (1999). Preparing teachers for diverse student populations: A critical race theory perspective. *Review of Research in Education, 24,* 211–247.

Ladson-Billings, G., & Tate, W. F. (1995). Toward a critical race theory of education. *Teachers College Record, 97*(1), 47–63.

MacLeod, J. (1987). *Ain't no makin' it: Aspirations and attainment in a low-income neighborhood.* Boulder, CO: Westview Press.

Maxwell, J. A. (1996). *Qualitative research design: An interactive approach.* Thousand Oaks, CA: Sage Publications.

Mehan, H., Hubbard, L., & Villanueva, I. (1994). Forming academic identities: Accommodation without assimilation among involuntary minorities, *Anthropology & Education Quarterly, 25*(2), 91–117.

Mickelson, R. A. (1990). The attitude-achievement paradox among Black adolescents. *Sociology of Education, 63*(1), 44–61.

O'Connor, C. (1997). Dispositions toward (collective) struggle and educational resilience in the inner city: A case analysis of six African-American high school students. *American Educational Research Journal, 34*(4), 593–629.

Ogbu, J. U. (1978). *Minority education and caste.* New York: Academic Press.

Ogbu, J. U. (1987). Variability in minority student performance: A problem in search of an explanation. *Anthropology & Education Quarterly, 18*(4), 312–334.

Ogbu, J. U. (1991). Immigrant and nonimmigrant minorities in comparative perspective. In M. Gibson & J. Ogbu (Eds.), *Minority status and schooling: A comparative perspective* (pp. 3–36). New York: Garland.

Ogbu, J. U. (2003). *Black American students in an affluent suburb: A study of academic disengagement.* Mahwah, NJ: Lawrence Erlbaum.

Ogbu, J. U., & Simons, H. D. (1998). Voluntary and involuntary minorities: A cultural-ecological theory of school performance with some implications for education. *Anthropology & Education Quarterly, 29*(2), 155–188.

Oyserman, D., Gant, L., & Ager, J. (1995). A socially contextualized model of African American identity: Possible selves and school persistence. *Journal of Personality and Social Psychology, 69*(6), 1216–1232.

Perry, T. (2003). Achieving in post–Civil Rights America: The outline of a theory. In T. Perry, C. Steele, & A. G. Hilliard (Eds.), *Young, gifted, and Black: Promoting high achievement among African-American students* (pp. 87–108). Boston, MA: Beacon Press.

Perry, T., Steele, C., & Hilliard, A. G. (2003). *Young, gifted, and Black: Promoting high achievement among African-American students.* Boston, MA: Beacon Press.

Roithmayr, D. (1999). Introduction to critical race theory in educational research and praxis. In L. Parker, D. Deyhle, & S. Villenas (Eds.), *Race is . . . race isn't: Critical race theory and qualitative studies in education* (pp. 1–6). Boulder, CO: Westview Press.

Sanders, M. (1997). Overcoming obstacles: Academic achievement as a response to racism and discrimination. *Journal of Negro Education, 66*(1), 83–93.

Seidman, I. E. (1998). *Interviewing as qualitative research: A guide for researchers in education and the social sciences* (2nd ed.). New York: Teachers College Press.

Sellers, R. M., Chavous, T. M., & Cooke, D. Y. (1998). Racial ideology and racial centrality as predictors of African American college students' academic performance. *Journal of Black Psychology, 24*(1), 8–27.

Sellers, R. M., Smith, M. A., Shelton, J. N., Rowley, A. J., & Chavous, T. M. (1998). Multidimensional model of racial identity: A reconceptualization of African American racial identity. *Personality and Social Psychology Review, 2*(1), 18–39.

Solórzano, D., Ceja, M., & Yosso, T. (2000, Winter/Spring). Critical race theory, racial microaggressions, and campus racial climate: The experiences of African American college students. *Journal of Negro Education, 69*(1/2), 60–73.

Solórzano, D. G., & Yosso, T. J. (2001). Critical race and Latcrit theory and method: Counterstorytelling. *International Journal of Qualitative Studies in Education, 14*(4), 471–497.

Steele, C. M. (1997). A threat in the air: How stereotypes shape intellectual identity and performance. *American Psychologist, 52*(6), 613–629.

Strauss, A., & Corbin, J. (1998). *Basics of qualitative research: Techniques and procedures for developing grounded theory* (2nd ed.). Thousand Oaks, CA: Sage Publications.

Tate, W. F. (1997). Critical race theory and education: History, theory and implications. *Review of Research in Education, 22*, 195–247.

Ward, J. V. (2000). *The skin we're in: Teaching our children to be emotionally strong, socially smart, spiritually connected.* New York: Free Press.

Waters, M. (1999). *Black identities: West Indian immigrant dreams and American realities.* New York: Russell Sage Foundation.

Weiner, B. (1986). *An attributional theory of motivation and emotion.* New York: Springer-Verlag.

FACT AND FICTION

STORIES OF PUERTO RICANS IN U.S. SCHOOLS

SONIA NIETO

Puerto Rican youths have been attending U.S. schools for nearly a century. As a result of the takeover of Puerto Rico after the Spanish-American War, in the early 1900s Puerto Ricans began arriving in New York and other northeastern cities in increasing numbers. Sociologist Clara Rodríguez has suggested that all Puerto Ricans, regardless of actual birthplace, have been "born in the U.S.A." because all are subject to federal laws and to an imposed U.S. citizenship that was neither sought nor particularly desired (1991). One result of this citizenship, however, has been that Puerto Ricans have been free of the travel restrictions and similar limitations faced by other immigrants to the United States.[1] At first Puerto Ricans came in small numbers, but after the 1917 Jones Act was passed, which made Puerto Ricans U.S. citizens, the numbers grew steadily (Sánchez Korrol, 1983/1994). By the 1940s, a massive out-migration from the island was in progress, and at present, approximately two-fifths of all Puerto Ricans, or 2.75 million people, reside in the United States, a dramatic example of a modern-day diaspora (Institute for Puerto Rican Policy, 1992).

The Puerto Rican community is constantly changing, as families seeking a better economic future regularly arrive in the United States and return often to the island. This circulatory migration, called vaivén ("coming and going"), has helped to redefine immigration from the life-transforming experience that it was for most European immigrants at the turn of the century to "a way of life" for a great many Puerto Ricans in the latter part of the century (National Puerto Rican Task Force, 1982). The nature of the migration has also profoundly influenced such issues as language use, identity , and cultural fusion and retention.

Schools and classrooms have been among the sites most seriously impacted by the Puerto Rican presence in the United States, especially during the past two decades, during which Latino children have become the fastest growing

Harvard Educational Review   Vol. 68   No. 2   Summer 1998

ethnic group in public schools. A small number of Puerto Rican students have fared very well academically, and some have expressed gratitude for opportunities offered in U.S. schools that might have never been available to poor, working-class children in Puerto Rico (see, for example, the comments of many of the writers interviewed in Hernandéz, 1997). The majority, however, have had difficult and unsatisfactory experiences, including low levels of academic achievement, severe ethnic isolation, and one of the highest dropout rates of all groups of students in the United States (National Center for Educational Statistics [NCES], 1995). The troubled history of the education of Puerto Ricans in U.S. schools is almost a century old, and although it has been chronicled for at least seventy years, it is, in the words of Catherine Walsh, "a disconcerting history of which most U.S. educators are totally unaware" (1991, p. 2). Thus, in spite of Puerto Ricans' growing visibility, much of their history in U.S. schools has yet to be heard.

More careful thought is now being given to that "disconcerting history," especially to the human face of the experiences of Puerto Rican students in U.S. schools, and such consideration is evident in the research literature, especially in more recent ethnographic research studies. It is also evident in a growing body of fiction as, over the past two decades, Puerto Ricans and their experiences in U.S. schools have become more visible as either a primary or an incidental topic in children's, young adult, and adult literature. As an educational researcher, I have concentrated much of my professional and personal attention and energy on the education of Puerto Rican youths, and I have learned a great deal about the promises and pitfalls of education in the United States. As a student of literature, I have also been fascinated by the growing number of fictional stories of Puerto Rican youngsters in U.S. schools, represented by such writers as Piri Thomas, Nicholasa Mohr, Judith Ortiz Cofer, Martín Espada, and others.

Yet fiction is not generally regarded as a legitimate source of data in the educational research community because it is thought to be overly subjective, emotional, and idiosyncratic. Precisely because of the emotional charge of fiction, however, it can be a rich source of knowledge about people's lives and experiences. As Anne Haas Dyson and Celia Genishi have asserted, "Stories are an important tool for proclaiming ourselves as cultural beings" (1994, p. 4). Santa Arias (1996) has suggested that Latino writers serve an important function in that they redefine "the border" as a place of multiple realities and of rebellion. The literature they write, she says, can be understood as a bridge between cultures: "They not only write in order to present a testimonial of survival, but to intervene at various levels in a definition of these borderlands, of what it is like to live in between geographical, linguistic, and cultural worlds" (p. 238).

Fiction can be used in schools to make the lives and experiences of Puerto Ricans more visible than they have been. Stories can also serve as liberating pedagogy in the classroom because they challenge the one-dimensional and largely negative image of Puerto Ricans pervasive in U.S. society. These negative depictions can motivate Puerto Rican writers to present another facet of their community through their writing. One such writer, Jack Agüeros, notes that he feels an obligation "to present our people as we know them, from the inside, from the heart, with all the details" (Hernandéz, 1997, p. 24). Such work can provide evidence of the debilitating experiences that some children have had, in addition to suggesting alternative and more positive possibilities for their future. Puerto Rican authors have written about schooling in the United States in numerous ways, from reports of confrontations with uncaring teachers and unthinking bureaucracies, to stories about teachers who have made a positive difference in the lives of children, to explorations of issues such as colonization, race, ethnicity, social class, and identity—all issues that are central to the lives of Puerto Rican youngsters. Jay Blanchard and Ursula Casanova (1996) suggest that fiction can be a convincing source of information for teachers, as well as a catalyst for thinking about teaching and learning, as demonstrated in their recent text of short stories geared to preservice and practicing teachers. In their book, Blanchard and Casanova use stories to help illustrate significant themes in teaching, such as the role of families, the need to develop meaningful relationships with students, and the world of imagination.

In summary, the growing body of fiction about Puerto Ricans in U.S. schools is a fertile avenue for exploring and analyzing issues that have heretofore been largely invisible in educational research. By using the title "Fact and Fiction" in this article, I do not mean to suggest that educational research always represents facts, or "the truth," and that fiction is make-believe. Quite the contrary: because the fiction I have used in my analysis includes the voices and experiences of students themselves (or authors' recollections of their experiences as students), stories can frequently teach lessons about life and reality more dramatically and candidly than educational research. A merging of these two arenas of literature—fact and fiction—can be both engaging and illuminating. Before considering the common themes in the literature, I first provide an overview of the education of Puerto Ricans in U.S. schools.

PUERTO RICAN STUDENTS IN U.S. SCHOOLS

Puerto Ricans have achieved the questionable distinction of being one of the most undereducated ethnic groups in the United States. The story of this miseducation is infused with controversy concerning Puerto Rico's political status, conflicts over the role of culture and language in U.S. schools and society, harsh experiences with discrimination based on race, ethnicity, language, and social class, and the Puerto Rican community's determination to define and defend itself.

Almost from the time Puerto Rican students started attending schools in the United States, they have experienced problems such as high dropout rates, virtual absence from top ability groups, massive levels of retention, and low academic achievement (Association of Assistant Superintendents, 1948; ASPIRA, 1968; Margolis, 1968; Morrison, 1958; NCES, 1995; Walsh, 1991). The high dropout rate, for instance, is an issue that was discussed as early as 1958 in *The Puerto Rican Study*, a massive three-year investigation into the educational problems of Puerto Rican youngsters in New York City schools, who by then numbered almost 54,000. In the intervening forty years, when the U.S. Puerto Rican school-age population grew to nearly a million (Institute for Puerto Rican Policy, 1996), dropout rates as high as 70 to 90 percent have been consistently reported in cities throughout the Northeast (ASPIRA, 1993; Cafferty & Rivera-Martínez, 1981; Frau-Ramos & Nieto, 1993; U.S. Commission on Civil Rights, 1976).

As we shall see below, the standard explanations for the failure of Puerto Rican youths in U.S. schools have been rooted in the students themselves: that is, their culture (or lack of it), poverty, limited English proficiency, and poor parenting, among other issues, have been blamed for students' poor achievement (Nieto, 1995). On the other hand, schools' low expectations of these students, the poor preparation of their teachers, the victimization and racism they have faced, and the extremely limited resources of the schools themselves have rarely been mentioned as contributing to the lack of success of Puerto Rican students. Some of these problems are graphically documented in the poem "Public School 190, Brooklyn 1963" by Martín Espada:

The inkwells had no ink.
The flag had 48 stars, four years
after Alaska and Hawaii.
There were vandalized blackboards
and chairs with three legs,
taped windows, retarded boys penned
in the basement.
Some of us stared in Spanish.
We windmilled punches
or hid in the closet to steal from coats
as the teacher drowsed, head bobbing.
We had the Dick and Jane books,
but someone filled in their faces
with a brown crayon.

When Kennedy was shot,
they hurried us onto buses,
not saying why,
saying only that
something bad had happened.
But we knew
something bad had happened,
knew that before
November 22, 1963. (1996, p. 25)

Another significant problem that has confounded the study of Puerto Ricans in U.S. schools is that historically much of the data have not been disaggregated according to ethnicity. Thus, Puerto Ricans are often lost in educational statistics labeled "Hispanic" or "Latino," as are Mexican Americans, Cubans, and Central and South Americans. There are valid reasons for using the overarching terms of Latino/a and Hispanic at times, including the fact that Latinos increasingly share physical space. This is the case, for example, with Puerto Ricans and Dominicans in the Northeast and Mexican Americans and Central Americans in California. Collectively, these groups have also tended to experience similar problems in education, housing, health care, and employment. However, the overarching terms do not recognize or take into consideration historic, regional, linguistic, racial, social class, and other important differences. Although many of the educational issues faced by Puerto Ricans are similar to those of Latinos in general, others are not. The tendency in research literature to lump all Latino groups together has resulted in muddling what might be sharp differences that could help explain how such issues as poverty, language dominance, political orientation, and school success or failure are manifested in different Latino ethnic groups.

As a subgroup within the Latino population, for instance, Puerto Ricans fare among the worst of all Latino groups in educational outcomes (Carrasquillo, 1991; Latino Commission, 1992; Meier & Stewart, 1991; Nieto, 1995), yet data to substantiate this situation are hard to find. For example, a national report by the National Council of La Raza found that more than one-third of all Latino children lived below the poverty line, compared with just one-eighth of White children (National Council of La Raza [NCLR], 1993). The even more distressing situation of Puerto Rican children is lost in these statistics, however, because the data were not disaggregated. Other research that centered specifically on Puerto Rican children found that they are at the greatest risk of being poor among other Latino ethnic groups, with a dramatic 58 percent living in poverty (ASPIRA, 1993; NCLR, 1993). Differences such as these may remain invisible unless the data are disaggregated. In this article, I use disaggregated data whenever possible, but I also use statistics on Latinos in general because they are more readily available.

RECURRING THEMES IN RESEARCH AND FICTION

Based on my reading of the literature in both educational research and fiction, I suggest that four interrelated and contrasting themes have emerged from the long history of stories told about Puerto Ricans in U.S. schools. They are: colonialism/resistance; cultural deficit/cultural acceptance; assimilation/identity; and marginalization/belonging. I explore here how each theme is illustrated in both research and fictional literature. To do this, I highlight significant literature in the educational arena, including historical analyses, commission findings and reports, and ethnographic studies. I also review and analyze works of fiction—short stories, novels, and poetry—that focus on the education of Puerto Rican students in U.S. schools. For every example of victimization or devaluation of Puerto Ricans there is a corresponding example of resistance or affirmation, and these examples can serve as important lessons for teachers and schools committed to helping Puerto Rican students succeed in school.

Ultimately, these four themes lead to the broader discussion concerning care as a significant motif missing from the research literature on the education of Puerto Rican children. I further argue that it is only through care that we can ensure that Puerto Rican students receive the affirmation they so urgently need in U.S. schools.

Colonialism/Resistance

The role that colonialism has played in the education of Puerto Ricans needs to be understood precisely because Puerto Rico and the United States are connected through colonial ties. Although officially called a "territory" by the United States, Puerto Rico has virtually no control over its own destiny. For the past five hundred years, it has been little more than a colony, first of Spain and later of the United States. The fact that Puerto Rico and the United States were joined as a result of conquest (Rodríguez, 1991) is overlooked by historians, educators, and researchers, or minimized in much of the research literature. As a result, Puerto Ricans are generally perceived as simply one of the latest "newcomers" in the traditional European-style model of the immigration experience (Rodríguez, 1991). In fact, early writers such as the sociologist/priest Joseph Fitzpatrick focused on overpopulation as the overriding reason for the migration of Puerto Ricans to the United States (Fitzpatrick, 1971/1987a). Conveniently sidestepped is the contribution of U.S. imperialism to creating the structural changes that adversely affected the Puerto Rican economy and that eventually led to the massive migration. These included the wholesale purchase of Puerto Rican farmlands by absentee U.S. landlords to grow and harvest sugar, in the process displacing an enormous number of local farmers. Many of these migrated to the United States (Melendez, 1991; Sánchez Korrol, 1983/1997). Later research, including Fitzpatrick's later work (1987b), challenged this initial analysis as overly simplistic (Bonilla & Campos, 1981; History Task Force, 1979; Melendez, 1991; Rodríguez, 1991; Sánchez Korrol, 1983/1994).

Recent critical research has focused more carefully on the impact that Puerto Rico's colonial status has had on education, both on the Island and in the United States (*Centro*, 1997; Nieto, 1995, 2000; Walsh, 1991). When people are stripped of their language and culture, they are also largely stripped of their identity as a people. However, dispossessing people of language and culture does not need to take place with the gun; it is frequently done more effectively through educational policies and practices, the effects of which can

can be even more brutal than those of the gun. The violence that takes place within schools and classrooms is more symbolic than real. According to Pierre Bourdieu (1977), symbolic violence refers to the maintenance of power relations of the dominant society through the manipulation of symbols.

Given Puerto Rico's long-standing colonial relationship with the United States, it is not surprising that the schools in Puerto Rico have been and continue to be sites of symbolic violence. In a groundbreaking study of the Americanization of schools in Puerto Rico, Aida Negrón de Montilla documented how the United States began to change educational policies and practices almost as soon as it took possession of the island in 1898. Some of these changes were blatant, such as language policies that attempted to wipe out the Spanish language. Within the first several decades, however, it became apparent that total obliteration of the language was impossible, both because the policy was not working and because many Puerto Ricans perceived it as a crude example of cultural imperialism. By the late 1940s, the United States had settled for enforced ESL instruction in all island schools. Other colonizing policies in the schools included the wholesale adoption of U.S. textbooks, curriculum, methods, and materials in island schools; the imposition of the Pledge of Allegiance and other patriotic rituals; and the preparation and expectations of teachers as agents of English and U.S. culture (Negrón de Montilla, 1971).

The symbolic violence represented in these policies is translated into stories that are usually told in sardonic but amusing ways. For instance, the stories of Abelardo Díaz Alfaro are hilarious examples of colonialism gone awry. In "Santa Cló va a La Cuchilla" (1962), Santa Claus, with all the trappings of his Yankee identity, including a sweltering red suit, shows up in La Cuchilla, a rural community with no understanding of this cultural icon. The story is a humorous example of how colonies are saturated with culturally meaningless symbols, while culturally meaningful ones—in this case Los Reyes Magos, or the Three Wise Men—are displaced or disparaged.

In another story, "Peyo Mercé Enseña Inglés" ("Peyo Mercé Teaches English"), Díaz Alfaro (1978) relates the panic experienced by a rural teacher who speaks only Spanish when he receives the mandate from the central office to teach his students English: Peyo Mercé is horrified when he realizes that he has to teach "inglés en inglés!" ("English in English!") (p. 98). The mandate, a historically accurate event, makes for a comical story told with great humanity and insight. Like all good teachers, Peyo Mercé tries to find something in the U.S.-imposed textbook to which his students can relate, and he comes upon a picture of a rooster. Using the picture, he instructs the children to say "cockle-doodle-doo," the sound that roosters make in English. As the story concludes, one of the young students can no longer accept the lie that he and his classmates are learning: he rejects both the English of the rooster and, presumably, the cultural imposition that it represents by stating emphatically that perhaps this is *another* kind of rooster, but that the roosters in *his* house clearly say "¡cocoroco!"—the sound made by roosters in Spanish.

Other examples of the link between politics and education in the early colonization of Puerto Rico by the United States were the establishment of para-educational organizations and activities—for example, the Boy Scouts, the Girl Scouts, and the Future Homemakers of America—and the substitution of Puerto Rican holidays with U.S. holidays, such as Washington's Birthday and Thanksgiving (Negrón de Montilla, 1971). Ironically, even the U.S. celebration of independence became an official holiday in the colony. In fact, the colonial presence can be felt through the manipulation of the tastes, values, and dispositions of the Puerto Rican people. In another scene from *When I Was Puerto Rican*, Esmeralda Santiago (1993) recounts how the mothers of the children in Miss Jiménez's class were asked to attend a meeting with experts from the United States who would teach them "all about proper nutrition and hygiene, so that we would grow up as tall and strong as Dick, Jane, and Sally, the *Americanitos* in our primers" (p. 64). At the meeting, the experts brought charts with unrecognizable food staples:

> There were carrots and broccoli, iceberg lettuce, apples, pears, and peaches. . . . There was no rice on the chart, no beans, no salted codfish. There were big White eggs, not at all like the small round ones our hens gave us. There was a tall glass of milk, but no coffee. . . . There were bananas but no plantains, potatoes but no *batatas* [sweet potatoes], cereal flakes but no oatmeal, bacon but no sausages. (p. 66)

At the end of the meeting, the mothers received peanut butter, cornflakes, fruit cocktail, peaches in heavy syrup, beets, tuna fish, grape jelly, and pickles, none of which formed part of the Puerto Rican diet, and the mother of the protagonist, Negi, concluded, "I don't understand why they didn't just give us a sack of rice and a bag of beans. It would keep this family fed for a month" (p. 68). Such educational policies thus imposed U.S. mainstream cultural values, tastes, and attitudes on Puerto Rican children and their families.

Along with their luggage and other prized possessions, Puerto Rican families also bring with them to the United States this legacy of colonialism. Officially U.S. citizens, Puerto Ricans are not national immigrants, and therefore it is their language, culture, and ethnicity, rather than their nationality, that separate them from their U.S. peers (Cafferty & Rivera-Martínez, 1981). Because the colonial relationship has made Puerto Rican migration a constant experience, in the process it has created "the students in between," those who spend time on both Island and mainland (Quality Education for Minorities Project, 1990). One consequence of colonialism is that issues of identity, belonging, and loyalty are at the very core of the psychological dilemmas faced by Puerto Rican youngsters, and even adults, who know only too well what it means to be a "cultural schizophrenic." In fact, the image of an air bus connecting Puerto Rico to New York has made its way into popular Puerto Rican fiction through Luis Rafael Sánchez's story, "The Flying Bus," in which Sánchez describes one of the passengers as "a well-poised woman . . . [who] informs us that she flies over *the pond* every month and that she has forgotten on which bank of it she really lives" (1987, p. 19; emphasis in original). Joy De Jesús has described the resulting identity crisis in this way:

> What makes growing up Puerto Rican unique is trying to define yourself within the unsettling condition of being neither here nor there: "Am I Black or White?" "Is my primary language Spanish or English?" "Am I Puerto Rican or American?" For the Puerto Rican child, the answers to these questions tend to be somewhere in between, and never simple. (1997, p. xviii)

Sandra María Estevez poetically expresses the same sentiment of being "in-between," in "Here":

> I am two parts / a person
> boricua/spic
> past and present
> alive and oppressed
> given a cultural beauty
> . . . and robbed of a cultural identity (1991, p. 186)

Stories about divided identities and loyalties, even among children, are common in the work of Puerto Rican writers. Abraham Rodríguez's "The Boy Without a Flag" is a classic example of this idea. After listening to his father denounce U.S. imperialism in Puerto Rico and throughout the world, the eleven-year-old protagonist decides that he will no longer salute the U.S. flag. When his teacher asks him to explain this decision, he announces, using the very same words he had heard his father use, "Because I'm Puerto Rican. I ain't no American. And I'm not no Yankee flag-waver" (1992, p. 18). The principal, who tries to convince him that this posture may in the long run jeopardize his future, asks: "You don't want to end up losing a good job opportunity in government or in the armed forces because as a child you indulged your imagination and refused to salute the flag?" (p. 26). The young boy is crestfallen when he realizes that his father is not only embarrassed by his behavior but has, in fact, sided with the principal, a position he has no doubt taken to protect his son. Martín Espada tells a similar story through the poem "The Year I Was Diagnosed with a Sacrilegious Heart":

> At twelve, I quit reciting
> the Pledge of Allegiance,
> could not salute the flag
> in 1969, and I,
> undecorated for grades or sports,
> was never again anonymous in school. (1993, pp. 72–74)

José Angel Figueroa echoes this theme in "Boricua," a poem that speaks of cultural and political conflict. Referring to education, he writes

schools
always wanted
to cave in your
PuertoRican Accent
& because you
wanted to make it
you had to pledge
allegiance lefthanded
because you
had lost your soul
during some english exam. (1991, p. 222)

These flag stories allegorically describe resistance to colonialism even among young children.

Colonial status cannot explain all of the educational problems experienced by Puerto Rican students in U.S. schools. Although it is true that the educational instability that results from moving back and forth can lead to low academic achievement, poor language skills, and high dropout rates, there are many Puerto Rican youngsters who do not move back and forth between Puerto Rico and the United States and therefore do not experience this kind of educational disruption. By and large, however, they also experience educational failure. Some theorists have even speculated that colonial status per se may have an impact on students' actual academic achievement (Gibson & Ogbu, 1991; Ogbu, 1987). John Ogbu's (1987) theory concerning voluntary and involuntary immigrants is helpful in understanding this phenomenon. According to Ogbu, it is important to look not simply at a group's cultural background, but also at its political situation in the host society and the perceptions it has of opportunities available in that society. Thus, the major problem in the academic performance of U.S. Puerto Ricans is not that they possess a different language, culture, or cognitive or communication style than students in the cultural mainstream. Rather, the nature of their history, subjugation, and exploitation, together with their own responses to their treatment, are at the heart of their poor academic achievement (Ogbu, 1987).

Because the problem of the poor academic achievement of Puerto Rican youngsters cannot be blamed simply on the legacy of colonialism, I now turn to an exploration of a related concept, the pressure to assimilate, and its effect on the education of Puerto Rican students.

Assimilation/Identity

In the United States, public schools have always had a pivotal role in assimilating immigrant and other non-mainstream students because they have historically stripped them of their native cultural identity in order to impose the majority culture on them. The creation of the common school during the nineteenth century was based in part on the perceived need to assimilate immigrant and other students of widely diverse backgrounds (Katz, 1975).

212

Hence, although the "melting pot" has been heralded as the chief metaphor for pluralism in the United States, a rigid Anglo-conformity has been in place for much of U.S. history. According to Joel Spring (1997), schools in the United States have assimilated students with practices that include flag ceremonies and other patriotic celebrations, the replacement in school curricula of local heroes with national ones, a focus on the history and traditions of the dominant White culture, and the prohibition of native language use in the school. The educational establishment repeated this process, at least in part, in schools in Puerto Rico, and it has been part of the educational landscape since the U.S. takeover of the island in 1898.

These socializing and assimilating agents, then, are no strangers to Puerto Rican students when they enter U.S. schools. Assimilation for Puerto Rican children continues in U.S.-based schools, usually in the urban centers of the Northeast. The image of decaying urban schools, graphically portrayed by a number of Puerto Rican writers, serves as a metaphor for the assimilation of newcomers. Historically, most newcomers to the United States have been poor, uneducated, and relegated to the urban ghettos from which earlier immigrants had fled. Schools in these urban ghettos often were old, worn, and dilapidated. Judith Ortiz Cofer, for instance, describes her first encounter with a school in Paterson, New Jersey, as follows:

> The school building was not a welcoming sight for someone used to the bright colors and airiness of tropical architecture. The building looked functional. It could have been a prison, an asylum, or just what it was: an urban school for the children of immigrants, built to withstand waves of change, generation by generation. (1990, p. 61)

In a powerful novel about a young girl's abuse-filled childhood, Alba Ambert compares the physical presence of her school in New York City with the apparent indifference of the staff who work there:

> Public School 9 was a red-brick structure built at the turn of the century. It loomed on 138th Street across from the Puerto Rico Theater like a huge armory vigilantly surveilling students, teachers, and staff who scuttled in and out of its wide staircase. . . . Teachers and principal lingered at the shore, their backs turned to the island of isolation in which the children lived. From the periphery, they looked away and refused to learn the language of the dispossessed. (1995, p. 113)

For El Cortes (2000), assimilation is portrayed through the rancid smells that are a result of the humiliation faced by children who throw up when they are prohibited from speaking Spanish, forced to eat strange foods, or ridiculed by their teachers for their customs and values:

> School smells is a mess of bad smells and altogether they make one great big bad stink. Vegetable soup with smelly onions in it and rotten orange peel smells get mixed up with the King Pine old mop bleach smell and all of that gets mixed up with . . . throw up. School smells.

Assimilation takes place in numerous ways, and examples of this process, as well as its detrimental effects, abound in fact and in fiction. For instance, the extensive 1976 report by the U.S. Commission on Civil Rights concerning Puerto Ricans in the United States found that young people identified the schools' unresponsiveness to their cultural backgrounds as a primary reason for dropping out of school. Underpinning the pressure to assimilate newcomers is the ideology of "colorblindness"; that is, the view that failing to see differences epitomizes fairness and equality. *The Losers*, one of the early comprehensive reports on the education of Puerto Rican students in the United States, was commissioned by ASPIRA, an educational and leadership advocacy organization focusing on Puerto Rican youths. The report, among the first to challenge the prevalent melting pot ideology, persuasively described the ideology of colorblindness by focusing on the Puerto Rican children's teachers—mostly White, middle-class women with little or no personal or professional experiences with the Puerto Rican community:

> Denying her prejudices, the teacher also denies genuine differences among her students. . . . There is, of course, something to be said for the egalitarian belief that all people are basically similar; but teachers who deny authentic cultural differences among their pupils are practicing a subtle form of tyranny. . . . That is how the majority culture imposes its standards upon a minority, a cruel sort of assimilation forced onto children in the name of equality. (Margolis, 1968, p. 7)

In some cases, the situation has changed very little in the intervening three decades. A recent ethnographic study by Ellen Bigler (1997) in a classroom with a sizable proportion of Puerto Rican students in a small upstate New York town documented that almost all the teachers, most of whom were White, were uncomfortable acknowledging cultural, racial, and ethnic differences among their students; they insisted that they wanted to treat all their students "the same."

Schools also promote assimilation by mythologizing what Bigler calls "ethnic success stories" (1997, p. 9). The model for these Horatio Alger-type success stories is the struggling European immigrant who makes good by learning English and adapting to the cultural mainstream. The teachers and other residents of the town who perpetuated these stories were unaware of how Puerto Rican migrants differed from earlier European immigrants, due to their experiences with colonization, racism, and a different economic situation. One middle-school teacher remarked: "Why are these kids doing this? Why are they not speaking English when they can? Why aren't they trying to fit into the mainstream? . . . They're no different than earlier waves. They worked, they learned the language, and that was your key to success" (p. 9).

One of the earliest and most exhaustively documented ethnographies concerning Puerto Rican children was carried out in 1965 in an East Harlem school (Bucchioni, 1982). Published years later, the study chronicled one case after another in which pressures toward assimilation took place in classrooms every day. In this particular study, the teacher recounted "the ethnic success story" when the children began to question why they lived in tiny, cramped apartments and shared a bathroom with other families, rather than in the kinds of spacious houses in middle-class neighborhoods that they were learning about in school. Juan, one of the children, mused aloud that only very rich people could live in those houses, to which his teacher Miss Dwight responded, "Not exactly rich, Juan. But they do work hard, and every day" (p. 210). When Juan answered that his father also worked hard, even on Sundays, Miss Dwight replied:

> It is difficult, sometimes, to earn enough money to do everything we want. It's important for you to remember that your work in school will some day help you to get a better job, earn more money, and live in a good home. . . . But let us remember that while we work toward something better, we must accept what we have now and try to appreciate the good things we have. (p. 210)

In the young-adult novel *Nilda*, Nicholasa Mohr articulates a cruder version of this myth through her character Miss Langhorn, who precedes the daily Pledge of Allegiance with "more or less the same speech": "Brave people they were, our forefathers, going into the unknown when man had never ventured. They were not going to permit the Indians to stop them. This nation was developed from a wild primitive forest into a civilized nation" (1986, p. 52).

The pressure to assimilate is also evident when schools identify the Spanish language as a problem. The first large-scale study of Puerto Rican children in the New York City schools, *The Puerto Rican Study* (Morrison, 1958), attempted to define and propose positive solutions to the problem of academic failure. It also identified the continuation of spoken Spanish in the home as "the chief deterrent" to Puerto Ricans' lack of academic progress. Several years later, the ASPIRA study roundly criticized this position and found the same message of "Spanish as a problem" still evident in many schools:

> In their eagerness to erase Spanish from the child's mind and substitute English, the schools are placing Puerto Rican children in an extremely ambiguous role. They are saying, "Forget where you came from, remember only where you are and where you are going." That is hardly the kind of message that inspires happy adjustments. (Margolis, 1968, p. 9)

Not only has the Spanish language been prohibited in the schools, but Puerto Rican students' accents and dialects have been disparaged as well. In Nicholasa Mohr's *Nilda*, she describes in comic detail how Miss Reilly, the Spanish teacher in the all-female school attended by Nilda, speaks with a thick American accent while insisting that Castilian Spanish is the "real Spanish." She continues, ". . . and I am determined, girls, that that is what we shall learn and speak in my class; nothing but the best!" (1986, p. 214). Castilian Spanish raises issues of power and privilege because the general public, as well as many non-Latino Spanish teachers, consider it to be the variety of Spanish of the highest prestige. Nilda's experience has been shared by many Puerto Ricans and other Latinos, who end up either failing Spanish or dropping it.

Over the years, both fiction and research have chronicled the practice of Anglicizing students' names. In *The Losers*, Margolis documents a typical example: "José González, a kindergartner, has given up trying to tell his teacher his name is not Joe. It makes her angry" (1968, p. 3). Thirty years later, Ellen Bigler found a remarkably similar situation in her ethnography of an upstate New York school. There, a teacher anglicized Javier to Xavier, saying that "it would be better in the long run for him to have a more American-sounding name" (1997, p. 13). The same scenario forms the basis for the story in Alma Flor Ada's novel for young children, *My Name is María Isabel* (1993). María Isabel Salazar López, a new third-grader, is given the name "Mary" by her teacher to distinguish her from the other two Marías in the classroom. María Isabel has a hard time remembering her new name and she is repeatedly scolded by her teacher for not responding when called on. María Isabel loves her name because it includes the names of both her grandmothers. When the teacher assigns her students a composition entitled "My Greatest Wish," María Isabel tells the teacher in her essay why her name is so important to her and why her greatest wish is to be called by her real name. In this case, there is a happy ending: the teacher, basically a sensitive and caring person, calls her María Isabel the very next day. Unfortunately, in real life, it is not always this way.

Puerto Rican resistance to assimilation has been visible in the educational literature, as well as in fiction. Educational literature has rationalized assimilation on many grounds: the very creation of the common school was based on the need to homogenize millions of European immigrants into U.S. mainstream culture (Appleton, 1983; Katz, 1975). The schools' reaction to the cultural and linguistic differences of Puerto Ricans and other students of color have been even more negative, and for many years they resulted, for example, in prohibitions on using Spanish in the schools (Crawford, 1992). Recent research on cultural and linguistic identity has challenged the long-standing conventional wisdom that in order to get ahead one must sacrifice one's identity. In the case of Spanish, for instance, Ana Celia Zentella's study (1997) of language practices among Puerto Rican children growing up in a low-income community in New York City found that the most academically successful students in the study were also the most fluent bilinguals. They also happened to be in bilingual rather than monolingual classes. The reluctance to drop Spanish has been found in reports as long ago as the ASPIRA study, *The Losers* (Margolis, 1968). A more recent study cited by Kenneth Meier and Joseph Stewart (1991) found that Puerto Rican parents, more than any other Latino parents, wanted their children to retain their Spanish while they also wanted their children to become fluent in English. Resisting the push for assimilation, Puerto Rican students and their communities have always attempted to claim and maintain their identities, even within the school setting. In the Puerto Rican community, there has been an insistence that one can be *both* Puerto

Rican *and* a good student, *both* English- *and* Spanish-speaking; in a word, that one can be bilingual and bicultural.

Linguistic and cultural maintenance have implications for academic success. For instance, a study by Jean Phinney (1993) of high school and college students of diverse racial and ethnic minority backgrounds found a significant correlation between ethnic identity and positive self-esteem. This link has important implications for student achievement. For example, in case studies of Puerto Rican and Vietnamese adolescents in a Boston bilingual program, Virginia Vogel Zanger (1987) found that the students' sense of stigmatization had a negative impact on their academic development. Another convincing counter-argument to the perceived need to assimilate is found in research on Cambodian refugee children by the Metropolitan Indochinese Children and Adolescent Service. In this study, researchers found that the more the children assimilated into U.S. mainstream culture, the worse was their emotional adjustment (*New voices*, 1988). Another study of Southeast Asian students found that higher grade point averages correlated with *maintaining*, rather than wiping out, traditional values, ethnic pride, and close social and cultural ties with members of the same ethnic group (Rumbaut & Ima, 1987).

In research with academically successful students of diverse backgrounds, I also found that there was a marked desire on the part of most to maintain their cultural and linguistic identification (Nieto, 1996). Further, in another study of high-achieving, college-bound Latino students in a comprehensive Boston high school, Zanger found similarly that these students voiced a tremendous resistance to assimilation. Referring to the pressure to assimilate that she felt from her teachers, one young woman stated, "They want to *monoculture* [you]" (1993, p. 172). These Latino students also demonstrated great pride in their cultural background and articulated a desire to be accepted for who they were. In the words of one student, "You don't need to change your culture to be American" (p. 175).

Cultural Deficit/Cultural Acceptance

In the search for explanations for the dismal educational failure of Puerto Rican students, a number of theories concerning cultural acceptance and "cultural deficit" have been used over the years. Numerous commissions, panels, and councils, as well as many individual researchers, who have studied the plight of Puerto Rican students in U.S. schools have used labels ranging from "problem" to "culturally deprived" to the more recent "at risk" to charcterize these students (Nieto, 1995). Such labels are at the very core of the deficit theories that began to define Puerto Rican students almost from the time they first entered U.S. schools. For example, a 1935 report by the New York City Chamber of Commerce described Puerto Rican students in general as "slow learners" (Sánchez Korrol, 1994). The previously cited *Puerto Rican Study* (Morrison, 1958) likewise indicated that teachers and schools were viewing Puerto Rican students' home language and culture as shortcomings and barriers to their education. Another early report stated that "some observers are of the opinion that the Puerto Rican, as well as members of the other Spanish-speaking groups, is less inclined to seek out educational advantages and follow them up by regular attendance than individuals of some of the other cultural groups" (Chenault, 1938/1970, p. 145). In another example, a teacher made the following comment about her Puerto Rican students: "The only way to teach them is to repeat things twenty-five times unless for some reason it means something to them" (Sexton, 1965, p. 58). Much of the early research literature similarly characterized Puerto Rican students as impulsive, undisciplined, and troublesome, all traits thought to be inherited from their families and which made them incapable of profiting from their education (Nieto, 1995).

That idea of cultural deficit has translated into lower teacher expectations for many Puerto Rican students. For instance, Virginia Vogel Zanger's (1993) research among high-achieving Latino students found that their perceptions of teachers' failure to push them was experienced emotionally as abandonment. Similar findings have been expressed over and over in the research literature (Darder & Upshur, 1993; Hidalgo, 1992; Margolis, 1968; National Commission, 1984). Fiction literature mimics this finding. A *Perfect Silence* (Ambert, 1995), for example, describes low expectations in depressing detail:

> Teachers never expected the children, who were mostly Puerto Rican and Black, with a smattering of Irish and Italians too poor to have fled the ghetto, to occupy the ivy-scented halls of distant universities or mark history with distinguished feats. Teachers felt grateful beyond their expectations when girls turned twelve without "getting themselves pregnant," and boys managed to elude reform school. (p. 113)

Clearly, teachers, schools, and society in general have assumed that the problem of Puerto Rican students' failure lies with the students themselves, be it in their culture, family, genes, or lack of English skills. Although such problems as poverty, racism, poor language skills, neglect, abuse, and crime cannot be dismissed as contributing to the academic failure that some Puerto Rican youngsters face, deficit explanations have rarely considered how schools and society have been complicitous in causing these failures. Instead, deficit explanations have often considered students and their families solely responsible for failure. These theories have influenced the framing of the problems, as well as proposed solutions to them.

The paradigm of cultural deficiency was nowhere more clearly and destructively articulated than in *La Vida*, an extensive anthropological investigation of one hundred Puerto Rican families living in poverty in New York City and San Juan, Puerto Rico (Lewis, 1965). *La Vida* personified "the culture of poverty" and its negative ramifications for future generations through an in-depth study of the Ríos family, whom author Oscar Lewis described as "closer to the expression of an unbridled id than any other people I have studied" (p. xxvi). A particularly insidious description of his subjects reads:

> The people in this book, like most of the other Puerto Rican slum dwellers I have studied, show a great zest for life, especially for sex, and a need for excitement, new experiences and adventures. . . . They value acting out more than thinking out, self-expression more than self-constraint, pleasure more than productivity, spending more than saving, personal loyalty more than impersonal justice. (Lewis, 1965, p. xxvi)

Characterizations such as these left a mark on how U.S. society in general, and schools and teachers in particular, were to view the Puerto Rican community for decades.

The schools' perceptions of Puerto Rican students have often echoed those of Lewis. For example, Eugene Bucchioni's ethnography of a school in Spanish Harlem documented the conversation of two teachers in the hall: "'The Puerto Ricans seem to learn absolutely nothing, either here or at home.' 'Yes,' said Miss Dwight, 'all they seem to care about is sleeping, eating, playing, and having parties'" (1982, p. 202). In Alba Ambert's novel *A Perfect Silence*, the narrator describes teachers' attitudes about their Puerto Rican students that speaks volumes about their teachers' lack of cultural knowledge:

> They expressed shock that little girls would have their ear lobes pierced, a savage tribal custom that, they thought, had to be some sort of child abuse. They criticized when children were absent from school to care for younger siblings if a mother had to run errands, or if they had to translate for a sick relative in the hospital. They accused children of cheating when they copied from each other's homework. (Ambert, 1995, p. 113)

The assumption that what needs changing are the students is still prevalent in many schools and is revealed in much of the research on Puerto Rican education. In their study of four public schools with large percentages of Latino children, Antonia Darder and Carol Upshur (1993) found that most teachers in the schools mentioned the problem of poor achievement as residing in the children's lack of conceptual understanding in English, lack of motivation, and lack of retention, while only occasionally mentioning the inadequate curriculum, the negative views of staff towards bilingual education, or their lack of cross-cultural understanding. Puerto Rican children in the four schools had quite different ideas about improving their schooling. When asked what they would like school to be like, they mentioned, among other things, the need to feel safe, to have newer and more interesting books and computers, and to have humorous and friendly teachers who would not yell at them (Darder & Upshur, 1993).

In *The Losers,* Margolis documents the following scene demonstrating how teachers assume Puerto Rican students' culture to be a barrier to their academic achievement: "An honor student asked her counselor for a chance to look at college catalogues. 'Is that Italian or Spanish?' asked the counselor, looking at the name on the girl's card. 'Spanish? Now this is just my opinion, but I think you'd be happier as a secretary'" (1968, p. 3). Another scene, striking in its similarity, was recounted several years later during the public hearings held by the U.S. Commission for Civil Rights in preparation for their report on Puerto Ricans in the United States. There, a high school student from Pennsylvania told the commission of her repeated attempts to gain admission to an academic course. Her counselor, she said, warned her that "I should not aim too high because I would probably be disappointed at the end result" (1976, p. 108).

For many years, another common practice in schools was to place students back at least a grade when they arrived from Puerto Rico, a practice based on the dubious assumption that this would help them learn English and catch up academically. The effect of retaining students was found to be "particularly acute" by the U.S. Commission on Civil Rights, and it was described by one witness from Massachusetts as a leading cause for the high dropout rate:

> They came from Puerto Rico, they're in the 10th, 11th, or senior year of high school. . . . They came to Boston and they placed them in the 6th and 7th grades. You're wondering why they dropped out. . . . Here's a kid trying to learn and he automatically gets an inferiority complex and quits. (1976, p. 101)

This experience is echoed in the novel *When I Was Puerto Rican*, when the author tells the story of Negi, unceremoniously put back a grade despite her excellent academic record simply because she does not speak English. Negi, however, fights back, convincing the principal that she is eighth-grade material: "I have A's in school Puerto Rico. I lern good. I no seven gray girl" (Santiago, 1993, p. 226). Fortunately, he changes his mind and places her in an eighth-grade class (albeit 8-23, the class for the lowest achieving students and those labeled as learning disabled). By the following year, Negi is placed in one of the top ninth-grade classes, and from there she goes on to a top-rated public high school and then to Harvard. Needless to say, this story is pure fiction for all but a tiny minority of Puerto Rican students, most of whom have neither the wherewithal nor the resources to make the demands that Negi was able to make.

Although U.S. public schools have been the setting of most stories of Puerto Ricans, a small number have focused on Catholic and independent schools (Rivera, 1982; Vega, 1996). The cultural rejection faced by Puerto Ricans in these settings has been of a different kind than that faced in public schools. In *Family Installments*, Edward Rivera (1982) tells the story of Santos Malánguez and his family, who move to New York City from Puerto Rico and enroll Santos in second grade at Saint Misericordia Academy (affectionately dubbed Saint Miseria's) for Boys and Girls in East Harlem. Catholic school differed from public schools in many ways—notably in the strict rules, the heavy doses of homework, the high expectations of all students, and the corporal punishment—but Puerto Ricans were still generally assumed to be of inferior genetic stock. These seemingly contradictory attitudes were well described in Rivera's story: "There was something both cold-hearted and generous about our nuns that gave at least some of us reason to be grateful our parents had signed us up at Saint Miseria's" (p. 74). Specifically, there is the humorous scene in which Sister Felicia, without consulting with Santos's parents, decides that he and a number of other children are charity cases. Since they are preparing for their First Communion, she marches off with them to *La Marqueta,* the Puerto Rican market in Spanish Harlem, to buy their outfits for the big day. Rivera describes the patronizing attitude of the nuns: "First they hit you and make certain embarrassing hints about your family habits and your man-eating ancestors, and then they treat you to a free purchase of clothes" (p. 78).

Deficit explanations for students' academic failure were accepted fairly consistently and uncritically until the late 1960s and 1970s, when Puerto Rican educators and researchers themselves were more visible in the research studies, commissions, and panels studying the education of Puerto Rican youths (Nieto, 1995). In short, the research literature until quite recently tended to highlight what Puerto Rican youngsters *did not have, did not know,* and *could not do,* and, as a result, neglected also to consider what students *already had, knew,* and *could do.*

The development of cultural awareness represents a step away from the view that students' native languages and cultures hinder their learning. For instance, in research that was part of the report of the Latino Commission of the New York City Board of Education, Clara Rodríguez (1991) found substantial differences between two high schools with high dropout rates and two with low dropout rates. At the schools with low dropout rates, she found that cultural sensitivity was either present or neutral, that is, there was a feeling among the students that their culture would not work against them, and that they would be treated fairly in spite of their culture. Rodríguez notes that "in the absence of cultural sensitivity, an acceptable surrogate seemed to be neutrality toward cultural differences combined with good teaching" (1991, pp. 45–46).

Teachers and schools step closer to cultural acceptance when they acknowledge the Spanish language and the Puerto Rican culture as important resources and talents. For instance, Lourdes Díaz Soto, in research with parents of both low- and high-achieving Puerto Rican children, discovered that the parents of the high-achieving children preferred a native language environment at home to a far greater extent than did the families of lower-achieving children (1993). Similarly, the Massachusetts Advocacy Center found that bilingual programs can actually act as a "buffer" to prevent some students from dropping out of high school (Massachusetts Advocacy Center, 1990). In the short story "School Smells," El Cortes lovingly recalls Miss Powell, her favorite teacher, who used the students' language and culture in positive ways:

In second grade when we spoke Spanish, we didn't get yelled at—SPEAK ENG-LISH. NO SPANISH. YOU'RE IN AMERICA NOW—like it was a sin. . . . Miss Powell had us teach her and the kids who didn't know Spanish some words and we wrote invitations to the mothers to visit. They came and told stories about how it was when they were kids in Puerto Rico and we told it in English for the kids who didn't know Spanish. (2000)

In recent research among Puerto Rican families, Carmen Mercado and Luis Moll (1997) demonstrate an even closer step to cultural acceptance. Using a "funds of knowledge" perspective based on the assumption that all families have cultural resources that can be used in the service of their children's learning, the researchers asked their graduate students, all bilingual teachers in New York City, to investigate the knowledge and practices that their students' families possessed. As a result of the research, the teachers, some of whom felt that they already knew their students quite well, were surprised at the wealth of sociocultural knowledge and practices in the families, resources of which even the families themselves are not always aware. These included entrepreneurial skills, knowledge of health and medicine, and musical talent.

Jo-Anne Wilson Keenan, Jerri Willett, and Judith Solsken, a classroom teacher and two university faculty members who engaged in collaborative research in the teacher's second-grade classroom for two years, described a similar finding. Their research (1993) focused on schools' need to change in order to accommodate and serve the children in them, in contrast to the conventional wisdom that students and their families need to do all the changing. Through a series of inspiring anecdotes, the authors documented how the families of the students changed the culture of the classroom. There was, for instance, the story of Blanca Pérez's father, a cartoonist and martial artist, who visited the classroom. The authors concluded: "Jimmy Pérez does not typically spend his days in an elementary school classroom. Yet this gentle and immensely talented man is capable of teaching many things" (p. 59). In addition, the authors explained how Jo-Anne, the teacher, attempted to learn Spanish, and how her attempts were appreciated by the parents: "As I risk speaking in another language, others feel free to take the same risk. As our struggle to appreciate each other's languages becomes public, language differences are no longer a barrier but common ground for generating conversations about language and cultural differences and similarities" (p. 63). When teachers and schools accept and, even better, when they affirm the language and culture of their Puerto Rican students, they also send students the message that their identity is not a barrier to their education. In the numerous examples above, we have seen that when teachers perceive only deficits in their students' backgrounds, the students' learning is not promoted. Conversely, when teachers see their students' individual and cultural talents, students are encouraged to continue their education.

Marginalization/Belonging

Marginalization has been a common theme in much of the research and fiction literature concerning Puerto Ricans in U.S. schools for many years, and it is no more poignantly expressed than in this segment of the poem "Broken English Dream" by Pedro Pietri:

To the united states we came
To learn how to misspell our name
To lose the definition of pride
To have misfortune on our side . . .
To be trained to turn on television sets
To dream about jobs you will never get
To fill out welfare applications
To graduate from school without an education . . . (1977, p. 22)

Puerto Rican youths have often felt that they simply did not belong in U.S. schools, and this feeling of alienation was well described by Piri Thomas in his 1967 novel, *Down These Mean Streets*: "School stunk. I hated school and all its teachers. I hated the crispy look of the teachers and the draggy-long hours they took out of my life from nine to three" (p. 64). In fact, for Thomas, sneaking out of school was like "escaping from some kind of prison" (p. 64). Research literature reflects these ideas. For example, ASPIRA conducted a survey in several schools to determine the adjustment of newly arrived students and found a good deal of alienation among Puerto Rican students:

> The conclusion of the survey, in short, was that despite the genuine good-will and effort of hundreds of teachers, many Puerto Rican children were being left out, were not participating in classroom activities, were not learning. Quietly and unobtrusively, they were "sitting out" months and years of their allotted school time. (Margolis, 1968, p. 125)

Almost two decades later, the National Commission on Secondary Education for Hispanics reached a similar conclusion:

> The fundamental finding of the National Commission on Secondary Education for Hispanics is that a shocking proportion of this generation of Hispanic young people is being wasted. Wasted because their education needs are neither understood nor met, their high aspirations unrecognized, their promising potential stunted. (1984, n.p.)

Marginalization often begins when Spanish-speaking students enter schools and find that their only means of communication is neither understood nor accepted. In the 1965 study, Eugene Bucchioni describes the role of the Spanish language for Puerto Rican students: "Its use symbolizes the cultural understanding and unity of Puerto Rican pupils, especially when confronted by an outsider who . . . represents the imposed authority and control of a superordinate group" (1982, p. 234). Using the Spanish language among themselves represents one of the few instances in which Puerto Rican students can create a sense of belonging. Marisol, one of the students I interviewed for a previous study, talked of her need to speak her native language in school even though she was fluent in English. She described a problem she had with a former teacher who had prohibited her from speaking Spanish in class: "I thought it was like an insult to us, you know? Just telling us not to talk Spanish, 'cause [we] were Puerto Ricans and, you know, we're free to talk whatever we want. . . . I could never stay quiet and talk only English, 'cause, you know, words slip in Spanish" (Nieto, 1996, p. 157).

For Puerto Rican students, speaking Spanish generally represents nothing more than solidarity and belonging, but it is often interpreted as a lack of respect.

In *Silent Dancing*, Judith Ortiz Cofer recounts her experience with a teacher who struck her on the head when she thought she was being disrespected. Actually, Judith did not understand English. This was to be a painful but quickly learned lesson: "I instinctively understood then that language is the only weapon a child has against the absolute power of adults," she concluded (1990, p. 62).

Alba Ambert also powerfully describes the alienating experience of school when her protagonist Blanca is placed in a class for the mentally retarded because she cannot speak English:

> During that year in a class for the mentally retarded, Blanca drew pumpkins in October, colored pine trees in December, and cut out White bunnies in April. She also picked up some English. When Blanca was able to communicate in English, school authorities no longer considered her retarded and placed her in a classroom for children without the deficiency of not knowing the English language. (Ambert, 1995, p. 79)

Marginalization, however, is not simply related to the lack of English-language skills. Many students have expressed feeling marginalized because their culture, their social class, their traditions, and the values of their families are different from the culture found in mainstream schools. Virginia Vogel Zanger's (1993) study of high-achieving, college-bound Latino students in a Boston high school exemplifies this marginalization. Even the words that the students in her study employed to describe their perceived status within the school were striking examples of alienation: these included terms such as "not joined in" and "out to the edge," and prepositions such as "below," "under," "low," and "down." Further, Johanna Vega, in recounting her experiences of going from the South Bronx to becoming a scholarship student at Groton, a posh independent school in Massachusetts, writes of the terrible "psychic wounding" that she underwent for four years (1996).

When my colleague Manuel Frau-Ramos and I questioned young people in an exploratory study of dropouts in Holyoke, Massachusetts, we heard one student explain, "I was an outsider." When we asked Pedro, one of the students who was still in school, if the alienation he felt was due to his level of English proficiency, he said, "No, it is not the English . . . that's not the problem. . . . I don't know how to explain it, I don't know" (Frau-Ramos & Nieto, 1993, p. 160). Another student, José, explained that he "felt alone" at school, adding, *"Tu sabes, no son los míos"* ["You know, they are not my people"]. When we asked Pedro if he had any recommendations for teachers and schools to help solve the dropout problem among Puerto Rican students, he said, *"Hacer algo para que los boricuas no se sientan aparte"* ["Do something so that the Puerto Rican students would not feel separate"] (p. 161). That feeling of separateness is another word for marginalization.

Contrasting that feeling of separateness documented by Manuel Frau-Ramos and me is an immensely successful program for Latino students studied by Jeannette Abi-Nader (1993), which suggests that a sense of belonging can counter the cultural isolation that Puerto Rican students feel. One of the keys to the program's success was the teacher who directed the program by incorporating motivational strategies that built on the students' culture and their need for family-like affection and caring. In other words, the teacher created a world in the classroom in which the students felt they "belonged." The students in turn described him as "a father, brother, and friend to us."

CONCLUSION: CARE AS THE MISSING INGREDIENT IN THE EDUCATION OF PUERTO RICANS

I began this article by stating that the general public knows very little of the history of Puerto Ricans in U.S. schools, and this is indeed true, although a great deal has been written on the subject. For instance, the ASPIRA report on the education of Puerto Ricans, written thirty years ago (Margolis, 1968), pointed out that an impressive bibliography of 450 articles and studies focusing on the issue of Puerto Rican children in U.S. schools had already been compiled by 1968. More research might point to better solutions, but it may also only point to more solutions that are rejected, ignored, or overlooked. The major problem, however, seems to be not the lack of data, but rather the lack of will and resources to remedy the educational problems that Puerto Rican students face.

This is the point at which the use of fiction with fact can make a difference in the education of Puerto Rican students. The examples of fiction used in this article, almost all written by Puerto Ricans, represent the lived experiences of Puerto Rican students themselves. They are not clinical or sterile descriptions of faceless students in nameless schools; instead, these works of fiction serve to make the educational research come alive and make it harder to ignore or reject the facts described in educational research literature. Using fact and fiction together can be a powerful way of making the problems that Puerto Rican students face more visible to those who can make schools caring and affirming places, that is, the teachers, administrators, and policymakers.

The message that emerges from this study of fact and fiction is one that underlies all the others: *the care or rejection experienced by Puerto Rican students in U.S. schools can have a significant impact on their academic success or failure.* Research by Victor Battistich, Daniel Solomon, Dong-il Kim, Meredith Watson, and Eric Schaps (1995) indicates important connections among caring communities, the identification that students make with learning, and their academic achievement. These researchers examined relationships between students' sense of school community, poverty level, and their attitudes, motives, beliefs, and behavior in twenty-four elementary schools. Because Puerto Rican students live in greater poverty than those from most other groups, one of the major conclusions of the study has especially important implications for them: "Although the deleterious effects of poverty are well known, the most encouraging aspect of the present findings is the suggestive evidence that some of its negative effects can be mitigated if the school is successful in creating a caring community for its members" (1995, p. 649).

According to the National Commission on Secondary Education for Hispanics (NCSEH), "Hispanic students almost unanimously identified 'someone caring' as the most important factor in academic success" (1984, p. 13). Students attribute academic success to this quality of "caring" in their schools. As one young woman in the NCSEH report explained, "I got pregnant and I thought I'd never be anybody but I came here and the teachers and the kids gave me love and I know I'll make it . . ." (p. 29). In an ethnographic study of Puerto Rican adolescents who had dropped out of school and were now attending an alternative school (Saravia-Shore & Martinez, 1992), the researchers documented numerous similar examples of conflicting values of home, peers, and schools. Students were happy with the alternative schools because they felt that teachers there cared about them, whereas criticisms of their previous schools included teachers' lack of respect, care, and concern: "They would say things like, 'Do you want to be like the other Puerto Rican women who never got an education? Do you want to be like the rest of your family and never go to school?'" (p. 242).

Research and fiction often associate caring with Puerto Rican or other Latino teachers (Hornberger, 1990; Latino Commission, 1992; Mercado & Moll, 1997; Montero-Sieburth & Pérez, 1987; National Commission on Secondary Education for Hispanics, 1984). It is important, however, to mention that, in both fact and fiction, caring is not exclusive to Latino teachers. Non-Latino teachers, who represent the vast majority of teachers of Puerto Rican youngsters, also show care and concern for their Puerto Rican students (Abi-Nader, 1993; Ada, 1993; Ambert, 1995; Cofer, 1990; Mercado & Moll, 1997; Mohr, 1979; Santiago, 1993; Vega, 1996). Many commissions and reports have called for hiring more Latino teachers (Latino Commission, 1992; Meier & Stewart, 1991; Morrison, 1958; National Commission on Secondary Education for Hispanics, 1984; U.S. Commission on Civil Rights, 1976), a recommendation that makes eminent good sense. However, the literature is clear that while being Puerto Rican can be an advantage to teaching Puerto Rican youths, non-Puerto Rican teachers can also be extremely effective with them.

Latino youngsters explicitly mention "love" as the factor that can make or break their experiences in school. Voices recorded in the research literature from the 1950s until today suggest that the importance of caring and the price of rejection have always been significant, but no one chose to listen to them. This was true in research as early as *The Puerto Rican Study* (Morrison, 1958), when children and their parents were interviewed: "There were instances where, from the child's viewpoint, the present teacher, compared with previous teachers in Puerto Rico, seemed uninteresting, lacking in affection or in kindness" (p. 133).

Almost thirty years later, research on the strategies used by a bilingual teacher to relate to her Latino students also identified *cariño*, or endearment—especially as evident in hugging and other displays of affection—as a key element in the success of Latino youngsters. She identified herself as a "teacher, friend, mother, social worker, translator, counselor, advocate, prosecutor, group therapist, hygienist, and monitor" (Montero-Sieburth & Pérez, 1987, p. 183). A few years later, Nancy Hornberger's (1990) study of successful learning contexts draws a similar conclusion: in the Puerto Rican classroom that she studied, she found that the teacher openly displayed tenderness and affection, as well as a "motherly concern" for her students, expressions typical of the Puerto Rican community. Nitza Hidalgo explains the importance of this kind of interpersonal support: "Because of the propensity to place value on interpersonal relationships within the culture, the relationship between the teacher and Puerto Rican student becomes vital to the educational achievement of the student. Students have to feel liked by the teacher; they gain strength from their relationship to their teachers (1992, p. 36). A young woman in Zanger's research described the experiences of Latino students and the cost of rejection: "They just feel left out, they feel like if no one loves them, no one cares, so why should they care?" (1993, p. 176). Still more recently, one of the Latina teachers in the research by Carmen Mercado and Luis Moll described how she viewed her profession: "It is not an 8:40 to 3:30 P.M. job but an extension of my life, as if it were part of my family" (1997, p. 31).

Fiction echoes the importance of caring that many have overlooked or ignored in the research literature. Alba Ambert's *A Perfect Silence* beautifully expresses this sentiment when she describes a number of exceptions to Blanca's generally uncaring and unfeeling teachers. Mrs. Wasserman, the teacher who first recognized the abuse Blanca had experienced, kept a collection of children's books in the classroom that Blanca transformed into "dreams of possible worlds" (1995, p. 114). Her second-grade teacher, Mrs. Kalfus, once kissed Blanca's swollen cheek when she had a toothache: "Years later, Blanca, who forgot much of her disrupted childhood, remembered that kiss" (p. 115).

Similarly, Mr. Barone, the guidance counselor in *When I Was Puerto Rican* (Santiago, 1993), sees promise in Negi and pushes her to go to an academic high school. The ensuing scene, in which Negi tries out for Performing Arts High School by reciting a monologue she memorized in a thick Puerto Rican accent using English that she does not understand, is a hilarious and touching example of care and concern in the fiction about Puerto Rican students in U.S. schools. By going out of his way to help Negi apply to a school with rigorous standards, Mr. Barone exemplifies how teachers and other educators can make caring and concern a vital part of the school community.

But what exactly does it mean to create such a caring community? The literature and research that we have seen describe "caring" as providing affection and support for students, building strong interpersonal relationships with them and their families, learning about and from them, respecting and affirming their language and culture and building on it, and having high expectations of them. Caring implies that schools' policies and practices also need to change because simply changing the nature of their relationships with teachers and schools will not by itself change the opportunities the children are given. Hence, changing both personal relationships among teachers and Puerto Rican students and the institutional conditions in their schools is essential if these students are to become successful learners.

These changes are, however, not enough. Care is demonstrated as well through the provision of adequate resources to ensure that learning can take place. The poignant plea of a student who addressed the National Commission on Secondary Education for Hispanics (1984) is even more explicit: "We work hard and we try and our teachers care, but we are not treated fairly. Our school is poor. If this commission cares, please make something happen" (n.p.). The commission's final word, that Latinos "are our children, a generation too precious to waste" (p. 45), is worth repeating if we are serious and truly care about creating the possibility of success for more Puerto Rican students.

NOTE

1. Puerto Ricans are not "immigrants" in the traditional sense of the word, since they arrive in the United States as citizens. They are also not strictly "migrants," since they have not simply moved from one geographic part of a culturally connected society to another. Some scholars refer to Puerto Ricans living in the United States as [im]migrants, highlighting the hybrid nature of their status. See, for example, Marquez (1995).

REFERENCES

Abi-Nader, J. (1993). Meeting the needs of multicultural classrooms: Family values and the motivation of minority students. In M. J. O'Hair & S. J. Odell (Eds.), *Diversity and teaching: Teacher education yearbook 1* (pp. 212–236). Ft. Worth, TX: Harcourt Brace Jovanovich.

Ada, A. F. (1993). *My name is María Isabel.* New York: Atheneum.

Ambert, A. (1995). *A perfect silence.* Houston, TX: Arte Público Press.

Appleton, N. (1983). *Cultural pluralism in education: Theoretical foundations.* New York: Longman.

Arias, S. (1996). Inside the worlds of Latino traveling cultures: Martín Espada's poetry of rebellion. *Bilingual Review/Revista Bilingüe, 21,* 231–240.

ASPIRA of New York. (1968). *Hemos trabajado bien: Proceedings of the ASPIRA National Conference of Puerto Ricans, Mexican-Americans, and Educators.* New York: Author.

ASPIRA Institute for Policy Research. (1993). *Facing the facts: The state of Hispanic education, 1993.* Washington, DC: ASPIRA.

Association of Assistant Superintendents (1948). *A program of education for Puerto Ricans in New York City.* Brooklyn: New York City Board of Education.

Battistich, V., Solomon, D., Kim, D., Watson, M., & Schaps, E. (1995). Schools as communities, poverty levels of student populations, and students' attitudes, motives, and performance: A multilevel analysis. *American Educational Research Journal, 32,* 627–658.

Bigler, E. (1997). Dangerous discourses: Language politics and classroom practices in Upstate New York. *Centro, 9*(9), 8–25.

Blanchard, J. S., & Casanova, U. (1996). *Modern fiction about schoolteaching: An anthology.* Needham Heights, MA: Allyn & Bacon.

Bonilla, F., & Campos, R. (1981). A wealth of poor: Puerto Ricans in the new economic order. *Daedalus, 110,* 133–176.

Bourdieu, P. (1977). *Outline of theory and practice.* Cambridge, Eng.: Cambridge University Press.

Bucchioni, E. (1982). The daily round of life in the school. In F. Cordasco & E. Bucchioni (Eds.), *The Puerto Rican community and its children on the mainland* (3rd rev. ed., pp. 201–238). Metuchen, NJ: Scarecrow Press.

Cafferty, P. S. J., & Rivera-Martínez, C. (1981). *The politics of language: The dilemma of bilingual education for Puerto Ricans.* Boulder, CO: Westview Press.

Carrasquillo, A. L. (1991). *Hispanic children and youth in the United States: A resource guide.* New York: Garland.

Centro. (1997). Special issue on the education of Puerto Ricans, 9(9).

Chenault, L. R. (1970). *The Puerto Rican migrant in New York City.* New York: Columbia University Press. (Original work published 1938)

Cofer, J. O. (1990). *Silent dancing: A partial remembrance of a Puerto Rican childhood.* Houston, TX: Arte Público Press.

Cortes, E. (2000). School smells. In S. Nieto (Ed.), *Puerto Rican students in U.S. schools.* Mahwah, NJ: Lawrence Erlbaum Associates.

Crawford, J. (1992). *Hold your tongue: Bilingualism and the politics of "English only."* Reading, MA: Addison-Wesley.

Darder, A., & Upshur, C. (1993). What do Latino children need to succeed in school? A study of four Boston public schools. In R. Rivera and S. Nieto (Eds.), *The education of Latino students in Massachusetts: Research and policy implications* (pp. 127–146). Boston: Gastón Institute for Latino Public Policy and Development.

De Jesús, J. L. (Ed.) (1997). *Growing up Puerto Rican.* New York: William Morrow.

Díaz Alfaro, A. (1962). Santa Cló va a La Cuchilla. In W. E. Colford (Ed. and Trans.), *Classic tales from Spanish America* (pp. 206–210). New York: Barrons Educational Series.

Díaz Alfaro, A. (1978). Peyo Mercé enseña inglés. In K. Wagenheim (Ed.), *Cuentos: An anthology of short stories from Puerto Rico* (pp. 98–107). New York: Schocken Books.

Díaz Soto, L. (1993). Native language for school success. *Bilingual Research Journal, 17* (1/2), 83–97.

Dyson, A. H., & Genishi, C. (1994). Introduction. In A. H. Dyson & C. Genishi (Eds.), *The need for story: Cultural diversity in classroom and community* (pp. 1–7). Urbana, IL: National Council of Teachers of English.

Espada, M. (1993). The year I was diagnosed with a sacrilegious heart. In M. Espada (Ed.), *City of coughing and dead radiators* (pp. 72–74). New York: W. W. Norton.

Espada, M. (1996). Public School 190, Brooklyn, 1963. In M. Espada, Ed.), *Imagine the angels of bread* (p. 25). New York: W. W. Norton.

Estevez, S. M. (1991). Here. In F. Turner (Ed.), *Puerto Rican writers at home in the U.S.A.: An anthology* (pp. 186–187). Seattle, WA: Open Hand.

Figueroa, J. A. (1991). Boricua. In F. Turner (Ed.), *Puerto Rican writers at home in the U.S.A.: An anthology* (pp. 221–224). Seattle, WA: Open Hand.

Fitzpatrick, J. P. (1987a). *Puerto Rican Americans: The meaning of migration to the mainland.* Englewood Cliffs, NJ: Prentice-Hall. (Original work published 1971)

Fitzpatrick, J. P. (1987b). *One church, many cultures: Challenge of diversity.* Kansas City, MO: Sheed & Ward.

Frau-Ramos, M., & Nieto, S. (1993). 'I was an outsider': Dropping out among Puerto Rican youths in Holyoke, Massachusetts. In R. Rivera and S. Nieto (Eds.), *The education of Latino students in Massachusetts: Research and policy implications* (pp. 147–169). Boston: Gastón Institute for Latino Public Policy and Development.

Gibson, M. A., & Ogbu, J. U. (Eds.). (1991). *Minority status and schooling: A comparative study of immigrant and involuntary minorities.* New York: Garland.

Hernández, C. D. (1997). *Puerto Rican voices in English: Interviews with writers.* Westport, CT: Praeger.

Hidalgo, N. M. (1992). *"i saw puerto rico once": A review of the literature on Puerto Rican families and school achievement in the United States* (Report No. 12). Boston: Center on Families, Communities, Schools and Children's Learning.

History Task Force, Centro de Estudios Puertorriqueños. (1979). *Labor migration under capitalism: The Puerto Rican experience.* New York: Monthly Review Press.

Hornberger, N. (1990). Creating successful learning contexts for biliteracy. *Teachers College Record, 92,* 212–229.

Institute for Puerto Rican Policy. (1992). The distribution of Puerto Ricans and other selected Latinos in the U.S.: 1990. *Datanote on the Puerto Rican community, 11.* New York: Author.

Institute for Puerto Rican Policy. (1996). The status of Puerto Rican children in the U.S. *IPR Datanote, 18.*

Katz, M. B. (1975). *Class, bureaucracy, and the schools: The illusion of educational change in America.* New York: Praeger.

Keenan, J. W., Willett, J., & Solsken, J. (1993). Constructing an urban village: School/home collaboration in a multicultural classroom. *Language Arts, 70,* 56–66.

Latino Commission on Educational Reform. (1992). *Toward a vision for the education of Latino students: Community voices, student voice* (Interim report of the Latino Commission on Educational Reform). Brooklyn: New York City Board of Education.

Lewis, O. (1965). *La vida: A Puerto Rican family in the culture of poverty, San Juan and New York.* New York: Vintage.

Margolis, R. J. (1968). *The losers: A report on Puerto Ricans and the public schools.* New York: ASPIRA.

Marquez, R. (1995). Sojourners, settlers, castaways, and creators: A recollection of Puerto Rico past and Puerto Ricans present. *Massachusetts Review, 36*(1), 94–118.

Massachusetts Advocacy Center. (1990). *Locked in/locked out: Tracking and placement practices in Boston public schools.* Boston: Author.

Meier, K. J., & Stewart, J., Jr. (1991). *The politics of Hispanic education: Un paso pa'lante y dos pa'tras.* Albany: State University of New York Press.

Melendez, E. (1991). *Los que se van, los que regresan: Puerto Rican migration to and from the United States, 1982–1988.* New York: Commonwealth of Puerto Rico, Department of Puerto Rican Community Affairs.

Mercado, C. I., & Moll, L. (1997). The study of funds of knowledge: Collaborative research in Latino homes. *Centro, 9*(9), 26–42.

Mohr, N. (1979). *Felita.* New York: Dial Press.

Mohr, N. (1986). *Nilda* (2nd ed). Houston, TX: Arte Público Press.

Montero-Sieburth, M., & Pérez, M. (1987). Echar pa'lante, moving onward: The dilemmas and strategies of a bilingual teacher. *Anthropology and Education Quarterly, 18,* 180–189.

Morrison, J. C. (1958). *The Puerto Rican study, 1953–1957.* Brooklyn: New York City Board of Education.

National Center for Educational Statistics. (1995). *The educational progress of Hispanic students.* Washington, DC: United States Department of Education, Office of Educational Research and Improvement.

National Commission on Secondary Education for Hispanics. (1984). *"Make something happen": Hispanics and urban school reform.* Washington, DC: Hispanic Policy Development Project.

National Council of La Raza. (1993). *Moving from the margins: Puerto Rican young men and family poverty.* Washington, DC: Author.

National Puerto Rican Task Force. (1982). *Toward a language policy for Puerto Ricans in the U.S.: An agenda for a community in movement.* New York: City University of New York Research Foundation.

Negrón de Montilla, A. (1971). *Americanization in Puerto Rico and the public school system, 1900–1930.* Río Piedras, PR: Editorial Edil.

New voices: Immigrant students in U.S. public schools. (1988). Boston: National Coalition of Advocates for Students.

Nieto, S. (1995). A history of the education of Puerto Rican students in U.S. mainland schools: "Losers," "outsiders," or "leaders"? In J. A. Banks & C. A. M. Banks (Eds.), *Handbook of research on multicultural education* (pp. 388–411). New York: Macmillan.

Nieto, S. (1996). *Affirming diversity: The sociopolitical context of multicultural education* (2nd ed.). White Plains, NY: Longman.

Nieto, S. (Ed.). (2000). *Puerto Rican students in U.S. schools.* Mahwah, NJ: Lawrence Erlbaum Associates.

Ogbu, J. U. (1987). Variability in minority school performance: A problem in search of an explanation. *Anthropology and Education Quarterly, 18,* 312–334.

Phinney, J. S. (1993). A three-stage model of ethnic identity development in adolescence. In M. E. Bernal & G. P. Knight (Eds.), *Ethnic identity: Formation and transmission among Hispanics and other minorities* (pp. 61–79). Albany: State University of New York Press.

Pietri, P. (1977). Broken English dream. In P. Pietri (Ed.), *Obituario puertorriqueño* (pp. 18–43). San Juan, PR: Instituto de Cultura Puertorriqueña.

Quality Education for Minorities Project. (1990). *Education that works: An action plan for the education of minorities.* Cambridge, MA: Author.

Rivera, E. (1982). *Family installments: Memories of growing up Hispanic.* New York: William Morrow.

Rodríguez, A., Jr. (1992). *The boy without a flag: Tales of the South Bronx.* Minneapolis, MN: Milkweed Editions.

Rodríguez, C. (1991). *Puerto Ricans: Born in the U.S.A.* Boulder, CO: Westview Press.

Rumbaut, R. G., & Ima, K. (1987). *The adaptation of Southeast Asian refugee youth: A comparative study* (Final Report.) San Diego, CA.: Office of Refugee Resettlement.

Sánchez, L. R. (1987). The flying bus. In A. Rodríguez de Laguna (Ed.), *Images and identities: The Puerto Rican in two world contexts* (pp. 17–25). New Brunswick, NJ: Transaction Books.

Sánchez Korrol, V. E. (1994). *From colonia to community: The history of Puerto Ricans in New York City.* Berkeley: University of California Press. (Original work published 1983)

Santiago, E. (1993). *When I was Puerto Rican.* Reading, MA: Addison-Wesley.
Saravia-Shore, M., & Martinez, H. (1992). An ethnographic study of home/school role conflicts of second generation Puerto Rican adolescents. In M. Saravia-Shore & S. F. Arvizu (Eds.), *Cross-cultural literacy: Ethnographies of communication in multiethnic classrooms* (pp. 227–251). New York: Garland.
Sexton, P. C. (1965). *Spanish Harlem.* New York: Harper & Row.
Spring, J. (1997). *Deculturalization and the struggle for equality: A brief history of the education of dominated cultures in the United States.* New York: McGraw-Hill.
Thomas, P. (1997). *Down these mean streets.* New York: Vintage Books.
U.S. Commission on Civil Rights. (1976). *Puerto Ricans in the continental United States: An uncertain future.* Washington, DC: Author.
Vega, J. (1996). From the South Bronx to Groton. In L. M. Carlson (Ed.), *Barrio streets, carnival dreams: Three generations of Latino artistry* (pp. 83–99). New York: Henry Holt.
Walsh, C. E. (1991). *Pedagogy and the struggle for voice: Issues of language, power, and schooling for Puerto Ricans.* New York: Bergin & Garvey.
Zanger, V. V. (1987). The social context of second language learning; An examination of barriers to integration in five case studies. Unpublished doctoral dissertation, Boston University.
Zanger, V. V. (1993). Academic costs of social marginalization: An analysis of the perceptions of Latino students at a Boston high school. In R. Rivera and S. Nieto (Eds.), *The education of Latino students in Massachusetts: Research and policy implications* (pp. 170–190). Boston: Gastón Institute for Latino Public Policy and Development.
Zentella, A. C. (1997). *Growing up bilingual: Puerto Rican children in New York.* Oxford, Eng.: Basil Blackwell.

A GAY-THEMED LESSON IN AN ETHNIC LITERATURE CURRICULUM

TENTH GRADERS' RESPONSES TO "DEAR ANITA"

STEVEN Z. ATHANASES

Beginning early in the school year, I watched Reiko Liu engage her students in literature study through discussions that required thinking about, and invited exploration of, such issues as cultural identity, subculture/dominant culture tensions, and ethnocentrism.* The works students read in her course, "The Ethnic Experience in Literature," also raised the difficult issues of cultural domination, racism, sexism, lynching, and rape. Reiko's class norms enabled her tenth graders to respond with curiosity, candor, and, at times, anger. Generally, however, they responded with sensitivity and maturity, despite the potential for awkwardness, tensions, and divisiveness that can occur when such issues arise in multiethnic urban public high school classrooms where racial and other tensions often run high.

In January, however, most of the class responded with little empathy to Marguerite, the character who struggles with her sexual identity in Maya Angelou's *I Know Why the Caged Bird Sings* (1969). Students remarked that being a lesbian is not normal, that gays choose to be gay and too often "go around talking about it." As with the entire curriculum, Reiko's goals for a unit on Ethnic Short Stories and Essays, to follow Angelou's book, included not only explorations of difference, but also recognition of common ground. She hoped her students would, as she put it, "take with them an understanding that people they thought were strange or different are not that strange or different after all." In that spirit, Reiko chose to "get gutsy" and include a piece dealing with

* The names of students, teachers, and the school have all been changed.

Harvard Educational Review   Vol. 66   No. 2   Summer 1996 gay experience. With the assistance of her best friend on the faculty, a gay man, she searched for readings, deciding on the essay, "Dear Anita: Late Night Thoughts of an Irish Catholic Homosexual," by Brian McNaught (1988a), a counselor and speaker on gay issues. For a workshop she later conducted, Reiko composed these notes on "Dear Anita":

> This article is addressed to Anita Bryant, who campaigned against the rights of gay people to teach in Dade County schools. McNaught discusses how he, like Anita, was raised to believe stereotypical notions of homosexuality as a sin and a mental disorder and of gay men as sexually interested in children. He effectively argues against each of these points and relates the painfulness of living in a society that denies him his human rights.

Reiko's purpose in the "Dear Anita" lesson fit her goals of teaching sensitivity to diversity and seeking common ground across marginalized groups. She told me she wanted her students to understand

> how it feels to be different, in this case as a gay person, how the whole world tells you that you're sinful, that you're a shame to the whole society, that you're a child molester, all these negative things. I want especially some of the more homophobic members of our class to understand where this person is coming from. And I want them to make a transition to how that's not too unlike having people tell you you're ignorant or you're stupid because of your racial background. These kids will probably say that being gay is different from being a member of an ethnic group. They've voiced that already. But I want them to understand that the effect on the person is not all that different.

What follows is background information detailing the inclusion of issues of sexual orientation in curriculum; an account of how the "Dear Anita" lesson unfolded; an analysis of the essay, the lesson, and the students' responses to these; and a close look at one student's role in the process. My analysis focuses on ways Reiko stimulated thoughtful discussions of literature and diversity and examines students' responses to such work.

BACKGROUND

Calls for more inclusive literature curricula from the English Coalition Conference (Lloyd-Jones & Lunsford, 1989), the Task Force on Racism and Bias (1986) for the National Council of Teachers of English, and other groups serving English and language arts teachers argue that "content integration" (Banks, 1993) can help insure that all students learn of the pluralistic nature of the United States, of contributions from all groups to U.S. culture and letters, and of the realities of racism and oppression lived by many in this country. To encourage inclusiveness and to work against stereotype formation, thoughtful educators can select texts by and about groups defined by not only race and ethnicity, but also gender, sexual orientation, religion, and other significant definitions of cultural and social group (Banks & Banks, 1993; Stotsky, 1994).

Despite the inclusion of sexual orientation in the language of some literature on diversified curricula, teachers, particularly in K-12 classrooms, seldom provide positive representations of gay and lesbian characters or address issues of sexual orientation or homophobia when they arise in lessons. Reasons for the dearth of such work in the classroom are numerous and varied. For example, the larger sociopolitical context within which schools operate has generally marginalized contributions of people of color and women, and concealed or avoided revealing the sexual orientation of prominent gays and lesbians. As a result, texts selected for class use have remained almost exclusively those authored by White men (Applebee, 1993); when authors are gay, this fact is generally repressed.

The deliberately limited use by teachers of gay and lesbian authors has been partially due to a lack of information and resources on diverse selections, although other reasons figure in this picture as well. Many teachers, for example, feel uncomfortable dealing with issues of sexual orientation, are not convinced it is a topic appropriate for study, or are themselves homophobic. Even when teachers are convinced of the importance of exploring gay and lesbian experiences in literature, they often still fear that community members will view such study as promoting homosexuality, thus instigating a backlash. For gay or lesbian teachers not out at school, such a backlash could lead to being "outed" or, for teachers already out, it could lead to accusations of "recruiting." In addition, some administrators who are unwilling to take risks censor their own teachers' efforts toward such inclusiveness (e.g., Hammett, 1992), while others use threats of dismissal to censor teachers. For example, a teacher in New Hampshire faced job loss because her twelfth graders were reading E. M. Forster's *Maurice* and May Sarton's *The Education of Harriet Hatfield*, which have, respectively, gay and lesbian protagonists (McVicar, 1995).

Other factors contribute to the lack of inclusion of gay and lesbian lives in curricula. Many teachers may avoid such issues as racism in schools that are fraught with racial tensions. In a similar way, some teachers fear responses to gay and lesbian issues by youth who are in the process of sexual identity formation. Some teachers may worry that male students in particular will resist such lessons, finding them objectionable or disturbing.

Finally, few published works describe ways teachers have managed such work and how students have responded, although essays in recent collections (e.g., Garber, 1994; Harbeck, 1992; Jennings, 1994) include mention of such work, and recent narratives describe the teaching of Rita Mae Brown's *Rubyfruit Jungle* (Boutilier, 1994) and Alice Walker's *The Color Purple* (Lankewish, 1992) in high schools. Additionally, the teaching of queer issues in Mexican American literature (Gonzalez, 1994) and of homophobia in writing courses in college settings (Hart & Parmeter, 1992) have been described. Harris (1990) also offered strategies for studying gay- and lesbian-themed literature at the secondary level. However, despite these efforts, descriptions of what occurs when lessons unfold and analyses of how students respond to and co-construct this work are still needed to aid in building theories of successful pedagogy in the teaching of gay- and lesbian-themed literature.

What follows is an account of a study that asked two questions. First, when a teacher working in a multiethnic setting includes a lesson on gay and lesbian experiences and homophobia in the context of an ethnic literature curriculum, how do students respond to the text and the lesson? Second, to what can those responses be attributed?

FRAMING THE STUDY

Reiko Liu, Her Curriculum, Her Students

My study of the "Dear Anita" lesson is part of a year-long ethnography in which I observed two tenth-grade English classes in two different urban public schools. In each case, the teachers worked to make text selections more diverse by using newly designed ethnic literature curricula, supported by instruction grounded in the elicitation of students' own literary responses rather than the pursuit of canonical interpretations, and by classroom discourse supportive of exploratory thinking rather than mere recitation of facts (Athanases, 1993b). I visited the sites two or more times weekly during the school year. My field notes were supported by audiotapes and videotapes of full-group and small-group discussions, student surveys and writing samples, and school and classroom artifacts. In total, I interviewed more than sixty teachers, students, parents, and other school personnel. Two years later, I returned to the school where Reiko taught and conducted a retrospective survey. I led a pair of group discussion interviews with all but three students from the original class, focusing on their reflections on the class from the distance of two years. I also conducted periodic informal follow-up interviews with both teachers in the two years following the focal study year. This discussion features Reiko's "Dear Anita" lesson, but draws on the larger study for elaboration and support.

Having immigrated to the United States from Japan as a teenager, Reiko experienced culture clash as an immigrant and later in marriage to a Chinese American. Seeing herself as a child of the sixties who had a vision of social change, Reiko remained committed to social justice and to public education as "the vehicle for equality and for participation in a democratic society." During her eighteen years of teaching, Reiko developed "freewheeling discussions" to enable her high school students to explore social issues arising from literature. She helped shape the district's new tenth-grade course on "The Ethnic Experience in Literature." In her first year of implementation, Reiko exposed her students to literature by and about people of a range of ethnicities and socialized students into discussions of diversity with the care that is her hallmark.

236

TABLE 1 *Reiko's students by ethnic identification*

African American	Alycia	European American	Andrea
	Cassandra		Celeste
	Demar		Mark
	LeTonia		
	Richard	Filipino American	Alberto
	Tanisha		Cristina
	Tyrone		Ferdy
			Robert
Chinese American	Genevieve		
	Irene		
	Li		
	Vanessa		
	Vicki		
	Vivian		
	Yong		

Richards High School where Reiko taught is a moderate sized school of grades 9-12 serving children of primarily middle- to low-income families. Reiko's tenth-grade English class was representative of the student body—of the twenty-one students, one-third were African American, one-third Chinese American, and the remaining third of Filipino and European ancestries (see Table 1). Despite the name of the course, Reiko's Honors English class included students at various academic levels.

While overt hostility or violence rarely occurred at the school, most students characterized the interethnic climate as one of avoidance and, at best, tolerance. Few at Richards reported appreciation among students for cultural difference, and, as attested to by letters to the editor in the school newspaper and comments by teachers, counselors, and students, some tensions existed between groups, particularly African Americans and Asian Americans. All of Reiko's students of color wrote of experiences with racial injustice.

Community Influences

All students shared two influences originating from the community—a strong religious presence and exposure to gay and lesbian life. In the predominantly African American neighborhood surrounding Richards, a large number of Baptist churches are set among small residences and businesses. All the churches operate out of small converted corner buildings, except for one large, traditional-looking church. For Chinese American students, the other large ethnic group at Richards, many of whom bus to school from Chinatown, the Catholic Church is as present in their neighborhoods as the Baptist Church is near Richards. Religion plays a central role in the lives of many Richards students, evidenced by remarks about church-going, stories of church activities, and, in the case of five of Reiko's students, firm devotion to the school's gospel choir.

Many of Richards' students have seen at least media images of gays and lesbians since they live in the San Francisco Bay Area, where lesbians and gays are relatively visible and hold some political power. In the school itself, one teacher, Ms. Salzman, came out five years earlier and keeps a photo of her partner on her desk. On the first day of school each year, she comes out so that students wanting to make schedule changes might do so (none ever did), and, as she puts it, to clear the air "so we [can] get on with the business of the class, which [is] learning history." It was clear to me that most students considered Ms. Salzman and Mr. Kendall (another out gay teacher and Reiko's best friend on the faculty) among the most effective and most caring teachers at Richards. Ms. Salzman sponsored safe, underground, district-supported, student gatherings for gay and lesbian students, made known through posters on corridor walls and announcements in daily bulletins. When Ms. Salzman's daughter was born to her and her partner, the principal posted a banner in the office. When Ms. Salzman and her partner chaperoned the prom, the principal remarked, "This has got to be a first for the district!"

Despite a strong gay and lesbian presence in local news and among educators, and despite the beginning of a school support group and some support from the principal, homophobia persisted at Richards. Rarely did students hear about the support group. In the early stages of the group's formation, the principal did not include announcements of the group in the school bulletin; when this changed, many teachers ignored or refused to read the announcements. Posters announcing the group were typically torn down. In addition, gay and lesbian students were sometimes harassed by peers, and a faculty member tore down the banner in the office that announced the birth of Ms. Salzman's daughter. A student, before graduation, told Ms. Salzman that if she prayed hard enough she could recover from being a lesbian. These community influences and school-life realities frame students' responses to Reiko's lesson.

THE "DEAR ANITA" LESSON

The Ethnic Short Stories and Essays Unit

Unable to locate an adequate anthology, Reiko searched libraries, bookstores, and friends' collections to assemble short prose works and excerpts for a five-week unit scheduled to begin in February (Table 2).

Reiko began the unit with a chapter from Martin Luther King Jr.'s book, *Stride Toward Freedom* (1958), noting that, "It sets a positive tone for more heated discussions that may arise later." Reiko wrote for her district teacher workshop:

TABLE 2   *Reiko's Unit of Ethnic Short Stories and Essays*

Author's Ethnicity	*Literary Title and Author*
African American	"A Pilgrimage to Nonviolence," from *Stride Toward Freedom*, Martin Luther King Jr. "How I Started Writing Poetry," Reginald Lockett
Chinese	"Four Directions," from *The Joy Luck Club*, Amy Tan "Boy Crazy," Wendy Ho Iwata
European/ Euro-American	"The Lift That Went Down into Hell," Par Lagerkwist
(Jewish)	"The Magic Barrel," Bernard Malamud
(Gay)	"Dear Anita: Late Night Thoughts of an Irish Catholic Homosexual," Brian McNaught
Filipino	*From America Is in the Heart*, Carlos Bulosan "A Scent of Apples," Bienvenido N. Santos
Japanese	From *No-No Boy*, John Okada
Native American	"Chee's Daughter," Juanita Platero and Siyowin Miller

King relates his search for a method of coping with injustice that would be both moral and effective. He gives a compelling rationale for the use of nonviolence and brings to life the age-old notions of love as a unifying force, of hating the sin but not the sinner.

During the five weeks, students read, discussed, and wrote about each text, including "Dear Anita," Brian McNaught's essay.

The Lesson

The lesson Reiko designed for "Dear Anita" covered two to three class periods. On the first day, she distributed the essay as homework and provided background, specifically Anita Bryant's efforts during the 1970's to ban gay and lesbian teachers from classrooms. On the second day, after a full-class discussion, Reiko asked students to do the following: "Write a 'Dear Brian' letter in response to the 'Dear Anita' article that you have read. Respond to each of the major points [the author] raises and tell whether or not he effectively addresses Anita's concerns. (Min. 300 words)." On a quiz at the end of the unit two weeks later, students wrote paragraphs on two of four questions, one dealing with "Dear Anita": "If Martin Luther King were to express his view on the plight of gay people as mentioned in the 'Dear Anita' article, what might he say, based on what you know of his philosophy?"

239

Analysis of "Dear Anita"

In his eleven-page essay, McNaught speaks to Bryant using language that masks how deliberately he has structured the work to teach and persuade. McNaught uses all three of what rhetoricians identify as Aristotle's persuasion categories: ethos (ethics of the speaker or writer), logos (logic or reasoning), and pathos (emotional appeals). Narrating his journey from childhood to adulthood, McNaught first establishes an ethos of a family-loving, religious, ethical citizen who Bryant would value "playing and praying" with if she did not know he were gay (McNaught, 1988a, p. 5). Next, as Table 3 demonstrates, one by one, McNaught logically refutes myths common in debates about homosexuality, many of which Bryant perpetuated in her anti-gay campaign. Most of these myths he spells out explicitly, some are implied, all are refuted.

Having established a credible ethos and having logically addressed myths in debates on homosexuality, McNaught then creates a scenario in which Bryant's thirteen-year-old son, Bob Jr., discovers he is gay. With this hypothetical story, McNaught itemizes each challenge a young gay man faces (Table 4).

In the process, McNaught creates strong emotional appeal, sharing his own painful journey through a suicide attempt, and noting that "Some people in this country, as we both know, would prefer I hadn't changed my mind [about taking his own life]. But not you, Anita" (p. 13). His persistent use of the direct address (appealing directly to Bryant throughout the essay) and his construction of her as a sensible and caring citizen and mother maintains the appeal that builds in the end to emotionally charged language about the "psychological terror" of being gay and the "primal scream" of the gay civil rights movement "pleading to straight society to refrain from forcing us to live in shadows of self-hate" (p. 14).

Having used ethos, logos, and pathos to persuade, McNaught closes firmly: "Gay civil rights are human civil rights" (p. 14) and no one has the right to interfere with another's development of "the wholeness of our being . . . unless it truly interferes with the rights of others" (p. 15). To challenge someone's right to life, liberty, and the pursuit of happiness, he argues, is to challenge both "the cornerstone of this country" and "the very fiber of our faith which we both claim to follow" (p. 15). In this way, McNaught closes by suggesting that if Bryant persists in her campaign against gays and lesbians, she is not a hero but someone who is anti-democracy and anti-faith.

DATA ANALYSIS

Data for the present study included an audiotape and a videotape of class discussion of "Dear Anita"; three audiotaped interviews with Reiko (before the lesson, immediately after the lesson, and on the following day); the "Dear Brian" writings; the set of unit quizzes; audiotaped interviews with eight case study students selected from the larger study as a varied and representative class sample in terms of gender, ethnicity, and writing and speaking perfor-

TABLE 3   Myths in Debates about Homosexuals and McNaught's Refutations in "Dear Anita"

Myths in Debates about Gays	Refutations
Come from bad backgrounds	McNaught, like many other gays, had strong family and religious upbringing
Psychologically imbalanced	Merely living in a hostile world
Promiscuous	His sexual encounters were late, tentative
Have shameful values	Often share same values with straights
Gays are a freakish few	Ten percent of U.S. population: 22 million
Sex is for procreation only	Many straights marry for reasons other than childbearing; human need for touch
God hates homosexuals	Easy to abuse Scripture
Good religion means literal reading of Scripture	Bible must be understood in cultural context
Cross-dressing is widespread	Most transvestites are heterosexual males
Gays and lesbians hate members of opposite sex	Must distinguish between friendships and object of desire for mates
Gays are child-molesters	Pederasts are rarely gay
Gay teachers will corrupt	Good teaching is good teaching
Gay pride is flaunting a lifestyle	Expression of self and culture are important to all individuals and in many groups
Homosexuality is a choice	It's an orientation, often "constitutional"
Gays want special rights	Gay civil rights are human civil rights

mance; two sets of surveys, one administered at the end of the unit, one two years later; and audiotapes of discussions conducted two years and three months after the lesson, just before the students graduated.

For analysis of the "Dear Anita" discussion, I transcribed the talk from audiotape, adding behavioral descriptions from the accompanying videotape. I used speaker turn (each time someone audibly took the floor) as the unit of analysis to analyze the talk structure and turn-taking patterns. I tracked the discussion content, charting topics, how they began, and who initiated them, and analyzed questions for who raised them, the functions they served, and what

TABLE 4 *Challenges Bob Bryant Jr. Would Face as a Gay Man, in McNaught's Scenario*

Difficulty understanding confusing feelings

Fear of losing parents' love

Being alone, with no one to talk to (not minister nor teacher)

Trying to be heterosexual but failing

Hearing and participating in anti-gay epithets and jokes (internalized homophobia)

Coping with family expectations of settling down with woman and having children

Contemplation of suicide and possible suicide attempt

Deciding: marry and hide, remain celibate, or seek same-sex companion

Coping with parents' failure to come out, their tolerating anti-gay epithets in the home

---

they yielded. I coded Reiko's questions and her other comments to analyze roles she played in shaping discussion. I examined the discourse for knowledge sources used during discussion to determine evidence speakers used to authenticate claims.

One student, Tanisha, took far more turns than any other student and played an enormous role in discussion. I pulled out all of her turns at talk and constructed a performance script, identifying a verb to clarify the verbal action (Long & Hopkins, 1982) of each of Tanisha's turns at talk (e.g., critiques, challenges, inquires, cites, reinforces). With the full transcript contextualizing her turns, I then used this script to describe patterns in Tanisha's discussion performance.

In my analysis of the "Dear Brian" essays, a broad set of themes emerged across them. I similarly identified themes in student quizzes, two sets of surveys, transcripts from case study interviews, and transcripts from the retrospective discussion. In addition to analyzing patterns in students' responses *within* each of these sets of data, I analyzed response patterns of case study students *across* data sets (i.e., each student's responses in writings, in discussions, in interviews). Also, I analyzed patterns of response across the various individual analyses.

Finally, analyses from the full ethnography were used to elaborate or provide comparison and contrast to those in the present study. The longitudinal nature of the study allowed for an investigation of patterns of language use and an examination of how teaching and learning evolved. Claims were strengthened by gaining multiple views of what occurred, including teacher and student perspectives, multiple student perspectives, and perspectives of a diverse group of case study students in terms of gender, ethnicity, academic preparedness, and frequency of participation in discussion.

STUDENTS' RESPONSES TO THE LESSON

The Discussion of "Dear Anita"

Structure of the discussion. From the third-floor classroom, its walls adorned with student poetry and Renaissance newscast posters from an earlier *Othello* unit, occasional shrieks could be heard through the open window from the P.E. class on the blacktop below. In class, as usual, students sat in a circle with Reiko and spoke without raising hands. Of eighteen students present, fifteen participated in discussion, fourteen of their own volition and one at Reiko's invitation. Conversation was fast paced and highly engaging. Many students took numerous short turns in a volleying manner, rather than few longer turns. This reflected in part the class norm of co-constructing interpretations, and in part the controversial nature of the topics. Nine of the eighteen students took ten or more turns during the discussion. As in other discussions during the year, Reiko asked questions but rarely evaluated students' responses, letting students respond to each other, build on each other's remarks, and challenge each other's ideas. As a result, students often engaged in long runs of talk without Reiko's intervention. Eight times during the discussion, students took more than ten consecutive turns without comment from Reiko, and three of these times, students continued for twenty-five turns or more without teacher remark. The videotape shows Reiko watching students closely, shaping discussion in a variety of ways. Of forty-four turns she took, exactly half were questions, half statements. For example, fourteen of Reiko's turns aided comprehension of the text by contextualizing it with cultural and background information and clarifying meaning. Six turns, mostly questions, worked toward interpretation, five challenged students to sharpen or elaborate claims, and seven were process-oriented turns to launch and guide discussion. Ten of Reiko's turns addressed the issue of empathy. Her questions pressed students to imagine struggles of gays and lesbians (e.g., "How can it be to be such a person . . . having the whole world telling you that you're sick and deranged and sinful?"), and, using textual details, she reminded students of McNaught's perspective on the plight of gays (e.g., when she said, "You tried your best to do what's expected of you. You try to be the best student, the best athlete, winner of all these trophies, and swimming and all this, playing the part of the All-American male, and yet inside, you know you're different."). In these ways, Reiko worked to move the discussion toward her goals.

Content of the discussion. Reiko began with a discussion of McNaught's Irish heritage and Catholic upbringing; specifically, she asked how these may have shaped his attitudes and sense of self, particularly given the view of homosexuality in Catholicism. Reiko pointed out the impact of cultural expectations, particularly to marry and raise a large family. Next, the class addressed the issue that inspired Bryant's movement, whether gay and lesbian teachers should be permitted to teach. The class easily reached an accord, agreeing that one's freedom to teach should be determined by competence in the classroom and not by sexual orientation. Ferdy, who is active in discussions, offered, "There should be no doubt about it that they should be in school. If they fit the qualifications, you know, then they should have the right to teach." Richard then raised a concern, which Tyrone and Tanisha challenged:

> *Richard:* If they start likin' one of their students, then they're like too far gone, it's gettin' personal.
>
> *Tyrone:* But if you were to think about it, a straight teacher could be eyein' a student just as well as a homosexual. Like male teachers, with a girl comin' to class.
>
> *Richard:* But I'm talkin' about with the same sex.
>
> *Tyrone:* I know, but I'm sayin' that it hurt your ego and your pride, but it's the same THING. A grown man lookin' at you just like a woman doin' it. But if it's a woman you gonna—
>
> *Tanisha:* Yeah, you're gonna say, "Oh yeah!"
>
> *Richard:* But you're talkin' about—
>
> *Reiko:* But Tyrone is saying either way is wrong.

Fifteen minutes into discussion, Richard asked if sexual orientation is a choice. He added that it seemed that Brian could have chosen to stay with women like when he dated them in high school. A few students joined him, and Reiko and Tanisha both challenged them repeatedly with questions like this one from Tanisha: "Why would he CHOOSE to do something that he KNEW was going to cause him a lot of grief and all of his family and a lot of people most likely and everybody around him a lot of grief?" Reiko later referred to this stretch as being "hung up on the element of choice." The class then discussed development of Brian's sexual identity, including his exploration of intimacy with women, and Cassandra asked if that made McNaught bisexual. Students named pop singers they thought were bisexual (Boy George, Prince), but Tyrone and Tanisha said these singers were in fact heterosexual. Reiko returned to the essay, asking how they would feel in Brian's shoes. Cassandra responded, "It would make you not want to be," and Tanisha added loudly and intensely, "That's why he tried to commit suicide!" Demar added, "It should turn you around." Before anyone could respond to Tanisha's remark or Tanisha could contest Demar's, Reiko had a question on the floor.

She asked the class the degree to which McNaught dispelled the myths of homosexuality, which was a goal of his essay. Students argued that he successfully countered gay stereotypes, especially the notion of gay men as pedophiles. Tanisha pointed out that McNaught refuted this myth by saying the majority of child molestation is committed by heterosexual males; she added that such acts are about abuse of power and not about sex, anyway. Richard returned to his earlier question about choice, asking Reiko, "Didn't he sort of like CHOOSE to be with the guys? So didn't he make that choice?" Tanisha argued that the only choice was about not hiding being gay, and Robert added that Brian was learning to accept his homosexuality: "Sometimes you gotta go where people will accept you and won't make fun of you." Tyrone added, "Where people aren't gonna try to kill you." They agreed that choice is, as Robert put it, "about where you want to live, but not about being gay."

After having her hand up for awhile, LaTonia asked about the impact on the child of a lesbian couple: "What do you think the chances are of the child growing up being a homosexual or lesbian or whatever?" The topic was not in the essay, but Reiko told me after class that she let the students explore it since there was intense interest. Six students, three male, three female, argued that the child of, say, Ms. Salzman and her partner would be unfairly hurt by peer pressure and therefore confused. Tanisha offered reasoned responses to these arguments: their daughter likes their male friends, they'll explain things to her, she'll be able to handle it if she can be strong. Five of the students (three male, two female), all African American like Tanisha, faced-off with Tanisha, pointing at her and arguing with increasing intensity that a child needs to know that she came from a mother and father. Tanisha stood her ground and gained intensity, too, as she appeared to align herself with Ms. Salzman and her partner. Things reached a crescendo when Tanisha finally dramatized the point that having two parents does not guarantee emotional health. She disclosed that after her parents were divorced she lived for five years with a step-mother who was jealous of her, who called her stupid, and who "beat me with a vacuum, with lots of stuff" that left scars all over her body. "I am really insecure about it," she went on. "Like when someone tells me to shut up, it REALLY hurts my feelings. I mean if somebody told you to shut up, I mean you're like, NO, don't tell me to shut up." Tyrone added, "I'll say, 'Your mama!'" Demar, a member of the group challenging Tanisha, said, "That's child abuse. This is entirely different." Tanisha could not find the words in that moment to explain how her emotional narrative supported her implied argument that having two heterosexual parents in the home does not ensure emotional well-being.

Ferdy then asked, "If a student came into our classroom and all of a sudden we broke out with a discussion like this, and that person was that girl we were talking about, how would SHE feel?" Demar responded, "She'd feel like dirt." Reiko used that moment to remind the class that 10 percent of the population is gay, and "There might be somebody here that might be suffering because you guys laugh and joke . . . doesn't this article say that gay teenagers have a really hard time, that the suicide rate is very high?" Her return to the core issues, away from the gay parenting topic that had occupied 20 percent of the discussion, appealed for empathy, in this case not just for Brian and other gays and lesbians "out there," but also for those at school and perhaps in this very class.

In response, the discussion closed with strong testimonials from three students on behalf of gay people, two of whom had objected to gay parenting. Tyrone argued, "If you wanna be gay, you know, that's fine, you know, it should be accepted as THAT, not as, 'You gay? I don't want to have anything to do with you.'" Robert addressed the myth of gay promiscuity, ending with, "The degree of desire is the same, but with *who* it's different." And Cassandra, who had challenged gay parenting, closed the discussion, pounding her fist dramatically on her desk for emphasis as she exclaimed each sexual orientation label: "Whether you're a lesbian, homosexual, heterosexual, or bisexual, you're a person, and you have the right to do whatever you want to do." As students filed out, Tyrone called from the door, "That was a very intelligent discussion we had." Celeste, however, lingered after the bell to reiterate her point: Ms. Salzman's daughter will be insecure "because her peers will never accept her parents."

Tanisha in discussion. Just as some students drew on their experiences as members of ethnic groups to better understand literature studied during the year in Reiko's class, Tanisha may have drawn strength for her convictions on gay issues from her personal experiences and feelings. In her senior year, one and a half years after the "Dear Anita" discussion, Tanisha came out as a lesbian and met with other gay and lesbian students in Ms. Salzman's group. Although Tanisha had generally been a frequent participant in discussions all year, her involvement increased during the "Dear Anita" discussion, in which she took sixty-five turns, or 27 percent of all student turns in the discussion. Other students often counted on Tanisha to simplify complexities in the readings, and her turns particularly served that purpose during this lesson. Additionally, her interactions refuted myths of homosexuality, and challenged both her peers and Anita Bryant. She expressed incredulity that anyone could believe a person would choose to be part of an oppressed group. She challenged her peers' problematizing of gay parenting with reasoned responses, and as classmates pointed at her and raised their voices, Tanisha held her ground. Throughout the discussion, she aligned herself with Ms. Salzman and her partner, and through them, all gays and lesbians interested in parenting. Finally she used her own story of a painful family life as support for her stand, though there is little evidence that her peers grasped the gist of this.

Tanisha, well-read and often articulate in class discussions, challenged the group to stay focused on the issues raised by the essay rather than utter remarks that perpetuated stereotypes. Nicknamed "Ms. Equality" by her mother, Tanisha often was a voice of justice. On issues of race and gender, she raged against unfairness and now she similarly challenged homophobia.

Themes in Student Writings

Moving beyond myths of homosexuality. The "Dear Anita" lesson helped break stereotypes and myths (many from Table 3) the students had held about gays and lesbians. In the "Dear Brian" letters, the most frequently cited stereotype was of gays as child molesters. Just as the class reached easy accord on this issue in discussion, students wrote of their appreciation for McNaught's clarification. Two girls pointed out that they used to think of homosexual men as a bad influence on children, but they both directly attributed a change in understanding of this issue to the essay. Cassandra also told Brian in her letter that she used to think of gays as child molesters, and "If you had not clarified that, I would have had a different attitude toward homosexuals because of my strong feelings for children" (she hoped to some day become a child psychologist). Two others cited experiences as reinforcement of McNaught's dispelling of this myth: Vanessa recalled a gay guest speaker in Family Living "who did not look at male students any different from females." Alicia said she used to think of gays as child molesters until she came to know a wonderful gay teacher at her previous school about whom she stated, "I loved [him] with all my heart, he was one of my best teachers, a good friend and confidant."

A second stereotype some students said the lesson dispelled was that of gay men as promiscuous. In addition to the remarks about McNaught's late-blooming sexuality and about "gay" meaning much more than sex, some students wrote in their letters to Brian that they now understood that homosexuality can also be about what Ferdy called "the company of another" and what Vanessa referred to as "feelings, love, understanding, and trust one feels for another." Students reported that the lesson refuted other myths. Vanessa came to understand that homosexuality is not a psychological disorder to be treated. She told me afterward that as she listened to the disagreement in the discussion about whether gays should get therapy to change or whether these are feelings that can't change, "I decided they can't change the feelings. It's not like a *disease* or something." She felt her one contribution to the discussion helped: "Homosexuals are just like normal people, just like us. It's just that their outlook on things is different." Some students noted that they understood now that notions of gays coming from bad backgrounds and holding shameful values were stereotypes, too. They were struck by McNaught's upbringing as a model child and teen, an athlete, a God-loving and family-oriented person. Demar wrote about Brian's stable childhood, saying, "Hell, you grew up better than I did." He continued, "For Anita to call your values shameful would almost be a sin. A matter of fact, if you and I met somewhere we would probably be pretty good friends."

Finally, in their writing, students reinforced other remarks about myths dispelled in their earlier talk. Demar argued for the importance of teachers' doing their jobs well, not their sexual orientation, as what truly matters: "I've had gay teachers and I and all the rest of the students turned out absolutely fine." Cassandra acknowledged that before reading McNaught's letter she thought that gays and lesbians all hated members of the opposite sex. Similarly, Vanessa used personal experience, recalling how the gay speaker in Family Living said he has women friends, something Tanisha echoed in an interview a few days later: "I know a lot of homosexuals. And they all have friends who are women. So if you're not a misogynist, well, of course you like women. It doesn't mean you have to jump in bed with them."

Developing empathy for gays and lesbians. In addition to changed understandings of the nature of homosexuality, some students wrote of empathy they now felt for lesbians and gay men. Five students referred in their writings as well as in the discussion to suicide attempts by gays and lesbians as something truly terrible. Yong said of Brian's attempted suicide, "Thank God you changed your mind after you drank the bottle of paint thinner." Three students reported feeling guilty for the prejudices they had felt toward gays. One apologized to Brian and hoped he would forgive her. Vicki said, "It was people like me that forced you to commit suicide. Your life means more than anything in the world." A few students wrote about Brian's early confusion over his sexual feelings and his struggle to try to conform to a heterosexual standard. One commented that sexuality is a gift and that she felt for Brian since so many people cannot accept homosexuality as natural. Robert remarked that he understood now how gays might fear ridicule based on religious beliefs. Vanessa summed up, saying, "Anyone with half a heart should have been moved or should have changed their stereotyped opinions when he/she read this article."

Equality and justice. The theme of equality and justice for gays and lesbians persisted in students' responses, especially in their responses to the quiz question. A fairly consistent response emerged in papers of students who chose to answer the question of how Martin Luther King Jr. would respond to the plight of gays and lesbians. Essentially, they argued that if King were alive today, he would support acceptance of and equality for gays and lesbians. All but two students, Richard and Celeste, whose responses are discussed later, stated that other than loving someone of their own gender, gays are no different and deserve support. Vivian, for example, argued that:

> No matter the situation, M. L. King will still practice his theory of agape. . . . He has expressed his point of view about many groups of people with different ideas and principles. Why should these . . . change towards people whose sexual preferences are different than that of the majority in the world? . . . Martin Luther King is against negative thoughts or feelings to even our enemies. He does not practice any form of hatred. . . . I'm sure this also applies to people who choose partners of their own sex.

Alberto argued for embracing gays beyond just tolerance, "God made all men and women equal, no matter what creed, religion, sex, or lifestyle, and . . . because God wants man happy." Alberto felt King would encourage people to "treat gays as part of society" and try to make friends with them and "learn about their lifestyle." A number of students mentioned that King would endorse equal rights for gays and lesbians, and that he would encourage gays to fight for these rights as he fought discrimination. Two students added that

King would have disagreed with Anita Bryant's efforts since, as Genevieve put it, "She is trying to teach exactly the opposite of what he believes in—equal rights for all." Tanisha went one step further in her response, envisioning King in a proactive role, staging sit-ins with gay and lesbian groups and building coalitions between anti-racism and anti-homophobia groups.

Cassandra and LaTonia, both Baptists and active in the school's gospel choir, whose responses shared some similarities with others' responses, nonetheless left the door slightly open for disapproval. Cassandra suggested that "God may not approve," and LaTonia stated that some religions or cultures may view homosexuality as sinful. Still, both felt King would support and accept gay rights. Mark, in contrast, offered a unique and sobering possibility, that King would offer gays support at best but would probably remain neutral: "[He] probably would not be any major mover for civil rights for homosexuals . . . since his religion probably would have forbidden it."

Identification and validation. Two students expressed feelings of identification and validation in their "Dear Brian" letters. Cristina, raised a Catholic, began her letter, "I am a fifteen year old girl who once questioned myself about my sexuality. . . . I share your [McNaught's] values and beliefs." Elaborating on ways society restricts and condemns people, particularly gays and lesbians, Cristina closed, saying,

> The worst thing that a homosexual person can do is hide his or her true identity. I chose to try to discover myself. In the process, I realized that I am a confused, young and naive person. Unlike the person I want to be, deep inside, I feel that I will eventually find happiness with the person that I all ready am. A friend, Cristina.

Reiko wrote on Cristina's letter, "I think you will, too, Cristina. Your letter is quite moving because it reaches out to another person as an equal." The essay struck a chord for Cristina, who identified with the struggle for sexual identity and self-definition.

A second student who may have found validation in the lesson was Tanisha. While she did not explicitly identify with Brian, Tanisha positioned herself with the oppressed groups in her alignment with him, Ms. Salzman, and other gays and lesbians. Part of this was due to Tanisha's sensitivity to the oppressed, her sense that "everybody seemed to be against" homosexuality. Tanisha referred to her earlier argument that people need "not be so narrow-minded. . . . You need to open up and think how other people feel, don't just go with what you feel and everybody else." In her writing, Tanisha critiqued Celeste's position on sin as "that old crock about how they don't condemn *you* but your sin." She continued, "If you think about it, it's just as bad, so you're really condemning the person. I mean it [homosexuality] comes from the person's being." Tanisha's capacity for empathy was evident throughout the year; she took on her peers directly in discussions of gay issues and continued as if speaking to them in her writings. She wrote, "Why should it matter if you love a woman and are a woman or if you love a man and are a man? If there is love there and it's pure, why should the form matter?" In a follow-up interview when she was a senior, she recalled how important the "Dear Anita" lesson was in her education about people considered "unnormal," a lesson that may have helped provide her with courage to be out and strong while still in high school, despite negative responses from peers. Ms. Salzman recalled this courage: after posters announcing the gay and lesbian support group were torn down, the group got a six-foot ladder, and Tanisha stood on it to hang posters out of reach of those wanting to destroy them.

Resistance based in religious teachings. The two students unmoved by McNaught's essay remained committed to the belief that homosexuality is sinful and, therefore, wrong. Richard, who argued in discussion that gays choose to be gay and argued against gay parenting, said in his letter to Brian that he should have "tried harder not to be gay" and that he should have gotten "more help and kept seeing a psychiatrist." While the main thrust of his argument is rooted in his religious beliefs, Richard also misread McNaught's rejection of his Catholic upbringing: "You say that you believe God condemns homosexuality but you are homosexual. And at that you are a Catholic homosexual. How can you live with that?" McNaught's remarks about such condemnation were in the context of the beliefs he was raised with, which he rejected and then refuted in the essay. Moreover, Richard either did not agree with or ignored McNaught's argument that scripture must be understood in historical context if rigid interpretations are to be avoided.

Celeste, a practicing Catholic who entered the class mid-year, steadfastly maintained that "homosexuality is an abomination before God." Following Martin Luther King Jr.'s stance toward racists, she argued that she could justifiably condemn the sin and not the sinner. She told Brian he must read scripture literally and stop trying to change his Catholic faith to justify his sin. Too many today, she explained, have

> accepted their sinful lives as a good way of life. . . . This is not only homosexuals, but adulterers, murderers, the power hungry, and the greed of those who seek only self-gratification. All of the above I would not want teaching my children because it does not promote life.

In the margin Reiko wrote, "This is rough company for anyone to be put in."

Like Richard, Celeste ignored or misunderstood portions of McNaught's essay. She wrote, "All through the whole entire thing, he's still having this like argument in his mind: 'Am I or am I not?' And he never really chooses at the end if he is." McNaught is, however, quite clear in the essay that he is gay; the subtitle for the essay, "Late night thoughts of an Irish Catholic homosexual," clarifies this. Celeste continued, "gay civil rights, according to you, are more important of an issue instead of the Civil Rights for all living in the United States." However, McNaught is also clear on this point: In response to Bryant's threat to remove gay teachers from schools, he argues, "Gay civil rights are human civil rights. Competent people should not be denied jobs because of what they do as consenting adults in the privacy of their homes" (McNaught, 1988a, p. 14).

Celeste's response may have been due, in part, to the fact that as an Irish Catholic she shares McNaught's ethnicity and religion. Celeste felt McNaught's essay painted Irish Catholics as inflexible and unloving, since this is how she judged McNaught, and she resented this and told Reiko so in an addendum to her essay. After responding to Celeste's letter, Reiko wrote to her that she saw McNaught as

> thoughtful and loving, not inflexible and unloving as you see him. My intent in having students read this article is to have them think about the issues and draw conclusions of right or wrong on their own. And, please understand, I in no way want to attack anyone's nationality or religion. That is the farthest thing from my mind! The author's being Irish Catholic just means that he faced religious and cultural prohibitions against the kind of lifestyle he leads.

In the retrospective discussions two years later, Tanisha reported her appreciation for Celeste's courage in standing up to outspoken peers, even when she did not appreciate Celeste's sometimes unpopular opinions. Celeste had only been in the tenth-grade class three weeks when the "Dear Anita" lesson occurred, and already she had enraged peers who found her insensitive and Eurocentric. On one occasion, when she protested Black History month ("I don't get an Irish History month"), one African American girl in class stood and exclaimed, "After four hundred years of oppression, you'd begrudge us one lousy month?!" She told Brian in her letter that his idea of living in a hostile world is ridiculous, that "we all live in a hostile world." Here she minimized oppression, flattened it out into something everyone feels in an imperfect world, perhaps, in part, a function of her lack of experience with the racism and injustice most of her peers knew first-hand. She also told Brian, "All sinners want their sins to be justified by others so they will continue to persist in actions towards gay rights, or any civil rights." Her claim that those who struggle for civil rights want their sins justified by others flies in the face of the community-building that occurred for five months in Reiko's class before Celeste entered. Nonetheless, Reiko addressed Celeste's issues head on in her response to her essay, handling her feelings sensitively. This was particularly important since Celeste's major support for her opinions came from her understanding of and faith in her religion, belief systems tied to her own sense of family and culture.

Students' Reflections on the Lesson

The effects of the "Dear Anita" lesson lasted beyond the unit. In a survey I conducted later that spring, seven students, a third of the class, described the "Dear Anita" discussion and lesson as memorable. Although one student criticized how the class got off the subject "discussing homosexuals but not relating to the story," others recalled the discussion as highly engaging and informative. One said he "learned much about gay stereotypes, gay fact and fiction." Another recalled the debate on choice and realized "you can't tell a person to change what they feel because it's impossible." In case study interviews in which I asked students to reflect on the unit and the full school year, most spoke of the impact of the "Dear Anita" lesson. Vivian thought King's chapter and McNaught's essay were the most interesting pieces from the unit. Cassandra remarked:

> Before I thought in the *Bible* it says when two people of the same sex come together it's earthquakes and the world's coming to an end. I was against it. But then I read "Dear Anita" and they have rights, too. . . . I was confused at first. Are they good people or bad people? But I came to realize they're just people, too.

Alberto, who is Filipino, remarked, "I'm a Catholic and the Catholic Church is supposed to be against it, and how could you be against a person when it says in the *Bible* you're supposed to love your neighbor as yourself?" He told me he had whispered to Mark during the discussion the question he eventually raised to the class: "If you have sex with a man does that make you gay, or is there more to it?" He said he spoke with his mother and wants to learn more about homosexuality.

In the survey I conducted two years and three months later, eighteen students reflected on the works of greatest impact from their tenth-grade year. Citing reasons such as identification and exposure to learning about difference, students selected Maya Angelou's (1969) autobiography and an excerpt from Amy Tan's *The Joy Luck Club* (1989) as particularly memorable. Three students selected "Dear Anita," which Genevieve called "an eye-opener" that made her feel she was "wrong in condemning them. I felt really bad. It has changed me a whole lot in my perception of homosexuals." Robert said, "I really had to rethink my feelings on homosexuality. . . . [It] really made me stop judging homosexuals by the ignorant opinions and stereotypes that were going around." During the accompanying retrospective discussions, students reflected on changed attitudes and new perceptions due to Reiko's class. Robert recalled the study of "Dear Anita":

> At first I was always calling gay people queers and stuff but then we kept talking about it and then like my homophobia just started to go away because whenever we talked about gay people it was just throwing stereotypes around, right? And then junior year and now . . . it's like, you start to see that all people are just like everyone else and you get to interact with them, and all that stuff just melts away, all those old fears and prejudices.

Clearly, the "Dear Anita" lesson had a strong impact on most of Reiko's students and may have had a lasting effect. To what can we attribute these results? A complex set of conditions made the impact of this lesson possible.

HOW CURRICULUM AND INSTRUCTION SHAPED STUDENTS' RESPONSES

Importance of Text Selection

As my analysis of McNaught's essay demonstrates, by sensitively describing his own story, McNaught's piece helps readers move beyond stereotypes (Tables 3 and 4). While some might critique McNaught as a gay apologist who asks, "Accept us because we're just like you," Reiko's choice of "Dear Anita" showed sensitivity to her students. Rather than deny her students' religious backgrounds, Reiko chose a work written from a religious perspective by a devout Catholic and loving, family-oriented man. This religious connection provided many students with a firm ground for identification as they grappled with the issues McNaught presents.

Reiko's choice of text followed principles articulated in the multicultural literature. First, the essay—about gay experiences—was written by a gay man, or "cultural insider," which made it more possible to achieve "cultural accuracy" (Bishop, 1992; Yokota, 1993). Students responded to this feature of the work, finding it a credible "inside view" of what it means to be gay. Second, the essay presented sociological perspectives on homosexuality, as important here as in treatment of racism and other atrocities in U.S. history, providing an analysis of institutional structures that have caused and continue to contribute to social inequities (Gibson, 1984; Hilliard, 1974; Mura, 1988). Reiko's lesson explored some of this, dealing with the oppression McNaught and other gays and lesbians experience, particularly through the use of Martin Luther King Jr.'s chapter as a way of invoking the issue of civil rights. Third, the essay showed a protagonist from a marginalized group in an empowered state, what is called in the literature "beyond victimization" (Greene, 1993; Pace, 1992). McNaught reports his suffering, but his convictions regarding human rights come through strongly in the end, and students responded to this strength of voice. Finally, effective multicultural education avoids perpetuation of "othering" that results from study of marginalized groups as purely different (Gibson, 1984). Thoughtful educators attend both to difference and to common ground across groups. Here again, invoking King in consideration of McNaught served this purpose well.

A Safe Environment for Explorations of Diversity

Reiko's students had practiced for months various strategies of openly exploring diversity. When students had questions about a culture different from their own, for example, they knew they could comfortably raise these questions without fear of either ridicule for their ignorance or accusations of insensitivity. Reiko frequently modeled this practice and invited students to share cultural knowledge that might shed light on issues under consideration.

In a discussion of an excerpt from Amy Tan's *The Joy Luck Club* (1989), for example, African American students asked Chinese American students about words and cultural norms they did not understand when reading the selection. Reiko used Tan's treatment of mother-child conflict as an opportunity for building common ground, by inviting students to engage in cross-cultural exchange of mother and grandmother tales (Athanases, 1993a). Such classroom practices made it easier for Reiko's students to ask candid questions, without embarrassment or criticism, about "choice" for homosexuals, the place of sex in sexual orientation, and the impact on children of gay parenting. While some of the students at times parroted myths and lines they had no doubt heard spoken by their elders or in the media, the videotape showed a group of students generally trying to understand the issues at hand and responding to Reiko's prompts for greater empathy. This was one goal of the entire curriculum, and was not new to them. They respected empathy as a worthy goal set by a teacher they respected highly and often looked to for clarity about complex cultural issues.

Discussion and Writing as Vehicles for Thinking and Feeling

Though Reiko had goals for her students that included enhanced empathy for gays and lesbians, her lesson invited thinking and not mere recitation of fact. Questions were generally authentic ones for which prespecified answers were not available. She raised "why" questions that invited thinking and perspective-taking on hypothetical questions that invited empathy. Nine students asked questions during the "Dear Anita" discussion, which is unusual for public school classrooms generally dominated by teacher-controlled talk with a strict pattern of teacher initiating talk with a question, student responding, and teacher evaluating (Cazden, 1986; Mehan, 1985). Important to this thinking climate is the use of evidence for support. Beyond the text, which Reiko and her students repeatedly cited for support, students used other sources for evidence and confirmation in their talk and writing: gay and lesbian teachers (Ms. Salzman, Mr. Kendall, a teacher from another school); media portrayals of gay lives (*A Current Affair* and another television show); a guest speaker in Family Living class; and personal encounters with gays and lesbians. Students tapped other literary works, making the intertextual connection Reiko fostered (such as the Martin Luther King-McNaught link) a way to reason through the issues of diversity. Finally, these students, most of whom had felt the pain of racism, tapped experiences of this pain in the language they used to reason with confidence that gays and lesbians deserve equality and a quality life. Demar, for example, wrote to Brian:

> It reminds me of racism. Like some incidents in racism when the qualifications are perfect. You walk in the office, he sees you're black, you're thrown out on your butt. So Brian I see where you are coming from, and you are right.

Cassandra used a civil rights oratorical style as she pounded her desk during her proclamation of rights for gays that closed the discussion. Finally, Reiko's use of a "Dear Brian" letter made the author and his struggle real as students addressed McNaught directly. This humanizing device aided the work to develop empathy that Reiko held as a goal for the lesson and for her entire curriculum.

DISCUSSION

This study provides evidence that a teacher can successfully integrate a gay-themed lesson into a curriculum of diverse literary works. Across data strands, students reported having myths of homosexuality dispelled, an emerging empathy for gays and lesbians, and a clear sense of the rights of gays and lesbians to be who they are without fearing the loss of their jobs, or harm. The students genuinely attempted to work through some of the issues. The study examined just one lesson in one small class of fairly motivated students, and to what degree such successes could occur in other classes is unclear. Still, the study demonstrates that even students at the point of early adolescence can discuss issues of sexual orientation and homophobia with candor, curiosity, and maturity when prompted by an appropriate text, a safe and structured climate for exploration of diversity, discussions and writing that invite thinking, and invitations for empathy.

The Need for Repeated Emphasis

While literature study can enable students to begin to alter their stereotyped notions of others, the realignment of beliefs based on preconceived notions is a slow process (Ramsey, 1987, 1992). Generally, repeated emphasis on such concerns is essential. Despite the overwhelming impact of McNaught's essay and Reiko's lesson on her students and their stated beliefs, Celeste resisted McNaught's reasoning and the lesson. Three months later, she and Tanisha, who disagreed strongly on gay issues, became sisters in outrage over the treatment of Native Americans as depicted in three novels they read for a Book Club assignment. For this assignment, students worked in groups to read and plan presentations on full-length literary works by ethnically diverse authors. Two years later, Celeste identified one of these, N. Scott Momaday's *House Made of Dawn* (1989), as the most memorable work from Reiko's class "because it showed me how much the government destroys a people['s] traditions, heritage. And how stubborn and stupid people are because they stick to stereotypes instead of finding out the truth." Clearly, Celeste was capable of enormous empathy, though not yet toward gays and lesbians in her tenth-grade year. And although I do not know where Celeste stood on gay/lesbian issues two years later, during the retrospective discussion, Celeste sat with her friend Tanisha, now an out lesbian, and laughed with Alycia and others as she recalled their tensions in the tenth grade over such issues as Black History Month.

For other students in Reiko's class who supported McNaught's refutations of myths about homosexuality, there were myths not yet dispelled that warranted further conversation and study. The notion of an orientation as something larger than sexual activity is one Alberto imagined to be true but could not yet grasp. Though three students refuted the myth of homosexuality as a choice, the class struggled to find language to distinguish between choosing to be gay and choosing an uncloseted life. Finally, while outside the purview of McNaught's essay, gay parenting aroused concern of a number of students.

The Need for Role Models

Despite evidence of homophobia in the worlds outside and inside school, Reiko's students had been exposed to positive models of lesbians and gay men and, as reported in anecdotes and studies (Sears & Williams, 1997), such exposure minimizes homophobia. As students read McNaught's essay and explored issues, they had positive examples to support this evolving empathy for gays and lesbians: beloved and respected gay and lesbian teachers, guest speakers, and media images. This gay presence enabled students to draw on a wider range of knowledge sources to sort through issues. This reinforces the importance of lesbian and gay role models in educating young people about difference, particularly for those who hear other messages from media, peers, adults, and those who rigidly interpret religious teachings. Even in the San Francisco Bay Area, which has a large population of out lesbians and gays, it was the personal relationships with gays and lesbians that students at Richards needed to draw on as support for McNaught's refuting of myths of homosexuality.

Importance of Literary Depictions of Gays and Lesbians

Literature curricula need to include works that explore the gay and lesbian experience, since little evidence exists that sex education dispels myths of homosexuality. Few counselors offer gay youth the support they need, which perpetuates their potentially dangerous isolation (Sears, 1992). Bringing gay and lesbian themed literature into the students' "orbit of attention" helps to ensure the cultural reproduction of such works (Smith, 1983) and their availability for all students, who can learn from and find validation in them. Inspired by McNaught's essay, Tanisha's discussion performance (aligning herself with the gay author, the lesbian teacher, all gays and lesbians, and challenging myths and homophobia expressed by her peers) prefigured her act of coming out two years later. McNaught notes in another essay, "I would guess that on an average day, the majority of gay men and lesbians are called upon to be courageous about their sexual orientation at least five times" (1988b, p. 72). Just as the course invited Tanisha to use her knowledge as a person of color and a young woman, and to voice feelings about these identities, it may have also allowed her early opportunities to claim voice on behalf of gays and to rehearse her own lesbian identity. Although she felt at odds with her peers in the discussion, the class provided her with the text, the structure, the forum, and the safety to voice what she did and to help educate her peers.

The Need for Coalition Building

Some educators fear that including sexual orientation and homophobia in a multicultural curriculum dilutes the focus on race and ethnicity that belongs at the heart of the multicultural agenda. Reiko's lesson shows that a lesson on gay and lesbian concerns need not detract from these issues but can, in fact, deepen students' understanding about identities and oppression and the ways in which marginal groups both share features and differ. Among the goals of a strong program in diversity is a deepened understanding of common ground for groups divided by difference, something Reiko's lesson achieved for many participants. Of the lesson, Robert said simply, "I learned that people are people are people. One must judge all people in the same way, and that is by who they are inside."

This search for common ground addressed the need many educators find in schools with students so often divided down lines defined by ethnicity, time of immigration, and class. It also speaks to the essential need for coalition building in struggles for civil rights and equality. Gates (1993) points out the folly of establishing "a pecking order of oppression" and identifies at least one point of common ground between African Americans and gays as groups: Just as Blacks have been portrayed as "sexually uncontrollable beasts . . . a similar vision of the predatory homosexual has been insinuated, often quite subtly, into the defense of the ban on gays in the military" (p. 43). Noting such connections, as Demar and a number of his peers did, is essential to the coalition-building needed to dispel myths about oppressed groups and to ward off hateful forces that would stereotype and bring harm to members of these groups. The same thoughtful principles that hold sensitive treatment of diversity as a central goal can guide the inclusion of stories of gay and lesbian experiences in any literature program, whether the context is a Mexican American literature course primarily for Hispanic university students (Gonzalez, 1994), a college course on women's studies (Kitch, 1994), or Reiko's course for tenth graders exploring The Ethnic Experience in Literature.

REFERENCES

Angelou, M. (1969). *I know why the caged bird sings.* New York: Bantam.

Applebee, A. N. (1993). *Literature in the secondary school: Studies of curriculum and instruction in the United States.* Urbana, IL: National Council of Teachers of English.

Athanases, S. Z. (1993a). Cross-cultural swapping of mother and grandmother tales in a tenth grade discussion of *The Joy Luck Club. Communication Education, 42,* 282–287.

Athanases, S. Z. (1993b). Discourse about literature and diversity: A study of two urban tenth-grade classes. *Dissertation Abstracts International, 54,* 05-A (Order No. AAD93-26420).

Banks, J. A. (1993). Multicultural education: Characteristics and goals. In J. A. Banks & C. A. McGee Banks (Eds.), *Multicultural education: Issues and perspectives* (pp. 3–28). Boston: Allyn and Bacon.

Banks, J. A., & Banks, C. A. McGee (Eds.). (1993). *Multicultural education: Issues and perspectives.* Boston: Allyn and Bacon.

Bishop, R. S. (1992). Multicultural literature for children: Making informed choices. In V. J. Harris (Ed.), *Teaching multicultural literature in grades K-8* (pp. 37–53). Norwood, PA: Christopher-Gordon.

Boutilier, N. (1994). Reading, writing, and Rita Mae Brown: Lesbian literature in high school. In L. Garber (Ed.), *Tilting the tower* (pp. 135–141). New York: Routledge.

Cazden, C. B. (1986). Classroom discourse. In M. C. Wittrock (Ed.), *Handbook of research on teaching* (3rd ed., pp. 432–463). New York: Macmillan.

Garber, L. (Ed.). (1994). *Tilting the tower.* New York: Routledge.

Gates, H. L., Jr. (1993, May 17). Blacklash? *New Yorker,* pp. 42–44.

Gibson, M. A. (1984). Approaches to multicultural education in the United States: Some concepts and assumptions. *Anthropology and Education, 15,* 94–119.

Gonzalez, M. C. (1994). Cultural conflict: Introducing the queer in Mexican-American literature class. In L. Garber (Ed.), *Tilting the tower* (pp. 56–62). New York: Routledge.

Greene, M. (1993). The passions of pluralism: Multiculturalism and the expanding community. *Educational Researcher, 22*(1), 13–18.

Hammett, R. F. (1992). A rationale and unit plan for introducing gay and lesbian literature into the grade twelve curriculum. In P. Shannon (Ed.), *Becoming political: Readings and writings in the politics of literacy education* (pp. 250–262). Portsmouth, NH: Heinemann.

Harbeck, K. M. (Ed.). (1992). *Coming out of the classroom closet: Gay and lesbian students, teachers, and curricula.* New York: Harrington Park Press.

Harris, S. (1990). *Lesbian and gay issues in the English classroom: The importance of being honest.* Philadelphia: Open University Press.

Hart, E. L., & Parmeter, S. (1992). "Writings in the margins": A lesbian-and-gay-inclusive course. In C. M. Hurlbert & S. Totten (Eds.), *Social issues in the classroom* (pp. 154–173). Urbana, IL: National Council of Teachers of English.

Hilliard, A. G. (1974). Restructuring teacher education for multicultural imperatives. In W. A. Hunter (Ed.), *Multicultural education through competency-based teacher education* (pp. 38–52). Washington, DC: American Association of Colleges for Teacher Education.

Jennings, K. (Ed.). (1994). *One teacher in ten: Gay and lesbian educators tell their stories.* Boston: Alyson.

King, M. L., Jr. (1958). *Stride toward freedom.* New York: Harper.

Kitch, S. L. (1994). Straight but not narrow: A gynetic approach to the teaching of lesbian literature. In L. Garber (Ed.), *Tilting the tower* (pp. 83–95). New York: Routledge.

Lankewish, V. A. (1992). Breaking the silence: Addressing homophobia with *The color purple.* In C. M. Hurlbert & S. Totten (Eds.), *Social issues in the classroom* (pp. 219–230). Urbana, IL: National Council of Teachers of English.

Lloyd-Jones, R., & Lunsford, A. A. (Eds.). (1989). *The English coalition conference: Democracy through language.* Urbana, IL: National Council of Teachers of English.

Long, B. W., & Hopkins, M. F. (1982). *Performing literature.* Englewood Cliffs, NJ: Prentice-Hall.

McNaught, B. (1988a). Dear Anita: Late night thoughts of an Irish Catholic homosexual. *On being gay: Thoughts on family, faith and love* (pp. 5–14). New York: St. Martin's Press.

McNaught, B. (1988b). Proud growls and courageous roars. *On being gay: Thoughts on family, faith and love* (pp. 72–75). New York: St. Martin's Press.

McVicar, D. M. (1995, September 3). Censored: Job on the line over gay books. *Providence (R.I.) Sunday Journal,* pp. 3, 16

Momaday, N. S. (1989). *House made of dawn.* New York: Harper Collins.

Mehan, H. (1985). The structure of classroom discourse. In T. A. Van Dijk (Ed.), *Handbook of discourse analysis, 3* (pp. 142–167). London: Academic Press.

Mura, D. (1988). Strangers in the village. In R. Simonson & S. Walker (Eds.), *The graywolf annual five: Multi-cultural literacy* (pp. 135–153). St. Paul, MN: Graywolf Press.

Pace, B. G. (1992). The textbook canon: Genre, gender, and race in U.S. literature anthologies. *English Journal, 81*(5), 33–38.

Ramsey, P. G. (1987). *Teaching and learning in a diverse world: Multicultural education for young children.* New York: Teachers College Press.

Ramsey, P. G. (1992, April). *Children's responses to a unit on Native American literature.* Paper presented at the annual meeting of the American Educational Research Association, San Francisco.

Sears, J. T. (1992). Educators, homosexuality, and homosexual students: Are personal feelings related to professional beliefs? In K. M. Harbeck (Ed.), *Coming out of the classroom closet: Gay and lesbian students, teachers, and curricula* (pp. 29–79). New York: Harrington Park Press.

Sears, J. T., & Williams, W. (1997). *Overcoming heterosexism and homophobia.* New York: Columbia University Press.

Smith, B. H. (1983). Contingencies of value. *Critical Inquiry, 10,* September, 1–35.

Stotsky, S. (1994). Academic guidelines for selecting multiethnic and multicultural literature. *English Journal, 83*(2), 27–34.

Tan, A. (1989). *The joy luck club.* New York: Ivy Books.

Task Force on Racism and Bias in the Teaching of English. (1986). *Expanding opportunities: Academic success for culturally and linguistically diverse students.* Urbana, IL: National Council of Teachers of English.

Yokota, J. (1993). Issues in selecting multicultural children's literature. *Language Arts, 70*(3), 156–167.

The research reported in this article was funded, in part, by a Spencer Dissertation-Year Fellowship from the Woodrow Wilson Foundation and by a Grant-in-Aid from the National Council of Teachers of English.

LOOKING FORWARD

ADVANCING A VISION OF WHAT EDUCATION IN A MULTICULTURAL SOCIETY COULD BE

PART III

LOOKING FORWARD

ADVANCING A VISION OF WHAT EDUCATION IN A MULTICULTURAL SOCIETY COULD BE

The previous articles have illuminated children and youth as co-constructors of knowledge and have featured multiple participants who challenge the dominant narratives that paralyze our imaginations and capacity to advance education. The last part of this volume summons us to pause and conceive what education *could* be—to imagine the kind of society we might achieve if we were to reenvision and redefine how we think about pedagogy and diversity, power and equality. Authors in this section take us on an intertextual journey intended to be transformative for both our practice and our thinking. From applying identity development theory while teaching about race to breaking away from the exhausted dialectic of oppression and domination and concretely experiencing liberation, these articles inspire us through their simple yet profound ways of imagining education. This final part of the volume moves readers to reconsider their own selves as educators, the first step in our collective struggle to embody these visions in a multicultural society.

We open with Beverly Daniel Tatum's (1992) critical examination of the writings and experiences of undergraduate students in her Psychology of Racism class. Published almost two decades ago, "Talking About Race, Learning About Racism: The Application of Racial Identity Development Theory in the Classroom" introduced readers to the intentionality and art of constructing a classroom where students come to understand not only their own racial identity development but also racism as a societal system. While the thinking on racial identity has changed since this article was written, what remains powerfully catalytic is the radically caring pedagogy that Tatum developed and practiced: maintaining a safe classroom atmosphere through discussion guidelines, creating opportunities for students to generate their own knowledge, providing a developmental model that students can use to understand their growth, and using strategies that empower students' sense of agency. These pedagogical practices push educators to address the resistance, apathy, tension, and silence that so often mark educational milieus where different people gather to learn about race together.

The purposeful intent with which Tatum reconfigures her classroom is also seen in "Using a Chicana Feminist Epistemology in Educational Research." Dolores Delgado Bernal (1998) asks educators to reevaluate and challenge the way knowledge is produced and validated. Delgado Bernal articulates an epistemology that "speaks to the failures of traditional patriarchal and liberal educational scholarship," which does not consider the intersection of gender, ethnic, and class oppressions in the lives of students and the structures of schooling (p. 296). This act of creation—the naming and describing of a different way of knowing—is not only visionary in terms of theory production but is also irrevocably linked to practice. Recalling the unique social and cultural history of Chicanas, Delgado Bernal proposes a Chicana feminist epistemology as a way of designing and conducting educational research. She extends the concept of theoretical sensitivity to coin the term "cultural intuition," which includes collective experience and community memory. Delgado Bernal invites educational researchers to uncover and reclaim their own subjugated knowledge, to believe that what research has constructed as knowledge is not *all* the knowledge that exists. With this belief, educational researchers can expand their epistemological horizons and connect new ways of knowing with new ways of doing—building research that restores justice and promotes equality in society.

Kathleen Weiler (1991) engages Delgado Bernal by complicating the relationship between theory and practice in her article, "Freire and a Feminist Pedagogy of Difference." She extends liberation pedagogy to be inclusive of people's specific experiences in the world, to be less abstract, and to be more mindful of the interrelated ways we are oppressed and in turn oppress others. In denying the Freirian notion of oppression as a "universal" experience untouched by our individual locations and histories, Weiler insists that our pedagogies start with who learners are as people, different from one another in myriad ways. She speaks to teachers who are not sure how to situate themselves in relation to the struggles of others; her solution to this challenge of teacher authority and power is to propose that the feminist teacher is "an intellectual and theorist" who helps students be "theorists of their own lives" (p. 333). This pedagogic stance reframes the relationship of teacher and student and their relationship with theory.

The final article in this section, Noah De Lissovoy's (2010) "Rethinking Education and Emancipation: Being, Teaching, and Power," asks readers to reconsider the very notion of education and to see teaching as an act of audacity against power and domination. De Lissovoy challenges critical pedagogy by arguing that humans already exist as bodies in struggle rather than in need of being developed. He questions the nature and purpose of education by reconstructing our notions of "emancipation," "human," and even "education." He declares:

"A truly liberatory education should be antisexist and antiracist and anticlassist, but beyond all these determinations it should be committed against the ubiquitous and parasitic action of power itself . . . Teaching, then, is a work on being and the invention of the possibility of an authentic encounter between beings outside of domination." (p. 352, 354)

In his challenge to the concept of "humanization," De Lissovoy invites readers to look for human moments in teaching that are free of deficit framing and to celebrate our simple, astonishing survival in the face of oppression. In the acknowledgement of the human as a being that exists before oppression, educators can concretely experience moments of liberation.

Across these articles, we hope readers have been inspired to transform their thinking about what education *is*. The tales of multicultural education in this volume momentarily pause here and then travel with us to create the stories we live and the stories that inspire possibilities for others. We hope this section renews the theorist and activist that lives in each of us and uplifts our eyes toward the visions we aspire to share and shape in solidarity. These are acts of transformation conceived by our imaginations—they begin with our roots and awaken our selves to discover the constructive inquiry through which liberation is born.

TALKING ABOUT RACE, LEARNING ABOUT RACISM

THE APPLICATION OF RACIAL IDENTITY DEVELOPMENT THEORY IN THE CLASSROOM

BEVERLY DANIEL TATUM

As many educational institutions struggle to become more multicultural in terms of their students, faculty, and staff, they also begin to examine issues of cultural representation within their curriculum. This examination has evoked a growing number of courses that give specific consideration to the effect of variables such as race, class, and gender on human experience—an important trend that is reflected and supported by the increasing availability of resource manuals for the modification of course content (Bronstein & Quina, 1988; Hull, Scott, & Smith, 1982; Schuster & Van Dyne, 1985).

Unfortunately, less attention has been given to the issues of process that inevitably emerge in the classroom when attention is focused on race, class, and/or gender. It is very difficult to talk about these concepts in a meaningful way without also talking and learning about racism, classism, and sexism.[1] The introduction of these issues of oppression often generates powerful emotional responses in students that range from guilt and shame to anger and despair. If not addressed, these emotional responses can result in student resistance to oppression-related content areas. Such resistance can ultimately interfere with the cognitive understanding and mastery of the material. This resistance and potential interference is particularly common when specifically addressing issues of race and racism. Yet, when students are given the opportunity to explore race-related material in a classroom where both their affective and intellectual responses are acknowledged and addressed, their level of understanding is greatly enhanced.

This article seeks to provide a framework for understanding students' psychological responses to race-related content and the student resistance that can result, as well as some strategies for overcoming this resistance. It is informed by more than a decade of experience as an African American engaged in teaching an undergraduate course on the psychology of racism, by thematic analyses of student journals and essays written for the racism class, and by an understanding and application of racial identity development theory (Helms, 1990).

SETTING THE CONTEXT

As a clinical psychologist with a research interest in racial identity development among African American youth raised in predominantly White communities, I began teaching about racism quite fortuitously. In 1980, while I was a part-time lecturer in the Black Studies department of a large public university, I was invited to teach a course called Group Exploration of Racism (Black Studies 2). A requirement for Black Studies majors, the course had to be offered, yet the instructor who regularly taught the course was no longer affiliated with the institution. Armed with a folder full of handouts, old syllabi that the previous instructor left behind, a copy of *White Awareness: Handbook for Anti-racism Training* (Katz, 1978), and my own clinical skills as a group facilitator, I constructed a course that seemed to meet the goals already outlined in the course catalogue. Designed "to provide students with an understanding of the psychological causes and emotional reality of racism as it appears in everyday life," the course incorporated the use of lectures, readings, simulation exercises, group research projects, and extensive class discussion to help students explore the psychological impact of racism on both the oppressor and the oppressed.

Though my first efforts were tentative, the results were powerful. The students in my class, most of whom were White, repeatedly described the course in their evaluations as one of the most valuable educational experiences of their college careers. I was convinced that helping students understand the ways in which racism operates in their own lives, and what they could do about it, was a social responsibility that I should accept. The freedom to institute the course in the curriculum of the psychology departments in which I would eventually teach became a personal condition of employment. I have successfully introduced the course in each new educational setting I have been in since leaving that university.

Since 1980, I have taught the course (now called the Psychology of Racism) eighteen times, at three different institutions. Although each of these schools is very different—a large public university, a small state college, and a private, elite women's college—the challenges of teaching about racism in each setting have been more similar than different.

In all of the settings, class size has been limited to thirty students (averaging twenty-four). Though typically predominantly White and female (even in coeducational settings), the class make-up has always been mixed in terms of both race and gender. The students of color who have taken the course include Asians and Latinos/as, but most frequently the students of color have been Black. Though most students have described themselves as middle class, all socioeconomic backgrounds (ranging from very poor to very wealthy) have been represented over the years.

The course has necessarily evolved in response to my own deepening awareness of the psychological legacy of racism and my expanding awareness of other forms of oppression, although the basic format has remained the same. Our weekly three-hour class meeting is held in a room with movable chairs, arranged in a circle. The physical structure communicates an important premise of the course—that I expect the students to speak with each other as well as with me.

My other expectations (timely completion of assignments, regular class attendance) are clearly communicated in our first class meeting, along with the assumptions and guidelines for discussion that I rely upon to guide our work together. Because the assumptions and guidelines are so central to the process of talking and learning about racism, it may be useful to outline them here.

Working Assumptions

1. Racism, defined as a "system of advantage based on race" (see Wellman, 1977), is a pervasive aspect of U.S. socialization. It is virtually impossible to live in U.S. contemporary society and not be exposed to some aspect of the personal, cultural, and/or institutional manifestations of racism in our society. It is also assumed that, as a result, all of us have received some misinformation about those groups disadvantaged by racism.

2. Prejudice, defined as a "preconceived judgment or opinion, often based on limited information," is clearly distinguished from racism (see Katz, 1978). I assume that all of us may have prejudices as a result of the various cultural stereotypes to which we have been exposed. Even when these preconceived ideas have positive associations (such as "Asian students are good in math"), they have negative effects because they deny a person's individuality. These attitudes may influence the individual behaviors of people of color as well as of Whites, and may affect intergroup as well as intragroup interaction. However, a distinction must be made between the negative racial attitudes held by individuals of color and White individuals, because it is only the attitudes of Whites that routinely carry with them the social power inherent in the systematic cultural reinforcement and institutionalization of those racial prejudices. To distinguish the prejudices of students of color from the racism of White students is *not* to say that the former is acceptable and the latter is not; both are clearly problematic. The distinction is important, however, to identify the power differential between members of dominant and subordinate groups.

3. In the context of U.S. society, the system of advantage clearly operates to benefit Whites as a group. However, it is assumed that racism, like other forms

of oppression, hurts members of the privileged group as well as those targeted by racism. While the impact of racism on Whites is clearly different from its impact on people of color, racism has negative ramifications for everyone. For example, some White students might remember the pain of having lost important relationships because Black friends were not allowed to visit their homes. Others may express sadness at having been denied access to a broad range of experiences because of social segregation. These individuals often attribute the discomfort or fear they now experience in racially mixed settings to the cultural limitations of their youth.

4. Because of the prejudice and racism inherent in our environments when we were children, I assume that we cannot be blamed for learning what we were taught (intentionally or unintentionally). Yet as adults, we have a responsibility to try to identify and interrupt the cycle of oppression. When we recognize that we have been misinformed, we have a responsibility to seek out more accurate information and to adjust our behavior accordingly.

5. It is assumed that change, both individual and institutional, is possible. Understanding and unlearning prejudice and racism is a lifelong process that may have begun prior to enrolling in this class, and which will surely continue after the course is over. Each of us may be at a different point in that process, and I assume that we will have mutual respect for each other, regardless of where we perceive one another to be.

To facilitate further our work together, I ask students to honor the following guidelines for our discussion. Specifically, I ask students to demonstrate their respect for one another by honoring the confidentiality of the group. So that students may feel free to ask potentially awkward or embarrassing questions, or share race-related experiences, I ask that students refrain from making personal attributions when discussing the course content with their friends. I also discourage the use of "zaps," overt or covert put-downs often used as comic relief when someone is feeling anxious about the content of the discussion. Finally, students are asked to speak from their own experience, to say, for example, "I think . . ." or "In my experience, I have found . . ." rather than generalizing their experience to others, as in "People say . . ."

Many students are reassured by the climate of safety that is created by these guidelines and find comfort in the nonblaming assumptions I outline for the class. Nevertheless, my experience has been that most students, regardless of their class and ethnic background, still find racism a difficult topic to discuss, as is revealed by these journal comments written after the first class meeting (all names are pseudonyms):

The class is called Psychology of Racism, the atmosphere is friendly and open, yet I feel very closed in. I feel guilt and doubt well up inside of me. (Tiffany, a White woman)

Class has started on a good note thus far. The class seems rather large and disturbs me. In a class of this nature, I expect there will be many painful and emotional moments. (Linda, an Asian woman)

I am a little nervous that as one of the few students of color in the class people are going to be looking at me for answers, or whatever other reasons. The thought of this inhibits me a great deal. (Louise, an African American woman)

I had never thought about my social position as being totally dominant. There wasn't one area in which I wasn't in the dominant group. . . . I first felt embarrassed. . . . Through association alone I felt in many ways responsible for the unequal condition existing in the world. This made me feel like shrinking in a hole in a class where I was surrounded by 27 women and 2 men, one of whom was Black and the other was Jewish. I felt that all these people would be justified in venting their anger upon me. After a short period, I realized that no one in the room was attacking or even blaming me for the conditions that exist. (Carl, a White man)

Even though most of my students voluntarily enroll in the course as an elective, their anxiety and subsequent resistance to learning about racism quickly emerge.

SOURCES OF RESISTANCE

In predominantly White college classrooms, I have experienced at least three major sources of student resistance to talking and learning about race and racism. They can be readily identified as the following:

1. Race is considered a taboo topic for discussion, especially in racially mixed settings.
2. Many students, regardless of racial-group membership, have been socialized to think of the United States as a just society.
3. Many students, particularly White students, initially deny any personal prejudice, recognizing the impact of racism on other people's lives, but failing to acknowledge its impact on their own.

Race as Taboo Topic

The first source of resistance, race as a taboo topic, is an essential obstacle to overcome if class discussion is to begin at all. Although many students are interested in the topic, they are often most interested in hearing other people talk about it, afraid to break the taboo themselves.

One source of this self-consciousness can be seen in the early childhood experiences of many students. It is known that children as young as three notice racial differences (see Phinney & Rotheram, 1987). Certainly preschoolers talk about what they see. Unfortunately, they often do so in ways that make adults uncomfortable. Imagine the following scenario: A White child in a public place points to a dark-skinned African American child and says loudly, "Why is that boy Black?" The embarrassed parent quickly responds, "Sh! Don't say that." The child is only attempting to make sense of a new observation (Derman-Sparks, Higa, & Sparks, 1980), yet the parent's attempt to silence the perplexed child sends a message that this observation is not okay to talk about. White children quickly become aware that their questions about race raise adult anxiety, and as a result, they learn not to ask questions.

When asked to reflect on their earliest race-related memories and the feelings associated with them, both White students and students of color often report feelings of confusion, anxiety, and/or fear. Students of color often have early memories of name-calling or other negative interactions with other children, and sometimes with adults. They also report having had questions that went both unasked and unanswered. In addition, many students have had uncomfortable interchanges around race-related topics as adults. When asked at the beginning of the semester, "How many of you have had difficult, perhaps heated conversations with someone on a race-related topic?", routinely almost everyone in the class raises his or her hand. It should come as no surprise then that students often approach the topic of race and/or racism with both curiosity and trepidation.

The Myth of the Meritocracy

The second source of student resistance to be discussed here is rooted in students' belief that the United States is a just society, a meritocracy where individual efforts are fairly rewarded. While some students (particularly students of color) may already have become disillusioned with that notion of the United States, the majority of my students who have experienced at least the personal success of college acceptance still have faith in this notion. To the extent that these students acknowledge that racism exists, they tend to view it as an individual phenomenon, rooted in the attitudes of the "Archie Bunkers" of the world or located only in particular parts of the country.

After several class meetings, Karen, a White woman, acknowledged this attitude in her journal:

> At one point in my life—the beginning of this class—I actually perceived America to be a relatively racist free society. I thought that the people who were racist or subjected to racist stereotypes were found only in small pockets of the U.S., such as the South. As I've come to realize, racism (or at least racially orientated stereotypes) is rampant.

An understanding of racism as a system of advantage presents a serious challenge to the notion of the United States as a just society where rewards are based solely on one's merit. Such a challenge often creates discomfort in students. The old adage "ignorance is bliss" seems to hold true in this case; students are not necessarily eager to recognize the painful reality of racism.

One common response to the discomfort is to engage in denial of what they are learning. White students in particular may question the accuracy or currency of statistical information regarding the prevalence of discrimination (housing, employment, access to health care, and so on). More qualitative data, such as autobiographical accounts of experiences with racism, may be challenged on the basis of their subjectivity.

It should be pointed out that the basic assumption that the United States is a just society for all is only one of many basic assumptions that might be challenged in the learning process. Another example can be seen in an interchange between two White students following a discussion about cultural racism, in which the omission or distortion of historical information about people of color was offered as an example of the cultural transmission of racism.

"Yeah, I just found out that Cleopatra was actually a Black woman."

"What?"

The first student went on to explain her newly learned information. Finally, the second student exclaimed in disbelief, "That can't be true. Cleopatra was beautiful!" This new information and her own deeply ingrained assumptions about who is beautiful and who is not were too incongruous to allow her to assimilate the information at that moment.

If outright denial of information is not possible, then withdrawal may be. Physical withdrawal in the form of absenteeism is one possible result; it is for precisely this reason that class attendance is mandatory. The reduction in the completion of reading and/or written assignments is another form of withdrawal. I have found this response to be so common that I now alert students to this possibility at the beginning of the semester. Knowing that this response is a common one seems to help students stay engaged, even when they experience the desire to withdraw.

Following an absence in the fifth week of the semester, one White student wrote, "I think I've hit the point you talked about, the point where you don't want to hear any more about racism. I sometimes begin to get the feeling we are all hypersensitive." (Two weeks later she wrote, "Class is getting better. I think I am beginning to get over my hump.")

Perhaps not surprisingly, this response can be found in both White students and students of color. Students of color often enter a discussion of racism with some awareness of the issue, based on personal experiences. However, even these students find that they did not have a full understanding of the widespread impact of racism in our society. For students who are targeted by racism, an increased awareness of the impact in and on their lives is painful, and often generates anger.

Four weeks into the semester, Louise, an African American woman, wrote in her journal about her own heightened sensitivity:

Many times in class I feel uncomfortable when White students use the term Black because even if they aren't aware of it they say it with all or at least a lot of the negative connotations they've been taught goes along with Black. Sometimes it just causes a stinging feeling inside of me. Sometimes I get real tired of hearing White people talk about the conditions of Black people. I think it's an important thing for them to talk about, but still I don't always like being around when they do it. I also get tired of hearing them talk about how hard it is for them, though I understand it, and most times I am very willing to listen and be open, but sometimes I can't. Right now I can't.

For White students, advantaged by racism, a heightened awareness of it often generates painful feelings of guilt. The following responses are typical:

After reading the article about privilege, I felt very guilty. (Rachel, a White woman)

Questions of racism are so full of anger and pain. When I think of all the pain White people have caused people of color, I get a feeling of guilt. How could someone like myself care so much about the color of someone's skin that they would do them harm? (Terri, a White woman)

White students also sometimes express a sense of betrayal when they realize the gaps in their own education about racism. After seeing the first episode of the documentary series *Eyes on the Prize,* Chris, a White man, wrote:

I never knew it was really that bad just 35 years ago. Why didn't I learn this in elementary or high school? Could it be that the White people of America want to forget this injustice? . . . I will never forget that movie for as long as I live. It was like a big slap in the face.

Barbara, a White woman, also felt anger and embarrassment in response to her own previous lack of information about the internment of Japanese Americans during World War II. She wrote:

I feel so stupid because I never even knew that these existed. I never knew that the Japanese were treated so poorly. I am becoming angry and upset about all of the things that I do not know. I have been so sheltered. My parents never wanted to let me know about the bad things that have happened in the world. After I saw the movie (Mitsuye and Nellie), I even called them up to ask them why they never told me this. . . . I am angry at them too for not teaching me and exposing me to the complete picture of my country.

Avoiding the subject matter is one way to avoid these uncomfortable feelings.

"I'm Not Racist, But . . ."

A third source of student resistance (particularly among White students) is the initial denial of any personal connection to racism. When asked why they have decided to enroll in a course on racism, White students typically explain their interest in the topic with such disclaimers as, "I'm not racist myself, but I know people who are, and I want to understand them better."

Because of their position as the targets of racism, students of color do not typically focus on their own prejudices or lack of them. Instead they usually express a desire to understand why racism exists, and how they have been affected by it.

However, as all students gain a better grasp of what racism is and its many manifestations in U.S. society, they inevitably start to recognize its legacy within themselves. Beliefs, attitudes, and actions based on racial stereotypes begin to be remembered and are newly observed by White students. Students of color as well often recognize negative attitudes they may have internalized about their own racial group or that they have believed about others. Those who previously thought themselves immune to the effects of growing up in a racist society often find themselves reliving uncomfortable feelings of guilt or anger.

After taping her own responses to a questionnaire on racial attitudes, Barbara, a White woman previously quoted, wrote:

> I always want to think of myself as open to all races. Yet when I did the interview to myself, I found that I did respond differently to the same question about different races. No one could ever have told me that I would have. I would have denied it. But I found that I did respond differently even though I didn't want to. This really upset me. I was angry with myself because I thought I was not prejudiced and yet the stereotypes that I had created had an impact on the answers that I gave even though I didn't want it to happen.

The new self-awareness, represented here by Barbara's journal entry, changes the classroom dynamic. One common result is that some White students, once perhaps active participants in class discussion, now hesitate to continue their participation for fear that their newly recognized racism will be revealed to others:

> Today I did feel guilty, and like I had to watch what I was saying (make it good enough), I guess to prove I'm really *not* prejudiced. From the conversations the first day, I guess this is a normal enough reaction, but I certainly never expected it in me. (Joanne, a White woman)

This withdrawal on the part of White students is often paralleled by an increase in participation by students of color who are seeking an outlet for what are often feelings of anger. The withdrawal of some previously vocal White students from the classroom exchange, however, is sometimes interpreted by students of color as indifference. This perceived indifference often serves to fuel the anger and frustration that many students of color experience, as awareness of their own oppression is heightened. For example, Robert, an African American man, wrote:

> I really wish the White students would talk more. When I read these articles, it makes me so mad and I really want to know what the White kids think. Don't they care?

Sonia, a Latina, described the classroom tension from another perspective:

> I would like to comment that at many points in the discussions I have felt uncomfortable and sometimes even angry with people. I guess I am at the stage where I am tired of listening to Whites feel guilty and watch their eyes fill up with tears. I do understand that everyone is at their own stage of development and I even tell myself every Tuesday that these people have come to this class by choice. Some days I am just more tolerant than others. . . . It takes courage to say things in that room with so many women of color present. It also takes courage for the women of color to say things about Whites.

What seems to be happening in the classroom at such moments is a collision of developmental processes that can be inherently useful for the racial identity development of the individuals involved. Nevertheless, the interaction may be perceived as problematic to instructors and students who are unfamiliar with the process. Although space does not allow for an exhaustive discussion of racial identity development theory, a brief explication of it here will provide additional clarity regarding the classroom dynamics when issues of race are discussed. It will also provide a theoretical framework for the strategies for dealing with student resistance that will be discussed at the conclusion of this article.

STAGES OF RACIAL IDENTITY DEVELOPMENT

Racial identity and racial identity development theory are defined by Janet Helms (1990) as

> a sense of group or collective identity based on one's *perception* that he or she shares a common racial heritage with a particular racial group . . . racial identity development theory concerns the psychological implications of racial-group membership, that is belief systems that evolve in reaction to perceived differential racial-group membership. (p. 3)

It is assumed that in a society where racial-group membership is emphasized, the development of a racial identity will occur in some form in everyone. Given the dominant/subordinate relationship of Whites and people of color in this society, however, it is not surprising that this developmental process will unfold in different ways. For purposes of this discussion, William Cross's (1971, 1978) model of Black identity development will be described along with Helms's (1990) model of White racial identity development theory. While the identity development of other students (Asian Latino/a, Native American) is not included in this particular theoretical formulation, there is evidence to suggest that the process for these oppressed groups is similar to that described for African Americans (Highlen et al., 1988; Phinney, 1990).[2] In each case, it is assumed that a positive sense of one's self as a member of one's group (which is not based on any assumed superiority) is important for psychological health.

276

Black Racial Identity Development

According to Cross's (1971, 1978, 1991) model of Black racial identity development, there are five stages in the process, identified as Preencounter, Encounter, Immersion/Emersion, Internalization, and Internalization-Commitment.
In the first stage of Preencounter, the African American has absorbed many
of the beliefs and values of the dominant White culture, including the notion
that "White is right" and "Black is wrong." Though the internalization of negative Black stereotypes may be outside of his or her conscious awareness, the
individual seeks to assimilate and be accepted by Whites, and actively or passively distances him/herself from other Blacks.[3]

Louise, an African American woman previously quoted, captured the
essence of this stage in the following description of herself at an earlier time:

> For a long time it seemed as if I didn't remember my background, and I guess in
> some ways I didn't. I was never taught to be proud of my African heritage. Like
> we talked about in class, I went through a very long stage of identifying with my
> oppressors. Wanting to be like, live like, and be accepted by them. Even to the
> point of hating my own race and myself for being a part of it. Now I am ashamed
> that I ever was ashamed. I lost so much of myself in my denial of and refusal to
> accept my people.

In order to maintain psychological comfort at this stage of development,
Helms writes:

> The person must maintain the fiction that race and racial indoctrination have
> nothing to do with how he or she lives life. It is probably the case that the Preen-
> counter person is bombarded on a regular basis with information that he or she
> cannot really be a member of the "in" racial group, but relies on denial to selec-
> tively screen such information from awareness. (1990, p. 23)

This de-emphasis on one's racial-group membership may allow the individual to think that race has not been or will not be a relevant factor in one's
own achievement, and may contribute to the belief in a U.S. meritocracy that
is often a part of a Preencounter worldview.

Movement into the Encounter phase is typically precipitated by an event or
series of events that forces the individual to acknowledge the impact of racism in one's life. For example, instances of social rejection by White friends
or colleagues (or reading new personally relevant information about racism)
may lead the individual to the conclusion that many Whites will not view him
or her as an equal. Faced with the reality that he or she cannot truly be White,
the individual is forced to focus on his or her identity as a member of a group
targeted by racism.

Brenda, a Korean American student, described her own experience of this
process as a result of her participation in the racism course:

> I feel that because of this class, I have become much more aware of racism that
> exists around. Because of my awareness of racism, I am now bothered by acts

277

and behaviors that might not have bothered me in the past. Before when racial comments were said around me I would somehow ignore it and pretend that nothing was said. By ignoring comments such as these, I was protecting myself. It became sort of a defense mechanism. I never realized I did this, until I was confronted with stories that were found in our reading, by other people of color, who also ignored comments that bothered them. In realizing that there is racism out in the world and that there are comments concerning race that are directed towards me, I feel as if I have reached the first step. I also think I have reached the second step, because I am now bothered and irritated by such comments. I no longer ignore them, but now confront them.

The Immersion/Emersion stage is characterized by the simultaneous desire to surround oneself with visible symbols of one's racial identity and an active avoidance of symbols of Whiteness. As Thomas Parham describes, "At this stage, everything of value in life must be Black or relevant to Blackness. This stage is also characterized by a tendency to denigrate White people, simultaneously glorifying Black people. . . ." (1989, p. 190). The previously described anger that emerges in class among African American students and other students of color in the process of learning about racism may be seen as part of the transition through these stages.

As individuals enter the Immersion stage, they actively seek out opportunities to explore aspects of their own history and culture with the support of peers from their own racial background. Typically, White-focused anger dissipates during this phase because so much of the person's energy is directed toward his or her own group- and self-exploration. The result of this exploration is an emerging security in a newly defined and affirmed sense of self.

Sharon, another African American woman, described herself at the beginning of the semester as angry, seemingly in the Encounter stage of development. She wrote after our class meeting:

> Another point that I must put down is that before I entered class today I was angry about the way Black people have been treated in this country. I don't think I will easily overcome that and I basically feel justified in my feelings.

At the end of the semester, Sharon had joined with two other Black students in the class to work on their final class project. She observed that the three of them had planned their project to focus on Black people specifically, suggesting movement into the Immersion stage of racial identity development. She wrote:

> We are concerned about the well-being of our own people. They cannot be well if they have this pinned-up hatred for their own people. This internalized racism is something that we all felt, at various times, needed to be talked about. This semester it has really been important to me, and I believe Gordon [a Black classmate], too.

The emergence from this stage marks the beginning of Internalization. Secure in one's own sense of racial identity, there is less need to assert the

"Blacker than thou" attitude often characteristic of the Immersion stage (Parham, 1989). In general, "pro-Black attitudes become more expansive, open, and less defensive" (Cross, 1971, p. 24). While still maintaining his or her connections with Black peers, the internalized individual is willing to establish meaningful relationships with Whites who acknowledge and are respectful of his or her self-definition. The individual is also ready to build coalitions with members of other oppressed groups. At the end of the semester, Brenda, a Korean American, concluded that she had in fact internalized a positive sense of racial identity. The process she described parallels the stages described by Cross:

> I have been aware for a long time that I am Korean. But through this class I am beginning to really become aware of my race. I am beginning to find out that White people can be accepting of me and at the same time accept me as a Korean.
>
> I grew up wanting to be accepted and ended up almost denying my race and culture. I don't think I did this consciously, but the denial did occur. As I grew older, I realized that I was different. I became for the first time, friends with other Koreans. I realized I had much in common with them. This was when I went through my "Korean friend" stage. I began to enjoy being friends with Koreans more than I did with Caucasians.
>
> Well, ultimately, through many years of growing up, I am pretty much in focus about who I am and who my friends are. I knew before I took this class that there were people not of color that were understanding of my differences. In our class, I feel that everyone is trying to sincerely find the answer of abolishing racism. I knew people like this existed, but it's nice to meet with them weekly.

Cross suggests that there are few psychological differences between the fourth stage, Internalization, and the fifth stage, Internalization-Commitment. However, those at the fifth stage have found ways to translate their "personal sense of Blackness into a plan of action or a general sense of commitment" to the concerns of Blacks as a group, which is sustained over time (Cross, 1991, p. 220). Whether at the fourth or fifth stage, the process of Internalization allows the individual, anchored in a positive sense of racial identity, both to proactively perceive and transcend race. Blackness becomes "the point of departure for discovering the universe of ideas, cultures and experiences beyond blackness in place of mistaking blackness as the universe itself" (Cross, Parham, & Helms, 1991, p. 330).

Though the process of racial identity development has been presented here in linear form, in fact it is probably more accurate to think of it in a spiral form. Often a person may move from one stage to the next, only to revisit an earlier stage as the result of new encounter experiences (Parham, 1989), though the later experience of the stage may be different from the original experience. The image that students often find helpful in understanding this concept of recycling through the stages is that of a spiral staircase. As a person ascends a spiral staircase, she may stop and look down at a spot below. When she reaches the next level, she may look down and see the same spot, but the vantage point has changed.[4]

White Racial Identity Development

The transformations experienced by those targeted by racism are often paralleled by those of White students. Helms (1990) describes the evolution of a positive White racial identity as involving both the abandonment of racism and the development of a nonracist White identity. In order to do the latter,

> he or she must accept his or her own Whiteness, the cultural implications of being White, and define a view of Self as a racial being that does not depend on the perceived superiority of one racial group over another. (p. 49)

She identifies six stages in her model of White racial identity development: Contact, Disintegration, Reintegration, Pseudo-Independent, Immersion/Emersion, and Autonomy.

The Contact stage is characterized by a lack of awareness of cultural and institutional racism, and of one's own White privilege. Peggy McIntosh (1989) writes eloquently about her own experience of this state of being:

> As a white person, I realized I had been taught about racism as something which puts others at a disadvantage, but had been taught not to see one of its corollary aspects, white privilege, which puts me at an advantage. . . . I was taught to see racism only in individual acts of meanness, not in invisible systems conferring dominance on my group. (p. 10)

In addition, the Contact stage often includes naive curiosity about or fear of people of color, based on stereotypes learned from friends, family, or the media. These stereotypes represent the framework in use when a person at this stage of development makes a comment such as, "You don't act like a Black person" (Helms, 1990, p. 57).

Those Whites whose lives are structured so as to limit their interaction with people of color, as well as their awareness of racial issues, may remain at this stage indefinitely. However, certain kinds of experiences (increased interaction with people of color or exposure to new information about racism) may lead to a new understanding that cultural and institutional racism exist. This new understanding marks the beginning of the Disintegration stage.

At this stage, the bliss of ignorance or lack of awareness is replaced by the discomfort of guilt, shame, and sometimes anger at the recognition of one's own advantage because of being White and the acknowledgment of the role of Whites in the maintenance of a racist system. Attempts to reduce discomfort may include denial (convincing oneself that racism doesn't really exist, or if it does, it is the fault of its victims).

For example, Tom, a White male student, responded with some frustration in his journal to a classmate's observation that the fact that she had never read any books by Black authors in any of her high school or college English classes was an example of cultural racism. He wrote, "It's not my fault that Blacks don't write books."

After viewing a film in which a psychologist used examples of Black children's drawings to illustrate the potentially damaging effect of negative cultural messages on a Black child's developing self-esteem, David, another White male student, wrote:

> I found it interesting the way Black children drew themselves without arms. The psychologist said this is saying that the child feels unable to control his environment. It can't be because the child has notions and beliefs already about being Black. It must be built in or hereditary due to the past history of the Blacks. I don't believe it's cognitive but more biological due to a long past history of repression and being put down.

Though Tom's and David's explanations seem quite problematic, they can be understood in the context of racial identity development theory as a way of reducing their cognitive dissonance upon learning this new race-related information. As was discussed earlier, withdrawal (accomplished by avoiding contact with people of color and the topic of racism) is another strategy for dealing with the discomfort experienced at this stage. Many of the previously described responses of White students to race-related content are characteristic of the transition from the Contact to the Disintegration stage of development.

Helms (1990) describes another response to the discomfort of Disintegration, which involves attempts to change significant others' attitudes toward African Americans and other people of color. However, as she points out,

> due to the racial naivete with which this approach may be undertaken and the person's ambivalent racial identification, this dissonance-reducing strategy is likely to be met with rejection by Whites as well as Blacks. (p. 59)

In fact, this response is also frequently observed among White students who have an opportunity to talk with friends and family during holiday visits. Suddenly they are noticing the racist content of jokes or comments of their friends and relatives and will try to confront them, often only to find that their efforts are, at best, ignored or dismissed as a "phase," or, at worst, greeted with open hostility.

Carl, a White male previously quoted, wrote at length about this dilemma:

> I realized that it was possible to simply go through life totally oblivious to the entire situation or, even if one realizes it, one can totally repress it. It is easy to fade into the woodwork, run with the rest of society, and never have to deal with these problems. So many people I know from home are like this. They have simply accepted what society has taught them with little, if any, question. My father is a prime example of this. . . . It has caused much friction in our relationship, and

he often tells me as a father he has failed in raising me correctly. Most of my high school friends will never deal with these issues and propagate them on to their own children. It's easy to see how the cycle continues. I don't think I could ever justify within myself simply turning my back on the problem. I finally realized that my position in all of these dominant groups gives me power to make change occur. . . . It is an unfortunate result often though that I feel alienated from friends and family. It's often played off as a mere stage that I'm going through. I obviously can't tell if it's merely a stage, but I know that they say this to take the attention off of the truth of what I'm saying. By belittling me, they take the power out of my argument. It's very depressing that being compassionate and considerate are seen as only phases that people go through. I don't want it to be a phase for me, but as obvious as this may sound, I look at my environment and often wonder how it will not be.

The societal pressure to accept the status quo may lead the individual from Disintegration to Reintegration. At this point the desire to be accepted by one's own racial group, in which the overt or covert belief in White superiority is so prevalent, may lead to a reshaping of the person's belief system to be more congruent with an acceptance of racism. The guilt and anxiety associated with Disintegration may be redirected in the form of fear and anger directed toward people of color (particularly Blacks), who are now blamed as the source of discomfort.

Connie, a White woman of Italian ancestry, in many ways exemplified the progression from the Contact stage to Reintegration, a process she herself described seven weeks into the semester. After reading about the stages of White identity development, she wrote:

I think mostly I can find myself in the disintegration stage of development. . . . There was a time when I never considered myself a color. I never described myself as a "White, Italian female" until I got to college and noticed that people of color always described themselves by their color/race. While taking this class, I have begun to understand that being White makes a difference. I never thought about it before but there are many privileges to being White. In my personal life, I cannot say that I have ever felt that I have had the advantage over a Black person, but I am aware that my race has the advantage.

I am feeling really guilty lately about that. I find myself thinking: "I didn't mean to be White, I really didn't mean it." I am starting to feel angry towards my race for ever using this advantage towards personal gains. But at the same time I resent the minority groups. I mean, it's not our fault that society has deemed us "superior." I don't feel any better than a Black person. But it really doesn't matter because I am a member of the dominant race. . . . I can't help it . . . and I sometimes get angry and feel like I'm being attacked.

I guess my anger toward a minority group would enter me into the next stage of Reintegration, where I am once again starting to blame the victim. This is all very trying for me and it has been on my mind a lot. I really would like to be able to reach the last stage, autonomy, where I can accept being White without hostility and anger. That is really hard to do.

Helms (1990) suggests that it is relatively easy for Whites to become stuck at the Reintegration stage of development, particularly if avoidance of people of color is possible. However, if there is a catalyst for continued self- examination, the person "begins to question her or his previous definition of Whiteness and the justifiability of racism in any of its forms . . ." (p. 61). In my experience, continued participation in a course on racism provides the catalyst for this deeper self-examination.

This process was again exemplified by Connie. At the end of the semester, she listened to her own taped interview of her racial attitudes that she had recorded at the beginning of the semester. She wrote:

> Oh wow! I could not believe some of the things that I said. I was obviously in different stages of the White identity development. As I listened and got more and more disgusted with myself when I was at the Reintegration stage, I tried to remind myself that these are stages that all (most) White people go through when dealing with notions of racism. I can remember clearly the resentment I had for people of color. I feel the one thing I enjoyed from listening to my interview was noticing how much I have changed. I think I am finally out of the Reintegration stage. I am beginning to make a conscious effort to seek out information about people of color and accept their criticism. . . . I still feel guilty about the feeling I had about people of color and I always feel bad about being privileged as a result of racism. But I am glad that I have reached what I feel is the Pseudo-Independent stage of White identity development.

The information-seeking that Connie describes often marks the onset of the Pseudo-Independent stage. At this stage, the individual is abandoning beliefs in White superiority, but may still behave in ways that unintentionally perpetuate the system. Looking to those targeted by racism to help him or her understand racism, the White person often tries to disavow his or her own Whiteness through active affiliation with Blacks, for example. The individual experiences a sense of alienation from other Whites who have not yet begun to examine their own racism, yet may also experience rejection from Blacks or other people of color who are suspicious of his or her motives. Students of color moving from the Encounter to the Immersion phase of their own racial identity development may be particularly unreceptive to the White person's attempts to connect with them.

Uncomfortable with his or her own Whiteness, yet unable to be truly any-thing else, the individual may begin searching for a new, more comfortable way to be White. This search is characteristic of the Immersion/Emersion stage of development. Just as the Black student seeks to redefine positively what it means to be of African ancestry in the United States through immer-sion in accurate information about one's culture and history, the White indi-vidual seeks to replace racially related myths and stereotypes with accurate information about what it means and has meant to be White in U.S. society (Helms, 1990). Learning about Whites who have been antiracist allies to peo-ple of color is a very important part of this process.

After reading articles written by antiracist activists describing their own process of unlearning racism, White students often comment on how helpful it is to know that others have experienced similar feelings and have found ways to resist the racism in their environments.[5] For example, Joanne, a White woman who initially experienced a lot of guilt, wrote:

> This article helped me out in many ways. I've been feeling helpless and frustrated. I know there are all these terrible things going on and I want to be able to do something. . . . Anyway this article helped me realize, again, that others feel this way, and gave me some positive ideas to resolve my dominant class guilt and shame.

Finally, reading the biographies and autobiographies of White individuals who have embarked on a similar process of identity development (such as Barnard, 1985/1987) provides White students with important models for change.

Learning about White antiracists can also provide students of color with a sense of hope that they can have White allies. After hearing a White antiracist activist address the class, Sonia, a Latina who had written about her impatience with expressions of White guilt, wrote:

> I don't know when I have been more impressed by anyone. She filled me with hope for the future. She made me believe that there are good people in the world and that Whites suffer too and want to change things.

For White students, the internalization of a newly defined sense of oneself as White is the primary task of the Autonomy stage. The positive feelings associated with this redefinition energize the person's efforts to confront racism and oppression in his or her daily life. Alliances with people of color can be more easily forged at this stage of development than previously because the person's antiracist behaviors and attitudes will be more consistently expressed. While Autonomy might be described as "racial self-actualization, . . . it is best to think of it as an ongoing process . . . wherein the person is continually open to new information and new ways of thinking about racial and cultural variables" (Helms, 1990, p. 66).

Annette, a White woman, described herself in the Autonomy stage, but talked at length about the circular process she felt she had been engaged in during the semester:

> If people as racist as C. P. Ellis (a former Klansman) can change, I think anyone can change. If that makes me idealistic, fine. I do not think my expecting society to change is naive anymore because I now *know* exactly what I want. To be naive means a lack of knowledge that allows me to accept myself both as a White person and as an idealist. This class showed me that these two are not mutually exclusive but are an integral part of me that I cannot deny. I realize now that through most of this class I was trying to deny both of them.
>
> While I was not accepting society's racism, I was accepting society's telling me as a White person, there was nothing I could do to change racism. So, I told

myself I was being naive and tried to suppress my desire to change society. This is what made me so frustrated—while I saw society's racism through examples in the readings and the media, I kept telling myself there was nothing I could do. Listening to my tape, I think I was already in the Autonomy stage when I started this class. I then seemed to decide that being White, I also had to be racist which is when I became frustrated and went back to the Disintegration stage. I was frustrated because I was not only telling myself there was nothing I could do but I also was assuming society's racism was my own which made me feel like I did not want to be White. Actually, it was not being White that I was disavowing but being racist. I think I have now returned to the Autonomy stage and am much more secure in my position there. I accept my Whiteness now as just a part of me as is my idealism. I will no longer disavow these characteristics as I have realized I can be proud of both of them. In turn, I can now truly accept other people for their unique characteristics and not by the labels society has given them as I can accept myself that way.

While I thought the main ideas that I learned in this class were that White people need to be educated to end racism and everyone should be treated as human beings, I really had already incorporated these ideas into my thoughts. What I learned from this class is being White does not mean being racist and being idealistic does not mean being naive. I really did not have to form new ideas about people of color; I had to form them about myself—and I did.

IMPLICATIONS FOR CLASSROOM TEACHING

Although movement through all the stages of racial identity development will not necessarily occur for each student within the course of a semester (or even four years of college), it is certainly common to witness beginning transformations in classes with race-related content. An awareness of the existence of this process has helped me to implement strategies to facilitate positive student development, as well as to improve interracial dialogue within the classroom.

Four strategies for reducing student resistance and promoting student development that I have found useful are the following:

1. the creation of a safe classroom atmosphere by establishing clear guidelines for discussion;
2. the creation of opportunities for self-generated knowledge;
3. the provision of an appropriate developmental model that students can use as a framework for understanding their own process;
4. the exploration of strategies to empower students as change agents.

Creating a Safe Climate

As was discussed earlier, making the classroom a safe space for discussion is essential for overcoming students' fears about breaking the race taboo, and will also reduce later anxieties about exposing one's own internalized racism. Establishing the guidelines of confidentiality, mutual respect, "no zaps," and speaking from one's own experience on the first day of class is a necessary step in the process.

Students respond very positively to these ground rules, and do try to honor them. While the rules do not totally eliminate anxiety, they clearly communicate to students that there is a safety net for the discussion. Students are also encouraged to direct their comments and questions to each other rather than always focusing their attention on me as the instructor, and to learn each other's names rather than referring to each other as "he," "she," or "the person in the red sweater" when responding to each other.[6]

The Power of Self-Generated Knowledge

The creation of opportunities for self-generated knowledge on the part of students is a powerful tool for reducing the initial stage of denial that many students experience. While it may seem easy for some students to challenge the validity of what they read or what the instructor says, it is harder to deny what they have seen with their own eyes. Students can be given hands-on assignments outside of class to facilitate this process.

For example, after reading *Portraits of White Racism* (Wellman, 1977), some students expressed the belief that the attitudes expressed by the White interviewees in the book were no longer commonly held attitudes. Students were then asked to use the same interview protocol used in the book (with some revision) to interview a White adult of their choice. When students reported on these interviews in class, their own observation of the similarity between those they had interviewed and those they had read about was more convincing than anything I might have said.

After doing her interview, Patty, a usually quiet White student, wrote:

> I think I learned a lot from it and that I'm finally getting a better grip on the idea of racism. I think that was why I participated so much in class. I really felt like I knew what I was talking about.

Other examples of creating opportunities for self-generated knowledge include assigning students the task of visiting grocery stores in neighborhoods of differing racial composition to compare the cost and quality of goods and services available at the two locations, and to observe the interactions between the shoppers and the store personnel. For White students, one of the most powerful assignments of this type has been to go apartment hunting with an African American student and to experience housing discrimination first-hand. While one concern with such an assignment is the effect it will have on the student(s) of color involved, I have found that those Black students who choose this assignment rather than another are typically eager to have their White classmates experience the reality of racism, and thus participate quite willingly in the process.

Naming the Problem

The emotional responses that students have to talking and learning about racism are quite predictable and related to their own racial identity development. Unfortunately, students typically do not know this; thus they consider their own guilt, shame, embarrassment, or anger an uncomfortable experience that they alone are having. Informing students at the beginning of the semester that these feelings may be part of the learning process is ethically necessary (in the sense of informed consent), and helps to normalize the students' experience. Knowing in advance that a desire to withdraw from classroom discussion or not to complete assignments is a common response helps students to remain engaged when they reach that point. As Alice, a White woman, wrote at the end of the semester:

> You were so right in saying in the beginning how we would grow tired of racism (I did in October) but then it would get so good! I have *loved* the class once I passed that point.

In addition, sharing the model of racial identity development with students gives them a useful framework for understanding each other's processes as well as their own. This cognitive framework does not necessarily prevent the collision of developmental processes previously described, but it does allow students to be less frightened by it when it occurs. If, for example, White students understand the stages of racial identity development of students of color, they are less likely to personalize or feel threatened by an African American student's anger.

Connie, a White student who initially expressed a lot of resentment at the way students of color tended to congregate in the college cafeteria, was much more understanding of this behavior after she learned about racial identity development theory. She wrote:

> I learned a lot from reading the article about the stages of development in the model of oppressed people. As a White person going through my stages of identity development, I do not take time to think about the struggle people of color go through to reach a stage of complete understanding. I am glad that I know about the stages because now I can understand people of color's behavior in certain situations. For example, when people of color stay to themselves and appear to be in a clique, it is not because they are being rude as I originally thought. Rather they are engaged perhaps in the Immersion stage.

Mary, another White student, wrote:

> I found the entire Cross model of racial identity development very enlightening. I knew that there were stages of racial identity development before I entered this class. I did not know what they were, or what they really entailed. After reading through this article I found myself saying, "Oh. That explains why she reacted this way to this incident instead of how she would have a year ago." Clearly this

person has entered a different stage and is working through different problems from a new viewpoint. Thankfully, the model provides a degree of hope that people will not always be angry, and will not always be separatists, etc. Although I'm not really sure about that.

Conversely, when students of color understand the stages of White racial identity development, they can be more tolerant or appreciative of a White student's struggle with guilt, for example. After reading about the stages of White identity development, Sonia, a Latina previously quoted, wrote:

> This article was the one that made me feel that my own prejudices were showing. I never knew that Whites went through an identity development of their own.

She later told me outside of class that she found it much easier to listen to some of the things White students said because she could understand their potentially offensive comments as part of a developmental stage.

Sharon, an African American woman, also found that an understanding of the respective stages of racial identity development helped her to understand some of the interactions she had had with White students since coming to college. She wrote:

> There is a lot of clash that occurs between Black and White people at college which is best explained by their respective stages of development. Unfortunately schools have not helped to alleviate these problems earlier in life.

In a course on the psychology of racism, it is easy to build in the provision of this information as part of the course content. For instructors teaching courses with race-related content in other fields, it may seem less natural to do so. However, the inclusion of articles on racial identity development and/or class discussion of these issues in conjunction with the other strategies that have been suggested can improve student receptivity to the course content in important ways, making it a very useful investment of class time. Because the stages describe kinds of behavior that many people have commonly observed in themselves, as well as in their own intraracial and interracial interactions, my experience has been that most students grasp the basic conceptual framework fairly easily, even if they do not have a background in psychology.

Empowering Students as Change Agents

Heightening students' awareness of racism without also developing an awareness of the possibility of change is a prescription for despair. I consider it unethical to do one without the other. Exploring strategies to empower students as change agents is thus a necessary part of the process of talking about race and learning about racism. As was previously mentioned, students find it very helpful to read about and hear from individuals who have been effective change agents. Newspaper and magazine articles, as well as biographical or autobiographical essays or book excerpts, are often important sources for this information.

I also ask students to work in small groups to develop an action plan of their own for interrupting racism. While I do not consider it appropriate to require students to engage in antiracist activity (since I believe this should be a personal choice the student makes for him/herself), students are required to think about the possibility. Guidelines are provided (see Katz, 1978), and the plans that they develop over several weeks are presented at the end of the semester. Students are generally impressed with each other's good ideas; and, in fact, they often do go on to implement their projects.

Joanne, a White student who initially struggled with feelings of guilt, wrote:

> I thought that hearing others' ideas for action plans was interesting and informative. It really helps me realize (reminds me) the many choices and avenues there are once I decided to be an ally. Not only did I develop my own concrete way to be an ally, I have found many other ways that I, as a college student, can be an active anti-racist. It was really empowering.

Another way all students can be empowered is by offering them the opportunity to consciously observe their own development. The taped exercise to which some of the previously quoted students have referred is an example of one way to provide this opportunity. At the beginning of the semester, students are given an interview guide with many open-ended questions concerning racial attitudes and opinions. They are asked to interview themselves on tape as a way of recording their own ideas for future reference. Though the tapes are collected, students are assured that no one (including me) will listen to them. The tapes are returned near the end of the semester, and students are asked to listen to their own tapes and use their understanding of racial identity development to discuss it in essay form.

The resulting essays are often remarkable and underscore the psychological importance of giving students the chance to examine racial issues in the classroom. The following was written by Elaine, a White woman:

> Another common theme that was apparent in the tape was that, for the most part, I was aware of my own ignorance and was embarrassed because of it. I wanted to know more about the oppression of people in the country so that I could do something about it. Since I have been here, I have begun to be actively resistant to racism. I have been able to confront my grandparents and some old friends from high school when they make racist comments. Taking this psychology of racism class is another step toward active resistance to racism. I am trying to educate myself so that I have a knowledge base to work from.
>
> When the tape was made, I was just beginning to be active and just beginning to be educated. I think I am now starting to move into the redefinition stage. I am starting to feel ok about being White. Some of my guilt is dissipating, and I do not feel as ignorant as I used to be. I think I have an understanding of racism; how it effects [sic] myself, and how it effects this country. Because of this I think I can be more active in doing something about it.

In the words of Louise, a Black female student:

One of the greatest things I learned from this semester in general is that the world is not only Black and White, nor is the United States. I learned a lot about my own erasure of many American ethnic groups. . . . I am in the (immersion) stage of my identity development. I think I am also dangling a little in the (encounter) stage. I say this because a lot of my energies are still directed toward White people. I began writing a poem two days ago and it was directed to White racism. However, I have also become more Black-identified. I am reaching to the strength in Afro-American heritage. I am learning more about the heritage and history of Afro-American culture. Knowledge = strength and strength = power.

While some students are clearly more self-reflective and articulate about their own process than others, most students experience the opportunity to talk and learn about these issues as a transforming process. In my experience, even those students who are frustrated by aspects of the course find themselves changed by it. One such student wrote in her final journal entry:

What I felt to be a major hindrance to me was the amount of people. Despite the philosophy, I really never felt at ease enough to speak openly about the feelings I have and kind of watched the class pull farther and farther apart as the semester went on. . . . I think that it was your attitude that kept me intrigued by the topics we were studying despite my frustrations with the class time. I really feel as though I made some significant moves in my understanding of other people's positions in our world as well as of my feelings of racism, and I feel very good about them. I feel like this class has moved me in the right direction. I'm on a roll I think, because I've been introduced to so much.

Facilitating student development in this way is a challenging and complex task, but the results are clearly worth the effort.

IMPLICATIONS FOR THE INSTITUTION

What are the institutional implications for an understanding of racial identity development theory beyond the classroom? How can this framework be used to address the pressing issues of increasing diversity and decreasing racial tensions on college campuses? How can providing opportunities in the curriculum to talk about race and learn about racism affect the recruitment and retention of students of color specifically, especially when the majority of the students enrolled are White?

The fact is, educating White students about race and racism changes attitudes in ways that go beyond the classroom boundaries. As White students move through their own stages of identity development, they take their friends with them by engaging them in dialogue. They share the articles they have read with roommates, and involve them in their projects. An example of this involvement can be seen in the following journal entry, written by Larry, a White man:

Here it is our fifth week of class and more and more I am becoming aware of the racism around me. Our second project made things clearer, because while watching T.V. I picked up many kinds of discrimination and stereotyping. Since the project was over, I still find myself watching these shows and picking up bits and pieces every show I watch. Even my friends will be watching a show and they will say, "Hey, Larry, put that in your paper." Since they know I am taking this class, they are looking out for these things. They are also watching what they say around me for fear that I will use them as an example. For example, one of my friends has this fascination with making fun of Jewish people. Before I would listen to his comments and take them in stride, but now I confront him about his comments.

The heightened awareness of the White students enrolled in the class has a ripple effect in their peer group, which helps to create a climate in which students of color and other targeted groups (Jewish students, for example) might feel more comfortable. It is likely that White students who have had the opportunity to learn about racism in a supportive atmosphere will be better able to be allies to students of color in extracurricular settings, like student government meetings and other organizational settings, where students of color often feel isolated and unheard.

At the same time, students of color who have had the opportunity to examine the ways in which racism may have affected their own lives are able to give voice to their own experience, and to validate it rather than be demoralized by it. An understanding of internalized oppression can help students of color recognize the ways in which they may have unknowingly participated in their own victimization, or the victimization of others. They may be able to move beyond victimization to empowerment, and share their learning with others, as Sharon, a previously quoted Black woman, planned to do.

Campus communities with an understanding of racial identity development could become more supportive of special-interest groups, such as the Black Student Union or the Asian Student Alliance, because they would recognize them not as "separatist" but as important outlets for students of color who may be at the Encounter or Immersion stage of racial identity development. Not only could speakers of color be sought out to add diversity to campus programming, but Whites who had made a commitment to unlearning their own racism could be offered as models to those White students looking for new ways to understand their own Whiteness, and to students of color looking for allies.

It has become painfully clear on many college campuses across the United States that we cannot have successfully multiracial campuses without talking about race and learning about racism. Providing a forum where this discussion can take place safely over a semester, a time period that allows personal and group development to unfold in ways that day-long or weekend programs do not, may be among the most proactive learning opportunities an institution can provide.

NOTES

1. A similar point could be made about other issues of oppression, such as anti-Semitism, homophobia and heterosexism, ageism, and so on.
2. While similar models of racial identity development exist, Cross and Helms are referenced here because they are among the most frequently cited writers on Black racial identity development and on White racial identity development, respectively. For a discussion of the commonalities between these and other identity development models, see Phinney (1989, 1990) and Helms (1990).
3. Both Parham (1989) and Phinney (1989) suggest that a preference for the dominant group is not always a characteristic of this stage. For example, children raised in households and communities with explicitly positive Afrocentric attitudes may absorb a pro-Black perspective, which then serves as the starting point for their own exploration of racial identity.
4. After being introduced to this model and Helms's model of White identity development, students are encouraged to think about how the models might apply to their own experience or the experiences of people they know. As is reflected in the cited journal entries, some students resonate to the theories quite readily, easily seeing their own process of growth reflected in them. Other students are sometimes puzzled because they feel as though their own process varies from these models, and may ask if it is possible to "skip" a particular stage, for example. Such questions provide a useful departure point for discussing the limitations of stage theories in general, and the potential variations in experience that make questions of racial identity development so complex.
5. Examples of useful articles include essays by McIntosh (1988), Lester (1987), and Braden (1987). Each of these combines autobiographical material, as well as a conceptual framework for understanding some aspect of racism that students find very helpful. Bowser and Hunt's (1981) edited book, *Impacts of Racism on Whites,* though less autobiographical in nature, is also a valuable resource.
6. Class size has a direct bearing on my ability to create safety in the classroom. Dividing the class into pairs or small groups of five or six students to discuss initial reactions to a particular article or film helps to increase participation, both in the small groups and later in the large group discussions.

REFERENCES

Barnard, H. F. (Ed.). (1987). *Outside the magic circle: The autobiography of Virginia Foster Durr.* New York: Simon & Schuster. (Original work published 1985)

Bowser, B. P., & Hunt, R. G. (1981). *Impacts of racism on Whites.* Beverly Hills: Sage.

Braden, A. (1987). Undoing racism: Lessons for the peace movement. *Nonviolent Activist* (April-May), 3–6.

Bronstein, P. A., & Quina, K. (Eds.). (1988). *Teaching a psychology of people: Resources for gender and sociocultural awareness.* Washington, DC: American Psychological Association.

Cross, W. E., Jr. (1971). The Negro to Black conversion experience: Toward a psychology of black liberation. *Black World, 20*(9), 13–27.

Cross, W. E., Jr. (1978). The Cross and Thomas models of psychological nigrescence. *Journal of Black Psychology, 5*(1), 13–19.

Cross, W. E., Jr. (1991). *Shades of Black: Diversity in African-American identity.* Philadelphia: Temple University Press.

Cross, W. E., Jr., Parham, T. A., & Helms, J. E. (1991). The stages of black identity development: Nigrescence models. In R. Jones (Ed.), *Black psychology* (3rd ed., pp. 319–338). San Francisco: Cobb and Henry.

Derman-Sparks, L., Higa, C. T., & Sparks, B. (1980). Children, race and racism: How race awareness develops. *Interracial Books for Children Bulletin, 11*(3/4), 3–15.

Helms, J. E. (Ed.). (1990). *Black and White racial identity: Theory, research and practice.* Westport, CT: Greenwood Press.

Highlen, P. S., Reynolds, A. L., Adams, E. M., Hanley, T. C., Myers, L. J., Cox, C., & Speight, S. (1988, August 13). *Self-identity development model of oppressed people: Inclusive model for all?* Paper presented at the American Psychological Association Convention, Atlanta, GA.

Hull, G. T., Scott, P. B., & Smith, B. (Eds.). (1982). *All the women are White, all the Blacks are men, but some of us are brave: Black women's studies.* Old Westbury, NY: Feminist Press.

Katz, J. H. (1978). *White awareness: Handbook for anti-racism training.* Norman: University of Oklahoma Press.

Lester, J. (1987). *What happens to the mythmakers when the myths are found to be untrue?* Unpublished paper, Equity Institute, Emeryville, CA.

McIntosh, P. (1988). *White privilege and male privilege: A personal a account of coming to see correspondences through work in women's studies.* Working paper, Wellesley College Center for Research on Women, Wellesley, MA.

McIntosh, P. (1989). White privilege: Unpacking the invisible knapsack. *Peace and Freedom,* (July/August), 10–12.

Parham, T. A. (1989). Cycles of psychological nigrescence. *Counseling Psychologist, 17*(2), 187–226.

Phinney, J. (1989). Stages of ethnic identity in minority group adolescents. *Journal of Early Adolescence, 9,* 34–39.

Phinney, J. (1990). Ethnic identity in adolescents and adults: Review of research. *Psychological Bulletin, 108*(3), 499–514.

Phinney, J. S., & Rotheram, M. J. (Eds.). (1987). *Children's ethnic socialization: Pluralism and development.* Newbury Park, CA: Sage.

Schuster, M. R., & Van Dyne, S. R. (Eds.). (1985). *Women's place in the academy: Transforming the liberal arts curriculum.* Totowa, NJ: Towman & Allanheld.

Wellman, D. (1977). *Portraits of White racism.* New York: Cambridge University Press.

USING A CHICANA FEMINIST EPISTEMOLOGY IN EDUCATIONAL RESEARCH

DOLORES DELGADO BERNAL

> Schools . . . presuppose and legitimate particular forms of history, community, and authority. . . . The question is what and whose history, community, knowledge, and voice prevails? Unless this question is addressed, the issues of what to teach, how to teach, how to engage our students, and how to function as intellectuals becomes removed from the wider principles that inform such issues and practices. (Giroux, 1992, p. 91)

Epistemological concerns in schools are inseparable from cultural hegemonic domination in educational research. The way educational research is conducted contributes significantly to what happens (or does not happen) in schools. In education, what is taught, how it is taught, who is taught, and whose fault it is when what is taught is not learned are often manifestations of what is considered the legitimate body of knowledge. For Chicanas, this is not merely an epistemological issue, but one of power, ethics, politics, and survival.[1] Employing a Chicana feminist epistemology in educational research thus becomes a means to resist epistemological racism (Scheurich & Young, 1997) and to recover untold histories.

In this article, I describe a Chicana epistemological perspective by providing an example of my research, which places Chicanas as central subjects and provides a forum in which Chicanas speak and analyze their stories of school resistance and grassroots leadership. I draw from the strong traditions of Black, Native American, and Chicana feminists in an attempt to articulate a Chicana feminist epistemology in educational research that reflects my history and that of the women I write about, a unique history that arises from the social, political, and cultural conditions of Chicanas. Most feminists of color recognize that gender, race, class, and sexual orientation—not gender alone—determine the allocation of power and the nature of any individual's identity, status, and circumstance (Collins, 1986; hooks, 1989; Hurtado, 1989; Pesquera & Segura, 1993). Therefore, "endarkened" feminist epistemologies are crucial, as they speak to the failures of traditional patriarchal and liberal educational scholarship and examine the intersection of race, class, gender, and sexuality.[2] Endarkened epistemologies in general, and Chicana feminism in particular, inform my perspective.

I first review briefly the failure of traditional mainstream educational scholarship and liberal feminist scholarship to provide a useful paradigm to examine the realities of working-class Chicana students. Second, I outline characteristics of a Chicana feminist epistemology by drawing from the work of Chicana scholars in various disciplines. Next, I use the work of Anselm Strauss and Juliet Corbin (1990) to describe four sources of what I call "cultural intuition"—that is, the unique viewpoints Chicana scholars bring to the research process. In doing so, I provide examples of my own cultural intuition as it relates to my research. In the last sections of this article, I clarify what I mean by a Chicana feminist epistemology and cultural intuition by describing an oral history study that examined a specific example of Chicana students' oppositional behavior as an act of school resistance and grassroots leadership (Delgado Bernal, 1997).[3] I demonstrate how, although not specifically articulated at the time of my study, my research was guided by my own cultural intuition and a Chicana feminist epistemology.

THE FAILURE OF LIBERAL EDUCATIONAL SCHOLARSHIP

Gender, ethnic, and class oppression contribute to the unique position of working-class Chicana students, yet liberal educational scholarship has failed to provide a useful paradigm to examine this intersection. For example, theories that attempt to understand how schools replicate the social relationships and attitudes needed to sustain the existing relations in a capitalist society have traditionally focused on White, working-class male students and ignored the role of female students (Bowles & Gintis, 1976). The goal of school resistance literature has been to better understand the role of agency in the process of social reproduction; however, most early studies are also grounded in a traditional, patriarchal epistemology that focuses on White working-class males and does not fully explain the resistance of female students (MacLeod, 1987; Willis, 1977). Theories of cognitive development (Piaget, 1952, 1954) still espoused in many teacher education and educational psychology programs are normed on the behaviors of White middle-class male students, and are ignored or misapplied to students of any other identities. Historically, traditional mainstream educational scholarship has not addressed the influence of gender, race/ethnicity, class, and sexuality on education policy and practice.

Most liberal feminist scholarship has also failed to provide a useful paradigm to examine the gender, ethnic, and class oppression that contribute to the unique positions of working-class Chicana students. Liberal feminist scholarship gives primacy to the domination of patriarchy without seriously addressing how institutional and cultural differences based on sexism, racism, and classism create a different range of choices and options for Chicanas (Zambrana, 1994). Another problematic position of liberal feminist scholarship is the notion that an analysis should begin with the commonalties of women's experience. By only looking at commonalties based on gender and omitting issues of race/ethnicity or class, one may overlook how institutional and cultural structures constrain and enable different groups of women differently. For example, very little is known about the educational mobility of women of color in general, and Chicanas in particular. Until recently, the educational paths of Chicanas were rarely explored. Today there are studies that have investigated the barriers to education experienced by Chicanas (Gándara, 1982; Segura, 1993; Vásquez, 1982), the marginality of Chicanas in higher education (Cuádraz, 1996), and in the college choice and resistance of Chicanas (Talavera-Bustillos, 1998). These studies go beyond the commonalties of women's experience and examine how family backgrounds, school practices, male privilege, and class and ethnic discrimination shape Chicanas' educational experiences and choices. More specifically, Denise Segura (1993) found that teachers' and counselors' actions channeled Chicanas into non-academic programs offering a lower quality of instruction, which restricted their range of life chances and options. Segura and other Chicana scholars address the shortcomings of liberal educational scholarship by embracing a Chicana feminist epistemology that examines Chicanas' experiences in relation to an entire structure of domination. Although it is impossible in this article to describe all the nuances of a Chicana epistemology or its evolution, in the next section I outline some of the defining characteristics of a Chicana feminist epistemology.

A CHICANA FEMINIST EPISTEMOLOGY

The relationship between methodology and a researcher's epistemological orientation is not always explicit, but is inevitably closely connected. Sandra Harding (1987) makes a distinction between epistemology, methodology, and method that is helpful in defining a Chicana feminist epistemology. "Method" generally only refers to techniques and strategies for collecting data. Although early feminist arguments defended qualitative approaches to studying and understanding women's lives over quantitative approaches, feminists today have reconsidered the false dichotomy of qualitative and quantitative methods (Maynard, 1994). Though quantitative methods are limited, both methods have been used in Chicana feminist research (e.g., Delgado-Gaitan,

1993; Flores-Ortiz, 1991; Pardo, 1990; Pesquera & Segura, 1990; Soldatenko, 1991), and as numerous educational researchers and feminists have pointed out, both methods have been used to objectify, exploit, and dominate people of color (Fine, 1994; Kelly, Burton, & Regan, 1994; Lather, 1991). A decision of whether to use qualitative or quantitative methods primarily depends on the topic and the research questions asked. Therefore, what becomes crucial in a Chicana feminist epistemology goes beyond quantitative versus qualitative methods, and lies instead in the methodology employed and in whose experiences and realities are accepted as the foundation of knowledge.

Methodology provides both theory and analysis of the research process, how research questions are framed, and the criteria used to evaluate research findings (Harding, 1987). Therefore, a Chicana methodology encompasses both the position from which distinctively Chicana research questions might be asked and the political and ethical issues involved in the research process. Liberal feminists have argued that what distinguishes feminist research from other forms of research is "the questions we have asked, the way we locate ourselves within our questions, and the purpose of our work" (Kelly, 1988, p. 6). However, these feminists (as well as mainstream scholars and Chicano male scholars) have too often failed to ask questions that analyze the interrelationships between classism, racism, sexism, and other forms of oppression, especially from Chicanas' perspectives. Liberal feminist research has insisted "on its political nature and potential to bring about change in women's lives" (Maynard, 1994, p. 16), yet this research has not addressed the lives of Chicanas.

Instead, it has been Chicana scholars who have challenged the historical and ideological representation of Chicanas, relocated them to a central position in the research, and asked distinctively Chicana feminist research questions, all important characteristics of a Chicana feminist epistemology (e.g., Alarcón et al., 1993; de la Torre & Pesquera, 1993; Flores-Ortiz, 1993; Mora & Del Castillo, 1980; Pérez, 1993; Romero, 1989; Zavella, 1993). By shifting the analysis onto Chicanas and their race/ethnicity, class, and sexuality, scholars are able to address the shortcomings of traditional patriarchal and liberal feminist scholarship (Castañeda, 1993; Castillo, 1995; Pardo, 1998; Pérez, 1993; Ruiz, 1998; Trujillo, 1993), thereby giving voice to Chicana experiences and bringing change to their lives. For example, Yvette Flores-Ortiz (1998) points to the need for and begins the process of creating a Chicana psychology. She points out that "the theory and practice of psychology have subjugated Chicanas by measuring their development, personality, and mental health against a male white upper-class model" (p. 102). Even feminist psychology that challenges patriarchal assumptions subsumes Chicanas under the variable of gender, and leaves them appearing deficient or dysfunctional when compared to White middle-class women. Flores-Ortiz's (1998) theoretical framework for a Chicana psychology relocates Chicanas to a central position and is informed by her twenty years as a clinical psychologist and her experience of immigration to the United States. Lara Medina's (1998) research documents the voices of how twenty-two Chicanas learned to substitute "patriarchal religion with their own cultural knowledge, sensibilities, and sense of justice" (p. 190). Her research challenges the spiritual and ideological representation of Chicanas in religion by asking how Chicanas recreate traditional cultural practices and look to non-Western philosophies as part of an ongoing process of spirituality. These and other Chicana scholars embrace and further develop a Chicana feminist epistemology by researching the lives and experiences of Chicanas, and framing their research questions in ways that give voice to these women. Inés Hernández-Avila (1995) speaks candidly about the importance of this kind of scholarship, and though a Chicana feminist epistemology may be unsettling for those operating within traditional research epistemologies, she affirms its importance in the academy:

> When I and other Native American women are central as subjects—as sovereign subjects—we often unsettle, disrupt, and sometimes threaten other people's, particularly many white people's, white scholars', white women feminists' sense of self as subjects. That may not have been my or our primary motivations, but it is necessarily inherent in Native women's claiming our right to speak for ourselves. (p. 494)

Epistemology involves the nature, status, and production of knowledge (Harding, 1987). Therefore, a Chicana epistemology must be concerned with the knowledge about Chicanas—about who generates an understanding of their experiences, and how this knowledge is legitimized or not legitimized. It questions objectivity, a universal foundation of knowledge, and the Western dichotomies of mind versus body, subject versus object, objective truth versus subjective emotion, and male versus female. In this sense, a Chicana epistemology maintains connections to indigenous roots by embracing dualities that are necessary and complementary qualities, and by challenging dichotomies that offer opposition without reconciliation. This notion of duality is connected to Leslie Marmon Silko's (1996) observation of a traditional Native American way of life: "In this universe there is no absolute good or absolute bad; there are only balances and harmonies that ebb and flow" (p. 64).

A Chicana feminist standpoint also acknowledges that most Chicanas lead lives with significantly different opportunity structures than men (including Chicano males) and White women. Patricia Hill Collins (1986) points out that Black feminists (similar to Chicana feminists) rarely describe the behavior of women of color without paying attention to the opportunity structures shaping their lives. Thus, adopting a Chicana feminist epistemology will expose human relationships and experiences that are probably not visible from a traditional patriarchal position or a liberal feminist standpoint. Within this framework, Chicanas become agents of knowledge who participate in intellectual discourse that links experience, research, community, and social change. Adela de la Torre and Beatríz Pesquera (1993) comment on this tradition, which places Chicanas as speaking subjects:

Rooted in the political climate of the late 1960s and early 1970s, our scholarship, like other currents of dissent, is a Chicana critique of cultural, political, and economic conditions in the United States. It is influenced by the tradition of advocacy scholarship, which challenges the claims of objectivity and links research to community concerns and social change. It is driven by a passion to place the Chicana, as speaking subject, at the center of intellectual discourse. (p. 1)

While acknowledging the diversity and complexity of Chicanas' relationships and experiences, we must also recognize that, as an indigenous/mestiza-based cultural group, our experiences are different from those of African Americans and Native Americans in the United States. A Chicana feminist epistemology is informed by and shares characteristics of endarkened feminist epistemologies (e.g., examinations of the influence of race, class, gender, and sexuality on opportunity structures), but is different from the "Black Feminist Thought" of Collins (1991) or the inter-tribal discourses of Elizabeth Cook-Lynn (1996) and Marmon Silko (1996). A unique characteristic of a Chicana feminist epistemology is that it also validates and addresses experiences that are intertwined with issues of immigration, migration, generational status, bilingualism, limited English proficiency, and the contradictions of Catholicism. In addition, through the process of naming dynamic identities and diverse cultural/historical experiences, these issues have been studied and written about by numerous Chicana feminists in a much different way than most Chicano male scholars (e.g., Alarcón, 1990; Anzaldúa, 1987; Castillo, 1995; Medina, 1998; Sandoval, 1998; Trujillo, 1998).

For example, concepts such as mestiza, borderlands, and Xicanisma are unique to a Chicana epistemology. A mestiza is literally a woman of mixed ancestry, especially of Native American, European, and African backgrounds. However, the term mestiza has come to mean a new Chicana consciousness that straddles cultures, races, languages, nations, sexualities, and spiritualities—that is, living with ambivalence while balancing opposing powers. Gloria Anzaldúa (1987) states that "the new mestiza copes by developing a tolerance for contradictions, a tolerance for ambiguity. She learns to be an Indian in Mexican culture, to be Mexican from an Anglo point of view. She learns to juggle cultures" (p. 79). Within a Chicana feminist epistemology, borderlands refers to the geographical, emotional, and/or psychological space occupied by mestizas. Anzaldúa believes that those individuals who are marginalized by society and are forced to live on the borderlands of dominant culture develop a sixth sense for survival. Therefore, Chicanas and other marginalized peoples have a strength that comes from their borderland experiences. Xicanisma, a term introduced by Ana Castillo (1995), describes Chicana feminisms that are developed from and carried out to "our work place, social gatherings, kitchens, bedrooms, and society in general" (p. 11).

Rather than use an epistemological framework that is based solely on the diverse social histories of other women of color (e.g., Black feminist thought) or the social history of the dominant race (e.g., liberal feminist thought), a

Chicana feminist epistemology offers a standpoint that borrows from endarkened feminist epistemologies and is grounded in the unique life experiences of Chicanas. For example, in educational research it is important to remember that Chicana students experience school from multiple dimensions, including their skin color, gender, class, and English-language proficiency. Castillo (1995) reflects on the trauma a Chicana may experience in regard to bilingualism:

> She was educated in English and learned it is the only acceptable language in society, but Spanish was the language of her childhood, family, and community. She may not be able to rid herself of an accent; society has denigrated her first language. By the same token, women may also become anxious and self conscious in later years if they have no or little facility in Spanish. (p. 39)

Bilingualism is often seen as un-American and is considered a deficit and an obstacle to learning. Prohibiting Spanish-language use among Mexican schoolchildren is a social philosophy and a political tool that has been and continues to be used to justify school segregation and to maintain a colonized relationship between Mexicans and the dominant society (Delgado Bernal, 1999). In my own research, I learned how Vickie Castro, a Los Angeles Unified School District board member, was physically separated from peers as a young girl because of the devaluation of Spanish:

> I do recall my first day of school. And I did not speak English. . . . I just recall being frightened and I recall not knowing what to do and I recall being told to just sit over there in the corner. And there was one other little girl and we were just scared out of our minds. (Castro, 1994, pp. 2, 3)

Historically, many Chicana and Chicano students have been segregated and stigmatized, with their perceived language deficiency used as justification. Students today continue to be segregated based on their limited English proficiency. In June 1998, California voters passed Proposition 227, the English Language Education for Immigrant Children initiative. The initiative does away with all bilingual education and English-language development programs that do not meet its rigid 180-day English-only approach.[4] It promotes stigmatization by allowing local schools "to place in the same classroom English learners of different ages but whose degree of English proficiency is similar."

To ground one's research within the experiences of Chicanas means that we deconstruct the historical devaluation of Spanish, the contradictions of Catholicism, the patriarchal ideology that devalues women, and the scapegoating of immigrants. Indeed, the everyday lives of Chicanas demonstrate that they are often at the center of these struggles against cultural domination, class exploitation, sexism, and racism. A Chicana feminist epistemology is therefore grounded in the rich historical legacy of Chicanas' resistance and translates into a pursuit of social justice in both research and scholarship.

A Chicana feminist epistemology that is based on the lives of Chicanas and is dedicated to achieving justice and equality combats what James Joseph Scheurich and Michelle Young (1997) call epistemological racism. As they define it, epistemological racism arises out of the social history and culture of the dominant race and is present in the current range of traditional research epistemologies—positivism to postmodernism and poststructuralism. Traditional research epistemologies reflect and reinforce the social history of the dominant race, which has negative results for people of color in general and students and scholars of color in particular. A Chicana feminist epistemology arises out of a unique social and cultural history, and demonstrates that our experiences as Mexican women are legitimate, appropriate, and effective in designing, conducting, and analyzing educational research. A Chicana cultural standpoint that is located in the interconnected identities of race/ethnicity, gender, class, and sexuality and within the historical and contemporary context of oppressions and resistance can also be the foundation for a theoretical sensitivity (Strauss & Corbin, 1990) that many Chicana scholars bring to their research.

FOUR SOURCES OF CULTURAL INTUITION

> The disciplines of Black and other ethnic studies and women's studies have opened the way for multiple theoretical and epistemological readings in the fields of educational research. A major contribution of these fields is that feminist and scholars of color (and those of us who identify as both) have argued that members of marginalized groups have unique viewpoints on our own experiences as a whole. (Dillard, 1997, p. 5)

I argue that Chicana researchers have unique viewpoints that can provide us with a perspective I call "cultural intuition." A Chicana researcher's cultural intuition is similar in concept to Strauss and Corbin's (1990) "theoretical sensitivity"—a personal quality of the researcher based on the attribute of having the ability to give meaning to data. Their construct of theoretical sensitivity indicates an understanding of the subtle meanings of data, and that "one can come to the research situation with varying degrees of sensitivity depending on one's previous reading and experience with or relevant to the data" (p. 41). They argue that theoretical sensitivity actually comes from four major sources: one's personal experience, the existing literature, one's professional experience, and the analytical research process itself. Having outlined in the last section important characteristics of a Chicana feminist epistemology, I propose that these four sources contribute to Chicana researchers' cultural intuition and are the foundation of a Chicana feminist epistemology in educational research. However, my concept of cultural intuition is different from theoretical sensitivity because it extends one's personal experience to include collective experience and community memory, and points to the importance of participants' engaging in the analysis of data. In the next sections, I briefly describe the four sources and how each contributes to my cultural intuition as a Chicana researcher. The sources do not include all possibilities, yet they provide a framework that facilitates an understanding of cultural intuition and therefore a Chicana feminist epistemology in educational research. My hope is that this framework helps demonstrate what forces shape a Chicana feminist epistemology without limiting the nuances that must be addressed in future work.

Personal Experience

First, one's personal experience represents a very important source of cultural intuition and is derived from the background that we each bring to the research situation. As many feminists contend, the researcher is a subject in her research and her personal history is part of the analytical process (Maynard, 1994; Stanley & Wise, 1993). Through past life experiences, individuals acquire an understanding of certain situations and why and what might happen in a particular setting under certain conditions. This often implicit knowledge helps us to understand events, actions, and words, and to do so more confidently than if one did not bring these particular life experiences into the research (Strauss & Corbin, 1990). For example, my life experiences as a Chicana, a student, and a participant in protest politics such as campus and community demonstrations and boycotts helped me to understand and analyze my data. The oral histories I collected in my study of Chicana student activists (Delgado Bernal, 1997) were not heard as merely random stories, but as testimonies of authority, preemption, and strength that demonstrate women's participation and leadership in school resistance. In other words, my personal experiences provided insight and a cultural intuition from which to draw upon during my research.

However, personal experience does not operate in a vacuum. To extend Strauss and Corbin's (1990) notion of personal experience, I argue that personal experience goes beyond the individual and has lateral ties to family and reverse ties to the past. Personal experience is partially shaped by collective experience and community memory, and as Marmon Silko (1996) states, "an individual's identity will extend from the identity constructed around the family" (p. 52). Through the experiences of ancestors and elders, Chicanas and Chicanos carry knowledge of conquest, loss of land, school and social segregation, labor market stratification, assimilation, and resistance. Community knowledge is taught to youth through legends, corridos,[5] storytelling, behavior, and most recently through the scholarship in the field of Chicana and Chicano Studies. As a child, my own family experience included learning through my grandmothers' stories, which were sprinkled with religion and mysticism, and my father's stories about the urban challenges of his childhood. As an adult, I began interviewing and recording the stories and knowledge that my family members shared with me. This knowledge that is passed from one generation to the next can help us survive in everyday life by providing an understanding of certain situations and explanations about why things happen under certain conditions. Sara Lawrence-Lightfoot (1994) discusses the unique knowledge that comes from the intertwinement of collective experience and intuition in African American communities:

> The development of this understanding is not rational—it comes from "the gut"; it is based on experience and intuition. There is the idea that this suspicion is passed down from the ancestors who teach the next generation the subtle dangers—through act and deed—who instruct their offspring in how to walk through treacherous minefields, who show them jungle posture. (p. 60)

Lawrence-Lightfoot writes of the "ancestral wisdom" that is taught from one generation to the next, and calls it "a powerful piece of our legacy" that is "healthy" and "necessary for survival." Likewise, Marmon Silko (1996) writes of how the Pueblo people have depended on the collective memory of many generations "to maintain and transmit an entire culture, a worldview complete with proven strategies for survival" (p. 30). For Chicana researchers, ancestral wisdom, community memory, and intuition influence one's own personal experiences. And it is personal experience that provides one source of cultural intuition from which to draw upon during research.

Existing Literature

Another source of cultural intuition is the existing literature on a topic. Technical literature includes research studies and theoretical or philosophical writings, while nontechnical literature refers to biographies, public documents, personal documents, and cultural studies writings (Strauss & Corbin, 1990). Having an understanding of this information provides some insight into what is going on with the events and circumstances we are studying. The technical literature may be used to stimulate theoretical sensitivity by providing concepts and relationships that are checked against actual data. For example, in my study of Chicana student activists, my readings of endarkened feminist theories, school resistance theories, and the socio-historical politics of Chicano schooling offered me a particular cultural intuition into the phenomenon I was studying by providing possible ways of approaching and interpreting data. My readings of descriptive materials, such as newspaper articles, also enhanced my cultural intuition by making me sensitive to what to look for in my data and helping me generate interview questions.

Professional Experience

One's professional experience can be yet another source of cultural intuition. Years of practice in a particular field often provides an insider view of how things work in that field (Strauss & Corbin, 1990). This knowledge, whether explicit or implicit, is taken into the research and helps one to understand differently than if one did not have this experience. My experiences as a bilingual teacher, a teacher educator, and my work with education programs in Latino community-based organizations have all contributed to the way I understand and analyze my data in educational research on Chicana students. Indeed,

Strauss and Corbin (1990) would argue that due to my professional experience I can move into the educational environment and gain insight into the lives of Chicana students more quickly than someone who has never worked in a school setting with Chicana students: "The more professional experience, the richer the knowledge base and insight available to draw upon in the research" (p. 42).

Analytical Research Process

Finally, the analytical research process itself provides an additional source of cultural intuition: "Insight and understanding about a phenomenon increase as you interact with your data" (Strauss & Corbin, 1990, p. 43). This comes from making comparisons, asking additional questions, thinking about what you are hearing and seeing, sorting data, developing a coding scheme, and engaging in concept formation. As one idea leads to another, we are able to look more closely at the data and bring meaning to the research. For example, in my study of Chicana student activists, my increased awareness of concepts, meanings, and relationships were influenced by my interaction with the interview data (e.g., transcribing, reading transcriptions, listening to taped interviews, and coding interviews). In addition, my awareness was also increased by including the women I interviewed in the analytical process of making sense of the data.

Extending Strauss and Corbin's analytical research process, I suggest that including Chicana participants in an interactive process of data analysis contributes to the researcher's cultural intuition. Pizarro (1998) calls for "a new methodological approach to research in Chicana/o communities" (p. 57) that includes participants as equals at all stages of the research. "This requires that researchers and participants deconstruct the epistemology of the participants and use it as the basis for the entire project" (p. 74). In the latter half of this article, I describe in detail how using a focus group strategy allowed me to incorporate the epistemological perspectives of the Chicanas I interviewed. This process allowed me to go beyond a simple feedback loop, and bring meaning to the data based on an interactive process.

Of course, researchers must be careful to not let any of the four sources block them from seeing the obvious or assume everyone's personal and professional experiences are equal to theirs. Early in my research, I learned that the women in my study were very diverse and the life experiences they shared with each other were very different from my own personal experiences. For example, all eight of these women shared the following similarities: they were second- or third-generation Chicanas, first-generation college students, grew up in working-class neighborhoods on the east side of Los Angeles, and were student activists in 1968. As a third-generation Chicana and first-generation college student, I grew up in the suburbs of Kansas City, was in preschool in 1968, and was not introduced to political activism until my early twenties. Therefore, my personal experiences did not automatically designate me an "insider." I, like any researcher, had to be concerned with how I was approaching and interpreting my subject's stories of activism. As hooks (1989) states, we have to consider the purpose and use of our research:

> When we write about the experiences of a group to which we do not belong, we should think about the ethics of our action, considering whether or not our work will be used to reinforce and perpetuate domination. (p. 43)

While I do not argue for an essentialist notion of who is capable of conducting research with various populations based on personal experiences, I do believe that many Chicana scholars achieve a sense of cultural intuition that is different from that of other scholars. Sofía Villenas (1996) indirectly addresses this issue as she examines her own emerging and changing identity as a Chicana researcher. In doing so, she asks what constitutes an insider to a community of research participants and asserts that it is based on "collective experiences and a collective space" at multiple levels, rather than on a singular identity (p. 722). Villenas explains how her practice in the field as a Chicana educational ethnographer cannot be explicated in the same manner as White, middle-class researchers' relationships with their research participants. She therefore argues for a process by which Chicanas "become the subjects and the creators of knowledge" (p. 730), essentially advocating for the use of a Chicana feminist epistemology in educational research.

Likewise, Dillard (1997) speaks of cultural intuition in her discussion of theoretical and conceptual standpoints of Black women educational researchers. She poses that the insights from being and living as African American researchers opens up possibilities for the research community to see phenomena in new ways. She views these standpoints of Black women as achieved rather than inherent in one's singular identity:

> While we will argue vehemently that Black women as a cultural group "theorize" and embody extensive life experiences which, while diverse, shape a coherent body, what we advance here is the notion that, in educational research, such theoretical and conceptual standpoints are achieved; they are not inherent in one's race, class, sex, or other identities. (pp. 5–6)

A Chicana researcher's cultural intuition is achieved and can be nurtured through our personal experiences (which are influenced by ancestral wisdom, community memory, and intuition), the literature on and about Chicanas, our professional experiences, and the analytical process we engage in when we are in a central position of our research and our analysis. Thus, cultural intuition is a complex process that is experiential, intuitive, historical, personal, collective, and dynamic.

Having defined cultural intuition and a Chicana feminist epistemology, I now attempt to illustrate what these concepts mean in educational research. In order to provide a concrete example of this conceptual discussion, the next section describes a research project I worked on over several years. As

I describe the oral history project, it is important to point out that I only became attentive to my own cultural intuition and the epistemology I brought to the research after I completed the project and had time to reflect on the research process. Though my theoretical framework was shaped by the school resistance theories in the sociology of education literature and interdisciplinary critical feminist theories, my self-reflections have allowed me to (re)interpret my epistemological framework from a Chicana feminist standpoint.[6] I now realize that the way I asked my research questions, designed the methodology, collected the data, and arrived at conclusions was greatly influenced by my cultural intuition. Even where the individual and focus group interviews were held, and my need to include the women in the data analysis process was unknowingly driven by a shared epistemology we all brought to the research. Therefore, it was both my cultural intuition and my epistemological orientation that served to resist dominant epistemologies and recover an ignored history of Chicana students.

RESISTANCE AND RECOVERY THROUGH AN ORAL HISTORY RESEARCH PROJECT

In 1968, people witnessed a worldwide rise in student movements in countries such as France, Italy, Mexico, and the United States. In March of that year, over ten thousand students walked out of schools in East Los Angeles to protest the inferior quality of their education. The event, which came to be known as the East L.A. Blowouts, focused national attention on the K–12 schooling of Chicanas and Chicanos and also set a precedent for school boycotts throughout the Southwest (Acuña, 1988). Though their stories are often excluded in written historical accounts, my research demonstrates that Chicanas played crucial leadership roles in these mass demonstrations and were intimately involved in the struggles for educational justice. As an educational researcher and a Chicana, I was interested in the women's voices and their unique experiences that had previously been omitted from the diverse accounts of the Blowouts. My historical-sociological case study, informed by my own achieved cultural intuition and a Chicana feminist epistemology, posed the following research question: How does pivoting the analysis onto key Chicana participants provide an alternative history of the 1968 Blowouts? This research question itself is distinctively Chicana, especially when compared to previous research that has examined the Blowouts. Chicano and White males have studied the event from a perspective of protest politics (Puckett, 1971), a spontaneous mass protest (Negrete, 1972), internal colonialism (Muñoz, 1973), the Chicano student movement (Gómez-Quiñones, 1978), and a political and social development of the wider Chicano movement (Rosen, 1973). Indeed, none of their historical accounts locate Chicanas in a central position in the research or address the many factors that restricted or enabled Chicana students to participate. My study, in contrast, examined how women interpret their participation in the Blowouts nearly thirty years later, and how their participation is important to an understanding of transformational resistance, grassroots leadership, and an alternative history of the Blowouts (Delgado Bernal, 1997, 1998).

To gain new perspectives and interpretations of the 1968 Blowouts and Chicana school resistance, my primary methods of data collection were in-depth, semistructured oral history interviews with eight key female participants from the Blowouts, a two-hour semistructured focus group interview, and phone interviews. Following a network sampling procedure (Gándara, 1995), I interviewed eight women who were identified by other female participants or resource individuals as "key participants" or "leaders" in the Blowouts. In scheduling these interviews, I allowed ample time, realizing that the length of each interview would vary. The interviews took place when and where it was most convenient for each woman—in their homes, their mother's home, or at work. I created an interview protocol with open-ended questions in order to elicit multiple levels of data that would address my research questions. Though the interview protocol was used as a guide, I realized that as the women spoke of very personal experiences, a less-structured approach allowed their voices and ways of knowing to come forth. I also asked probing questions to follow up on responses that were unclear or possibly incomplete in order to understand how the women interpreted the reasons and ways in which they participated in the Blowouts.

The oral histories were not merely heard as random stories, but as testimonies of authority, preemption, and strength that demonstrate women's participation and leadership in school resistance. My life experiences as a Chicana provided a source of cultural intuition that helped me both to listen to and to hear the interviewees. For example, in six of the eight individual interviews, religion was discussed in terms of Catholic values, contradictions of Catholicism, or spirituality. I understood Rosalinda Méndez González's feelings of disillusionment and betrayal when she passionately talked to me about the contradictions of her Catholic upbringing and the influence it had on her activism. Having been exposed to these contradictions myself, and still identifying as a "cultural Catholic" (Medina, 1998), I heard her story as a very personal one. She remembers:

> And then from my Catholic upbringing we were taught about compassion and charity, and how Jesus healed the ill and took care of the poor, and all of that. . . . And I go to college and find out that every religion in the world claims the same thing, that they're all the only true one, and that all of them have committed atrocities in the name of God, in the name of their religion, that the Catholic church tortured people and killed people in the name of God. (Interview with author)

After conducting individual oral history interviews, I corresponded with each woman twice. The first time I sent a complete copy of the interview transcript with a letter describing their role in the analysis of the data. The following is a portion of that letter:

I've decided to send transcriptions back to the women I've interviewed so that you each have a chance to see my initial interpretation. I believe it's important that you have an opportunity to reflect and respond to what you said in the interview. This will not only strengthen my analysis, but it allows each woman to interact with and "dialogue" with her own interview. The interview transcription with comments and questions in the margins is the one I'd like for you to review. These comments and questions are specific to areas that I'm curious or not quite clear about (that is, other women commented on the same issue, or I've since thought of a related issue). If possible I'd love for you to respond in writing on the transcription and/or a separate page. Please bring this copy and your comments with you to the focus group interview. At that time, we can further address any areas you'd like to elaborate on or additional questions I may have. The second clean copy is for you to hold on to—an interesting keepsake.

Closer to our meeting, I wrote the women informing them where we would be holding the group interview and the agenda for our meeting. Here is a portion of that letter:

Well, the date of our group interview is drawing near and I wanted to send you this update. On Saturday, February 17th we will hold our event in East Los Angeles' Self-Help Graphics from 4:00 to 7:00 p.m. Tomás Benitez, assistant director of Self-Help (and Mita Cuaron's husband) was able to secure space for us in the art gallery. The art gallery will be particularly special given the beautiful exhibit, La Vida Indigena, and the fact that the interview will be filmed. . . .

The agenda for the actual group interview will follow a semi-structured format. That is, based on your responses in the individual interviews, I will identify a few topics I would like to ask the group to respond to. In addition, I would also like each of you to bring up any blowout-related issues or events that are particularly interesting to you. . . . I'm not as interested in reconstructing the "Truth" of what happened as I am interested in your individual experiences and their similarities and differences.

When we met for the two-hour focus group, all but one of the women had read and reflected on their transcripts prior to the group meeting, and three of them returned their transcript with responses to my queries actually written in the margins. Their comments ranged from yes/no responses and name spelling corrections to several emotional sentences elaborating on their activism and a paragraph explaining why someone considered herself a leader. The written reflections were of course helpful to my analysis, as they provided me with additional information and clarified specific points from the individual interviews. The impact of the written reflections, however, was small in comparison to the lessons I gained from the subsequent group dialogue. My real interest in conducting a focus group interview was to incorporate the explicit use of group interaction to produce data and insights that might have been less accessible otherwise (Krueger, 1988).

I now realize that the focus group process seemed natural to me partially because of the cultural intuition I brought to the research project. I was used to my grandmothers' storytelling in which absolute "Truth" was less important to me than hearing and recording their life experiences. It was my familiarity with and respect for ancestral wisdom taught from one generation to the next and a regard for collective knowledge that allowed me to approach the research project with complete respect for each woman's testimony of school resistance. Indeed, the women shared their community knowledge through a form of storytelling in which all the women talked about their resistance by invoking stories about their families, quoting their parents, and mentioning where their parents were born. To make a point about democratic ideals and the right to question authority, Rosalinda contrasted her upbringing and socialization with that of her mother's a generation earlier:

> I remember when I was a kid growing up in Texas and going to school and being taught these things about democracy and how different my response was from my mother's response. My mother was born and raised in Mexico, in Chihuahua. And if you spoke up against the government, the next day your body would be found. . . . And she was terrified of standing up for her rights or speaking against any authority figure, and that included teachers. (Unpublished focus group data)

The interaction among the participants also produced new information and differing viewpoints. For instance, several women were reminded of something based on another woman's recollections and made comments such as, "I was listening to Mita talk and I hadn't thought about it till right now . . .". The group interaction also allowed them to compare and contrast their experiences with each other. Three of the women come from politically progressive families who had been concerned with justice struggles for many years, and one of them stated, "I was born into this family of struggle, protest, rebellion, [and] . . . equal rights." In contrast, the other women spoke of coming from a more "traditional family." Whatever their personal family experiences were, they all agreed that during the time of their activism there was a knowledge or "gospel" in Mexican homes in East Los Angeles that did not question the Church or schoolteachers' absolute authority: "The church, whatever they say and the teachers, whatever they say." The women's interactions were a form of storytelling in which they were able to compare and contrast their memories and experiences. Their group dialogue also provided me with invaluable lessons in relation to the data analysis process.

LESSONS FROM THE FOCUS GROUP

Prior to the focus group interview, I sorted data by integrating key themes that emerged from the women's individual oral histories with the existing literature. During the focus group, I presented four themes related to the women's school resistance and asked them to respond to my preliminary interpretations of how these themes shaped their student activism: dual identity, patriotism,

310

dimensions of leadership, and awareness/agency. Presenting my preliminary findings to the women was one way of including their knowledge and a means of avoiding "authenticity of interpretation and description under the guise of authority" (Villenas, 1996, p. 713). Indeed, my cultural intuition and the women's knowledge helped shape my final analysis.

For example, I was originally attempting to interpret the women's behavior within the common duality of "good girl" and "bad girl" discussed and critiqued by a number of Chicana authors (Anzaldúa, 1987; Castillo, 1995; Hurtado, 1996; Trujillo, 1993). These imposed constructions of Chicanas' identity are couched in women's sexuality and in what is perceived as acceptable and unacceptable behavior. The two polarized roles of Virgin Mary and whore exemplify the ultimate "good girl" and "bad girl." Aida Hurtado (1996) states that these are "social locations that are given cultural space to exist" (p. 50). During the individual interviews the women talked about their "good schoolgirl" behavior in terms of being "college-bound," "real straightlaced," "a star student," "head cheerleader," and in the "goody-goody camp." Yet in the same breath they discussed their very bold resistant behavior that was considered "bad activist student" behavior and deviant by most of society. The women wrote articles for community activist newspapers regarding the poor conditions in their schools, stood up to accusations of being communists, provided testimony about the inferior quality of their education to the U.S. Commission on Civil Rights, and were arrested by police and expelled from school because of their activism. Because shifting from "deviant (and therefore defiant) locations . . . to culturally sanctioned locations is . . . difficult" (Hurtado, 1996, p. 50), I was interested in how they were able to move between these social locations. Therefore, I asked the women how the social, cultural, and sexual realities of their lives were manifested in the duality of "good schoolgirl" and "bad activist student."

The women expressed a belief that my preliminary analysis was slightly off target. In fact, they believed that rather than moving between these two social locations, they were engaging in the same type of behaviors as "good schoolgirls" and as "bad activist students." It was the perceptions of their behaviors that changed. Their good schoolgirl behavior of speaking up in class, asking questions, and offering leadership to sanctioned student organizations was acceptable behavior (and even encouraged). However, when they practiced these same behaviors during the school boycotts, they were perceived as deviant. Their behavior had not changed—others' interpretation of their behavior had. In other words, they helped me to see that their "good schoolgirl" behavior that was so openly rewarded by good grades, student council positions, and respect from teachers was the exact same behavior that was unfairly punished when they used it to protest the inferior quality of their education. Their insight contributed to my reorganization of themes and altered my preliminary analysis.

In another case, the women confirmed my preliminary analysis regarding the complexity of gender's influence on their different dimensions of leadership. For example, during the oral history interviews, women made statements ranging from "Nobody ever said that you couldn't do this because you were a girl" to "I know that the females were not the leaders," and from "Being a female was not an issue, it was just a non-issue" to "I'm sure I knew that there was sexism involved . . . but we probably didn't talk about it." During the focus group interview the influence of gender continued to be perceived in a somewhat nebulous way. The diversity of statements found within interviews, between interviews, and at the focus group interview led me to conclude that there was no one distinct and precise viewpoint on gender's influence. Rather, the women's individual and collective thoughts on gender represent the indeterminate and complex influence of gender within a structure of patriarchy—a system of domination and unequal stratification based on gender.

Including these women in the analytical process of making sense of the data helped shape my research findings and was an important source of my own cultural intuition. Just as importantly, their participation in this process made them not just subjects of research, but also creators of knowledge—an important characteristic of a Chicana feminist epistemology. Thus, contrary to patriarchal historical accounts of the 1968 East L.A. School Blowouts, a Chicana feminist standpoint exposes human relationships and experiences that were previously invisible.

CONCLUSION

> The issue of subjectivity represents a realization of the fact that who we are, how we act, what we think, and what stories we tell become more intelligible within an epistemological framework that begins by recognizing existing hegemonic histories. . . . [Thus], uncovering and reclaiming of subjugated knowledges is one way to lay claim to alternative histories. (Mohanty, 1994, p. 148)

How educational research is conducted significantly contributes to what and whose history, community, and knowledge is legitimated. A Chicana feminist epistemology addresses the failure of traditional research paradigms that have distorted or omitted the history and knowledge of Chicanas. Though similar endarkened feminist epistemologies exist in specific segments of women's studies and ethnic studies, acknowledging a Chicana feminist epistemology in educational research is virtually unprecedented. And yet, a disproportionate number of all Chicana and Chicano Ph.D.s receive their doctoral degrees in the field of education (Solorzano, 1995). Without an articulated Chicana epistemology or an acknowledgment of cultural intuition within the field of education, these scholars are restricted by cultural hegemonic domination in educational research.

Therefore, one of the major contributions of this article is an emerging articulation of a new epistemology in educational research. This epistemology gives license to both Chicana and Chicano education scholars to uncover and reclaim their own subjugated knowledge. It also allows them to place some trust in their own cultural intuition so that they move beyond traditional areas of research situated in existing paradigms that overlook the particular educational experiences of Chicanas or Chicanos. To illustrate this point, consider the experience of Chicano scholar Octavio Villalpando when he conducted his doctoral dissertation research. Villalpando's (1996) investigation yielded very significant quantitative evidence demonstrating that Chicana and Chicano college students benefit substantially from affiliating primarily with other Chicanas and Chicanos during college. These benefits were particularly noteworthy for Chicano students, spanning a range of several important post-college outcomes. Although these are significant findings in the field of higher education, they could not be completely explained by preexisting higher education paradigms. Villalpando's analysis might have been taken further had he been able to access his cultural intuition (Villalpando, personal communication, 1998). A Chicana feminist epistemology gives Chicana and Chicano education scholars some freedom to interpret their research findings outside of existing paradigms, and hopefully develop and propose policies and practices that better meet the needs of Chicanas and Chicanos.

Given the significant and growing Chicana and Chicano student population, particularly in the Southwest, it certainly is not my intent to suggest an end to all educational research on Chicanas that is not conducted by Chicana scholars. Indeed, I hope that others will read this article and think about their own epistemological framework and that of the Chicana and Chicano communities they research. Borrowing from a Chicana epistemology may help all scholars to raise more appropriate research questions and avoid asking questions based on a cultural deficit model or incorrect stereotypes. Chicana sociologist Mary Pardo (1998) provides an insightful example of a White woman colleague who asked an inappropriate question based on stereotypes rather than the knowledge base of the East Los Angeles Chicanas she was reporting on. During Pardo's research, she and her colleague were having a meal with women from Mothers of East Los Angeles (MELA), a group of working-class community activists. Her colleague asked the group how they might mobilize around a hypothetical case of false imprisonment of an alleged youth gang member. Pardo describes why silence engulfed the room:

> Her question about the alleged gang member reflected the media assumption that gang activity constituted the most significant problem facing Eastside Los Angeles residents. But the women from MELA were long-time, stable home owners, most of whose children had already graduated from college. They had . . . directed collective efforts at getting summer jobs for youth. . . . Rebuilding a neighborhood park and opposing the prison and toxic-waste incinerator consumed most of their time. (p. 12)

A new epistemological approach in educational research has the potential to avoid these type of inappropriate questions and focus on questions that may expose important school issues and community experiences that are otherwise not visible.

A major tenet of cultural intuition and a Chicana feminist epistemology is the inclusion of Chicana research participants in the analysis of data. This allows Chicana participants—whether they are students, parents, teachers, or school administrators—to be speaking subjects who take part in producing and validating knowledge. A focus group interview is one data collection strategy that helps Chicana scholars and non-Chicana scholars include the epistemology of their research participants in the analysis of data. The example I provide in this article demonstrates how focus groups can be paired with an oral history methodology to include Chicana participants in the interpretation of data. In addition, it seems that focus groups can be effectively used with other qualitative and quantitative research methods and methodologies such as school ethnography, student interviews, survey research, and classroom observations. In the future, we must look for additional strategies that provide opportunities for Chicanas and Chicanos to participate in the construction of knowledge and research that is dedicated to achieving social justice. Hopefully, "an analysis of the Chicana/o experience can . . . assist us in forging a new epistemological approach to academic life and can help us uncover a methodology that is true to and helpful in the struggle of these people as it 'creates' a new knowledge base" (Pizarro, 1998, p. 72).

NOTES

1. "Chicana" is a cultural and political identity composed of multiple layers and is often an identity of resistance that we consciously adopt later in life. "Chicana is not a name that women (or men) are born to or with, as is often the case with 'Mexican,' but rather it is consciously and critically assumed and serves as a point of redeparture for dismantling historical conjunctures of crisis, confusion, political and ideological conflict . . ." (Alarcón, 1990, p. 250). The term *Chicana* is used to discuss women of Mexican origin and/or women who identify with this label. While many of the issues addressed in this article apply to Chicano males and other Latinas and Latinos, the focus here is on Chicanas.
2. Cynthia Dillard (1997) proposes that "endarkened feminist ideology described as inherently cultural, positional, political, strategic, relational, and transformative is offered as possible criteria and catalyst for future educational research. In contrast to our common use of the term 'enlightening' as a way of expressing the having of new and important insights, we use the term endarkening to suggest epistemological roots of Black feminist thought which embody a distinguishable difference in cultural standpoint" (pp. 3–4). I use endarkened in a similar way, and include not only Black feminist thought, but the feminist thought of all women of color.
3. In this study, school resistance was defined as students' acknowledging problems in oppressive educational settings and demanding changes.
4. Proposition 227 requires that "all children in California public schools shall be taught English by being taught in English." This requirement counters educational research that demonstrates that English immersion is one of the least effective ways to teach the English language to children with limited English proficiency. The proposition also

requires local schools to place students in English immersion classrooms for up to one year, based on their degree of English proficiency (Article 2). Parental exception waivers for the English immersion requirement may only be granted to parents who personally visit the school to apply and whose children meet certain requirements, including children who already know English, are over ten years old, or have special needs (Article 3).

5. The *corrido* is a Mexican ballad and is one means of oral tradition in which history and culture are preserved and shared through song. Corridos often tell stories of the struggles and resistance of Mexican people.

6. My self-reflections have been greatly influenced by earlier and recent Chicana scholars and writers. Unfortunately, much of the early work by Chicanas is difficult to find and has often gone unrecognized—indicative of the Eurocentric culture of academia. In the 1980s there was a reemergence of Chicana scholarship that not only repositioned class and ethnicity in relationship to gender, but also addressed the many aspects of sexuality. In the last few years the work of several progressive Chicana scholars has been particularly influential in helping me develop an articulation of Chicana feminist epistemology in educational research (Castillo, 1995; de la Torre & Pesquera, 1993; Hurtado, 1996; Pardo, 1998; Ruiz, 1998; Trujillo, 1998).

REFERENCES

Acuña, R. (1988). *Occupied America: A history of Chicanos.* New York: HarperCollins.

Alarcón, N. (1990). Chicana feminism: In the tracks of "the" native woman. *Cultural Studies, 4,* 248–256.

Alarcón, N., Castro, R., Pérez, E., Pesquera, B., Sosa-Riddell, A., & Zavella, P. (Eds.). (1993). *Chicana critical issues.* Berkeley: Third Woman Press.

Anzaldúa, G. (1987). *Borderlands, la frontera: The new mestiza.* San Francisco: Aunt Lute Books.

Bowles, S., & Gintis, H. (1976). *Schooling in capitalist America.* New York: Basic Books.

Castañeda, A. (1993). Sexual violence in the politics and policies of conquest: Amerindian women and the Spanish conquest of Alta California. In A. de la Torre & B. Pesquera (Eds.), *Building with our hands: New directions in Chicano studies* (pp. 15–33). Berkeley: University of California Press.

Castillo, A. (1995). *Massacre of the dreamers: Essays on Xicanisma.* New York: Plume.

Collins, P. H. (1986). Learning from the outsider within: The sociological significance of Black feminist thought. *Social Problems, 33*(6), S14–S32.

Collins, P. H. (1991). *Black feminist thought: Knowledge, consciousness, and the politics of empowerment.* New York: Routledge.

Cook-Lynn, E. (1996). *Why I can't read Wallace Stegner and other essays: A tribal voice.* Madison: University of Wisconsin Press.

Cuádraz, G. (1996). Experiences of multiple marginality: A case study of "Chicana scholarship women." In C. Turner, M. García, A. Nora, & L. Rendón (Eds.), *Racial and ethnic diversity in higher education* (pp. 210–222). New York: Simon & Schuster.

de la Torre, A., & Pesquera, B. (Eds.). (1993). *Building with our hands: New directions in Chicana studies.* Berkeley: University of California Press.

Delgado Bernal, D. (1997). *Chicana school resistance and grassroots leadership: Providing an alternative history of the 1968 East Los Angeles blowouts.* Doctoral dissertation, University of California, Los Angeles.

Delgado Bernal, D. (1998). Grassroots leadership reconceptualized: Chicana oral histories and the 1968 East Los Angeles school blowouts. *Frontiers: A Journal of Women Studies, 19*(2), 113–142.

Delgado Bernal, D. (1999). Chicana/o education from the civil rights era to the present. In J. F. Moreno (Ed.), *The elusive quest for equality: 150 years of Chicano/Chicana education.* Cambridge, MA: Harvard Educational Review.

Delgado-Gaitan, C. (1993). Researching change and changing the researcher. *Harvard Educational Review, 63,* 389–411.

Dillard, C. B. (1997, April). *The substance of things hoped for, the evidence of things not seen: Toward an endarkened feminist ideology in research.* Paper presented at the annual meeting of the American Educational Research Association, Chicago.

Fine, M. (1994). Working the hyphens: Reinventing self and other in qualitative research. In N. Denzin & Y. Lincoln (Eds.), *Handbook of qualitative research* (pp. 70–82). Thousand Oaks, CA: Sage.

Flores-Ortiz, E. (1998). Voices from the couch: The co-creation of a Chicana psychology. In C. Trujillo (Ed.), *Living Chicana theory* (pp. 102–122). Berkeley: Third Woman Press.

Flores-Ortiz, Y. (1991). Levels of acculturation, marital satisfaction, and depression among Chicana workers: A psychological perspective. *Aztlán, 20*(1/2), 151–175.

Flores-Ortiz, Y. (1993). La mujer y la violencia: A culturally based model for the understanding and treatment of domestic violence in Chicana/Latina communities. In N. Alarcón et al. (Eds.), *Chicana critical issues* (pp. 169–182). Berkeley: Third Woman Press.

Gándara, P. (1982). Passing through the eye of the needle: High-achieving Chicanas. *Hispanic Behavioral Sciences, 4,* 167–179.

Gándara, P. (1995). *Over the ivy walls: The educational mobility of low-income Chicanos.* Albany: State University of New York Press.

Giroux, H. A. (1992). *Border crossings: Cultural workers and the politics of education.* New York: Routledge.

Gómez-Quiñones, J. (1978). *Mexican students por La Raza: The Chicano student movement in Southern California 1967–1977.* Santa Barbara, CA: Editorial La Causa.

Harding, S. (Ed.). (1987). Feminism and methodology. Milton Keynes, Eng.: Open University Press.

Hernández-Avila, I. (1995). Relocations upon relocations: Home, language, and Native American women's writings. *American Indian Quarterly, 19,* 491–507.

hooks, b. (1989). *Talking back: Thinking feminist, thinking Black.* Boston: South End Press.

Hurtado, A. (1989). Relating to privilege: Seduction and rejection in the subordination of White women and women of color. *Signs: Journal of Women in Culture and Society, 14,* 833–855.

Hurtado, A. (1996). *The color of privilege: Three blasphemies on race and feminism.* Ann Arbor: University of Michigan Press.

Kelly, L. (1988). *Surviving sexual violence.* Cambridge, Eng.: Polity Press.

Kelly, L., Burton, S., & Regan, L. (1994). Researching women's lives or studying women's oppression? Reflections on what constitutes feminist research. In M. Maynard & J. Purvis (Eds.), *Researching women's lives from a feminist perspective* (pp. 27–48). Bristol, PA: Taylor & Francis.

Krueger, R. A. (1988). *Focus groups: A practical guide for applied research.* Newbury Park, CA: Sage.

Lather, P. (1991). *Getting smart: Feminist research and pedagogy with/in the postmodern.* New York: Routledge.

Lawrence-Lightfoot, S. (1994). *I've known rivers: Lives of loss and liberation.* New York: Penguin Books.

MacLeod, J. (1987). *Ain't no makin' it: Leveled aspirations in a low-income neighborhood.* Boulder, CO: Westview Press.

Marmon Silko, L. (1996). *Yellow woman and a beauty of the spirit: Essays on Native American life today.* New York: Touchstone.

Maynard, M. (1994). Methods, practice and epistemology: The debate about feminism and research. In M. Maynard & J. Purvis (Eds.), *Researching women's lives from a feminist perspective* (pp. 10–26). Bristol, PA: Taylor & Francis.

Medina, L. (1998). Los espíritus siguen hablando: Chicana spiritualities. In C. Trujillo (Ed.), *Living Chicana theory* (pp. 189–213). Berkeley: Third Woman Press.

Mohanty, C. T. (1994). On race and voice: Challenges for liberal education in the 1990's. In H. A. Giroux & P. McLaren (Eds.), *Between borders: Pedagogy and the politics of cultural studies* (pp. 145–166). New York: Routledge.

Mora, M., & Del Castillo, A. R. (Eds.). (1980). *Mexican women in the United States: Struggles past and present.* Los Angeles: University of California, Los Angeles, Chicano Studies Research Center.

Muñoz, C., Jr. (1973). *The politics of Chicano urban protest: A model of political analysis.* Unpublished doctoral dissertation, Claremont Graduate School.

Negrete, L. R. (1972). Culture clash: The utility of mass protest as a political response. *Journal of Comparative Cultures, 1,* 25–36.

Pardo, M. (1990). Mexican American women grassroots community activists: "Mothers of East Los Angeles." *Frontiers: A Journal of Women Studies, 11,* 1–7.

Pardo, M. (1998). *Mexican American women activists: Identity and resistance in two Los Angeles communities.* Philadelphia: Temple University Press.

Pérez, E. (1993). Speaking from the margin: Uninvited discourse on sexuality and power. In A. de la Torre & B. Pesquera (Eds.), *Building with our hands: New directions in Chicana studies* (pp. 57–71). Berkeley: University of California Press.

Pesquera, B. M., & Segura, D. A. (1990). *Feminism in the ranks: Political consciousness and Chicana/Latina white collar workers.* Paper presented at the annual meeting of the National Association for Chicana and Chicano Studies, Albuquerque, NM.

Pesquera, B. M., & Segura, D. A. (1993). There is no going back: Chicanas and feminism. In N. Alarcón et al. (Eds.), *Chicana critical issues* (pp. 95–115). Berkeley: Third Woman Press.

Piaget, J. (1952). *The origins of intelligence in children.* New York: International Universities Press.

Piaget, J. (1954). *The construction of reality in the child.* New York: Basic Books.

Pizarro, M. (1998). "Chicana/o Power!" Epistemology and methodology for social justice and empowerment in Chicana/o communities. *International Journal of Qualitative Studies in Education, 11*(1), 57–80.

Puckett, M. (1971). *Protest politics in education: A case study in the Los Angeles Unified School District.* Unpublished doctoral dissertation, Claremont Graduate School.

Romero, M. (1989). Twice protected? Assessing the impact of affirmative action on Mexican American women. *Journal of Hispanic Policy, 3,* 83–101.

Rosen, G. (1973). The development of the Chicano movement in Los Angeles from 1967–1969. *Aztlán, 4,* 155–183.

Ruiz, V. (1998). *From out of the shadows: Mexican women in twentieth-century America.* Oxford, Eng.: Oxford University Press.

Sandoval, C. (1998). Mestizaje as method: Feminists of color challenge the canon. In C. Trujillo (Ed.), *Living Chicana theory* (pp. 352–370). Berkeley: Third Woman Press.

Scheurich, J. J., & Young, M. D. (1997). Coloring epistemologies: Are our research epistemologies racially biased? *Educational Researcher, 26*(4), 4–16.

Segura, D. (1993). Slipping through the cracks: Dilemmas in Chicana education. In A. de la Torre & B. Pesquera (Eds.), *Building with our hands: New directions in Chicana studies* (pp. 199–216). Berkeley: University of California Press.

Soldatenko, M. A. (1991). Organizing Latina garment workers in Los Angeles. *Aztlán, 20*(1/2), 73–96.

Solorzano, D. G. (1995). The baccalaureate origins of Chicana and Chicano doctorates in the social sciences. *Hispanic Journal of Behavioral Science, 17*(1), 3–32.

Stanley, L., & Wise, S. (1993). *Breaking out again.* London: Routledge.

Strauss, A., & Corbin, J. (1990). *Basics of qualitative research: Grounded theory procedures and techniques.* Newbury Park, CA: Sage.

Talavera-Bustillos, V. (1998). *Chicana college choice and resistance: An exploratory study of first-generation Chicana college students.* Unpublished doctoral dissertation, University of California, Los Angeles.

Trujillo, C. (1993). Chicana lesbians: Fear and loathing in the Chicano community. In N. Alarcón et al. (Eds.), *Chicana critical issues* (pp. 117–125). Berkeley: Third Woman Press.

Trujillo, C. (1998). La Virgen de Guadalupe and her reconstruction in Chicana lesbian desire. In C. Trujillo (Ed.), *Living Chicana theory* (pp. 214–231). Berkeley: Third Woman Press.

Vásquez, M. (1982). Confronting barriers to the participation of Mexican American women in higher education. *Hispanic Journal of Behavioral Sciences, 4,* 147–165.

Villalpando, O. (1996). *The long term effects of college on Chicano and Chicana students: "Other oriented" values, service careers, and community involvement.* Unpublished doctoral dissertation, University of California, Los Angeles.

Villenas, S. (1996). The colonizer/colonized Chicana ethnographer: Identity marginalization, and co-optation in the field. *Harvard Educational Review, 66,* 711–731.

Willis, P. E. (1977). *Learning to labour: How working-class kids got working-class jobs.* Aldershot, Eng.: Gower.

Zambrana, R. (1994). Toward understanding the educational trajectory and socialization of Latina women. In L. Stone & G. M. Boldt (Eds.), *The education feminism reader* (pp. 135–145). New York: Routledge.

Zavella, P. (1993). The politics of race and gender: Organizing Chicana cannery workers in Northern California. In N. Alarcón et al. (Eds.), *Chicana critical issues* (pp. 127–153). Berkeley: Third Woman Press.

I am indebted to the many Chicana scholars, activists, writers, and artists who have influenced my (ongoing) epistemological journey and helped me to better understand my cultural intuition. I am particularly grateful to Adaljiza Sosa-Riddell, Daniel Solorzano, Octavio Villalpando, and Harvard Educational Review Editorial Board members Romina Carrillo and Matthew Hartley for their invaluable insights and suggestions on this article. I take responsibility for my interpretations and, because producing knowledge must be part of an ongoing conversation, I welcome comments and constructive criticism.

FREIRE AND A FEMINIST
PEDAGOGY OF DIFFERENCE

KATHLEEN WEILER

We are living in a period of profound challenges to traditional Western epistemology and political theory. These challenges, couched in the language of postmodernist theory and in postcolonialist critiques, reflect the rapid transformation of the economic and political structure of the world order: the impact of transnational capital; the ever more comprehensive integration of resources, labor, and markets; the pervasiveness of media and consumer images. This interdependent world system is based on the exploitation of oppressed groups, but the system at the same time calls forth oppositional cultural forms that give voice to the conditions of these groups. White male bourgeois dominance is being challenged by people of color, women, and other oppressed groups, who assert the validity of their own knowledge and demand social justice and equality in numerous political and cultural struggles. In the intellectual sphere, this shifting world system has led to a shattering of Western metanarratives and to the variety of stances of postmodernist and cultural-identity theory. A major theoretical challenge to traditional Western knowledge systems is emerging from feminist theory, which has been increasingly influenced by postmodernist and cultural-identity theory. Feminist theory, like other contemporary approaches, validates difference, challenges universal claims to truth, and seeks to create social transformation in a world of shifting and uncertain meanings.

In education, these profound shifts are evident on two levels: first, at the level of practice, as excluded and formerly silenced groups challenge dominant approaches to learning and to definitions of knowledge; and second, at the level of theory, as modernist claims to universal truth are called into question.[1] These challenges to accepted truths have been raised not only to the institutions and theories that defend the status quo, but also to the critical or liberatory pedagogies that emerged in the 1960s and 1970s. Feminist educa-

Harvard Educational Review   Vol. 61   No. 4   November 1991

tional critics, like other theorists influenced by postmodernism and theories of difference, want to retain the vision of social justice and transformation that underlies liberatory pedagogies, but they find that their claims to universal truths and their assumptions of a collective experience of oppression do not adequately address the realities of their own confusing and often tension-filled classrooms. This consciousness of the inadequacy of classical liberatory pedagogies has been particularly true for feminist educators, who are acutely aware of the continuing force of sexism and patriarchal structures and of the power of race, sexual preference, physical ability, and age to divide teachers from students and students from one another.

Paulo Freire is without question the most influential theorist of critical or liberatory education. His theories have profoundly influenced literacy programs throughout the world and what has come to be called critical pedagogy in the United States. His theoretical works, particularly *Pedagogy of the Oppressed,* provide classic statements of liberatory or critical pedagogy based on universal claims of truth.[2] Feminist pedagogy as it has developed in the United States provides a historically situated example of a critical pedagogy in practice. Feminist conceptions of education are similar to Freire's pedagogy in a variety of ways, and feminist educators often cite Freire as the educational theorist who comes closest to the approach and goals of feminist pedagogy.[3] Both feminist pedagogy as it is usually defined and Freirean pedagogy rest upon visions of social transformation; underlying both are certain common assumptions concerning oppression, consciousness, and historical change. Both pedagogies assert the existence of oppression in people's material conditions of existence and as a part of consciousness; both rest on a view of consciousness as more than a sum of dominating discourses, but as containing within it a critical capacity—what Antonio Gramsci called "good sense"; and both thus see human beings as subjects and actors in history and hold a strong commitment to justice and a vision of a better world and of the potential for liberation.[4] These ideals have powerfully influenced teachers and students in a wide range of educational settings, both formal and informal.

But in action, the goals of liberation or opposition to oppression have not always been easy to understand or achieve. As universal goals, these ideals do not address the specificity of people's lives; they do not directly analyze the contradictions between conflicting oppressed groups or the ways in which a single individual can experience oppression in one sphere while being privileged or oppressive in another. Feminist and Freirean teachers are in many ways engaged in what Teresa de Lauretis has called "shifting the ground of signs," challenging accepted meanings and relationships that occur at what she calls "political or more often micropolitical" levels, groupings that "produce no texts as such, but by shifting the 'ground' of a given sign . . . effectively intervene upon codes of perception as well as ideological codes."[5] But in attempting to challenge dominant values and to "shift the ground of signs," feminist and Freirean teachers raise conflicts for themselves and for their students, who also are historically situated and whose own subjectivities are often contradictory and in process. These conflicts have become increasingly clear as both Freirean and feminist pedagogies are put into practice. Attempting to implement these pedagogies without acknowledging the conflict not only of divided consciousness—what Audre Lorde calls "the oppressor within us"— but also the conflicts among groups trying to work together to name and struggle against oppression—among teachers and students in classrooms, or among political groups working for change in very specific areas—can lead to anger, frustration, and a retreat to safer or more traditional approaches.[6] The numerous accounts of the tensions of trying to put liberatory pedagogies into practice demonstrate the need to reexamine the assumptions of the classic texts of liberatory pedagogy and to consider the various issues that have arisen in attempts at critical and liberatory classroom practice.[7]

As a White feminist writing and teaching from the traditions of both critical pedagogy and feminist theory, these issues are of particular concern to me. In this article, I examine and critique the classic liberatory pedagogy of Paulo Freire, particularly as it is presented in *Pedagogy of the Oppressed,* his most famous and influential text. I then examine the development and practice of feminist pedagogy, which emerged in a particular historical and political moment in the United States, and which, as a situated pedagogy, provides an example of some of the difficulties of putting these ideals into practice and suggests at the same time some possible theoretical and practical directions for liberatory pedagogies in general. I argue that an exploration of the conflicts and concerns that have arisen for feminist teachers attempting to put into practice their versions of a feminist pedagogy can help enrich and re-envision Freirean goals of liberation and social progress. This emerging pedagogy does not reject the goals of justice—the end of oppression, and liberation—but frames them more specifically in the context of historically defined struggles and calls for the articulation of interests and identity on the part of teacher and theorist as well as student. This approach questions whether the oppressed cannot act also as oppressors and challenges the idea of a commonality of oppression. It raises questions about common experience as a source of knowledge, the pedagogical authority of the teacher, and the nature of political and pedagogical struggle.

THE PEDAGOGY OF PAULO FREIRE

Freire's pedagogy developed in particular historical and political circumstances of neocolonialism and imperialism. As is well known, Freire's methods developed originally from his work with peasants in Brazil and later in Chile and Guinea-Bissau.[8] Freire's thought thus needs to be understood in the context of the political and economic situation of the developing world. In Freire's initial formulation, oppression was conceived in class terms and education was viewed in the context of peasants' and working people's revolutionary struggles. Equally influential in Freire's thought and pedagogy were the influence of radical Christian thought and the revolutionary role of liberation theology in Latin America. As is true for other radical Christians in Latin America, Freire's personal knowledge of extreme poverty and suffering challenged his deeply felt Christian faith grounded in the ethical teachings of Jesus in the Gospels. Freire's pedagogy is thus founded on a moral imperative to side with the oppressed that emerges from both his Christian faith and his knowledge and experience of suffering in the society in which he grew up and lived. Freire has repeatedly stated that his pedagogical method cannot simply be transferred to other settings, but that each historical site requires the development of a pedagogy appropriate to that setting. In his most recent work, he has also addressed sexism and racism as systems of oppression that must be considered as seriously as class oppression.[9] Nonetheless, Freire is frequently read without consideration for the context of the specific settings in which his work developed and without these qualifications in mind. His most commonly read text still is his first book to be published in English, *Pedagogy of the Oppressed*. In this classic text, Freire presents the epistemological basis for his pedagogy and discusses the concepts of oppression, conscientization, and dialogue that are at the heart of his pedagogical project, but as he enacted it in settings in the developing world and as it has been appropriated by radical teachers in other settings.

Freire organizes his approach to liberatory pedagogy in terms of a dualism between the oppressed and the oppressors and between humanization and dehumanization. This organization of thoughts in terms of opposing forces reflects Freire's own experiences of literacy work with the poor in Brazil, a situation in which the lines between oppressor and oppressed were clear. For Freire, humanization is the goal of liberation; it has not yet been achieved, nor can it be achieved so long as the oppressors oppress the oppressed. That is, liberation and humanization will not occur if the roles of oppressor and oppressed are simply reversed. If humanization is to be realized, new relationships among human beings must be created:

> Because it is a distortion of being more fully human, sooner or later being less human leads the oppressed to struggle against those who made them so. In order for this struggle to have meaning, the oppressed must not, in seeking to regain their humanity (which is a way to create it), become in turn oppressors of the oppressors, but rather restorers of the humanity of both.[10]

The struggle against oppression leading to humanization is thus utopian and visionary. As Freire says elsewhere, "To be utopian is not to be merely idealistic or impractical but rather to engage in denunciation and annunciation."[11] By denunciation, Freire refers to the naming and analysis of existing structures of oppression; by annunciation, he means the creation of new forms of relationships and being in the world as a result of mutual struggle against oppression. Thus Freire presents a theoretical justification for a pedagogy that aims to critique existing forms of oppression and to transform the world, thereby creating new ways of being, or humanization.

Radical educators throughout the world have used *Pedagogy of the Oppressed* as the theoretical justification for their work. As an eloquent and impassioned statement of the need for and possibility of change through reading the world and the word, there is no comparable contemporary text.[12] But when we look at *Pedagogy of the Oppressed* from the perspective of recent feminist theory and pedagogy, certain problems arise that may reflect the difficulties that have sometimes arisen when Freire's ideas are enacted in specific settings. The challenges of recent feminist theory do not imply the rejection of Freire's goals for what he calls a pedagogy for liberation; feminists certainly share Freire's emphasis on seeing human beings as the subjects and not the objects of history. A critical feminist rereading of Freire, however, points to ways in which the project of Freirean pedagogy, like that of feminist pedagogy, may be enriched and re-envisioned.

From a feminist perspective, *Pedagogy of the Oppressed* is striking in its use of the male referent, a usage that was universal when the book was written in the 1960s.[13] Much more troublesome, however, is the abstract quality of terms such as humanization, which do not address the particular meanings imbued by men and women, Black and White, or other groups. The assumption of *Pedagogy of the Oppressed* is that in struggling against oppression, the oppressed will move toward true humanity. But this leaves unaddressed the forms of oppression experienced by different actors, the possibility of struggles among people oppressed differently by different groups—what Cameron McCarthy calls "nonsynchrony of oppression."[14] This assumption also presents humanization as a universal, without considering the various definitions this term may bring forth from people of different groups. When Freire speaks of the oppressed needing to fight the tendency to become "sub-oppressors," he means that the oppressed have only the pattern of oppression before them as a way of being in a position other than the one they are in. As Freire writes, "Their ideal is to be men; but for them, to be men is to be oppressors. This is their model of humanity."[15] What is troubling here is not that "men" is used for human beings, but that the model of oppressor implied here is based on the immediate oppressor of men—in this case, bosses over peasants or workers. What is not addressed is the possibility of simultaneous contradictory positions of oppression and dominance: the man oppressed by his boss could at the same time oppress his wife, for example, or the White woman oppressed by sexism could exploit the Black woman. By framing this discussion in such abstract terms, Freire slides over the contradictions and tensions within social settings in which overlapping forms of oppression exist.

This usage of "the oppressed" in the abstract also raises difficulties in Freire's use of experience as the means of acquiring a radical literacy, "reading the world and the word." At the heart of Freire's pedagogy is the insistence that all people are subjects and knowers of the world. Their political literacy will emerge from their reading of the world—that is, their own experience. This reading will lead to collective knowledge and action. But what if that experience is divided? What if different truths are discovered in reading the world from different positions? For Freire, education as the practice of freedom "denies that men are abstract, isolated, independent, and unattached to the world. . . . Authentic reflection considers neither abstract man nor the world without men, but men in their relations with the world."[16] But implicit in this vision is the assumption that, when the oppressed perceive themselves in relation to the world, they will act together collectively to transform the world and to move toward their own humanization. The nature of their perception of the world and their oppression is implicitly assumed to be uniform for all the oppressed. The possibility of a contradictory experience of oppression among the oppressed is absent. As Freire says:

> Accordingly, the point of departure must always be with men in the "here and now," which constitutes the situation within which they are submerged, from which they emerge, and in which they intervene. Only by starting from this situation—which determines their perception of it—can they begin to move.[17]

The assumption again is that the oppressed, these men, are submerged in a common situation of oppression, and that their shared knowledge of that oppression will lead them to collective action.

Central to Freire's pedagogy is the practice of conscientization; that is, coming to a consciousness of oppression and a commitment to end that oppression. Conscientization is based on this common experience of oppression. Through this reading of the world, the oppressed will come to knowledge. The role of the teacher in this process is to instigate a dialogue between teacher and student, based on their common ability to know the world and to act as subjects in the world. But the question of the authority and power of the teacher, particularly those forms of power based on the teacher's subject position as raced, classed, gendered, and so on, is not addressed by Freire. There is, again, the assumption that the teacher is "on the same side" as the oppressed, and that as teachers and students engage together in a dialogue about the world, they will uncover together the same reality, the same oppression, and the same liberation. In *Pedagogy of the Oppressed*, the teacher is presented as a generic man whose interests will be with the oppressed as they mutually discover the mechanisms of oppression. The subjectivity of the Freirean teacher is, in this sense, what Gayatri Chakravorty Spivak refers to as "transparent."[18] In fact, of course, teachers are not abstract; they are women or men of particular races, classes, ages, abilities, and so on. The teacher will be seen and heard by students not as an abstraction, but as a particular person with a certain defined history and relationship to the world. In a later book, Freire argues that the teacher has to assume authority, but must do so without becoming authoritarian. In this recognition of the teacher's authority, Freire acknowledges the difference between teacher and students:

> The educator continues to be different from the students, but, and now for me this is the central question, the difference between them, if the teacher is democratic, if his or her political dream is a liberating one, is that he or she cannot permit the necessary difference between the teacher and the students to become "antagonistic."[19]

In this passage, Freire acknowledges the power of the teacher by virtue of the structural role of "teacher" within a hierarchical institution and, under the best of circumstances, by virtue of the teacher's greater experience and knowledge. But Freire does not go on to investigate what the other sources of "antagonism" in the classroom might be. However much he provides a valuable guide to the use of authority by the liberatory teacher, he never addresses the question of other forms of power held by the teacher by virtue of race, gender, or class that may lead to antagonisms. Without naming these sources of tension, it is difficult to address or build upon them to challenge existing structures of power and subjectivities. Without recognizing more clearly the implicit power and limitations of the position of teacher, calls for a collective liberation or for opposition to oppression slide over the surface of the tensions that may emerge among teachers and students as subjects with conflicting interests and histories and with different kinds of knowledge and power. A number of questions are thus left unaddressed in *Pedagogy of the Oppressed*: How are we to situate ourselves in relation to the struggle of others? How are we to address our own contradictory positions as oppressors and oppressed? Where are we to look for liberation when our collective "reading of the world" reveals contradictory and conflicting experiences and struggles? The Freirean vision of the oppressed as undifferentiated and as the source of unitary political action, the transparency of the subjectivity of the Freirean teacher, and the claims of universal goals of liberation and social transformation fail to provide the answers to these questions.

Calling into question the universal and abstract claims of *Pedagogy of the Oppressed* is certainly not to argue that Freire's pedagogy should be rejected or discarded. The ethical stance of Freire in terms of praxis and his articulation of people's worth and ability to know and change the world are an essential basis for radical pedagogies in opposition to oppression. Freire's thought illuminates the central question of political action in a world increasingly without universals. Freire, like liberation theologians such as Sharon Welch, positions himself on the side of the oppressed; he claims the moral imperative to act in the world. As Peter McLaren has commented in reference to Freire's political stand, "The task of liberating others from their suffering may not emerge from some transcendental fiat, yet it nevertheless compels us to affirm our humanity in solidarity with victims."[20] But in order better to seek the affirmation of our own humanity and to seek to end suffering and oppression, I am arguing for a more situated theory of oppression and subjectivity, and for the need to consider the contradictions of such universal claims of truth or process.

In the next section of this article, I explore feminist pedagogy as an example of a situated pedagogy of liberation. Like Freirean pedagogy, feminist pedagogy is based on assumptions of the power of consciousness raising, the existence of oppression and the possibility of ending it, and the desire for social transformation. But in its historical development, feminist pedagogy has revealed the shortcomings that emerge in the attempt to enact a pedagogy that assumes a universal experience and abstract goals. In the attempt of feminist pedagogy to address these issues, a more complex vision of a liberatory pedagogy is being developed and explored.

FEMINIST PEDAGOGY, CONSCIOUSNESS RAISING, AND WOMEN'S LIBERATION

Feminist pedagogy in colleges and universities has developed in conjunction with the growth of women's studies and what is inclusively called "the new scholarship on women." These developments within universities—the institutionalization of women's studies as programs and departments and the challenge to existing canons and disciplines by the new scholarship on women and by feminist theory—are reflected in the classroom teaching methods that have come to be loosely termed feminist pedagogy. Defining exactly what feminist pedagogy means in practice, however, is difficult. It is easier to describe the various methods used in specific women's studies courses and included by feminist teachers claiming the term feminist pedagogy than it is to provide a coherent definition.[21] But common to the claims of feminist teachers is the goal of providing students with the skills to continue political work as feminists after they have left the university. Nancy Schniedewind makes a similar claim for what she calls "feminist process," which she characterizes as "both a feminist vision of equalitarian personal relations and societal forms and the confidence and skills to make their knowledge and vision functional in the world."[22]

The pedagogy of feminist teachers is based on certain assumptions about knowledge, power, and political action that can be traced beyond the academy to the political activism of the women's movement in the 1960s. This same commitment to social change through the transformative potential of education underlay Freire's pedagogy in Brazil during the same period. Women's studies at the university level have since come to encompass a wide variety of political stances and theoretical approaches. Socialist feminism, liberal feminism, radical feminism, and postmodern feminism all view issues from their different perspectives. Nonetheless, feminist pedagogy continues to echo the struggles of its origins and to retain a vision of social activism. Virtually all women's studies courses and programs at least partially reflect this critical, oppositional, and activist stance, even within programs now established and integrated into the bureaucratic structures of university life. As Linda Gordon points out:

> Women's studies did not arise accidentally, as the product of someone's good idea, but was created by a social movement for women's liberation with a sharp critique of the whole structure of society. By its very existence, women's studies constitutes a critique of the university and the body of knowledge it imparts.[23]

Despite tensions and splits within feminism at a theoretical level and in the context of women's studies programs in universities, the political commitment of women's liberation that Gordon refers to continues to shape feminist pedagogy. Thus, like Freirean pedagogy, feminist pedagogy is grounded in a vision of social change. And, like Freirean pedagogy, feminist pedagogy rests on truth claims of the primacy of experience and consciousness that are grounded in historically situated social change movements. Key to understanding the methods and epistemological claims of feminist pedagogy is an understanding of its origins in more grassroots political activity, particularly in the consciousness-raising groups of the women's liberation movement of the late 1960s and early 1970s.

Women's consciousness-raising groups began to form more or less spontaneously in northeastern and western U.S. cities in late 1967 among White women who had been active in the civil rights and new left movements.[24] In a fascinating parallel to the rise of the women's suffrage movement out of the abolitionist movement in the mid-nineteenth century, these activist and politically committed women came to apply the universal demands for equality and justice of the civil rights movement to their own situation as women.[25] While public actions such as the Miss America protest of 1968, mass meetings, and conferences were organized in this early period, the unique organizational basis for the women's liberation movement was grounded in the small groups of women who came together for what came to be known as consciousness raising. Early consciousness-raising groups, based on friendship and common political commitment, focused on the discussion of shared experiences of sexuality, work, family, and participation in the male-dominated left political movement. Consciousness raising focused on collective political change rather than on individual therapy. The groups were unstructured and local—they could be formed anywhere and did not follow formal guidelines—but they used the same sorts of methods because these methods addressed common problems. One woman remembers the first meeting of what became her consciousness-raising group:

> The flood broke loose gradually and then more swiftly. We talked about our families, our mothers, our fathers, our siblings; we talked about our men; we talked about school; we talked about "the movement" (which meant new left men). For hours we talked and unburdened our souls and left feeling high and planning to meet again the following week.[26]

Perhaps the clearest summary of consciousness raising from this period can be found in Kathie Sarachild's essay, "Consciousness Raising: A Radical Weapon."[27] In this article, Sarachild, a veteran of the civil rights movement in the South and a member of Redstockings, one of the earliest and most influential women's groups, presents an account that is both descriptive and prescriptive.[28] She makes it clear that consciousness raising arose spontaneously among small groups of women and that she is describing and summarizing a collective process that can be used by other groups of women. Fundamental to Sarachild's description of consciousness raising is its grounding in the need for political action. She describes the emergence of the method of consciousness raising among a group of women who considered themselves radicals in the sense of demanding fundamental changes in society. As Sarachild comments:

> We were interested in getting to the roots of problems in society. You might say we wanted to pull up weeds in the garden by their roots, not just pick off the leaves at the top to make things look good momentarily. Women's liberation was started by women who considered themselves radicals in this sense.[29]

A second fundamental aspect of consciousness raising is the reliance on experience and feeling. According to Sarachild, the focus on examining women's own experience came from a profound distrust of accepted authority and truth. These claims about what was valuable and true tended to be accepting of existing assumptions about women's "inherent nature" and "proper place." In order to call those truths into question (truths we might now call hegemonic and that Foucault, for example, would tie to structures of power), women had nowhere to turn except to their own experience. Sarachild describes the process in her group:

> In the end the group decided to raise its consciousness by studying women's lives by topics like childhood, jobs, motherhood, etc. We'd do any outside reading we wanted to and thought was important. But our starting point for discussion, as well as our test of the accuracy of what any of the books said, would be the actual experience we had in these areas.[30]

The last aspect of consciousness raising was a common sharing of experience in a collective, leaderless group. As Michele Russell points out, this sharing is similar to the practice of "testifying" in the Black church, and depends upon openness and trust in the group.[31] The assumption underlying this sharing of stories was the existence of commonality among women; as Sarachild puts it, "we made the assumption, an assumption basic to consciousness raising, that most women were like ourselves—not different."[32]

The model for consciousness raising among the Redstockings, as with other early groups, came from the experiences of many of the women as organizers in the civil rights movement in the South. Sarachild, for instance, cites the example of the Student Nonviolent Coordinating Committee, and quotes Stokely Carmichael when she argues for the need for people to organize in order to understand their own conditions of existence and to fight their own struggles. Other sources cited by Sarachild include the nineteenth-century suffragist Ernestine Rose, Mao Zedong, Malcolm X, and the practice of "speaking bitterness" in the Chinese revolution described by William Hinton in Fansh-en.[33] Both the example of the civil rights movement and the revolutionary tradition of the male writers that provided the model for early consciousness raising supported women's commitment to political action and social change.[34] As Sarachild comments:

> We would be the first to dare to say and do the undareable, what women really felt and wanted. The first job now was to raise awareness and understanding, our own and others—awareness that would prompt people to organize and to act on a mass scale.[35]

Thus consciousness raising shared the assumptions of earlier revolutionary traditions: that understanding and theoretical analysis were the first steps to revolutionary change, and that neither was adequate alone; theory and prac-tice were intertwined as praxis. As Sarachild puts it, "Consciousness raising was seen as both a method for arriving at the truth and a means for action and organizing."[36] What was original in consciousness raising, however, was its emphasis on experience and feeling as the guide to theoretical understand-ing, an approach that reflected the realities of women's socially defined sub-jectivities and the conditions of their lives. Irene Peslikis, another member of Redstockings, wrote, "When we think of what it is that politicizes people it is not so much books or ideas but experience."[37]

While Sarachild and other early feminists influenced by a left political tra-dition explored the creation of theory grounded in women's feelings and experiences, they never lost the commitment to social transformation.[38] In their subsequent history, however, consciousness raising and feminist peda-gogy did not always retain this political commitment to action. As the women's movement expanded to reach wider groups of women, consciousness raising tended to lose its commitment to revolutionary change. This trend seems to have been particularly true as the women's movement affected women with a less radical perspective and with little previous political involvement. Without a vision of collective action and social transformation, consciousness raising held the possibility of what Berenice Fisher calls "a diversion of energies into an exploration of feelings and 'private' concerns to the detriment of politi-cal activism."[39] The lack of structure and the local natures of consciousness-raising groups only reinforced these tendencies toward a focus on individual rather than collective change. The one site in which the tradition of conscious-ness raising did find institutional expression was in academia, in the growth of women's studies courses and programs stimulated by the new scholarship on women. The founders of these early courses and programs tended to be politi-cally committed feminists who themselves had experienced consciousness rais-ing and who, like Freire, assumed that education could and should be a means of social change.

The first women's studies courses, reflecting the growth of the women's movement in what has come to be called the second wave of feminism, were

taught in the late 1960s.[40] In 1970, Paul Lauter and Florence Howe founded
The Feminist Press, an important outlet for publishing early feminist scholarship and recovering lost texts by women writers.[41] In 1977, the founding
of the National Women's Studies Association provided a national organization, a journal, and yearly conferences that gave feminists inside and outside
of academia a forum to exchange ideas and experiences. By the late 1980s,
respected journals such as *Signs* and *Feminist Studies* were well established, and
women's studies programs and courses were widespread (if not always enthu-
siastically supported by administrations) in colleges and universities.[42] At the
same time, feminist research and theory—what has come to be called "the
new scholarship on women"—put forth a profound challenge to traditional
disciplines.[43] The growth of women's studies programs and feminist scholarship thus provided an institutional framework and theoretical underpinning
for feminist pedagogy, the attempt to express feminist values and goals in the
classroom. But while feminist scholarship has presented fundamental challenges to traditional androcentric knowledge, the attempt to create a new
pedagogy modeled on consciousness raising has not been as successful or
coherent a project. Serious challenges to the goal of political transformation
through the experience of feminist learning have been raised in the attempt
to create a feminist pedagogy in the academy. The difficulties and contradictions that have emerged in the attempt to create a feminist pedagogy in traditional institutions like universities raise serious questions for all liberatory
pedagogies and echo some of the problems raised by the unitary and universal approach of *Pedagogy of the Oppressed*. But in engaging these questions,
feminist pedagogy suggests new directions that can enrich Freirean pedagogies of liberation.

Feminist pedagogy has raised three areas of concern that are particularly
useful in considering the ways in which Freirean and other liberatory pedagogies can be enriched and expanded. The first of these concerns the role and
authority of the teacher; the second addresses the epistemological question of
the source of the claims for knowledge and truth in personal experience and
feeling; the last, emerging from challenges by women of color and postmodernist feminist theorists, raises the question of difference. Their challenges
have led to a shattering of the unproblematic and unitary category "woman,"
as well as of an assumption of the inevitable unity of "women." Instead, feminist theorists have increasingly emphasized the importance of recognizing difference as a central category of feminist pedagogy. The unstated assumption
of a universal experience of "being a woman" was exploded by the critiques
of postmodern feminists and by the growing assertion of lesbians and women
of color that the universal category "woman" in fact meant "White, heterosexual, middle-class woman," even when used by White, heterosexual, socialist
feminists, or women veterans of the civil rights movement who were committed to class or race struggles.[44] These theoretical challenges to the unity of
both "woman" and "women" have in turn called into question the authority of

330

women as teachers and students in the classroom, the epistemological value of both feeling and experience, and the nature of political strategies for enacting feminist goals of social change. I turn next to an exploration of these key issues of authority, experience, feeling, and difference within feminist pedagogy and theory.

The Role and Authority of the Teacher

In many respects, the feminist vision of the teacher's authority echoes that Freirean image of the teacher who is a joint learner with students and who holds authority by virtue of greater knowledge and experience. But as we have seen, Freire fails to address the various forms of power held by teachers depending on their race, gender, and the historical and institutional settings in which they work. In the Freirean account, they are in this sense "transparent." In the actual practice of feminist pedagogy, the central issues of difference, positionality, and the need to recognize the implications of subjectivity or identity for teachers and students have become central. Moreover, the question of authority in institutional settings makes problematic the possibility of achieving the collective and nonhierarchical vision of early consciousness-raising groups within university classrooms. The basic elements of early consciousness-raising groups—an emphasis on feeling, experience, and sharing, and a suspicion of hierarchy and authority—continue to influence feminist pedagogy in academic settings. But the institutionalized nature of women's studies in the hierarchical and bureaucratic structure of academia creates tensions that run counter to the original commitment to praxis in consciousness-raising groups. Early consciousness-raising groups were homogeneous, antagonistic to authority, and had a commitment to political change that had directly emerged from the civil rights and new left movements. Feminist pedagogy within academic classrooms addresses heterogeneous groups of students within a competitive and individualistic culture in which the teacher holds institutional power and responsibility (even if she may want to reject that power).[45] As bell hooks comments, "The academic setting, the academic discourse [we] work in, is not a known site for truthtelling."[46] The very success of feminist scholarship has meant the development of a rich theoretical tradition with deep divisions and opposing goals and methods.[47] Thus the source of the teacher's authority as a "woman" who can call upon a "common woman's knowledge" is called into question; at the same time the feminist teacher is "given" authority by virtue of her role within the hierarchical structure of the university.

The question of authority in feminist pedagogy seems to be centered around two different conceptions. The first refers to the institutionally imposed authority of the teacher within a hierarchical university structure. The teacher in this role must give grades, is evaluated by administrators and colleagues in terms of expertise in a body of knowledge, and is expected to take responsibility for meeting the goals of an academic course as it is understood within the wider university. This hierarchical structure is clearly in opposition to the collective goals of a common women's movement and is miles from the early structure-less consciousness-raising groups in which each woman was an expert on her own life. Not only does the university structure impose this model of institutional authority, but students themselves expect it. As Barbara Hillyer Davis comments: "The institutional pressure to [impart knowledge] is reinforced by the students' well-socialized behavior. If I will tell them 'what I want,' they will deliver it. They are exasperated with my efforts to depart from the role of dispenser of wisdom."[48] Feminist educators have attempted to address this tension between their ideals of collective education and the demands of the university by a variety of expedients: group assignments and grades, contracts for grades, pass/fail courses, and such techniques as self-revelation and the articulation of the dynamics of the classroom.[49]

Another aspect of institutionalized authority, however, is the need for women to *claim* authority in a society that denies it to them. As Culley and Portuges have pointed out, the authority and power of the woman feminist teacher is already in question from many of her students precisely because she is a woman:

> As women, our own position is precarious, and the power we are supposed to exercise is given grudgingly, if at all. For our own students, for ourselves, and for our superiors, we are not clearly "us" or "them." The facts of class, of race, of ethnicity, of sexual preference—as well as gender—may cut across the neat divisions of teacher/student.[50]

Thus the issue of institutional authority raises the contradictions of trying to achieve a democratic and collective ideal in a hierarchical institution, but it also raises the question of the meaning of authority for feminist teachers, whose right to speak or to hold power is itself under attack in a patriarchal (and racist, homophobic, classist, and so on) society. The question of asserting authority and power is a central concern to feminists precisely because as women they have been taught that taking power is inappropriate. From this perspective, the feminist teacher's acceptance of authority becomes in itself liberating to her and to her students. It becomes a claim to authority in terms of her own value as a scholar and a teacher in a patriarchal society that structurally denies or questions that authority as it is manifest in the organization and bureaucracy of the university. Women students, after all, are socialized to be deferential, and both men and women students are taught to accept male authority. It is instructive for students to see women assert authority. But this use of authority will lead to positive social change only if those teachers are working also to empower students in a Freirean sense.[51] As Susan Stanford Friedman argues:

> What I and other women have needed is a theory of feminist pedagogy consistent with our needs as women operating at the fringes of patriarchal space. As we attempt to move on to academic turf culturally defined as male, we need a theory that first recognizes the androcentric denial of all authority to women

and, second, points out a way for us to speak with an authentic voice not based on tyranny.[52]

These concerns lead to a conception of authority and power in a positive sense, both in terms of women asserting authority as women, and in terms of valuing intellectual work and the creation of theory as a means of understanding and, thus, of changing the world.

The authority of the intellectual raises issues for feminists in the academy that are similar to those faced by other democratic and collective political movements, such as those described by Freire. There is a contradiction between the idea of a women's movement including all women and a group of what Berenice Fisher calls "advanced women."[53] Feminists who question the whole tradition of androcentric thought are deeply suspicious of women who take a position of "experts" who can translate and interpret other women's experiences. Fisher articulates these tensions well:

> Who are intellectuals in relation to the women's movement? . . . Are intellectuals sorts of leaders, sage guides, women who give voice to or clarify a broader urge toward social change? Is intellectual work essentially elitist, a matter of mere privilege to think, to write, to create? Is it simply a patriarchal mode of gaining and maintaining power, a way of negating women's everyday experience, a means of separating some women from the rest of the "community?"[54]

Fisher argues that feminist intellectuals are struggling with these questions in their scholarship, teaching, and roles within the universities and the wider women's movement. She does not reject the authority of the feminist intellectual, but she also does not deny the need to address and clarify these contradictions. She, like Charlotte Bunch, is an embodiment of this attempt to accept both the authority and responsibility of the feminist intellectual who is creating theory.

In terms of feminist pedagogy, the authority of the feminist teacher as intellectual and theorist finds expression in the goal of making students themselves theorists of their own lives by interrogating and analyzing their own experience. In an approach very similar to Freire's concept of conscientization, this strategy moves beyond the naming or sharing of experience to the creation of a critical understanding of the forces that have shaped that experience. This theorizing is antithetical to traditional views of women. As Bunch points out, traditionally

> women are supposed to worry about mundane survival problems, to brood about fate, and to fantasize in a personal manner. We are not meant to think analytically about society, to question the ways things are, to consider how things could be different. Such thinking involves an active, not a passive, relationship to the world.[55]

Thus feminist educators like Fisher and Bunch accept their authority as intellectuals and theorists, but they consciously attempt to construct their pedagogy to recognize and encourage the capacity of their students to theorize and to recognize their own power.[56] This is a conception of authority not in the institutional terms of a bureaucratized university system, but rather an attempt to claim the authority of theorist and guide for students who are themselves potential theorists.

Feminist concerns about the authority of the feminist teacher address questions of classroom practice and theory ignored by Freire—in his formulation of the teacher and student as two "knowers" of the world, and in his assertion that the liberatory teacher should acknowledge and claim authority but not authoritarianism. The feminist exploration of authority is much richer and addresses more directly the contradictions between goals of collectivity and hierarchies of knowledge. Feminist teachers are much more conscious of the power of various subject positions than is represented in Freire's "transparent" liberatory teacher. An acknowledgment of the realities of conflict and tensions based on contradictory political goals, as well as of the meaning of historically experienced oppression for both teachers and students, leads to a pedagogy that respects difference not just as significant for students, but for teachers as well.

Personal Experience as a Source of Knowledge and Truth

As feminists explore the relationship of authority, theory, and political action, they raise questions about the categories and claims for truth underlying both consciousness raising and feminist pedagogy. These claims rest on categories of experience and feeling as guides to theoretical understanding and political change. Basic to the Freirean method of conscientization is the belief in the ability of all people to be knowers and to read both the word and the world. In Freirean pedagogy, it is through the interrogation of their own experiences that the oppressed will come to an understanding of their own power as knowers and creators of the world; this knowledge will contribute to the transformation of their world. In consciousness-raising groups and in feminist pedagogy in the university, a similar reliance on experience and feeling has been fundamental to the development of a feminist knowledge of the world that can be the basis for social change. Underlying both Freirean and early feminist pedagogy is an assumption of a common experience as the basis for political analysis and action. Both experience and feeling were central to consciousness raising and remain central to feminist pedagogy in academia; they are claimed as a kind of "inner knowing," shaped by society but at the same time containing an oppositional quality. Feeling is looked to as a guide to a deeper truth than that of abstract rationality. Experience, which is interpreted through ideologically constructed categories, also can be the basis for an opposition to dominant schemes of truth if what is experienced runs counter to what is set forth and accepted as "true." Feminist educators, beginning with women in the early consciousness-raising groups, have explored both experience and feeling as sources of knowledge, and both deserve closer examination.

In many ways, feeling or emotion has been seen traditionally as a source of women's knowledge about the world. As we have seen, in the early consciousness-raising groups, feelings were looked to as the source of a "true" knowledge of the world for women living in a society that denied the value of their perceptions. Feelings or emotions were seen as a way of testing accepted claims of what is universally true about human nature or, specifically, about women. Claims such as Freud's theory of penis envy, for example, were challenged by women first because these theoretical descriptions of women's psychology did not match women's own feelings about their lives. As feminist pedagogy has developed, with a continued emphasis on the function of feelings as a guide to knowledge about the world, emotions have been seen as links between a kind of inner truth or inner self and the outer world—including ideology, culture, and other discourses of power.[57] However, as feminist educators have explored the uses of feeling or emotion as a source of knowledge, several difficulties have become clear. First of all, there is a danger that the expression of strong emotion can be simply cathartic and can deflect the need for action to address the underlying causes of that emotion. Moreover, it is not clear how to distinguish among a wide range of emotions as the source of political action. At a more theoretical level, there are contradictions involved in claiming that the emotions are a source for knowledge and at the same time arguing that they are manipulated and shaped by dominant discourses. Both consciousness-raising groups and feminist theorists have asserted the social construction of feelings and their manipulation by the dominant culture; at the same time, they look to feelings as a source of truth. Berenice Fisher points to the contradiction implicit in these claims:

> In theoretical terms, we cannot simultaneously claim that all feelings are socially conditioned and that some feelings are "true." We would be more consistent to acknowledge that society only partly shapes our emotions, leaving an opening where we can challenge and change the responses to which we have been socialized. That opening enables the consciousness-raising process to take place and gives us the space in which to reflect on the new emotional responses that our process evokes.[58]

In this formulation, Fisher seems to be arguing for a kind of Gramscian "good sense," a locus of knowing in the self that is grounded in feeling as a guide to theoretical understanding. Feelings thus are viewed as a kind of cognition—a source of knowledge.

Perhaps the most eloquent argument for feelings as a source of oppositional knowledge is found in the work of Audre Lorde. Lorde, a Black lesbian feminist theorist and poet, writes from the specificity of her own socially defined and shaped life. For her, feeling is the source of poetry, a means of knowing that challenges White, Western, androcentric epistemologies. She specifically ties her own feelings as a Black woman to a non-Western way of knowing. She writes:

> As we come more into touch with our own ancient, non-European conscious-
> ness of living as a situation to be experienced and interacted with, we learn more
> and more to cherish our feelings, to respect those hidden sources of power from
> where true knowledge and, therefore, lasting action comes.[59]

Lorde is acutely aware of the ways in which the dominant society shapes
our sense of who we are and what we feel. As she points out, "Within living
structures defined by profit, by linear power, by institutional dehumanization,
our feelings were not meant to survive."[60] Moreover, Lorde is conscious of the
oppressor within us: "For we have, built into all of us, old blueprints of expectation and response, old structures of oppression, and these must be altered
at the same time as we alter the living conditions which are the result of those
structures."[61] But although Lorde does not deny what she calls "the oppressor
within," she retains a belief in the power of deeper feeling to challenge the
dominant definitions of truth and to point the way to an analysis that can lead
to an alternative vision:

> As we begin to recognize our deepest feelings, we begin to give up, of necessity,
> being satisfied with suffering and self-negation, and with the numbness which
> so often seems like their only alternative in society. Our acts against oppression
> become integral with self, motivated and empowered from within.[62]

For Lorde, then, feelings are a guide to analysis and to action. While they
are shaped by society and are socially constructed in that sense, Lorde insists
on a deeper reality of feeling closer in touch with what it means to be human.
This formulation echoes the Freirean vision of humanization as a new way of
being in the world other than as oppressor and oppressed. Both Freire and
Lorde retain a Utopian faith in the possibility that human beings can create
new ways of being in the world out of collective struggle and a human capacity to feel. Lorde terms this the power of the erotic; she speaks of the erotic as
"a measure between the beginnings of our sense of self and the chaos of our
strongest feelings," a resource "firmly rooted in the power of our unexpressed
or unrecognized feeling."[63] Because the erotic can challenge the dominant,
it has been denied as a source of power and knowledge. But for Lorde, the
power of the erotic provides the basis for visionary social change.

In her exploration of feelings and of the erotic as a source of knowledge
about the world, Lorde does not reject analysis and rationality. But she questions the depth of critical understanding of those forces that shape our lives
that can be achieved using only the rational and abstract methods of analysis
given to us by dominant ideology. In Foucault's terms, she is seeking a perspective from which to interrogate dominant regimes of truth; central to her
argument is the claim that an analysis framed solely in the terms of accepted
discourse cannot get to the root of structures of power. That is what her well-
known phrase, "The Master's Tools Will Never Dismantle the Master's House,"
implies. As she argues:

Rationality is not unnecessary. It serves the chaos of knowledge. It serves feeling. It serves to get from this place to that place. But if you don't honor those places, then the road is meaningless. Too often, that's what happens with the worship of rationality and that circular, academic analytic thinking. But ultimately, I don't see feel/think as a dichotomy. I see them as a choice of ways and combinations.[64]

Lorde's discussion of feeling and the erotic as a source of power and knowledge is based on the assumption that human beings have the capacity to feel and know, and can engage in self-critique; people are not completely shaped by dominant discourse. The oppressor may be within us, but Lorde insists that we also have the capacity to challenge our own ways of feeling and knowing. When tied to a recognition of positionality, this validation of feeling can be used to develop powerful sources of politically focused feminist education.

For Lorde and Fisher, this kind of knowing through an exploration of feeling and emotion requires collective inquiry and constant reevaluation. It is a contingent and positioned claim to truth. Similar complexities arise in the use of experience as the basis for feminist political action. Looking to experience as the source of knowledge and the focus of feminist learning is perhaps the most fundamental tenet of feminist pedagogy. This is similar to the Freirean call to "read the world" to seek the generative themes that codify power relationships and social structures. The sharing of women's experiences was the touchstone of early consciousness-raising groups and continues to be a fundamental method of feminist pedagogy. That women need to examine what they have experienced and lived in concrete ways, in their own bodies, is a materialistic conception of experience. In an early essay, Adrienne Rich pointed to this materiality of experience: "To think like a woman in a man's world means . . . remembering that every mind resides in a body; remaining accountable to the female bodies in which we live; constantly retesting given hypotheses against lived experience."[65] As became clear quite early in the women's movement, claims about experience as a source of women's knowledge rested on certain assumptions about commonalities in women's lives. Women were conceived of as a unitary and relatively undifferentiated group. Sarachild, for example, spoke of devising "new theories which . . . reflect the actual experience and feelings and necessities of women."[66] Underlying this approach was the assumption of a common woman's experience, one reflecting the world of the White, middle-class, heterosexual women of the early feminist movement. But as the critiques of lesbians, women of color, and postmodernist feminist theorists have made clear, there is no single woman's experience to be revealed. Both experience and feeling thus have been called into question as the source of an unproblematic knowledge of the world that will lead to praxis. As Diana Fuss comments: "'female experience' is never as unified, as knowable, as universal, and as stable as we presume it to be."[67]

Challenges to the concept of a unitary women's experience by both women of color and by postmodern critics has not meant the abandonment of experience as a source of knowledge for feminist teachers. Of course experience, like feeling, is socially constructed in the sense that we can only understand it and speak about it in ideas and terms that are part of an existing ideology and language. But in a stance similar to that of Lorde in her use of the erotic, feminist teachers have explored the ways in which women have experienced the material world through their bodies. This self-examination of lived experience is then used as a source of knowledge that can illuminate the social processes and ideology that shape us. As Fuss suggests, "Such a position permits the introduction of narratives of lived experience into the classroom while at the same time challenging us to examine collectively the central role social and historical practices play in shaping and producing these narratives."[68] One example of this approach is found in the work of Frigga Haug and the group of German feminists of which she is a part.[69] Haug and this group use what they call collective memory work to explore their feelings about their own bodies in order to uncover the social construction of their selves:

> Our collective empirical work set itself the high-flown task of identifying the ways in which individuals construct themselves into existing structures, and are thereby themselves formed; the way in which they reconstruct social structures; the points at which change is possible, the points where our chains chafe most, the point where accommodations have been made.[70]

This collective exploration of "the point where . . . chains chafe most" recalls the Freirean culture circles, in which peasants would take such examples as their personal experiences with the landlord as the starting point for their education or conscientization. Basic to their approach is a belief in reflection and a rejection of a view of people as "fixed, given, unchangeable." By working collectively on "memory work," a sharing and comparison of their own lives, Haug and her group hope to uncover the workings of hegemonic ideology in their own subjectivities. Another example of such collective work can be found in the Jamaican women's theater group, Sistren. Founded in 1977, Sistren is a collaborative theater group made up of working-class Jamaican women who create and write plays based on a collaborative exploration of their own experiences. The life histories of the women of Sistren have been collected in *Lionheart Girl: Life Stories of Jamaican Women*. In the compilation of this book, the Sistren collective used the same process of the collective sharing and analysis of experience that is the basis for their theater work. As the company's director Honor Ford-Smith writes:

> We began meeting collectively at first. Starting with our childhood, we made drawings of images based on such themes as where we had grown up, symbols of oppression in our lives, our relationships with men, our experience with race and the kind of work we had done.[71]

For Haug and her group, the Sistren collective, the early consciousness-raising groups, and the Freirean culture circles, collective sharing of experience is the source of knowledge of the forces that have shaped and continue to shape them. But their recognition of the shifting meaning of experience as it is explored through memory insists on the profoundly social and political nature of who we are.

The Question of Difference

Both women of color writing from a perspective of cultural feminism and postmodernist feminist theorists converge in their critique of the concept of a universal "women's experience." While the idea of a unitary and universal category "woman" has been challenged by women of color for its racist assumptions, it has also been challenged by recent analyses of feminist theorists influenced by postmodernism, who point to the social construction of subjectivity and who emphasize the "unstable" nature of the self. Postmodernist feminist critics such as Chris Weedon have argued that socially given identities such as "woman" are "precarious, contradictory, and in process, constantly being reconstituted in discourse each time we speak."[72] This kind of analysis considers the ways in which "the subject" is not an object; that is, not fixed in a static social structure, but constantly being created, actively creating the self, and struggling for new ways of being in the world through new forms of discourse or new forms of social relationships. Such analysis calls for a recognition of the positionality of each person in any discussion of what can be known from experience. This calling into question the permanence of subjectivities is what Jane Flax refers to as the "unstable self."[73] If we view individual selves as being constructed and negotiated, then we can begin to consider what exactly those forces are in which individuals shape themselves and by which they are shaped. The category of "woman" is itself challenged as it is seen more and more as a part of a symbolic system of ideology. Donna Haraway calls all such claims of identity into question:

> With the hard-won recognition of their social and historical constitution, gender, race, and class cannot provide the basis for belief in "essential" unity: There is nothing about being "female" that naturally binds women. There is not even such a state as "being" female, itself a highly complex category constructed in contested sexual discourses and other social practices. Gender, race, or class consciousness is an achievement forced on us by the terrible historical experience of the contradictory social realities of patriarchy, colonialism, and capitalism.[74]

These analyses support the challenges to assumptions of an essential and universal nature of women and women's experience that have come from lesbian critics and women of color.[75]

Both women of color and lesbian critics have pointed to the complexity of socially given identities. Black women and other women of color raise challenges to the assumption that the sharing of experience will create solidarity and a theoretical understanding based upon a common women's standpoint. Lesbian feminists, both White and of color, point to the destructive nature of homophobia and what Adrienne Rich has called compulsory heterosexuality. As is true of White, heterosexual, feminist educators, these theorists base their analysis upon their own experiences, but those experiences reveal not only the workings of sexism, but of racism, homophobia, and class oppression as well. This complex perspective underlies the Combahee River Collective Statement, a position paper written by a group of African American feminists in Boston in the 1970s. This statement makes clear what a grounded theory of experience means for women whose value is denied by the dominant society in numerous ways. The women in the Combahee River Collective argue that "the most profound and potentially most radical politics come directly out of our own identity, as opposed to working to end somebody else's oppression."[76] For African American women, an investigation of the shaping of their own identities reveals the ways in which sexism and racism are interlocking forms of oppression:

> As children we realized that we were different from boys and that we were treated differently. For example, we were told in the same breath to be quiet both for the sake of being "ladylike" and to make us less objectionable in the eyes of white people. As we grew older we became aware of the threat of physical and sexual abuse from men. However, we had no way of conceptualizing what was so apparent to us, what we knew was really happening.[77]

When African American teachers like Michele Russell or Barbara Omolade describe their feminist pedagogy, they ground that pedagogy in an investigation of experience in material terms. As Russell describes her teaching of an introductory Black Studies class for women at Wayne County Community College in Detroit: "We have an hour together. . . . The first topic of conversation—among themselves and with me—is what they went through just to make it in the door, on time. That, in itself becomes a lesson."[78] And Omolade points out in her discussion of her teaching at Medgar Evers College in New York, a college whose students are largely African American women:

> No one can teach students to "see," but an instructor is responsible for providing the coherent ordering of information and content. The classroom process is one of information-sharing in which students learn to generalize their particular life experiences within a community of fellow intellectuals.[79]

Thus the pedagogy of Russell and Omolade is grounded in experience as a source of knowledge in a particularly materialistic way; the knowledge generated reveals the overlapping forms of oppression lived by women of color in this society.

The investigation of the experiences of women of color, lesbian women, women whose very being challenges existing racial, sexual, heterosexual, and class dominance, leads to a knowledge of the world that both acknowledges differences and points to the need for an "integrated analysis and practice based upon the fact that the major systems of oppression are interlocking."[80]

The turning to experience thus reveals not a universal and common women's essence, but, rather, deep divisions in what different women have experienced, and in the kinds of knowledge they discover when they examine their own experience. The recognition of the differences among women raises serious challenges to feminist pedagogy by calling into question the authority of the teacher/theorist, raising feelings of guilt and shame, and revealing tensions among students as well as between teacher and students. In classes of African American women taught by African American teachers, the sharing of experience can lead to the same sense of commonality and sharing that was true of early consciousness-raising groups. But in settings in which students come from different positions of privilege or oppression, the sharing of experience raises conflicts rather than building solidarity. In these circumstances, the collective exploration of experience leads not to a common knowledge and solidarity based on sameness, but to the tensions of an articulation of difference. Such exploration raises again the problems left unaddressed by Freirean pedagogy: the overlapping and multiple forms of oppression revealed in "reading the world" of experience.

CONCLUSION

Both Freirean and feminist pedagogies are based on political commitment and identification with subordinate and oppressed groups; both seek justice and empowerment. Freire sets out these goals of liberation and social and political transformation as universal claims, without exploring his own privileged position or existing conflicts among oppressed groups themselves. Writing from within a tradition of Western modernism, his theory rests on a belief of transcendent and universal truth. But feminist theory influenced by postmodernist thought and by the writings of women of color challenges the underlying assumptions of these universal claims. Feminist theorists in particular argue that it is essential to recognize, as Julie Mitchell comments, that we cannot "live as human subjects without in some sense taking on a history."[81] The recognition of our own histories means the necessity of articulating our own subjectivities and our own interests as we try to interpret and critique the social world. This stance rejects the universalizing tendency of much "malestream" thought, and insists on recognizing the power and privilege of who we are. As Biddy Martin and Chandra Mohanty comment:

> The claim to a lack of identity or positionality is itself based on privilege, on the refusal to accept responsibility for one's implication in actual historical or social relations, or a denial that positionalities exist or that they matter, the denial of one's own personal history and the claim to a total separation from it.[82]

Fundamental to recent feminist theory is a questioning of the concept of a coherent subject moving through history with a single essential identity. Instead, feminist theorists are developing a concept of the constant creation

341

and negotiation of selves within structures of ideology and material constraints.[83] This line of theoretical analysis calls into question assumptions of the common interests of the oppressed, whether conceived of as women or peasants; it challenges the use of such universal terms as oppression and liberation without locating these claims in a concrete historical or social context. The challenges of recent feminist theory and, in particular, the writings of feminists of color point to the need to articulate and claim a particular historical and social identity, to locate ourselves, and to build coalitions from a recognition of the partial knowledges of our own constructed identities. Recognizing the standpoint of subjects as shaped by their experience of class, race, gender, or other socially defined identities has powerful implications for pedagogy, in that it emphasizes the need to make conscious the subject positions not only of students but of teachers as well. These lines of theoretical analysis have implications for the ways in which we can understand pedagogy as contested, as a site of discourse among subjects, teachers, and students whose identities are, as Weedon puts it, contradictory and in process. The theoretical formulation of the "unstable self," the complexity of subjectivities, what Giroux calls "multi-layered subjects," and the need to position ourselves in relation to our own histories raise important issues for liberatory pedagogies. If all people's identities are recognized in their full historical and social complexity as subject positions that are in process, based on knowledges that are partial and that reflect deep and conflicting differences, how can we theorize what a liberatory pedagogy actively struggling against different forms of oppression may look like? How can we build upon the rich and complex analysis of feminist theory and pedagogy to work toward a Freirean vision of social justice and liberation?

In the complexity of issues raised by feminist pedagogy, we can begin to acknowledge the reality of tensions that result from different histories, from privilege, oppression, and power as they are lived by teachers and students in classrooms. To recognize these tensions and differences does not mean abandonment of the goals of social justice and empowerment, but it does make clear the need to recognize contingent and situated claims and to acknowledge our own histories and selves in process. One significant area of feminist work has been grounded in the collective analysis of experience and emotion, as exemplified by the work of Haug and her group in Germany or by the Jamaican women's theater group, Sistren. In many respects, these projects look back to consciousness raising, but with a more developed theory of ideology and an acute consciousness of difference. As Berenice Fisher argues, a collective inquiry "requires the slow unfolding of layers of experience, both the contradictory experiences of a given woman and the conflicting experiences of different women."[84] Another approach builds on what Bernice Reagon calls the need for coalition building, a recognition and validation of difference. This is similar to what has come to be known as identity politics, exemplified in what Minnie Bruce Pratt is seeking in her discussion of trying to come to terms with her own identity as a privileged Southern White woman.[85] Martin and Mohanty speak of this as a sense of "home," a recognition of the difficulties of coming to terms with privilege or oppression, of the benefits of being an oppressor, or of the rage of being oppressed.[86] This is a validation of both difference and conflict, but also an attempt to build coalitions around common goals rather than a denial of differences.[87] It is clear that this kind of pedagogy and exploration of experiences in a society in which privilege and oppression are lived is risky and filled with pain. Such a pedagogy suggests a more complex realization of the Freirean vision of the collective conscientization and struggle against oppression, one which acknowledges difference and conflict, but which, like Freire's vision, rests on a belief in the human capacity to feel, to know, and to change.

NOTES

1. See as representative Henry Giroux, ed., *Postmodernism, Feminism and Cultural Politics* (Albany: State University of New York Press, 1991); Cleo Cherryholmes, *Power and Criticism: Poststructural Investigations in Education* (New York: Teachers College Press, 1988); Henry Giroux and Roger Simon, eds., *Popular Culture, Schooling and Everyday Life* (Westport, CT: Bergin & Garvey, 1989); Deborah Britzman, *Practice Makes Practice* (Albany: State University of New York Press, 1991); Patti Lather, *Getting Smart: Feminist Research and Pedagogy With/in the Postmodern* (New York: Routledge, 1991).
2. Paulo Freire, *Pedagogy of the Oppressed* (New York: Herder & Herder, 1971), p. 28.
3. Margo Culley and Catherine Portuges, "Introduction," in *Gendered Subjects* (Boston: Routledge & Kegan Paul, 1985). For comparisons of Freirean and feminist pedagogy, see also Frances Maher, "Classroom Pedagogy and the New Scholarship on Women," in *Gendered Subjects*, pp. 29–48, and "Toward a Richer Theory of Feminist Pedagogy: A Comparison of 'Liberation' and 'Gender' Models for Teaching and Learning," *Journal of Education, 169,* No. 3 (1987), 91–100.
4. Antonio Gramsci, *Selections from the Prison Notebooks* (New York: International Publishers, 1971).
5. Teresa de Lauretis, *Alice Doesn't: Feminism, Semiotics, Cinema* (Bloomington: Indiana University Press, 1984), p. 178.
6. Audre Lorde, *Sister Outsider* (Trumansburg, NY: The Crossing Press, 1984).
7. See, for example, Elizabeth Ellsworth, "Why Doesn't This Feel Empowering? Working through the Repressive Myths of Critical Pedagogy," *Harvard Educational Review, 59* (1989), 297–324; Ann Berlak, "Teaching for Outrage and Empathy in the Liberal Arts," *Educational Foundations, 3,* No. 2 (1989), 69–94; Deborah Britzman, "Decentering Discourses in Teacher Education: Or, the Unleashing of Unpopular Things," in *What Schools Can Do: Critical Pedagogy and Practice,* ed. Candace Mitchell and Kathleen Weiler (Albany: State University of New York Press, 1992).
8. Freire's method of codifications and generative themes have been discussed frequently. Perhaps the best introduction to these concrete methods can be found in Paulo Freire, *Education for Critical Consciousness* (New York: Seabury, 1973).
9. See, for example, Paulo Freire, *The Politics of Education* (Westport, CT: Bergin & Garvey, 1985); Paulo Freire and Donaldo Macedo, *Literacy: Reading the Word and the World* (Westport, CT: Bergin & Garvey, 1987); Paulo Freire and Ira Shor, *A Pedagogy For Liberation* (London: Macmillan, 1987); Myles Horton and Paulo Freire, *We Make the Road by Walking: Conversations on Education and Social Change,* ed. Brenda Bell, John Gaventa, and John Peters (Philadelphia: Temple University Press, 1990).

10. Freire, *Pedagogy of the Oppressed*, p. 28.

11. Paulo Freire, "The Adult Literacy Process as Cultural Action for Freedom," in *The Politics of Education*, p. 57.

12. Freire and Macedo, *Literacy: Reading the Word and the World*.

13. See Simone de Beauvoir, *The Second Sex* (New York: Knopf, 1953), for a more striking use of the male referent.

14. Cameron McCarthy, "Rethinking Liberal and Radical Perspectives on Racial Inequality in Schooling: Making the Case for Nonsynchrony," *Harvard Educational Review, 58* (1988), 265–280.

15. Freire, *Pedagogy of the Oppressed*, p. 30.

16. Freire, *Pedagogy of the Oppressed*, p. 69.

17. Freire, *Pedagogy of the Oppressed*, p. 73.

18. Gayatri Chakravorty Spivak, "Can the Subaltern Speak?," in *Marxism and the Interpretation of Culture*, ed. Cary Nelson and Lawrence Grossberg (Urbana: University of Illinois Press, 1988), pp. 271–313.

19. Freire and Shor, *A Pedagogy for Liberation*, p. 93.

20. Peter McLaren, "Postmodernity and the Death of Politics: A Brazilian Reprieve," *Educational Theory, 36* (1986), p. 399.

21. When definitions of feminist pedagogy are attempted, they sometimes tend toward generalization and such a broad inclusiveness as to be of dubious usefulness. For example, Carolyn Shrewsbury characterizes feminist pedagogy as follows:

    > It does not automatically preclude any technique or approach. It does indicate the relationship that specific techniques have to educational goals. It is not limited to any specific subject matter but it does include a reflexive element that increases the feminist scholarship component involved in the teaching/learning of any subject matter. It has close ties with other liberatory pedagogies, but it cannot be subsumed under other pedagogical approaches. It is transformative, helping us revision the educational enterprise. But it can also be phased into a traditional teaching approach or another alternative pedagogical approach. (Shrewsbury, "What Is Feminist Pedagogy?," *Women's Studies Quarterly, 15,* Nos. 3–4 [1987], p. 12)

    Certain descriptions of feminist pedagogy show the influence of group dynamics and interactionist approaches. See, for example, Nancy Schniedewind, "Feminist Values: Guidelines for Teaching Methodology in Women's Studies," *Radical Teacher, 18,* 25–28. Methods used by feminist teachers include cooperation, shared leadership, and democratic process. Feminist teachers describe such techniques as keeping journals, soliciting students' responses to readings and to the classroom dynamics of a course, the use of role playing and theater games, the use of self-revelation on the part of the teacher, building leadership skills among students by requiring them to teach parts of a course, and contracting for grades. For accounts of classroom practice, see the articles in the special issue on feminist pedagogy of *Women's Studies Quarterly, 15,* Nos. 3–4 (1987); Culley and Portuges, *Gendered Subjects*; Charlotte Bunch and Sandra Pollack, eds., *Learning Our Way* (Trumansburg, NY: The Crossing Press, 1983); Gloria Hull, Patricia Bell Scott, and Barbara Smith, ed., *But Some of Us Are Brave* (Old Westbury, NY: The Feminist Press, 1982); and numerous articles in *Women's Studies Newsletter* and *Radical Teacher*.

22. Nancy Schniedewind, "Teaching Feminist Process," *Women's Studies Quarterly, 15,* Nos. 3–4 (1987), p. 29.

23. Linda Gordon, "A Socialist View of Women's Studies: A Reply to the Editorial, Volume 1, Number 1," *Signs, 1* (1975), p. 559.

24. A discussion of the relationship of the early women's liberation movement to the civil rights movement and the new left can be found in Sara Evans, *Personal Politics* (New York: Vintage Press, 1980). Based on extensive interviews as well as pamphlets and private documents, Evans shows the origins of both political goals and methods in the ear-

lier male-dominated movement, particularly the model of Black student organizers and the Black church in the South.

25. While mid-nineteenth-century suffragists developed their ideas of human equality and justice through the abolitionist movement, by the late nineteenth century, White suffragists often demonstrated racist attitudes and employed racist strategies in their campaigns for suffrage. This offers another instructive parallel to the White feminist movement of the 1960s. Here, once again, feminist claims emerged out of an anti-racist struggle for civil rights, but later too often took up the universalizing stance that the experiences and issues of White women represented the lives of all women. See bell hooks, *Ain't I a Woman?* (Boston: South End Press, 1981) and *Feminist Theory from Margin to Center* (Boston: South End Press, 1984) for powerful discussions of these issues.
26. Nancy Hawley as quoted in Evans, *Personal Politics,* p. 205.
27. Kathie Sarachild, "Consciousness Raising: A Radical Weapon," in *Feminist Revolution,* ed. Redstockings (New York: Random House, 1975).
28. Redstockings included a number of women who were influential in the women's movement; Shulamith Firestone, Rosalyn Baxandall, Ellen Willis, and Robin Morgan were among a number of other significant feminist writers and activists who participated.
29. Sarachild, "Consciousness Raising," p. 144.
30. Sarachild, "Consciousness Raising," p. 145.
31. Michele Russell, "Black-Eyed Blues Connection: From the Inside Out," in Bunch and Pollack, *Learning Our Way,* pp. 272–284.
32. Sarachild, "Consciousness Raising," p. 147.
33. William Hinton, *Fanshen* (New York: Vintage Books, 1966).
34. See Berenice Fisher, "Guilt and Shame in the Women's Movement: The Radical Ideal of Political Action and Its Meaning for Feminist Intellectuals," *Feminist Studies, 10* (1984), 185–212, for an extended discussion of the impact of the methods and goals of the civil rights movement on consciousness raising and the early women's liberation movement.
35. Sarachild, "Consciousness Raising," p. 145.
36. Sarachild, "Consciousness Raising," p. 147.
37. Irene Peslikis, "Resistances to Consciousness," in *Sisterhood Is Powerful,* ed. Robin Morgan (New York: Vintage Books, 1970), p. 339.
38. See, for example, Kathy McAfee and Myrna Wood, "Bread and Roses," in *Voices from Women's Liberation,* ed. Leslie Tanner (New York: New American Library, 1970) for an early socialist feminist analysis of the need to connect the women's movement with the class struggle.
39. Berenice Fisher, "What is Feminist Pedagogy?," *Radical Teacher, 18,* 20–25. See also bell hooks, "on self-recovery," in *talking back: thinking feminist, thinking black* (Boston: South End Press, 1989).
40. Marilyn Boxer, "For and about Women: The Theory and Practice of Women's Studies in the United States," in *Reconstructing the Academy: Women's Education and Women's Studies,* ed. Elizabeth Minnich, Jean O'Barr, and Rachel Rosenfeld (Chicago: University of Chicago Press, 1988), p. 71.
41. See Florence Howe, *Myths of Coeducation* (Bloomington: University of Indiana Press, 1984), for a collection of essays documenting this period.
42. Boxer estimates there were over 300 programs and 30,000 courses in women's studies given in 1982. See "For and about Women," p. 70.
43. The literature of feminist challenges to specific disciplines is by now immense. For general discussions of the impact of the new scholarship on women, see Ellen DuBois, Gail Kelly, Elizabeth Kennedy, Carolyn Korsmeyer, and Lillian Robinson, eds., *Feminist Scholarship: Kindling in the Groves of Academe* (Urbana: University of Illinois Press, 1985), and Christie Farnhum, ed., *The Impact of Feminist Research in the Academy* (Bloomington: Indiana University Press, 1987).

44. See, for example, Diana Fuss, *Essentially Speaking* (New York: Routledge, 1989); hooks, *talking back*; Britzman, *Practice Makes Practice*.

45. Susan Stanford Friedman, "Authority in the Feminist Classroom: A Contradiction in Terms?" in Culley and Portuges, *Gendered Subjects*, 203–208.

46. hooks, *talking back*, p. 29.

47. See Alison Jaggar, *Feminist Politics and Human Nature* (Sussex, Eng.: Harvester Press, 1983), for an excellent discussion of these perspectives.

48. Barbara Hillyer Davis, "Teaching the Feminist Minority," in Bunch and Pollack, *Learning Our Way*, p. 91.

49. See, for example, Evelyn Torton Beck, "Self-disclosure and the Commitment to Social Change," *Women's Studies International Forum*, 6 (1983), 159–164.

50. Margo Culley and Catherine Portuges, "The Politics of Nurturance," in *Gendered Subjects*, p. 12. See also Margo Culley, "Anger and Authority in the Introductory Women's Studies Classroom," in *Gendered Subjects*, pp. 209–217.

51. See Davis, "Teaching the Feminist Minority," for a thoughtful discussion of the contradictory pressures on the feminist teacher both to nurture and challenge women students.

52. Friedman, "Authority in the Feminist Classroom," p. 207.

53. Fisher, "What is Feminist Pedagogy?" p. 22.

54. Fisher, "Guilt and Shame in the Women's Movement," p. 202.

55. Charlotte Bunch, "Not by Degrees: Feminist Theory and Education," in Bunch and Pollack, *Learning Our Way*, p. 156.

56. See Berenice Fisher, "Professing Feminism: Feminist Academics and the Women's Movement," *Psychology of Women Quarterly*, 7 (1982), 55–69, for a thoughtful discussion of the difficulties of retaining an activist stance for feminists in the academy.

57. See Arlie Russell Hochschild, *The Managed Heart* (Berkeley: University of California Press, 1983), for a discussion of the social construction of emotions in contemporary society. Hochschild argues that emotion is a "biologically given sense . . . and a means by which we know about our relation to the world" (p. 219). At the same time she investigates the ways in which the emotions themselves are manipulated and constructed.

58. Berenice Fisher, "The Heart Has Its Reasons: Feeling, Thinking, and Community Building in Feminist Education," *Women's Studies Quarterly*, 15, Nos. 3–4 (1987), 48.

59. Lorde, *Sister Outsider*, p. 37.

60. Lorde, *Sister Outsider*, p. 34.

61. Lorde, *Sister Outsider*, p. 123.

62. Lorde, *Sister Outsider*, p. 58.

63. Lorde, *Sister Outsider*, p. 53.

64. Lorde, *Sister Outsider*, p. 100.

65. Adrienne Rich, "Taking Women Students Seriously," in *On Lies, Secrets, and Silence*, ed. Adrienne Rich (New York: W. W. Norton, 1979), p. 243.

66. Sarachild, "Consciousness Raising," p. 148.

67. Fuss, *Essentially Speaking*, p. 114.

68. Fuss, *Essentially Speaking*, p. 118.

69. Frigga Haug, *Female Sexualization* (London: Verso Press, 1987).

70. Haug, *Female Sexualization*, p. 41.

71. Sistren Collective with Honor Ford-Smith, *Lionheart Gal: Life Stories of Jamaican Women* (London: Woman's Press, 1986), p. 15.

72. Chris Weedon, *Feminist Practice and Poststructuralist Theory* (Oxford: Basil Blackwell, 1987), p. 33.

73. Jane Flax, "Postmodernism and Gender Relations in Feminist Theory," *Signs*, 12 (1987), 621–643.

74. Donna Haraway, "A Manifesto for Cyborgs," *Socialist Review*, 80 (1985), 72.

75. As representative, see Johnella Butler, "Toward a Pedagogy of Everywoman's Studies," in Culley and Portuges, *Gendered Subjects*; hooks, *talking back*; Hull, Scott, and Smith, *But Some of Us Are Brave*; Gloria Joseph and Jill Lewis, *Common Differences: Conflicts in Black and White Perspectives* (New York: Anchor Books, 1981); Chierrie Moraga and Gloria Anzaldua, eds., *This Bridge Called My Back* (Watertown, MA: Persephone Press, 1981); Barbara Omolade, "A Black Feminist Pedagogy," *Women's Studies Quarterly, 15,* Nos. 3–4 (1987), 32–40; Russell, "Black-Eyed Blues Connection," pp. 272–284; Elizabeth Spellman, "Combatting the Marginalization of Black Women in the Classroom," in Culley and Portuges, *Gendered Subjects*, pp. 240–244.
76. Combahee River Collective, "Combahee River Collective River Statement," in *Home Girls,* ed. Barbara Smith (New York: Kitchen Table—Women of Color Press, 1983), p. 275.
77. Combahee River Collective, "Combahee River Collective Statement," p. 274.
78. Russell, "Black-Eyed Blues Connection," p. 155.
79. Omolade, "A Black Feminist Pedagogy," p. 39.
80. Combahee River Collective, "Combahee River Collective Statement," p. 272.
81. Juliet Mitchell, *Women: The Longest Revolution* (New York: Pantheon Books, 1984).
82. Biddy Martin and Chandra Mohanty, "Feminist Politics: What's Home Got to Do With It?" in *Feminist Studies/ Critical Studies*, ed. Teresa de Lauretis (Bloomington: University of Indiana Press, 1986), p. 208.
83. See, for example, Flax, "Postmodernism and Gender Relations in Feminist Theory"; Sandra Harding, *The Science Question in Feminism* (Ithaca: Cornell University Press, 1986); Dorothy Smith, *The Everyday World as Problematic* (Boston: Northeastern University Press, 1987); Haraway, "A Manifesto for Cyborgs," *Socialist Review, 80* (1985), 64–107; Nancy Hartsock, *Money, Sex, and Power* (New York: Longman, 1983); Mary O'Brien, *The Politics of Reproduction* (Boston: Routledge & Kegan Paul, 1981); Irene Diamond and Lee Quinby, eds., *Feminism and Foucault* (Boston: Northeastern University Press, 1988); Linda Alcoff, "Cultural Feminism versus Post Structuralism: The Identity Crisis in Feminist Theory," *Signs, 13* (1988), 405–437; Special Issue on Feminism and Deconstruction, *Feminist Studies, 14,* No. 1 (1988); Judith Butler, *Gender Trouble* (New York: Routledge, 1990); Linda Nicholson, ed., *Feminism/Postmodernism* (New York: Routledge, 1990).
84. Fisher, "The Heart Has Its Reasons," p. 49.
85. Minnie Bruce Pratt, "Identity: Skin Blood Heart," in *Yours in Struggle,* ed. Elly Bulkin, Minnie Bruce Pratt, and Barbara Smith (Brooklyn, NY: Long Hand Press, 1984).
86. Martin and Mohanty, "What's Home Got to Do With It?"
87. Bernice Reagon, "Coalition Politics: Turning the Century," in Smith, *Home Girls,* pp. 356–369.

RETHINKING EDUCATION AND EMANCIPATION

BEING, TEACHING, AND POWER

NOAH DE LISSOVOY

In an inhuman world, the problem of education is the problem of articulating a human voice against the machineries of violence visited persistently upon persons—a voice against the truth of power, the dead and finished truth of what is decided, the truth of the inert and incontrovertible. The problem of education is the problem of unwinding the human body and soul from this intricate clockwork of not merely the correct and commendable but also the apparently self-evident and inevitable. It is the problem of rescuing *being* from *what is*, a *what is* that has conquered every other possibility to give itself the status of fact and truth. This *what is* is not just an apparatus of painful training; it is a machine of assimilation and destruction. The experiences that theorists have identified variously as exploitation, marginalization, and normalization should not be fought over as to their priority since they all participate in the same process. They represent the various modes of an assault on the human by power and by the reality that power has assembled for itself.[1] The exposure of and challenge to this violence is the real problem of education.

The first part of this essay describes the process of domination and then provides an account of the project of emancipation that confronts it. This problematic is generally made invisible in educational research, which tends to overlook the logic of dominative power altogether, to distort it through a structural-functionalist perspective focused on social reproduction, or to deflect attention from it through an emphasis on power as discursive and constructive. By contrast, I argue that domination is a social end rather than only a means, that it works pervasively across both material and immaterial levels of social life, and that it persistently acts *against* human beings in obscuring and injuring them. Emancipation means recognizing these beings and affirming their integrity and survival against power; this implies a consideration of the domain of *being* in relation to education.

The second section argues for an understanding of the *human* as the abiding ontological kernel of the selves of students and teachers, as it asserts itself *before* the more familiar scenes of struggle over identity, beliefs, and values. I argue for a sense of humanism in education that pushes the familiar perspective of the critical traditions by conceptualizing the human as a fact to be verified rather than a capacity to be constructed. Rooted in this understanding, as the third part of this essay describes, emancipatory education discovers an essential equality between students and teachers to which any (even critical or democratic) authority must be subordinated, an equality that is systematically concealed by dominant (and even progressive) pedagogies. In addition, I argue that a new ground for agency is possible, one that depends on a recognition that students are already effective as beings against power, rather than on the existential enlargement of the subject that is assumed in familiar conceptions of development. This human determination should be affirmed as the condition of any larger educational and social struggle.

This project is inspired by contemporary work in philosophy and cultural studies that confronts the domain of being as a political problem; although in synthesizing the discoveries of the different theoretical currents I draw from, and in considering them in the educational context, I take them in new directions. The purpose of this essay is not to describe a method but, rather, to specify the grounding concepts and principles that should inform a contemporary emancipatory education. In developing these concepts and principles, I contrast them with familiar senses of the nature and purpose of education. This involves a significant reconstruction of the notions of "emancipation," "human," and even "education." In the course of this discussion, I offer a critique of both mainstream and poststructuralist understandings, which I believe obscure the process of domination and in this way make efforts to contest it more difficult. In addition, while my argument starts from a standpoint located within the critical education tradition and remains committed to this tradition, I nevertheless challenge several of its key assumptions in order to press it toward a more radically democratic conception of agency and emancipation. This essay has important implications for educational researchers and practitioners concerned with social justice, transformation, and the struggle against oppression, since it proposes a reconceptualization of the problematic of power upon which such efforts are built. At the same time, it identifies the indispensable core of the idea and experience of emancipation that can truly allow for a liberatory approach to pedagogy.

UNDERSTANDING DOMINATION AND EMANCIPATION

The problem of education cannot be resolved by finding the proper organization of schools, or the correct professional development for teachers, or the most efficient curriculum, as mainstream approaches in policy and practice set out to do. Reforms and reorganizations in these domains—conservative and progressive—ultimately end up refreshing and refining processes of alienation and subjection. For example, the bright face put on accountability initiatives (as ostensible expressions of egalitarianism) only conceals the inner principle of domination that lives in the heart of these reforms. However, the main problem is not that official efforts are governed by a technical rhetoric and reason that hide their true political interests, as the critical perspective would put it. The problem, rather, is the basic meaning and purpose of education that inhabit these efforts and that they systematically disavow. In other words, oppression in education does not merely function to preserve privilege; education as it in fact exists oppresses students because its central sense and purpose is domination and subjection—the subjection of bodies and minds to the tyranny of the actual. In refusing to confront this inner determination of education as they tinker with its expressions in policy and pedagogical technique and obsessively invent new efficiencies, mainstream approaches to reform are complicit in preserving it.

If mainstream efforts disguise the dominative meaning of education as it actually exists, alternative perspectives often miss the essence of domination in their own conceptualizations. In their incessant exposure of the hidden architecture of hegemony and stratification that makes education into a machine for social reproduction (e.g., Apple, 2004; Anyon, 2005; Bourdieu & Passeron, 1979), critical approaches risk obscuring the active violence of domination, which is in each moment willed, and which in its "tacit intentionality" (Gillborn, 2005) always exceeds the passive character of a structural effect. In becoming the cleverest and most determined explicators of social reproduction, these approaches sometimes risk also becoming celebrants, in spite of themselves, of its implacable force. Even work that has emphasized the resistance of students depends on the persistent backdrop of the process of social reproduction against which this resistance finds its meaning, especially when it is imagined as ultimately participating in the maintenance of school and social structures (Willis, 1977).

With regard to ideology, critical theorists have demonstrated the depth and complexity of the way consciousness and common sense are organized and how this organization preserves the sense, structure, and privileges of power (Gramsci, 1971). But ideology in this sense only provides the excuse, not the reason, for domination. We should not overlook the extent to which domination is its own motive and reward—the way in which the organization of social structures and relationships is in place to allow power the most efficient and complete expression of its force, rather than the other way around. The inertia of the system is never simply an expression of the accumulated weight of history but, rather, is always an active violence (Fanon, 1963). For the notion of ideology to retain its usefulness, we have to stretch it to include the original violence that sets the very conditions of possibility for the coherent emergence of self and society.

The postructuralist perspective in education, by contrast, seeks to trouble the dominant discourse without permitting itself to endorse any consistent and different purpose. The attention in this perspective to the imbrication of power and knowledge allows for a recognition of the dangers in the science of educational progress (Lather, 2004; Popkewitz, 1998; Walkerdine, 1998). At the same time, poststructuralism's antipathy toward the notions of truth and emancipation means the very questions that most urgently need to be confronted are declared off-limits (e.g., What does an authentically liberatory education look like?), since any *positive* response to them is taken to represent a form of discursive violence. This perspective's compulsive suspicion tends to lead to political paralysis. In short, in contrast to the accounts I have just described, I argue that the point is not to propose modifications to the current experience of education, or to more perfectly expose the intricacies of its organization and persistence, or to exorcise the issue of power altogether as the insoluble problem of discourse, but to recognize the essentially dominative meaning of education and to contest and counter it with a different truth and purpose.

Domination operates through a colonizing impulse that opportunistically invades bodies across a range of modalities—as gendered, raced, and culturally constructed; as economic and socially productive; even as imaginative, communicative, and emotional potentialities (West, 2009). A truly liberatory education should be antisexist and antiracist and anticlassist, but beyond all these determinations it should be committed against the ubiquitous and parasitic action of power itself. It should undertake the decolonial project of deracinating the logic of power from the space of self and social life and unraveling its sway over being. As Maldonado-Torres (2008) shows, the Eurocentrism that has defined the West politically and culturally as a project of conquest extends even to the domains of ethics and ontology as an underlying will to violence. Similarly, Mills (1997) describes a "racial contract" that organizes racist hierarchies of being and knowing as a first principle of social life. Capitalism, too, can be seen as a dominion over and within being: its original violence is its forcing into intelligible existence the very social subjects that it then exploits and alienates (Althusser, 1971).

In all of these respects, education has been a crucial location for the introduction and consolidation of the principle of domination; it has to become a crucial site in the struggle against this principle. But education here means something much more than the space of classrooms or the choice of methods; it means the site where the core truth of society and social relationships is articulated. For instance, the unacknowledged naturalization and redemption of European imperialism in curricula—through the apparently objective narration of the (distant, detached, decided) *past*—is a *contemporary* act of violence against present beings and possibilities. Education is the deliberate repetition and inculcation of the senses of self, relationship, and collectivity that define our being together. The possibility of liberation depends on confronting these basic understandings that incessantly repeat the wound—at the levels of identity, knowledge, and even being—which colonialism and capitalism have inflicted historically as political projects (Mignolo, 2005).

In this way, education takes shape within a society in which the relation of violation constitutes the organizing principle. Therefore, the basic referentiality and relationality that philosophers have argued is characteristic of human being as *being-with* (Heidegger, 1996) is exposed as essentially dominative. This relationality is concretely elaborated in the historical passages of racism, patriarchy, and war (Maldonado-Torres, 2008). Further, this violation is more than a form of reason or knowledge. Theorists have critiqued the instrumental rationality that both calculates and naturalizes exploitation in capitalist society (Horkheimer & Adorno, 2002). But dominative power does not just *know* the world inhumanly; it institutes itself as the inner principle of that world through a persistent denial of the human meanings and beings that outrage it. This principle determines not just what can officially come to count as true but also what can *come to be* in the first place. Teaching has to struggle against domination on these difficult terms. Refusing to choose between styles of authoritarianism, it has to challenge the underlying principle of authority that is already given by power.

In countering the project of domination that lives at the heart of education, emancipation is less a project of *humanization* than an insistence on the necessity of constructing education—*to begin with*—as a human encounter. That is, in the context of a society organized by the process of domination, the truly transformative act is to constitute a moment *outside* of that logic (De Angelis, 2007). In care theory, ethical relationships between teachers and students serve the purpose of training students to be caring adults (Noddings, 1992). But in order to create a human encounter between teacher and students, and among students themselves, the weight of a dominative society must be confronted. As critical pedagogy has recognized, no ethical space in education can be created as if in a vacuum, without a conscious negation of oppression and exploitation (McLaren, 2000). This is the mistake of progressive approaches that seek to work on attitudes as if they were isolable and accidental. But critical approaches also oversimplify the problem, in their own way, by emphasizing the process of critique as the central route to liberation. Power works on *being* itself; it constitutes the ontological conditions that set the parameters of subjectivization and consciousness. The order of the real already has a fundamental political determination, even before this politics is determined by familiar interests (Žižek, 2008). And it is this determination of being that is power's central purpose and triumph, rather than the particular forms of reason and belief that follow and express this fundamental fact. While the importance of a political consideration of being in education has begun to be recognized (e.g., Brayboy & Maughan, 2009; Lewis, 2008), it has not yet been adequately specified. I argue that the determination of being is at the same time a hiding of the reality and possibility that outrages power: the human. In this sense, power simultaneously obscures the fact that the human being is persistently present as an ontological minimum, violates the development of that human potential, and requires the articulation of meaning and subjectivity within its own inhuman universe.

To create a human situation—and discover a moment of human being—is to challenge the essence of power, and this depends on an analysis that goes deeper than an exposure of hegemonic representations and valuations. The dominant forms of knowledge and discourse that discipline, humiliate, and exclude students, and refuse their entry into the circle of the "good," are ultimately only expressions of the more fundamental work of domination itself. That is, these representations are simply occasions among others for a violence that is continuous in its action across the material and immaterial—reducing the fundamental social meanings of and for young people at the same time that it expels them from spaces of material support (e.g., well-resourced schools and communities) and organizes concrete assaults on their psychical and physical integrity (e.g., in both systematic impoverishment and police violence). Against this pervasive force, which twists bodies, encounters, and relationships into rituals of violation, a liberatory pedagogy has to first find a human moment (Dussel, 2003). These moments are more than local triumphs; they open a breach in the universe of the actual and its truth (Badiou, 2001)—the truth of domination and inevitability. Only from such moments, in which the veil (to recall Du Bois's [1995] term) of oppression is torn, can a different world be glimpsed. We can analyze and deconstruct the actual forever, and still never depart from it. But the given forms and structures of society depend on the economy of domination proper, which posits us in the first place as the inhuman objects of power. To find a human moment is to open a hole in this inner armature.

Teaching, then, is *a work on being* and the invention of the possibility of an authentic encounter between beings outside of domination. It is not, however, simply an ethical problem, at least in the terms that the ethical has usually been understood. It is not a matter of specifying conceptually the correct principles for human relationship or human society generally, as if this could be done outside of the historical and material condition of domination (Deloria, 1999). If teaching has an ethical horizon, this horizon is constructed from the process itself of struggle: the material searching and resistance; the unraveling of oppressive modalities of feeling, saying, seeing, and knowing; and the articulation of different modalities, which then have to be fought for and protected (Anzaldúa, 1987). This articulation demands an act of will against power, since for power we are always broken, always *after the fact*—and if not dead exactly, then undead, living the life of objects. And yet this struggle and discovery depend on the persistence of a human substrate that survives power and whose recognition is the founding moment of any extended humanist pedagogy or politics. Teaching in this sense does not really *construct* humanity along the high road of a coming to critical consciousness, but instead knows and names human beings here and now against their violation—*verifies* them, as Rancière (1991) says, against the doctrine and practice of their denial and destruction.

From the starting point of the intimate refusal of the determinations of power in teaching—within the space of a self or a relationship—a larger project of liberation can be undertaken. The ordeal of education, in which power works to bend and break selves in order that they conform to the real, in order that they *get real*, is shared across society as bodies are cast off by the social machine—which proves their superfluousness by assigning them to permanent unemployment, incarceration, or, at best, the purely formal life of incessant consumption and spectacle. Teaching threatens this order, these foregone conclusions, not first in convincing students that things *can be* different but in knowing students already *as* different—"announcing" their humanity against domination.[2]

LISTENING FOR THE HUMAN

As Fanon (1963) has shown, the human being which emancipation recognizes, and for which it struggles, is neither a transcendental essence outside of history nor the simple virtual possibility of resistance. Rather, it is the *fact* of a body in struggle, the material process of suffering and refusal of suffering. However, the emergence of this body, and the project of solidarity with it, require a naming and recognition within which it is disclosed as human, rather than a purely contingent juncture of forces and effects. The process of domination, as it assimilates experience and communication to its own flattened grammars, seeks to render human suffering invisible or at least make it unremarkable and natural. Solidarity with human being means a navigation through these distorted surfaces—from the intimate spaces of conversation to the wider terrains of public life—and a registration of the being of the human against the twisted images that are propagated to deny it or to replace it with specters (De Lissovoy, 2007). This solidarity also means exposing the violence of punishment, exploitation, and incarceration as they work their way through society generally as well as through schools and the textures of teaching, as can be seen in the elaborate practices of detention, retention, remediation, expulsion, and probation. The point is not a comparison in quantitative terms but rather an exposure of the common participation of diverse moments of social life in the logic of domination. The *human* does not name some universal and abstract essence, the pure bearer of rights and responsibilities that the law is supposed to defend but, rather, a shared experience, a shared social body, and a shared being.

Emancipatory teaching listens for this human being in the conversation of pedagogy. Emancipatory teaching hears their injuries as they are communicated by students within the everyday idioms made available to them. Emancipatory teaching speaks *to* human beings, against the official idiom and curriculum that do not believe or know they are there and that see them as only the occasion for assessment, management, or "interaction." Emancipatory teaching speaks *from* human beings, whereas the recommended instruction proposes the teacher as a "caring" functionary whose job is to move the students through a series of procedures. The tradition of critical pedagogy, and especially the work of Paulo Freire, has provided the crucial foundation for this emancipatory and radical humanism in education.[3] It is this tradition that ultimately grounds my argument and that I aim to develop in this essay. However, I believe that faithfulness to this emancipatory project means pressing critical pedagogy itself to recognize human being and emancipatory agency even where they have not yet been engaged in any formal process of conscientization (Freire, 1997) and where educators up to now have tended to see merely petrification and disempowerment.

Emancipatory teaching means more than the familiar injunction to dialogue—it means determined struggle against the injury to human being that happens through standardized testing, scripted instruction, and hyperdiscipline. This belief in and experience of the human—this particular *humanism*—which some might disparage as a reactionary attachment to an outmoded foundationalism, is in fact a material performance of solidarity. Against Foucault (1995), I argue that the "human" is not the name for the normal and normative subject as it is reproduced through rituals of punishment but, rather, the name for the being that absorbs these blows, and the name for the possibility of identifying with this being against power. This identification does not imply an erasure of the cultural, gender, racial, and class differences that are constituted through this history of violence. But it does suggest a commonality extrapolated and uncovered through a range of experiences of struggle (Mohanty, 2003). This collective being opens a location of solidarity for teachers and students. On this basis, listening for the fact and possibility of the human means refusing to endorse the familiar machineries and moralities of education.

How do we find that human moment in both students and teachers? Given the terrain of power I have described, this must be more than a process of demystification. Beyond the embedded cultures of indignity that construct schools, and beyond the popular discourses that hegemony circulates in curricula and students appropriate against themselves, we are already prepared for participation in and submission to domination in our organization as effective social subjects in the first place. This process of interpellation—in which we are *hailed*, or called into intelligible subjectivity, by the state (Althusser, 1971)—is centrally operated in education by the discourse of achievement and failure that produces teaching always as a measurement, from the local moment of correction in the classroom to the federal apparatus of testing that distributes rewards and punishments on the broadest scale (Lipman, 2004; McNeil, 2000). The texture of assessment that forms the very meaning of contemporary education is a mode of subjection before it is any particular index of performance.[4] In this way, students are organized in the first place as empty spaces waiting to be named and known, to have their inner truth told by power.

Nevertheless, that we are named and organized by power does not mean there is no point or possibility outside of this process. Butler (1993) suggests that identification happens according to a rule or grammar and that there is no substance to the self outside of the citation or transgression of that rule. By contrast, I argue that if the process of becoming a subject is a moment of violence, this is ultimately because this violence acts on or against *something*. This something (even if it is not yet a *someone*) is the human. Challenging this violence means discovering and starting from that human moment. In short, a commitment to the process of emancipation in education means locating the human moment that we are, beyond the selves that have been given to us. For teachers to challenge the oppression of students by the structures of schooling also means challenging their own performances of identity in teaching (Zemblyas, 2003), but in the context of a faith that these official performances do not exhaust the meaning or content of being. It is clear that the architecture of the school, with its series of cells for study, recreation, and punishment, is repeated in the architecture of the subject of the teacher, with its carefully organized impulses toward correction and "care." Making social violence visible in the space of education means making visible the violence of the meaning of teaching—and of the meaning of the teacher as a subject. But in challenging this meaning, the project of emancipation proceeds by way of the human, which is the consistent residue that proves the failure of domination.

As a teacher in relationship to a student, I find you not through a confirmation of the accomplished self that you present; I find you through a recognition of the human limit in you that refuses your determinations by society. This human limit is also my own. It is the shared and identical condition of our reality as more than figures of domination or subjection. In knowing that I am more than the broken forms given to me to live in, I can begin to recognize you as more than the object of my instruction—or (in the case of the student's view of the teacher) as more than the agent of my punishment. In our justified efforts to affirm student identities against their pathologization by the system, we should not enforce a closure that imitates the dominant essentialisms (Orellana & Bowman, 2003). Dialogue within a pedagogy of emancipation takes place on the terrain not only of who we are but also of who we are not. To put it another way, emancipation is built on the ground of *what* we are; this *what* is the shared moment of meaning beyond power—the unacknowledged fact of the human. For example, when in solidarity a teacher resists a dominative image of working-class students (e.g., as unconcerned with education) without at the same time essentializing them (e.g., as inherently resistant), while remembering the force and context of oppression that surrounds them, the teacher assumes a minimal ethical and agentic core in the student that is nevertheless open to diverse expression.

The idea of emancipation is often assumed to have been surpassed by our sophistication about power, which is supposed to inhabit (and sabotage) every liberatory impulse (Spivak, 1988). But this view underestimates the scope and sense of emancipation, which is a freeing not merely from the grip of simple subjugation or prohibitive law, but even from the constructive and articulatory modes of power. We can recognize the depth and complexity of domination—its intimacy and productivity—and still challenge it. Teaching is a crucial instance of this complexity of power: in confronting the meaning and process of teaching, we confront power itself in all its intricacy and we open the possibility of a refusal of its pervasive sense and force.

EDUCATION AGAINST DOMINATION: EQUALITY AND AGENCY

My reconceptualization of emancipation, and the understanding of humanism and the human that informs it, set the parameters for a contemporary liberatory education. I further develop these starting points to indicate the principles for pedagogical orientation and practice they suggest. Two of these principles— equality and agency—show how emancipatory education should approach the central problems, respectively, of the relationship between teacher and students and of the possibility for empowerment and social action.

Pedagogy and Equality

The foregoing discussion suggests a particular kind of relationship between teacher and student. This is not a relationship between expert and novice, in which the student is bound to the teacher by the process of apprenticeship. It is not a paternalistic relationship, in which the teacher's concern for the student is grounded in the charge to develop the student as an ethical person. Instead, it is a relationship of solidarity between beings finding a commitment together against the social, institutional, and discursive violence that denies their shared humanness. To the extent that the classroom is both built from and shot through by dominative structures and processes, this is a journey through a difficult wilderness in which faith in and love for others takes precedence over the moral authority and certitude that educators have usually sought to appropriate for themselves.

Emancipatory dialogue can only have meaning within the context of this sense of solidarity. A notion of dialogue that reserves for the teacher the final or better word, or which is premised on the idea that the teacher's role is to bring the student around to the proper understanding—or even to the properly developed critical consciousness—violates this relationship and repeats the subjection of the student. The teacher can propose to students the possibility of an opening, of a refusal of domination, but the teacher cannot propose to govern this process. Dialogue must take place under the sign of equality rather than authority (Rancière, 2007). This does not mean that the teacher and student have the same roles, but it does mean that teaching is authentic to the extent that it discloses their essential equality. This pedagogy is different from one that is grounded in a notion of freedom as the result of the progression of the unformed to the status of proficiency or in which students are still defined by a lack—even if it is the lack of social consciousness rather than intellectual ability or cultural capital.

The habits and textures of established teaching vibrate to a frequency— the frequency of domination. To the extent that they recombine the same set of given understandings and practices, progressive approaches cannot overcome this determination of education. The logic of domination saturates the space of education as a cognitive, emotional, and physical experience. That basic frequency, which sets the reason and meaning of education, rather than the organization of the ingredients of the process, is what needs to be transformed. In this regard, while discourse-oriented approaches (e.g., Walkerdine, 1998) are sensitive to the depth and breadth of power, they are less able to recognize the process of domination itself. Whether in attacking or constructing students' selves, this domination continues to act against the human. In this way, the labels and academic-clinical discourses that increasingly diagnose students' differences are first of all basic injuries to human being, even as they are articulations of new identifications. An awareness of the intimacy of this scene of power, and of the implication of even progressive efforts in it, should not mean ignoring the fact of domination and the struggle of human beings against it. Emancipation remains a negation rather than a redeployment of power.

Teacher and student work to find each other through a set of difficulties produced not only by school organization or curriculum but also by basic senses of what it is to be, to learn, and to know. This means a sensitivity both to difference and to identity. On the one hand, the teacher should be attentive to students' differences, not only from the dominant or mainstream but also from the pedagogical expectation of what the student will become. That is, the teacher should insist on the radical openness of the trajectory of the meaning of selves (Giroux, 1992). This implies a refusal of the violence of cultural norms as well as a refusal to decide the identity of students even in the name of struggle (Delpit, 1995). On the other hand, the teacher should recognize the essential sameness of the student—with regard to humanity, agency, and intelligence—in relation to the teacher herself or himself. Teachers and students participate equally in human being. In contrast to the idea of education as a process of gradual *humanization*, which suggests a process of development toward a fuller and in some sense *more human* subjectivity, emancipatory education starts from the premise of equality—not an eventual equality but an original one. From this perspective, the difference between the teacher and student, while real, is nevertheless secondary, contingent, and practical. It is the difference between two positions in an essentially shared process and moment. Even the sociocultural model of a "community of learners" (Rogoff, 2001) emphasizes the *expert* position occupied by the teacher in relation to knowledge. However, if this community is grounded instead in the identical relationship students and teachers ultimately have to knowing and learning, this sense of expertise can be deflated. If the teacher has the role of opening up the possibility of learning, of suggesting and inviting it, it no more belongs to her or him than it does to the student, nor should the teacher have any more say over its meaning than does the student.

In the dialogue of teaching, an *I* and a *You* find themselves; this is the ethics of pedagogy that comes to us from Freire (1997) and Buber (1970). But this is, at the same time, humanity finding itself, finding itself constituted in relationship to itself, discovering its repetition against and in spite of what colonizes, exploits, and oppresses it. Human relationships, including pedagogical ones, are relationships of identity to the extent that there are no advanced degrees of humanity, no elevated or special forms of it. Being faithful to this principle means challenging the assumption of *deficit* that has plagued conceptions of education up to the present, however sophisticated its cultural and theoretical repackaging (Akom, 2008; Valencia & Solórzano, 1997). Until this assumption is evicted from the full spectrum of educational theories and practices, education will continue to teach students that they are *less than*—in the name of teaching them to be better.

Emancipatory Agency

In sociology and education, *agency* has traditionally been imagined as the relative power of individuals to act within the structural constraints that condition them (Giddens, 1979). In the more radical version of this idea, these constraints are revealed to be historical constructions and their force is shown to be the product of collective human action. From this perspective, agency means achieving an authentic subjecthood that sees through the apparently immutable organization of the present and that recognizes this present as susceptible to transformation through struggle (Lukács, 1971). On the other hand, from a poststructuralist perspective, power operates as much to construct the subject as to oppress or repress it. So, rather than a flight from or opposition to power, poststructuralists call for a subversion of it and of the law and structure it sediments. In their view, agency is not a separate moment from the articulation of subjectivity but, rather, is identified with it. That is, agency is expressed in resignifications or alternative performances of identity, which exploit the generativity of power as discourse to subvert its authority from within (Butler, 2006).

This poststructuralist understanding of agency is, I believe, opposed in a dangerous way to the very prospect of emancipation. It ends up refusing the possibility of emancipatory action altogether, since the goal becomes a perpetual retelling or reauthoring of the terms of identity rather than a praxis that moves against the space and force of power. From this perspective, the possibilities of the subject are already *drowned* in power—which is why poststructuralism is forced into the paradoxical idea of an agency without emancipation.

On the other hand, while the familiar critical-sociological perspective is a cru-cial starting point, it is in its own way not fully adequate. This conceptualiza-tion of agency tends to pull away with one hand what it offers with the other. This perspective contests the common sense that dooms persons to the status of objects within society. But the enlarged and empowered subject it imag-ines is nevertheless exhausted by the existential situation that is its dialectical antagonist, and whose persistent interference is in fact necessary to confirm the subject as authentic—as a subject always in development.

An emancipatory perspective believes in the presence of the human, and its integrity, in spite of and against the assaults of power (Dussel, 2003). This is not simply a potential to be developed through the proper series of choices and acts; the human is present as the ontological minimum that confronts and absorbs the force of domination—even if this presence only becomes evident to us through struggle. For instance, in whatever ways students of color are hurt by the systematic racism of schooling, their integrity in being remains; the recognition of that integrity is the starting point for a human teaching. In this teaching, as Ladson-Billings (1994) puts it, "their complete personhood is never doubted" (p. 76). More generally, to recognize domination is at the same time to recognize the fact and integrity of the human beings that domi-nation acts against—the cast-off and forgotten ones who are brought to life again in resistance (Marcos, 1995). The human both absorbs and resists domi-nation; it is the surplus that continually outrages power, and which power—even in its pervasiveness and inventiveness—can never finally master.

Emancipatory education knows this humanity in students and communities not merely as a possibility but as a present fact. For instance, while mainstream curricula deemphasize the historical and contemporary resistance of African Americans against racial violence (as Brown & Brown [2010] show), emanci-patory education affirms this human moment against the power that seeks both to overwhelm and to obscure it—as the prison seeks both to conquer and to bury the prisoner. To the extent that alternative educational perspec-tives reproduce in their own way this obscurity of humanity in students (e.g., as epistemologically compromised or developmentally incomplete), they are partly complicit in the disempowerment of students. Further, this humanity is not equivalent in a simple way to students' contingent *identifications*. Rather, emancipatory teaching first names the single human thread that weaves its way through all participants in the classroom. The complexity of emancipation is in the relationship of the contingent and contextual expression of self to the human instant that belongs equally to all (Badiou, 2001).

In its persistence, that human instant defeats domination. Emancipatory education exposes, names, and celebrates that instant; the reminder of its truth is the starting point for a more consistent and organized project of strug-gle for students and teachers. Youth persist through a culture that more often than not despises them; working-class children face down a society that daily takes more opportunities away from them; students of color confront, and come through, a persistent racism that continually reinvents itself (in spite of the frequent announcements of its disappearance). All of these are human acts and achievements. In this way, agency depends not on the hope for some distant and total triumph, or on a philosophical sleight of hand that displaces the scene of struggle altogether, but instead on *the recognition of a continuous series of present victories against power.*

Living and surviving are the first of these victories. "Celebrating survival" (Smith, 1999, p. 145) is the second. Communicating this celebration is the third. All of these depend on a knowledge of self that, even as it is injured, is ultimately uncompromised by domination (Collins, 2000). Emancipatory education extends this series of victories, recognizing and repeating them within the community of the classroom and beyond. This means that teaching should not just expose the general fact and form of oppression, and not only recognize the understandings that students bring with them from their own communities, but should also acknowledge the specific acts of courage and resistance by which students have personally overcome the violence directed at them by power. Collective social and political action, in turn, depend on the experience and acknowledgment of these victories that then form the basis of broader movements. It is not that the recognition of an individual humanity is a small event that makes possible the hope for a larger and different one. Instead, the victories of broader political struggles consist in a repetition of this simple one: the fact of survival and recognition of humanity against domination. In this way, agency is not achieved at the end of a process of pedagogical development; it always already *is.* Struggle shows agency always in fact to have *been,* as it is proven in the survival, communication, and action of students and teachers. The political task is to defeat the discourse and practice of power that assail this agency with doubts and hide it under the body of structure and system, and to open the way for its proliferation within subjects and across society.

CONCLUSION

Through a faith in and recognition of the human instant that remains alive and active through experiences of domination, emancipatory education makes possible a more radical materialization of equality in teaching and learning and a new understanding of agency. These discoveries should lead us to focus less on the slow construction of citizen-subjects, and more on recognizing the actuality of survival and struggle against domination and the original openings this recognition makes available to students. In this context, we can begin to see that our immediate interventions are not just preludes to a grander public project of transformation but in fact are themselves continuous with this transformation. In challenging a dominative word, in finding a lovingness in the classroom, in refusing "to ignore anything that concerns the human person" (Freire, 1998, p. 127), as well as in acting collectively against oppression, we uncover the truth of emancipation—we constitute and reconstitute its reality. These moments are then repeated and connected to create a more extensive and public movement; understanding the nature of emancipation reveals the common determination of "local" and "global" moments of struggle. The process of emancipation depends on this proliferating recognition of the human; in this process there are no lesser or greater forms, but only the same participation in humanness across a multiplicity of instances.

In this project we should start from an awareness of the urgency of the present as well as of the emancipatory possibilities that are already ubiquitously at work in it. Instead of tempering the impatience of students for transformation, teachers should learn from and reinforce it. This is not recklessness but, rather, a sensitivity to the historical moment. The present crises of power, which extend to an unprecedented depth in social, economic, and ideological terms, signal also an unprecedented condition of possibility—not the end of the road but rather an exit from the exhausted dialectic of oppression and domination, and the beginning of the concrete experience of liberation. In contrast to an existential orientation to human being and liberation as perpetual futurity, this perspective understands emancipation as a fact in the present—a persistent and pervasive experience, already fundamentally transforming the real.

The recognition of domination—the naming of the principle of actually existing society and education—is what makes possible our release from it, since in naming domination we recognize both its real force and its real limits. Once we realize that at the level of its historical intention education has been fundamentally tied to the project of dominative power, we can find permission to imagine both another education and another society and to recognize the tendrils of their emergence in the present. In its assaults on being, knowing, and doing, domination depends on a violent repertoire of words and actions. In beginning to speak and act in a different language—the language of human being—we acknowledge the force of power while at the same time indicating the fact of a reality it does not command. In the conversation that it creates, teaching can demonstrate this departure, proving the possibility of an audacity against power and indicating the real openings that can lead us out from its miserable assumptions and economies and into a different and human world.

NOTES

1. I use "power" to refer to the social force and agent of domination. There are also, of course, forms of relational and liberatory power. However, precisely because of the hegemonic role played by the dominative form of "power-over," as Holloway (2002) puts it (as opposed to a collective and emancipatory "power-to"), even the more democratic usages of "power" are partly inflected in spite of themselves by power's expression as domination. For this reason, I reserve "power" for "power-over" and use other terms to name emancipatory agency. My sense of power is rooted in a critique of capital. In

naming both a fundamental social logic and a political position of command, "power" is roughly equivalent to "capital," as I conceptualize it. However, "power" also evokes a subjective force and drive and a domain that extends to every level of culture and society, which are important to my description of the process of domination and that are not always attributed to capital.

2. Although Rancière (1991, 2007) begins from somewhat different notions of power and the human than I do here, his insistence on equality and humanity as present possibilities (to be "announced"), rather than eventual gifts of the teacher (or philosopher), is an important foundation for my own conception of emancipation.

3. In relation to my particular argument in this essay, see especially Freire's *Pedagogy of the Oppressed* (1997) and *Pedagogy of Freedom* (1998), Giroux's (2001) seminal work on the meanings of resistance in education, McLaren's (2005) argument for a Marxist humanist pedagogy, and Darder's (2002) emphasis on the notion of humanity in Freire's work.

4. This can clearly be seen in the elaborate nomenclature of "exemplary," "recognized," and "low-performing" (etc.) schools that the discourse of accountability continually produces.

REFERENCES

Akom, A. A. (2008). Ameritocracy and infra-racial racism: Racializing social and cultural reproduction theory in the twenty-first century. *Race Ethnicity and Education, 11*(3), 205–230.

Althusser, L. (1971). *Lenin and philosophy and other essays* (B. Brewster, Trans.). New York: Monthly Review Press.

Anyon, J. (2005). *Radical possibilities: Public policy, urban education, and a new social movement.* New York: Routledge.

Anzaldúa, G. (1987). *Borderlands/La Frontera: The new Mestiza.* San Francisco: Aunt Lute.

Apple, M. W. (2004). *Ideology and curriculum* (3rd ed.). New York: RoutledgeFalmer.

Badiou, A. (2001). *Ethics: An essay on the understanding of evil.* London: Verso.

Bourdieu, P., & Passeron, J. C. (1979). *The inheritors: French students and their relation to culture* (R. Nice, Trans.). Chicago: University of Chicago Press.

Brayboy, B. M. J., & Maughan, E. (2009). Indigenous knowledges and the story of the bean. *Harvard Educational Review, 79*(1), 1–21.

Brown, A. L., & Brown, K. D. (2010). Strange fruit indeed: Interrogating contemporary textbook representations of racial violence toward African Americans. *Teachers College Record, 112*(1), 31–67.

Buber, M. (1970). *I and thou* (W. Kaufmann, Trans.). New York: Scribner's.

Butler, J. (1993). *Bodies that matter: On the discursive limits of sex.* New York: Routledge.

Butler, J. (2006). *Gender trouble: Feminism and the subversion of identity.* New York: Routledge.

Collins, P. H. (2000). *Black feminist thought: Knowledge, consciousness, and the politics of empowerment.* New York: Routledge.

Darder, A. (2002). *Reinventing Paulo Freire: A pedagogy of love.* Boulder, CO: Westview Press.

De Angelis, M. (2007). *The beginning of history: Value struggles and global capitalism.* London: Pluto Press.

De Lissovoy, N. (2007). History, histories, or historicity? The time of educational liberation in the age of empire. *Review of Education, Pedagogy, and Cultural Studies, 29*(5), 441–460.

Deloria, V., Jr. (1999). *Spirit and reason: The Vine Deloria, Jr. reader.* Golden, CO: Fulcrum.

Delpit, L. (1995). *Other people's children: Cultural conflict in the classroom.* New York: New Press.

Du Bois, W. E. B. (1995). *The souls of black folk.* New York: Penguin Putnam. (Original work published 1903).

Dussel, E. (2003). *Beyond philosophy: Ethics, history, Marxism, and liberation theology.* Lanham, MD: Rowman & Littlefield.

Fanon, F. (1963). *The wretched of the earth* (C. Farrington, Trans.). New York: Grove Press.

Foucault, M. (1995). *Discipline and punish* (A. Sheridan, Trans.). New York: Random House.

Freire, P. (1997). *Pedagogy of the oppressed* (M. B. Ramos, Trans.). New York: Continuum.

Freire, P. (1998). *Pedagogy of freedom: Ethics, democracy, and civic courage* (P. Clarke, Trans.). Lanham, MD: Rowman & Littlefield.

Giddens, A. (1979). *Central problems in social theory: Action, structure, and contradiction in social analysis.* Berkeley: University of California Press.

Gillborn, D. (2005). Education policy as an act of white supremacy: Whiteness, critical race theory, and education reform. *Journal of Education Policy, 20*(4), 485–505.

Giroux, H. A. (1992). *Border crossings: Cultural workers and the politics of education.* New York: Routledge.

Giroux, H. A. (2001). *Theory and resistance in education: Towards a pedagogy for the opposition.* Westport, CT: Bergin & Garvey.

Gramsci, A. (1971). *Selections from the prison notebooks* (Q. Hoare & G. N. Smith, Trans.). New York: International.

Heidegger, M. (1996). *Being and time* (J. Stambaugh, Trans.). Albany: State University of New York Press.

Holloway, J. (2002). *Change the world without taking power: The meaning of revolution today.* London: Pluto Press.

Horkheimer, M., & Adorno, T. W. (2002). *Dialectic of enlightenment* (E. Jephcott, Trans.). Stanford, CA: Stanford University Press.

Ladson-Billings, G. (1994). *The dreamkeepers: Successful teachers of African American children.* San Francisco: Jossey-Bass.

Lather, P. (2004). Scientific research in education: A critical perspective. *British Educational Research Journal, 30*(6), 759–772.

Lewis, T. (2008). Defining the political ontology of the classroom: Toward a multitudinous education. *Teaching Education, 19*(4), 249–260.

Lipman, P. (2004). *High stakes education: Inequality, globalization, and urban school reform.* New York: RoutledgeFalmer.

Lukács, G. (1971). *History and class consciousness* (R. Livingstone, Trans.). Cambridge, MA: MIT Press.

Maldonado-Torres, N. (2008). *Against war: Views from the underside of modernity.* Durham, NC: Duke University Press.

Marcos. (1995). *Shadows of tender fury: The letters and communiqués of Subcomandante Marcos and the Zapatista Army of National Liberation* (F. Bardacke & L. López, Trans.). New York: Monthly Review Press.

McLaren, P. (2000). *Che Guevara, Paulo Freire, and the pedagogy of revolution.* New York: Rowman & Littlefield.

McLaren, P. (2005). *Capitalists and conquerors: A critical pedagogy against empire.* Lanham, MD: Rowman & Littlefield.

McNeil, L. M. (2000). *Contradictions of school reform: Educational costs of standardized testing.* New York: Routledge.

Mignolo, W. D. (2005). *The idea of Latin America.* Malden, MA: Blackwell.

Mills, C. W. (1997). *The racial contract.* Ithaca, NY: Cornell University Press.

Mohanty, C. T. (2003). *Feminism without borders: Decolonizing theory, practicing solidarity.* Durham, NC: Duke University Press.

Noddings, N. (1992). *The challenge to care in schools: An alternative approach to education.* New York: Teachers College Press.

Orellana, M. F., & Bowman, P. (2003). Cultural diversity research on learning and development: Conceptual, methodological, and strategic considerations. *Educational Researcher, 32*(5), 26–32.

Popkewitz, T. S. (1998). The culture of redemption and the administration of freedom as research. *Review of Educational Research, 68*(1), 1–34.

Rancière, J. (1991). *The ignorant schoolmaster: Five lessons in intellectual emancipation* (K. Ross, Trans.). Stanford, CA: Stanford University Press.

Rancière, J. (2007). *On the shores of politics* (L. Heron, Trans.). London: Verso.

Rogoff, B. (2001). Becoming a cooperative parent in a parent co-operative. In B. Rogoff, C. G. Turkanis, & L. Bartlett (Eds.), *Learning together: Children and adults in a school community* (pp. 145–155). Oxford: Oxford University Press.

Smith, L. T. (1999). *Decolonizing methodologies: Research and indigenous peoples.* London and Dunedin: Zed Books/University of Otago Press.

Spivak, G. C. (1988). Can the subaltern speak? In C. Nelson & L. Grossberg (Eds.), *Marxism and the interpretation of culture* (pp. 271–313). Chicago: University of Illinois Press.

Valencia, R. R., & Solórzano, D. G. (1997). Contemporary deficit thinking. In R. R. Valencia (Ed.), *The evolution of deficit thinking: Educational thought and practice* (pp. 160–210). London: Falmer Press.

Walkerdine, V. (1998). *Counting girls out: Girls and mathematics.* London: Falmer Press.

West, C. (2009). *Keeping faith: Philosophy and race in America.* New York: Routledge.

Willis, P. (1977). *Learning to labor: How working class kids get working class jobs.* New York: Columbia University Press.

Zemblyas, M. (2003). Interrogating "teacher identity": Emotion, resistance, and self-formation. *Educational Theory, 53*(1), 107–127.

Žižek, S. (2008). *The sublime object of ideology.* London: Verso.

I would like to thank Irene Liefshitz, Thomas Nikundiwe, Carla Shalaby, and the Editorial Board for their thoughtful comments on earlier versions of this manuscript.

ABOUT THE EDITORS

Kolajo Paul Afolabi is a fourth-year doctoral student in higher education at the Harvard Graduate School of Education. His current research focuses on transfer from two- to four-year public colleges. Prior to attending Harvard, Kolajo worked in educational research, evaluating programs and policies designed to improve schooling and other services for children and youth. During his tenure as an educational researcher, he focused on out-of-school time programs for youth, youth development programs, teacher professional development, and federal education policy. Kolajo now spends most of his time studying higher education and is broadly interested in the transition to college, community colleges, non-traditional college students, and immigrant students in higher education. Kolajo holds an EdM from the Harvard Graduate School of Education and an AB in public policy and American institutions from Brown University.

Candice Bocala is a doctoral student in education policy, leadership, and instructional practice at the Harvard Graduate School of Education. Her research interests include teamwork and collaboration, new teacher and school leader preparation, school improvement, and social justice in education. Previously, Candice taught elementary school in Washington, DC. She has supervised and taught student teachers as an adjunct instructor at American University and at the Harvard Graduate School of Education. She also works as a research assistant at WestEd, where she has co-authored two studies about special education published through the federally funded Regional Educational Laboratory network. She holds a BA in government from Cornell University, an MA in policy analysis and evaluation from Stanford University, and an MAT in elementary education from American University. She currently serves as one of the cochairs of the *Harvard Educational Review*.

Raygine C. DiAquoi is a fourth-year doctoral student in culture, communities, and education. Her current research focuses on the role of segregated schools in the lives of African Americans pre-and post-integration. Prior to matriculating at the Harvard Graduate School of Education, Raygine worked for a leadership development program for minority youth and taught second and sixth grades at predominantly Black and Latino schools in Harlem. The explicit attention devoted to students' racialized academic identities and the processes created by each program to uphold students' biculturalism, which prized both dominant and non-dominant forms of cultural capital, are the inspiration for her current work. She holds a BA in sociology from Columbia University.

Julia M. Hayden is a manuscript editor for the *Harvard Educational Review*. She is a Larsen Fellow and a doctoral candidate in human development and education at the Harvard Graduate School of Education. In her research, she explores how autobiographical memory, narrative, and identity are enacted and transmitted within family relationships. Her dissertation focuses on the ways in which mothers' talk about the past plays a role in the development of preschool-aged children's autobiographical memory, narrative skills, and theory of mind. Prior to matriculating at Harvard, Julia worked on several longitudinal research projects at the Child Study Center at Yale University, where she was a Zigler Fellow in Child Development and Social Policy. Julia holds an EdM in education from the Harvard Graduate School of Education and a BA in psychology from Connecticut College.

Irene A. Liefshitz is a third year doctoral student in education policy, leadership, and instructional practice. Prior to Harvard, Irene worked for fifteen years as an educator in New York City public schools. She was a teacher, assistant principal, mathematics instructional coach, and professional development consultant. Her current research interests include stories and metaphors employed to talk about the work of teaching, the intersection of identity and culture, and phenomenology. Born in Russia and an immigrant to the United States, Irene is also interested in bringing the educational philosophy of Anton Makarenko to a wider American audience. Irene holds a BA in religion from Bryn Mawr College, an MS in education from Fordham University, permanent NYS school supervisory certification, and an EdM from Harvard.

Soojin Susan Oh is a doctoral candidate in human development and education at Harvard. Her broad research agenda entails advancing theory and innovative methods to examine critical dimensions of immigrant childhood in U.S. context. In particular, she focuses on how multiple linguistic, cultural, and ethnic contexts shape immigrant children's development and learning. Another focus of her research—related yet distinct—considers how policy can expand systemic efforts to address social inequalities and improve the well-being of children in U.S. and international contexts. As a meta-analysis research assistant at the Center on the Developing Child, Soojin examines the causal impact of early childhood interventions and parenting services on developmental outcomes. Through her involvement with a UNICEF-sponsored study, she investigates how low- and middle-income nations develop, finance, and implement a multisectoral policy to provide accessible, equitable, and high-quality early childhood education and care for all children. She also writes columns on child development, and consults for schools and nonprofit organizations evaluating early childhood assessments, teacher quality, home visiting, and literacy interventions. Prior to coming to Harvard, Soojin taught kindergarten and first grade in Philadelphia. Soojin holds a BA in psychology from the University of Pennsylvania and an EdM in education policy and management from Harvard.

ABOUT THE CONTRIBUTORS

Dorinda J. Carter Andrews (formerly Carter) is an assistant professor in the Department of Teacher Education at Michigan State University. Her research focuses on race and equity in education, with a particular emphasis on black student achievement in urban and suburban schools. Drawing on qualitative methodologies and race-based theories, she studies how the racial and achievement identities and ideologies of black students shape their adaptive and maladaptive behaviors for schooling. She also conducts research on urban teacher preparation and closing achievement gaps in schools.

Steven Z. Athanases (PhD, Stanford University, 1993) is a professor in the school of education at the University of California, Davis. A former high school English teacher, Athanases conducts research and teaches about diversity and equity in English teaching and in teacher education and development. Supported by postdoctoral fellowships from the McDonnell and Spencer Foundations, Athanases studied the teaching and learning of English in urban public schools. He received NCTE's Promising Researcher Award and the Association of Teacher Educators' Distinguished Research Award. His recent articles have appeared in *Teachers College Record, Teaching and Teacher Education, Journal of Teacher Education, Journal of Curriculum Studies,* and *Multicultural Education.* He co-edited *Mentors in the Making: Developing New Leaders for New Teachers* (Teachers College Press). Athanases' current research examines the potential of preservice teacher inquiry to develop teachers' abilities to meet the needs of culturally and linguistically diverse youth in mostly high-poverty urban and rural schools.

Dolores Delgado Bernal is Professor of Education, Culture, and Society and Ethnic Studies at the University of Utah. Her research focuses on the schooling of Chicana/o and Latina/o students, the experiences of students and faculty of color in higher education, and community engaged scholarship. She teaches courses in critical race theory, feminist epistemology, Chicana/o studies, and ethnic studies. She is co-editor of *Chicana/Latina Education in Everyday Life: Feminista Perspectives on Pedagogy and Epistemology* (2006) and is the author of numerous chapters and articles some of which appear in *Harvard Educational Review, International Journal of Qualitative Studies in Education, Urban Education,* and *Social Justice.* She is co-PI and co-director of Adelante, a university-school-community partnership at Jackson Elementary School, which is dedicated to creating educational opportunities and college-going expectations through community engagement, research, and reciprocity.

Bryan McKinley Jones Brayboy is an enrolled member of the Lumbee Tribe of North Carolina. He is Borderlands Associate Professor of Educational Leadership and Policy Studies, co-director of the Center for Indian Education, co-editor of the *Journal of American Indian Education* at Arizona State University, and Visiting President's Professor of Indigenous Education at the University of Alaska Fairbanks. He is currently finishing a book manuscript on American Indians in higher education. He lives in Phoenix with his spouse, Doris S. Warriner, and their two sons, Quanah and Ely.

Noah De Lissovoy is an assistant professor of curriculum studies in the Department of Curriculum and Instruction at the University of Texas at Austin, where he teaches in the areas of curriculum theory, sociocultural foundations, and educational philosophy. His research centers on critical and emancipatory approaches to curriculum, pedagogy, and educational theory. He is the author of *Power, Crisis, and Education for Liberation: Rethinking Critical Peda-*

369

gogy, which received the 2010 Critics Choice Book Award from the American Educational Studies Association. His work has appeared in many journals and edited collections, including the *Harvard Educational Review, Curriculum Inquiry, Discourse: Studies in the Cultural Politics of Education, Educational Philosophy and Theory, Review of Education, Pedagogy, and Cultural Studies, Cultural Studies—Critical Methodologies,* and the *Journal of Education Policy.*

Lisa D. Delpit, executive director and eminent scholar at the Center for Urban Education and Innovation at Florida International University in Miami, is interested in improving urban education, particularly for children of color, and in the perspectives and aspirations of teachers of color. Her recent publications include *The Skin That We Speak: Thoughts on Language and Culture in the Classroom* (coedited with J. Kilgour Dowdy, 2003) and *The Real Ebonics Debate* (coedited with T. Perry, 1998). She received a MacArthur Fellowship in 1990 and the Horace Mann Humanity Award in 2003.

Signithia Fordham, the former Susan B. Anthony Professor of Gender and Women's Studies, is a cultural anthropologist at the University of Rochester. She is the author of the ethnography *Blacked Out: Dilemmas of Race, Identity and Success at Capital High* (1996). Her research and essays have appeared in public media, including *Education Week,* the *Chicago Sun-Times, The Washington Post, The New York Times,* and the *London Times,* as well as academic journals such as T*ransforming Anthropology: The Official Journal of the Association of Black Anthropology, The Urban Review, Anthropology and Education Quarterly, Teachers College Record,* and the *Harvard Educational Review.* Her current research, and the subject of her book manuscript, tentatively titled *Downed by Friendly Fire: Black Girls, White Girls and Female Competition at UGRH (Underground Railroad High),* focuses on female competition, bullying, and aggression.

Emma Maughan is an adjunct professor in the school of teacher education and leadership at Utah State University. Previously she worked as a research associate at the Center for the Study of Empowered Students of Color, University of Utah. Her research interests include epistemologies and knowledge systems, writing in the university, American Indian education, and race in education. She is the recent coauthor of a chapter in *Structure and Agency in the Neoliberal University* and an article scheduled to appear in the *Review of Research in Education.*

Sonia Nieto is Professor Emerita of Language, Literacy, and Culture at the University of Massachusetts, Amherst. She continues to write, speak, and consult on multicultural education, the education of students of diverse backgrounds, and teacher education. Her books include *Affirming Diversity: The Sociopolitical Context of Multicultural Education, What Keeps Teachers Going?, The Light in Their Eyes,* and a number of edited volumes including *Puerto Rican Students in U.S. Schools, Why We Teach,* and *Dear Paulo,* among others. She has received many awards for her scholarship, teaching, and advocacy, including four honorary doctorates.

Django Paris is an assistant professor in the English education program at Arizona State University. His research focuses on understanding how pluralism works in multiethnic youth communities and how we can re-vision language and literacy learning to foster understanding within and across difference. Paris spent six years as an English language arts teacher in California, Arizona, and the Dominican Republic. His work appears in the *Journal of Language, Identity, and Education,* the journal *English Education,* and the *International Journal of Qualitative Studies in Education.* His first book, *Language Across Difference: Ethnicity, Communication, and Youth Identities in Changing Urban Schools* (forthcoming, Cambridge University Press), explores the ways the everyday oral and written language of youth of color challenges and reinforces ethnic difference and division in multiethnic and multilingual high schools. His research has been supported by fellowships from the Spencer, Ford, and NCTE foundations.

Patricia J. Saylor was the director of Circle of Friends, a federally-funded, demonstration bilingual preschool program for Deaf and hearing children in Durham, NC from 1995–2000. In 1993 and 1995 she adopted two Deaf children, and in spite of a request for a "Deaf baby," a "brown baby like me," and "a girl," in 1998 birthed a Hearing White Boy. He is, nevertheless, well-loved by his siblings. She now runs a private tutoring and educational consulting business called Solterra Way Cottage School (http://www.solterrawaycottageschool.com) and teaches academically gifted children in a public Montessori school in Durham, NC. She holds teaching credentials in seven areas by the North Carolina Department of Public Instruction as well as the American Montessori Society and the National Board for Professional Teaching Standards. Her professional interest continues to be designing individual instruction to meet the needs of diverse learners.

Paul Skilton-Sylvester is currently the Lower School Director at the Wissahickon Charter School—an urban, environmentally focused K–8 charter school in a refurbished radio factory in Philadelphia. Previously, he was Associate Director of Teacher Education at the University of Pennsylvania and, before that, an elementary school teacher in Boston and Philadelphia. He is the author of "Less Like a Robot: A Comparison of Change in an Inner City School and a Fortune 500 Company," which was published in the *American Educational Research Journal*.

Beverly Daniel Tatum is president of Spelman College in Atlanta. A clinical psychologist with 28 years of experience in higher education as a professor and administrator, she is a noted author and race relations expert. A fifth anniversary edition of her critically acclaimed book, *"Why are All the Black Kids Sitting Together in the Cafeteria?" and Other Conversations about Race* was released in 2003. She is also the author of *Can We Talk about Race? and Other Conversations in an Era of School Desegregation* (2007) and *Assimilation Blues: Black Families in a White Community* (1987). In 2005 she was awarded the Brock International Prize for Innovation in Education.

Kathleen Weiler is a professor of education at Tufts University in Medford, Massachusetts. She has published widely on gender and education. Her books include *Feminist Engagements* (2001), *Country Schoolwomen: Teaching in the California Countryside, 1850–1950* (1998), and *Women Teaching for Change* (1988). She is currently working on a joint biography of two twentieth-century female progressive educators, Helen Heffernan and Corinne Seeds.

Arlette Ingram Willis received her PhD from the Ohio State University. She is currently a professor at the University of Illinois at Urbana-Champaign in the Department of Curriculum and Instruction, the Division of Language and Literacy. Her publications include *Teaching and Using Multicultural Literature in Grades 9–12: Moving Beyond the Canon* (1998), *Reading Comprehension Research and Testing in the US: Undercurrents of Race, Class, and Power in the Struggle for Meaning* (2008), three co-edited books including *Multiple and Intersecting Identities in Qualitative Research* (with B. Merchant, 2001); *Multicultural Issues in Literacy Research and Practice* (with G. Garcia, R. Barrera, and V. Harris, 2003); *On Critically Conscious Research: Approaches to Language and Literacy Research* (with M. Montovan, H. Hall, C. Hunter, L. Burke, and A. Herrera, A., 2008); and numerous referred articles, book chapters, book reviews, and monographs. She also has served as co-editor (with David Bloome) of the National Council of Teachers of English Literacy Book Series and is co-editor (with Violet J. Harris) of the American Education Research Journal, Teaching, Learning, and Human Development section.